ISBN 978-0-484-47799-4
PIBN 10554034

This book is a reproduction of an important historical work. Forgotten Books uses state-of-the-art technology to digitally reconstruct the work, preserving the original format whilst repairing imperfections present in the aged copy. In rare cases, an imperfection in the original, such as a blemish or missing page, may be replicated in our edition. We do, however, repair the vast majority of imperfections successfully; any imperfections that remain are intentionally left to preserve the state of such historical works.

Luftspiel in 3 Akten

(nach Varin und Michel Delaporte).

eopold Karl Kohl Von von Kohlenegg

L. K. von Kohlenegg (Poly Henrion).

Wien, 1865.

Druck von Waldheim & Förster.

Personen:

Conrad Reimer, ehemals Kaufmann, jetzt Rentier.
Mathilde, seine Frau zweiter Ehe.
Wally, seine Nichte.
Therese Müllner, Reimer's Schwester.
Clärchen, deren Tochter.
Edmund Feldern.
Julius Kleinlich.
Frau Pariser, Direktrice eines Mädchen=Pensionates.
Sabine, Stubenmädchen bei Reimer.
Adele, Modistin.
Ein Diener Reimer's.
Eine Magd bei Frau Müllner.

Ort der Handlung: eine große Stadt; Zeit: die Gegenwart.

(Rechts und links vom Schauspieler.)

Erster Akt.

(Bei Reimer. Reich und luxuriös möblirter Salon. Rechts erste Coulisse ein Fauteuil; zweite Coulisse ein Kamin mit Spiegel, Uhr, Vasen 2c.; vor dem Kamin gegen die Mitte der Bühne ein Sopha. Links erste Coulisse ein ovaler Tisch mit zwei Fauteuils; auf dem Tische Albums, Bücher, Blumenvasen u. dgl. Zweite Coulisse ein Fenster mit Blumentöpfen. In der Mitte des Hintergrundes die allgemeine Eingangsthür. Rechts und links, schräge gegen die letzten Coulissen, Seitenthüren. Zwischen den Seiten= und der Mittelthür Tischchen mit Stühlen. An den Wänden: Bilder, Statuen 2c.; unter den größeren Möbeln bunte Teppiche.)

Erste Szene.
Sabine, Adele.

Adele.
(Aus der Seitenthür rechts kommend und zurücksprechend.)

Wenn Sie befehlen, so werde ich warten, aber es pressirt wirklich nicht.

Sabine (aufräumend).

Ah! Mamsell Adele, schon fertig? Nun, ist die gnädige Frau mit bem Kleide zufrieden?

Adele (vorkommend).

Ziemlich; Sie wissen ja wie schwer die zufrieden zu stellen ist.

Sabine (seufzend.)

Leider!

Adele.

Sie will durchaus, daß ich Herrn Reimer hier erwarte, um gleich die Bezahlung zu empfangen.

1*

Sabine.

Ja der Herr zahlt immer — und Alles — und handelt nie! Ist d e r verliebt in seine Frau!

Adele.

Das ist auch ganz in der Ordnung, es ist zwischen Beiden ein so großer Unterschied im Alter! — — — Und s i e, liebt sie ihn auch?

Sabine.

Wer kann das wissen. Aber übellaunisch ist sie oft genug; Fräulein Wally hat auch ihren eigenen Kopf und da gibt's dann Scenen — — —!

Adele.

Da haben S i e wohl einen recht schweren Stand im Hause.

Sabine.

Ach nein, ich bin recht zufrieden. Der Herr kümmert sich nur um die gnädige Frau, die Frau kümmert sich nur um ihre Toiletten, — um m i ch kümmert sich also Niemand und . . . . das weiß ich zu benützen. Doch, da kommt der Herr. (Geht nach rechts und beginnt wieder aufzuräumen.)

Zweite Szene.

Vorige, Reimer (von links.)

Reimer.

So, Mamsell Adele, da bin ich; wo ist die Rechnung?

Adele (gibt ihm dieselbe).

Hier, Herr Reimer.

Reimer (nach einem raschen Blick auf die Rechnung).

Donnerwetter, die ist nicht klein!

Adele.

Ich versichere, daß ich meine Kunden so billig als möglich bediene. Fragen Sie die gnädige Frau, die sich gewiß darauf versteht — — —

Reimer.

Ist meine Frau mit dem neuen Kleide zufrieden?

Adele.

Sie ist entzückt davon.

Reimer.

Dann ist es nicht zu theuer. (Er zählt Geld auf den Tisch links, indem er sich an jenes Ende desselben stellt, welches der Coulisse am nächsten ist, während Adele an das andere Ende des Tisches, gegen die Mitte der Bühne zu, tritt.)

Dritte Szene.

Vorige, Frau Müllner mit Clärchen (durch die Mittelthür eintretend. Beide in eleganten Sommertoiletten mit Hüten und Mantillen.).

Frau Müllner.

Da haben wir's! Mein Bruder gibt schon wieder Geld aus! Weiter thut er jetzt gar nichts mehr!

Sabine (bei Seite).

Die Frau Brummtante, wie Fräulein Wally immer sagt.

Reimer.

Grüß Dich Gott, Schwester.

Frau Müllner (höhnisch).

Abermals eine kleine Putzrechnung? Hat die Frau Gemahlin wieder neue Toiletten nöthig?

Clärchen.

Guten Morgen Onkelchen. (Sie tritt an den Tisch links, an Adelens Stelle.)

Reimer.

Guten Morgen liebes Clärchen! (er küßt Clärchen auf die Stirne, indem er sich über den Tisch lehnt und dann wieder fortfährt, das Geld aufzuzählen.)

Clärchen.

Ist Wally nicht hier?

Frau Müllner.

Schweig, mein Kind, Du störst Deinen Onkel im Geldausgeben!

Clärchen (die Unterwürfige spielend).

Wie Du befiehlst, liebe Mutter. (Setzt sich auf's Sopha.)

Reimer (zu Frau Müllner.)

Nein, nein, laß sie nur — ich bin schon fertig. (Zu Adele). Ist's so in der Ordnung?

Adele (ist wieder an den Tisch getreten und steckt das Geld ein.)

Vollkommen, Herr Reimer — und morgen werde ich die Ehre haben die neuen Muster zu bringen.

Reimer.

Neue Muster?

Adele.

Ja, die gnädige Frau braucht noch ein Kleid für alle Tage.

Frau Müllner.

No ch ein Kleid?! Sie hat schon so viele Kleider als es Tage im Jahre gibt — jetzt braucht sie noch eines für a l l e Tage!!

Reimer (beschwichtigend).

Je nun, wenn Sie eines benöthigt — die Kleider sind ja so billig —

Frau Müllner (bei Seite).

Das findet d e r billig?! (Sie setzt sich zu Clärchen auf's Sopha.)

Reimer (zu Adele).

Kommen Sie morgen, liebe Mamsell, da meine Frau es wünscht, und bringen sie recht hübsche Muster mit.

Adele.

Schön, Herr R e i m e r! (Nach einer Verbeugung durch die Mitte ab.)

Sabine (im Abgehen zu Adele leise.)

Ist das ein Ehemann, was?! (Mit Adele ab.)

Vierte Szene.

Reimer, Frau Müllner, Clärchen.

Frau Müllner.

Conrad! Du bist unbegreiflich!

Reimer (lustig).

Wie so? (Er setzt sich auf den Fauteuil rechts im Vordergrund, dem Publikum halb den Rücken kehrend.)

Frau Müllner.

Das will ich gar nicht a n f a n g e n zu erörtern, sonst käme ich schwerlich so schnell damit zu Ende! — Lassen wir das! — Ich bin gekommen, Dich und deine Frau einzuladen, der Prüfung meiner Tochter beizuwohnen, die heute über acht Tage im Pensionat stattfindet.

Reimer.

Wir werben nicht ermangeln, umsomehr (zu Clärchen) da uns mein Clärchen gewiß viel Freube und Ehre machen wird.

Clärchen (bescheiden die Augen niederschlagend).

Wer weiß, lieber Onkel!

Frau Müllner (fest).

Ich weiß es! (Zu Reimer.) Es gibt gar kein fleißigeres und namentlich kein sittsameres Mädchen als meine Tochter.

Clärchen (wie oben.)

Das ist mir so angeboren, liebe Mutter.

Frau Müllner.

Weiß ich auch.

Clärchen.

Und dann Ihr Beispiel, — die steten, weisen Lehren, die tief eingegraben sind in meinem Innern — — —

Reimer (aufstehend und nach links gehend).

Nun also — Du wirst das Glück und den Stolz Deiner Familie ausmachen — hoffen wir's!

Frau Müllner (steht ebenfalls auf.)

Ich bin davon schon überzeugt.

Clärchen (ebenso).

Onkelchen, wie geht es Wally?

Reimer.

Ganz vortrefflich, liebes Kind; willst Du sie sehen?

Frau Müllner.

Das verbiete ich! Du weißt, daß Du nie allein mit ihr sein darfst.

Reimer.

So geh' Du mit ihr.

Frau Müllner.

Ich habe mit Dir zu sprechen, Conrad.

Reimer (seufzend bei Seite).

Oh weh!

Frau Müllner (deutet nach links zu Clärchen).

Geh' da hinein in das Cabinet Deines Onkels und warte bis ich Dich rufe.

Clärchen.

Wie Du befiehlst, liebe Mutter! (Bei Seite im Abgehen.) Diese Langeweile! (Links ab.)

Fünfte Szene.

Reimer. Frau Müllner.

Reimer (nach rechts gehend).

Du bist ein Bischen streng mit Deiner Tochter.

Frau Müllner.

Und Du bist es zu wenig mit deiner Nichte! Ich bin ent=
rüstet über die Art und Weise, wie Wally bei dir erzogen wird.

Reimer.

Ich finde Deinen Tadel ungerecht. Wally ist eine Waise. Als
ihre Eltern starben, war das Kind arm und verlassen, weit weg
in der Provinz, und kam auf's Land zu ... Bauern! Ich
hätte sie zwar dort lassen können und mich nicht um sie beküm=
mern, allein ... (Lehnt sich mit dem Rücken an den Kamin.)

Frau Müllner (sich Reimer nähernd).

Du fürchtetest das Urtheil der Welt; wolltest für keinen
schlechten Onkel gelten!

Reimer.

Und die Welt hätte vollkommen recht gehabt, wenn sie mich
dafür gehalten hätte. Ich war reich, Witwer, ohne Kinder, hatte
mich von den Geschäften zurückgezogen und also nichts
Besseres zu thun, als mich meiner armen Nichte anzunehmen,
deren natürlicher Vormund ich war. Deßhalb habe ich sie in
mein Haus genommen und sorge für sie wie für mein eigenes
Kind.

Frau Müllner.

Schöne Fürsorge! Sie ißt, trinkt, schläft, allerdings mehr
als nöthig ist, für das Materielle sorgst Du ganz außerordent=
lich und bildest Dir ein, damit sei Alles gethan, weil Du eben
selbst nur materiell bist vom Wirbel bis zur Zehe.

Reimer (lächelnd).

So?! Ich glaubte ich wäre geistreich!

Frau Müllner.

Zum Erbarmen! Kümmerst Du Dich um ihre Seele, um
ihren Geist, um ihre Moral — (stärker) um ihre Moral,
so wie ich die meiner Tochter überwache.

Reimer.

Mich dünkt, Du übst diesen Wachtdienst ein wenig zu strenge.

Frau Müllner.

Eine sehr wohlthätige Strenge! die Du ebenso bei Wally anwenden solltest! — Conrad, mir hättest Du das Kind anvertrauen sollen, ich hätte ihre schlechten Anlagen mit der Wurzel ausgerissen und ein ordentliches Mädchen aus ihr gemacht.

Reimer (sich auf's Sopha setzend).

Ei — ich hoffe Du hältst sie nicht für das Gegentheil!

Frau Müllner.

So wird sie's werden, — (Reimer zuckt ungeduldig mit den Achseln) wenn sie länger in Deinem Hause bleibt. (Sie setzt sich zum Tische links.) Deine Frau, die ihr mit gutem Beispiele vorangehen sollte, gibt ihr nur das des Luxus und der Frivolität.

Reimer (ungeduldig).

So — nun geht's wieder über meine Frau los!

Frau Müllner.

Und Du selbst! Du, — ein Mann, — (verächtlich) Pantoffelheld! — stehst unter dem Commando Deiner Frau! Sie hat Dich in die große Welt gezogen; läßt Dich allen Vergnügungen nachlaufen, umgibt Dich nur mit jungen Menschen und macht aus Dir selbst einen alten lächerlichen Gecken! (Reimer will sprechen.) Einen alten lächerlichen Gecken, der sich wie ein junger Dandy kleidet und sich des Morgens alle grauen Haare ausrupft um Abends hübsch braun zu sein! Mußt Du bei der Arbeit müde werden?

Reimer (lächelnd).

So ein kleiner Betrug ist kein Verbrechen und wird mit der Zeit sogar nöthig. Meine Frau ist jung und ich . . . wünsche zu vergessen daß ich es nicht mehr bin!

Frau Müllner.

Du hättest überhaupt gescheidter gethan, Witwer zu bleiben.

Reimer.

Na, zu diesen Reflexionen ist's jetzt zu spät.

Frau Müllner.

Ich habe diese Heirat nie begreifen können.

Reimer (steht auf).

Vielleicht wirst Du mit jener mehr einverstanden sein, die ich für Wally beschlossen habe.

Frau Müllner (ebenfalls aufstehend.)

Du willst Wally verheiraten?

Reimer.

Ja — es ist höchste Zeit! Sie und meine Frau können sich weder verstehen noch vertragen. Mathilde ist ein Bischen heftig, Wally ist gerade auch kein Lamm, und widerspricht ihr fortwäh=rend, so kommt's zu steten Reibungen und ich, zwischen den bei=den Frauen, ich . . . ich will mich nicht länger reiben lassen!

Frau Müllner (pathetisch).

Und deßhalb willst Deine Nichte hinopfern?

Reimer.

Hinopfern? Ich opfere sie ja nicht! Ich habe ihr einen char=manten jungen Mann ausgesucht, mit dessen Vater ich lauge Zeit in Geschäftsverbindung stand. Das junge Herrchen kommt eben aus Brasilien zurück, wohin sein Vater ihn gesandt hatte, um große Minengeschäfte und andere industrielle Unternehmungen einzuleiten; die Partie ist vortrefflich, eine bessere als ich je hoffen durfte für Wally zu finden.

Frau Müllner.

Das glaube ich! (Bei Seite.) Mir paßte der auch für mein Clärchen. (Laut.) Kennt ihn Wally?

Reimer.

Nein, sie weiß noch gar nichts davon.

Frau Müllner (boshaft).

Und glaubst Du, daß sie mit einem, ewig auf dem Meere schwimmenden Herru Gemal zufrieden sein wird?

Reimer.

Sein Vater wird ihn hier in der Residenz etabliren.

Frau Müllner (wie oben).

Ich wünsche daß es gut ausgehen möge! Wenigstens kommt Wally aus der . . . gefährlichen Nachbarschaft.

Reimer (erblickt Mathilde).

Ach, da ist ja mein Thildchen!

Sechſte Szene.

Vorige. Mathilde (von rechts).

Mathilde (in die Couliſſe zurückſprechend).

Nein, das iſt denn doch zu arg — das halte ich nicht länger aus.

Reimer.

Was haſt Du denn, mein Herzchen?

Mathilde.

Meine Geduld iſt zu Ende. (Geht rechts zum Kaminſpiegel und ordnet ſich das Haar).

Reimer.

Was hat es denn gegeben?

Mathilde (immer mit ihrem Haarputz beſchäftigt).

Zank, Ungehorſam, Widerſpänſtigkeit — wie gewöhnlich!

Reimer.

Wally ſchon wieder?

Mathilde.

Wer ſonſt? (Sie kommt vor ohne Frau Müllner zu ſehen welche ſich zum Tiſche links ſetzt und in einem Album blättert.) Ich gebe ihr eine Mantille, um ein Spitzenendchen, das abgetrennt war, wieder anzunähen! Glaubſt Du ſie hätte es gethan? Keine Spur! Sie meinte, ſpäter habe es wohl auch noch Zeit, — ich hätte ja mehr Mantillen — ich könnte ja eine andere nehmen! — Und als ich ſie zwingen wollte, mir zu folgen, — ging ſie in den Garten Federball ſpielen!

Reimer.

Was Du ſagſt!

Frau Müllner (immer in dem Album blätternd).

Das war allerdings ſehr ungezogen von ihr, — aber Feder-ball ſpielen oder Spitzen annähen, iſt eines ſo nützlich wie das andere, und ich wundere mich, daß man in dieſem Hauſe die Zeit mit ſolchen Lappalien verbringt.

Mathilde.

Frau Schwägerin, ich kümmere mich nicht um Ihre Haus= ordnung, wollen Sie ſo freundlich ſein, gegen mich dieſelbe Rückſicht zu haben.

Frau Müllner (wie oben).

Schön; ich ſehe es auch täglich mehr ein, wie thöricht es

ift, für gewiffe Perfonen Theilnahme oder Intereffe zu haben. . . .

Mathilde.

Ich, für meinen Theil, difpenfire Sie davon . . .

Reimer (zwifchen beiden ftehend).

Na — na! Kinder — fchließen wir die Diskuffion!

Mathilde.

Ich erkläre Dir, lieber Mann, daß ich nicht länger mit Wally unter einem Dache bleibe. Es geht über meine Kräfte. Eine folche Exiftenz kann ich nicht weiter führen.

Frau Müllner (immer wie oben).

Wenn fie fich über Wally zu beklagen haben, meine Liebe, find Sie nur felbft daran Schuld! Waren fie nicht ihre Erzieherin ihre Gouvernante? Hätten fie den Charakter ihrer Schülerin beffer gezogen, hätten Sie beffer Ihre Pflicht gethan . . .

Mathilde.

Frau Schwägerin, ich verbiete mir alle unberufenen Bemerkungen. Ich weiß was ich zu thun hatte, und weiß daß ich jetzt Herrin hier im Haufe bin!

Reimer.

Meine Damen, nun ift's genug! Wenn ich zwifchen drei Frauen einen Frieden herzuftellen nöthig hätte, müßte ich mindeftens einen Congreß zufammenberufen.

Mathilde.

Lieber Mann, ich ertrage es nicht länger.

Reimer.

So fei doch nur ruhig — es hat Alles jetzt ein Ende — Wally wird heiraten.

Mathilde.

Heiraten?

Reimer.

Sogar fehr bald.

Mathilde.

Du haft mir ja kein Wort davon gefagt?

Reimer.

Heute Morgens wurde erft Alles abgemacht — ich wollte Dich überrafchen . . .

Mathilde.

Wer ift der Zukünftige?

Reimer.

Du wirst ihn gleich kennen lernen, ich erwarte ihn eben.

Mathilde.

Gott sei Dank — ich bin mit Jedem einverstanden, daß nur wieder Ruhe im Hause wird!

Siebente Szene.

Vorige. Wally, dann Sabine.

Wally (eine Federball=Raquette in der Hand, durch die Mitte).

Pardon, Onkelchen, ich komme nur meinen Federball zu holen, der sich dort einquartirt hat (deutet auf das Fenster.)

Reimer.

Leg' das Zeug da weg und höre mich ruhig an.

Wally.

Ach laß' mich zuerst meinen Federball holen.

Reimer.

Nein, stillgestanden! Ich muß Dich auszanken.

Wally (schelmisch).

Ist das so nothwendig?

Reimer.

Ja; Du beträgst Dich nicht achtungsvoll genug gegen Mathilde.

Wally.

Nicht achtungsvoll?

Reimer.

Sie verlangt Gehorsam, Respekt —

Wally.

Respekt? Freundschaft wäre vielleicht besser! Vor Frau Müllner habe ich gewiß sehr viel Respekt — sie ist in einem Alter ! . . .

Frau Müllner (grob).

Mein Alter kümmert Sie nichts, Mamsell Naseweis!

Wally.

Auch gut! Aber mein kleines Tantchen . . . die fast ebenso jung ist wie ich . . . (schelmisch) Ei ich glaubte ihre Eitelkeit zu verletzen, wenn ich zu viel Respekt vor ihr hätte.

Mathilde.

Es handelt sich nicht um meine Jugend sondern um die Stellung, die ich in diesem Hause einnehme! Du scheinst die Güte zu vergessen, mit der man dich hier aufnahm!

Wally.

Das wäre schwer . . . man erinnert mich ja täglich an dieselbe.

Reimer.

Das war schon wieder eine Bemerkung, die . . .

Wally.

Hättest Du mich lieber in meinem Dörfchen, bei meinen guten Bauern gelassen! — Die waren nicht reich, nicht meine Verwandten und nahmen mich dennoch liebevoll auf . . . ohne mir ihre Güte täglich vorzuwerfen! Und als ich von ihnen wegzog, weinten sie! Es scheint, daß ich denn doch nicht gar so . . . schlimm bin!

Mathilde.

Nun, ich denke, die Erziehung, die Du hier genossen hast . . .

Wally.

Mein Gott! wenn Jene mich hätten erziehen können, hätte ich keine Gouvernante nöthig gehabt — (Reimer nicht lächelnd zustimmend) und Sie wären dann auch schwerlich die Frau meines Onkels geworden! (Sie umarmt Reimer, der von den letzten Worten unangenehm berührt scheint und mit Wally mehr in den Hintergrund geht, nachdem diese ihren Federball vom Fenster geholt hat.)

Mathilde (wüthend bei Seite).

Die Unverschämte!

Frau Müllner (noch mit dem Album beschäftigt).

Ja — Glück muß der Mensch haben. Vom Lectionengeben zur Millionärin avanciren! — hübscher Sprung! Es gibt Frauen, die eben so glücklich sind als . . . schlau!

Mathilde.

Und es gibt andere, die nicht einmal so viel Geschicklichkeit besitzen, ihren Mann sich zu erhalten. Ich kenne eine, die schon wenige Monate nach der Hochzeit von dem ihrigen verlassen wurde, und die ihn dann fern, allein und verlassen sterben ließ.

Frau Müllner (auffspringend.)

Madame! (sie geht wüthend auf Mathilden zu; Reimer stürzt ängstlich zwischen Beide). Wenn mein Mann mich verlassen hat, so waren meine **guten Augen** daran **Schuld**! (Reimer zupft sie beschwichtigend am Kleide; sie fährt aber stets heftiger, ohne auf ihn zu achten, fort.) Ich war nicht blind, nicht kindisch leicht= gläubig — (sich plötzlich zu Reimer wendend, losplatzend) wie an= dere gewisse Menschen . . . deren Name mir auf der Zungen= spitze schwebt!

Reimer.

Sapperlot! wird heute Ruhe werden oder nicht! Soll ich mich auch noch ärgern?!

Wally (mit dem Federball spielend).

Onkelchen, ich möchte wieder nach dem Garten gehen!

Reimer.

Nein, ich habe mit Dir zu sprechen! (Frau Müllner setzt sich auf's Sopha.)

Wally (wie oben).

Könntest Du das nicht auf später verschieben?

Reimer.

Nein! — Uebrigens habe ich dir etwas mitzutheilen, was Dich jedenfalls sehr erfreuen wird!

Wally (wie oben).

Das wäre was Neues! (Sie läßt den Federball fallen und hebt ihn wieder auf.)

Reimer.

Es handelt sich um . . . einen Bräutigam!

Wally (immer spielend.)

Um einen Bräutigam? Für wen? (Der Federball fällt wieder herab).

Reimer (denselben aufhebend und Wally gebend).

Für Dich!

Wally (spielt wieder).

Für mich?! (Sie läßt den Ball zum dritten Male fallen, Rei= mer hebt ihn abermals auf und will ihn Wally wieder geben, besinnt sich aber und steckt ihn in die Tasche.) Ist das Spaß oder Ernst? (Geht zu Mathilde.) Wirklich Tantchen, für mich? (Legt die Raquette auf den Tisch rechts.)

Reimer.

Also würdest Du Dich gerne verheiraten?

Wally.

Außerordentlich gerne! Ich werde meinen Bräutigam wie einen geliebten Retter empfangen, der mich von vielen... Unannehmlichkeiten befreit, und wenn er nicht zu alt und häßlich ist...

Reimer.

Sei unbesorgt, ich habe Dir ein Männchen ausgesucht...

Sabine (durch die Mitte eintretend).

Herr Reimer!

Reimer.

Was gibt's?

Sabine.

Eine Visitenkarte; ich habe den Herrn in den kleinen Salon eintreten lassen.

Reimer (wirft einen Blick auf die Karte).

Er ist es!

Mathilde (zu Wally gehend).

Man kann sie ihm doch nicht in diesem Hauskleidchen vorstellen!

Frau Müllner.

Weshalb nicht? Die Einfachheit ist die schönste Zierde eines jungen Mädchens.

Mathilde.

Ja, Einfachheit und... eine hübsche Toilette.

Reimer (zu Mathilde und Frau Müllner).

Lassen wir den jungen Mann nicht länger warten. (Zu Wally). Mache Dich so schön als möglich!

Wally (trocken).

Ich werde mir Mühe geben!

(Frau Müllner und Mathilde sind an der rechten Seitenthür angelangt, und machen sich gegenseitig ceremonielle Verbeugungen, um der Andern den Vortritt zu lassen.)

Reimer (dies bemerkend).

Welche Umstände! — Schwester, geh' Du voraus — Du bist ohnehin die Aelteste! (Frau Müllner macht erzürnt einen Schritt gegen Reimer, bezwingt sich aber und geht stolz ab; die beiden Andern folgen lachend.)

Achte Szene.

Wally, dann Clärchen.

Wally.

Sie sind alle neugieriger auf meinen Zukünftigen als ich — und dennoch begrüße ich ihn als meinen Befreier, meinen Erretter! — —

Clärchen (steckt den Kopf zur linken Seitenthür heraus).
Wally! bist Du allein?

Wally.

Was, Clärchen, Du hier?

Clärchen (kommt vor und umarmt Wally).
Mama hatte mit dem Onkel allein zu sprechen und exilirte mich da hinein! Aber es ging ein Bischen lebhaft hier zu; gab es denn einen kleinen Zank?

Wally (schmunzelnd).
Ja, wie gewöhnlich hier im Hause. Deine Mutter und Tante Mathilde sind beständig auf dem Kriegsfuße, und wenn die Eine das Schlachtfeld räumt, nimmt die Andere die Feind= seligkeiten mit mir wieder auf! Gekämpft muß immer werden!

Clärchen.

Mir schien, . . . ich horchte zwar nicht, Gott bewahre, das thu' ich nie . . .

Wally.

Ich sehr oft!

Clärchen.

Aber man sprach so laut, daß ich von einer Heirat zu hören glaubte!

Wally.

Ganz richtig! Der Unglückliche ist bereits im Gefängniß angelangt! (Deutet nach rechts.)

Clärchen.

Kennst Du ihn?

Wally.

Nein, ich habe ihn nie gesehen.

Clärchen.

Und willst ihn heiraten?

Wally.

So schnell als möglich.... um von hier fortzukommen!

Clärchen.

Fühlst Du Dich denn hier so unglücklich?

Wally.

Unglücklich... ist nicht das richtige Wort.... ich bin auch nicht von d e r Sorte, die so rasch aus Kummer sterben... Auch habe ich Onkel Conrad recht lieb; er ist gut, gerecht und ich bin überzeugt, daß er mich — im Geheimen — auch sehr gern hat! Aber seine Frau kann mich nicht leiden, nicht daß sie bösartig wäre, nein — aber sie ist hoffärtig, eigensüchtig, möchte die ganze Welt terrorisiren.... und das paßt mir nicht! Ich wiedersetze mich, opponire — ich bin immer auf der äußersten Linken!

Clärchen.

Das finde ich ganz natürlich und stimme Dir auch vollkommen bei! Also bist Du ganz Sklavin? Hast keinen freien Augenblick?

Wally.

Oh, im Gegentheil, nur zu viel! Es kümmert sich kein Mensch um mich! Onkel Conrad und die Tante sind ja meistens verreist...

Clärchen.

Warum nehmen sie Dich nie mit?

Wally.

Weiß ich nicht! Ich bleibe immer allein mit Sabine — die von Früh Morgens bis spät Abends spazieren geht.

Clärchen.

Allein, so oft, so lange, und in Deinem Alter ... das ist sehr gefährlich.

Wally.

Ja — ein Bischen!... Hauptsächlich ist es langweilig!... Freilich muß ich auch oft auf meiner Hut sein... so allein, mir selbst überlassen...

Clärchen.

Da Du Niemanden liebst, ist die Gefahr nicht so groß... aber, wenn Du auch noch gegen die Liebe zu kämpfen hättest....

Wally.

Gegen die Liebe — das wäre allerdings... Das heißt, es ist schwer hierauf zu antworten. Was würdest Du in dem Falle thun?

Clärchen (sehr züchtig und unschuldsvoll).

Ich — wie sollte ich darüber sprechen können?! Du weißt, wie man mich bewacht und hütet... was eigentlich überflüssig ist, da mein eigenes Gefühl für Sittsamkeit und Tugend —

Wally.

Hm hm! In Deinem Pensionat geht's sehr anständig zu?

Clärchen.

Außerordentlich! Die Professoren sind lauter alte Herren, sehr ehrwürdig und langweilig; — die Lehrerinnen fürchterlich streng und von einer Moralität.... (Sich vergessend und einen andern Ton anschlagend.) Apropos, eine kannte Frau Reimer noch von früher...

Wally.

Da sie auch Erzieherin war, ist das nichts Merkwürdiges.

Clärchen.

Es scheint, daß sie als Mädchen ziemlich ... lustig war und kokett...!

Wally.

Wie ich merke, wird in Eurem moralischen Pensionat denn doch auch ein wenig geklatscht.

Clärchen.

Nun... Erholungsstunden müssen wir doch haben. Aber das ist noch nicht Alles, man behauptet, daß Tante Mathilde vor ihrer Verheiratung....

Wally.

Wenn es etwas Schlechtes ist, was man behauptet — so sag' mir's lieber nicht! Sie ist die Frau meines Onkels, und was ihm unangenehm wäre, will auch ich nicht wissen!

2 *

Neunte Szene.

Vorige. Frau Müllner.

Frau Müllner (durch die Mitte eintretend).

Stecken schon wieder beisammen! — (Zu Clärchen.) Weshalb hast Du das Kabinet verlassen, in welches ich Dich internirt habe?

Clärchen.

Verzeih' Mama, Wally kam zufällig in jenes Zimmer ....

Wally (bei Seite, erstaunt).

Sie lügt ja?!

Clärchen.

Und da traten wir dann hier ein und plauderten ...

Frau Müllner.

Wovon?

Wally.

Wir sprachen von ....

Clärchen (rasch einfallend).

Von meiner Prüfung und ich lud Wally ein mitzukommen.

Wally (wie oben).

Ah! Die lügt nicht schlecht!

Clärchen.

Trachte nur, dabei zu sein — wir werden Komödie spielen.

Wally.

Kannst Du das auch?

Frau Müllner (stolz).

Oh, ganz vortrefflich!

Clärchen.

Du wirst Dich selbst überzeugen — leider, daß es das letzte Mal sein wird!

Wally.

Du verläßt die Pension?

Frau Müllner.

Ja, von nun an wird sie bei ihrer Mutter bleiben! —

Wally.

Da bist Du wohl recht zufrieden?

Clärchen.

Ah ja! (Die Hand ihrer Mutter ergreifend, in schmeichelndem Tone.) Wenn man eine, so zärtliche, aufopfernde Mutter hat — so sehnt man sich nach dem Augenblick, wieder ganz i h r anzugehören! Und doch verlasse ich so manche treue Jugendfreundin, so manches schöne Bündniß, das von nun an nur mehr in der Erinnerung wird leben können.

Wally.

Das kann ich mir wohl denken — indeß — nun werde ich da sein, mein Mühmchen, und meine Liebe soll Dich für Manches entschädigen, das Du dort verlassen mußt.

Frau Müllner.

Du vergißt, daß bald ein Gatte all' Dein Denken und Fühlen in Anspruch nehmen wird!

Wally.

Richtig — daran dacht' ich gar nicht mehr! Sahen Sie ihn?

Frau Müllner.

Ja; — der junge Mann scheint mir viel Muth zu besitzen....

Wally.

Ah?

Frau Müllner.

Da er Dich heiraten will, ohne Dich zu kennen.

Wally (knixend, ironisch).

Danke! — Wie sieht er denn aus?

Frau Müllner.

Na... sein Physisches ist annehmbar, allein... Aeußerlichkeiten haben so geringen Werth!

Clärchen (sich vergessend).

Oh doch, Mama, ein Mann der..

Frau Müllner.

Schweig' still, meine Tochter!

Wally.

Nun, und was meint denn mein Onkel?

Frau Müllner.

Der hat ihn natürlich mit offenen Armen aufgenommen! Seine Frau hingegen...

Wally.

Hat sie ihn schlecht empfangen?

Frau Müllner.

Das hätte sie nicht wagen dürfen, allein sie fingirte ein plötzliches Unwohlsein und verließ stolz den Salon.

Wally.

Das ist sonderbar!

Frau Müllner.

Oh nein... ganz natürlich! Sie ärgert sich, daß Du einen jungen Mann bekömmst, während sie selbst einen... alten hat.

Clärchen.

Das begreife ich, denn ein alter Ehemann...

Frau Müllner.

Aber so schweig' doch! Was sprichst Du denn von Dingen, die Du noch gar nicht zu verstehen hast!

Zehnte Szene.

Vorige. Mathilde (durch die Mitte).

Mathilde (bei Seite).

Noch immer hier!

Frau Müllner.

Ah, Frau Schwägerin! Nun, Ihr Unwohlsein, das ich übrigens begreiflich finde...

Mathilde.

Sie finden es begreiflich?

Frau Müllner.

Ist wohl schon vorüber...? und ich staune, daß das neue Familien=Schooßkind Sie nicht hieher begleitete — ich hätte ihn für galanter, für (mit einem Blick auf Wally) sehnsüchtiger gehalten!

Clärchen (bei Seite).

Ich möchte ihn gerne sehen! (Sie versucht, ungesehen, theils durch die Mittel=, theils durch die rechte Seitenthür in die anstoßenden Gemächer zu blicken.)

Mathilde.

Das neue Familien=Schooßkind, wie Sie den Bewerber Wally's zu nennen belieben, wäre auch sicher bereits hier, wenn mein Mann ihn nicht zurückgehalten hätte... und aufrichtig ge= standen, sind Sie ein wenig daran Schuld.

Frau Müllner.

Ich?

Mathilde.

Conrad wollte sich nicht in Gegenwart des fremden jungen Mannes Ihren gewöhnlichen schwesterlichen Bemerkungen aus= setzen und will mit der Brautwerbung lieber warten....

Frau Müllner.

Bis ich fort bin?

Mathilde (mit einer zierlichen Verbeugung).

Sie sind so freundlich, meine Rede selbst zu beenden.

Frau Müllner (ebenso).

Und ich bin Ihnen sehr verbunden, daß Sie mir die längst präparirte Pille so liebenswürdig überzuckern.

Mathilde (wie oben).

Frau Schwägerin!

Frau Müller (wie oben).

Frau Schwägerin! (Den Ton ändernd.) Uebrigens paßt mir das gerade so! Mein Clärchen braucht bei derartigen Manö= vern gar nicht dabei zu sein! Komm, Kind! Geh'n wir ein Bischen frische Luft schöpfen! (Nimmt Clärchen barsch bei der Hand und geht rasch durch die Mitte mit ihr ab.)

Eilfte Szene.

Wally. Mathilde.

Wally.

Sie verabschieden sie ziemlich barsch.

Mathilde.

Das geschah mit Absicht... denn die Augenblicke sind kostbar... und ich habe mit Dir zu sprechen, mein theures Kind.

Wally (bei Seite).

Ihr theures Kind?

Mathilde.

Ich weiß, Du liebst mich nicht... Du mußt mich sogar
haffen...

Mally.

Ich hätte nichts fehnlicher gewünscht, als Sie vom Herzen
lieben zu können, — und wenn Sie es nur gewollt
hätten...

Mathilde.

Ja, nur meine Schuld ist's! Aber ich bin so nervös —
so leicht erregbar... Wie oft war ich hart und ungerecht gegen
Dich... aber ich bereue es — denn jetzt erkenne ich, daß Du
beffer bist als ich — b'rum vergib mir, wenn ich Dich gekränkt,
wenn ich Deinem Herzen wehe gethan habe.

Wally.

Ich Ihnen vergeben? (Bei Seite.) Die will was!

Mathilde.

Beffer wär' es gewesen, Dich wie eine Schwester, wie eine
Freundin zu behandeln...

Wally (herzlich).

O, da hätten Sie mich auch viel glücklicher gemacht...

Mathilde.

Nun denn... es ist noch Zeit... ich bin gekommen, Dir
die Hand zu reichen... willst Du mir die Deinige geben, Wally?

Wally.

Hier ist sie... und von ganzem Herzen! (Sie reichen sich
die Hände.) Mir fehlte viel in diesem Haufe, da mir Ihre
Freundschaft, Ihre Liebe fehlte... jetzt aber — — —

Mathilde.

Haft Du sie, da Du sie in reichem Maße verdienst! Und
den erften und beften Beweis meiner Theilnahme für Dich kann
ich Dir gleich jetzt geben, indem ich jene Heirat verhindere, zu
der man Dich zwingen will!

Wally (enttäuscht).

Verhindern? Weßhalb?

Mathilde (von nun an immer unsicherer).

Weil der Mann, den man Dir bestimmt hat, Dich nicht
glücklich machen würde.

Wally.

Woraus schließen Sie das?

Mathilde.

Aus seinem Vorleben . . . aus seinen früheren Verbindungen! Er würde Dir wohl sagen daß er Dich liebe . . . er würde es Dir schwören . . . allein seine Versprechungen, seine Eide sind **Lügen**! Er würde Dich betrügen, wie er Andere betrogen hat!

Wally.

Sie kennen ihn also?

Mathilde.

Willige nicht in diese Heirat, Wally, verweigere ihm Deine Hand . . . Du würdest mit diesem Manne grenzenlos unglücklich werden.

Wally (immer erstaunter).

Ich soll ihn zurückweisen?

Mathilde.

Das kann Dir ja kein Opfer sein . . . Du kennst ihn ja gar nicht.

Wally.

Das bleibt sich gleich. Mein Onkel hat mit väterlicher Fürsorge diese Wahl getroffen, wie kann ich ohne Grund, auf vielleicht **irrthümliche** Voraussetzungen hin . . .

Mathilde.

Du mußt es . . . Du mußt es um jeden Preis!

Wally (ruhig).

Ich werde meinen Onkel um Rath fragen.

Mathilde (aufschreiend).

Meinen Mann?

Wally (bei Seite).

Sie erschrickt?

Mathilde.

Um Gotteswillen nicht! Siehst Du denn nicht meine Angst, meine Aufregung? . . . Muß ich Dir erst noch **gestehen**, was Du vielleicht schon errathen hast?!

Wally (bei Seite).

Fast fürchte ich's!

Mathilde.

Nun denn, ja! Besser ich vertraue mich Dir an . . . ich kenne Dein Herz, Du wirst mich nicht verrathen! —

Wally (theilnahmsvoll).

Ich, Sie verrathen?! —

Mathilde.

Du sollst Alles wissen!... und wenn es noch eine Ent-
schuldigung gibt, so liegt sie in den Verhältnissen welche meine
Jugend trübten. Wir waren einst reich; allein mein Vater liebte
das Spiel leidenschaftlich, meine Mutter, eine vortreffliche Frau,
war die Mildthätigkeit selbst und wandte ihr ganzes Herz jenen
unglücklichen Kindern zu, die das harte Schicksal heimsuchte...
elternlos zu sein. Sie war die wohlthätige Fee aller Waisen...
und fühlte nicht, daß sie dadurch ihr eigenes Kind fast zur Waise
machte!... Mir selbst überlassen, fand ich nur Trost und Zer-
streuung in Studien und Erwerbung wissenschaftlicher Kenntnisse.
Man hielt mir die besten Lehrer, die berühmtesten Meister...
ich machte rasche Fortschritte... und als die Verschwendung
meines Vaters, das übertriebene Mitleid meiner Mutter uns zu
Grunde gerichtet hatten... hieß es arbeiten um unser Brod
zu erwerben! (Wally macht eine theilnehmende Bewegung). Ich
bildete mich vollständig zur Lehrerin aus und gab Lektionen.

Wally.

Aber das war ja sehr rechtschaffen, sehr ehrenvoll!

Mathilde (düster).

Und ward mein Unglück!... Eine meiner Schülerinnen
hatte einen Bruder... Herrn Edmund Feldern.

Wally.

Am Ende gar der mir bestimmte Bräutigam?

Mathilde (verlegen).

Ja, Wally, er ist's (erregt.) Und wenn Du ihn heirathest
... wenn er in unsere Familie träte... wenn ich gezwungen
wäre seine Gegenwart zu ertragen, ihn täglich zu sehen... ihn
... zwischen mir und meinem Gatten...! Nein, nein, Wally,
lieber sterben!

Wally (nach kurzer Pause entschlossen).

Ich begreife Alles... zählen Sie auf mich!

Mathilde.

Du willst ihm entsagen?

Wally.

Ja!

Mathilde.

O Dank! Dank, Wally — (sie küßt sie.) Du rettest mich!

Wally (bei Seite).

Mein armer Onkel! — (Beide gehen nach rechts in den Vordergrund).

Zwölfte Szene.

Vorige, Reimer, Edmund.

Reimer.

Treten Sie nur ein, lieber Edmund!

Wally (bei Seite).

Das ist er also!

Edmund (grüßend).

Meine Damen! (Allgemeine Begrüßung — Mathilde setzt sich auf den Fauteuil im Vordergrunde rechts, Wally auf das Sopha).

Reimer (längs dem Camin zu Mathilde tretend).

Nun, mein Herzchen, ist Dir besser!

Mathilde.

Es war nur ein kleiner Anfall von Migraine.

Reimer.

Wir bedauerten daß Du uns deßhalb so schnell verlassen mußtest.

Edmund.

Und ich kam um das Vergnügen, Ihre liebenswürdige Bekanntschaft zu machen! (Er verbeugt sich gegen Mathilden).

Mathilde (bei Seite).

Er besitzt noch immer die alte Kühnheit!

Reimer (ist hinter dem Sopha wieder zu Edmund getreten).

Nun, Sie werden wohl künftig mehr Gelegenheit dazu finden! — Aber vorerst will ich Sie mit aller Feierlichkeit vorstellen.

Edmund (bei Seite).

Vor ihr . . . das ist störend!

Reimer (zu Wally).

Liebe Nichte, Herr Edmund Feldern! (Wally nickt kalt mit dem Kopfe.) Lieber Edmund, meine Nichte Wally! (Edmund verbeugt sich ebenfalls.) So, die nöthigen Formalitäten wären beendet . . . jetzt wollen wir gemüthlich sein! (Er nimmt einen Fauteuil von links und schiebt ihn Edmund zu, der sich darauf setzt; Reimer bleibt zwischen Wally und Edmund stehen).

Edmund.

Mein Fräulein, Ihr Herr Oheim beglückt mich mit so viel Wohlwollen, daß ich doppelt erfreut wäre, Sie dasselbe theilen zu sehen.

Wally.

Mein Herr . . .! (bei Seite.) Er ist sehr hübsch!

Edmund.

Nur hat Herr Reimer mich falsch über Sie berichtet.

Reimer.

Ich?

Edmund.

Sie sagten mir Ihr Fräulein Nichte sei reizend . . .

Reimer (hinter dem Sopha sich Wally nähernd).

Und ist sie es etwa nicht?

Edmund.

Bezaubernd . . . entzückend hätten Sie sagen müssen.

Wally (geschmeichelt bei Seite).

Sehr galant!

Mathilde (bei Seite verletzt).

Und in meiner Gegenwart!

Reimer.

Es ist mir sehr angenehm das von Ihnen zu hören und da Wally den Zweck Ihres Besuches bereits kennt, so . . . gehen Sie gerade auf's Ziel los! — — — Sie haben das Wort!

Edmund.

Das Fräulein wußte gewiß im Vorhinein, welchen günstigen Eindruck sie auf mich machen würde . . . allein das genügt nicht! Auch mein Urtheil muß gesprochen werden . . . und ich bin linkisch, schüchtern . . .

Mathilde (bei Seite).

Davon merkt man nichts.

Edmund.

Früher war ich allerdings mehr Weltmann . . . ich hatte mehr Vertrauen zu mir selbst, allein die Geschäftsunternehmungen unseres Hauses führten mich unter einen anderen Himmelsstrich und wenn sonst das Reisen die Jugend bildet... mich haben sie wieder — entbildet! In fernen Welt-

theilen, unter Wilden und Negern . . . wurde ich selbst ein kleiner
Wilder und als ich jetzt wieder den deutschen Boden betrat, da
fühlte ich mich den gesellschaftlichen Formen ganz entfremdet . . .
sah ein, daß ich alle guten Lehren und alle feine Sitte bei mei=
nen Löwen= und Bärenjagden in Brasilien verlernt hatte und
daß es wohl nöthig sein wird, meine Erziehung von Neuem zu
beginnen.

     R e i m e r (wieder zu Edmund tretend).

Spaßvogel! Sie haben da unten in Bahia und Bernam=
buco nichts v e r l o r e n, sondern im Gegentheil ein großes
Vermögen e r w o r b e n!

       E d m u n d (lächelnd).

Nun, ich mußte doch mit E t w a s zurückkommen . . . und
mein Vermögen ist auch vielleicht . . . meine einzige gute Eigen=
schaft! (Aufstehend zu Wally.) Wird d i e s e vorläufig genügen, mich
in Ihren Augen Gnade finden zu lassen?

      W a l l y (bei Seite naiv).

Ist es nicht jammerschade, daß ich den nun nicht heira=
ten soll!

        R e i m e r.

Also, Wally, Du hörst; die Frage war klar und deutlich!

        W a l l y.

Ja, lieber Onkel! (bei Seite.) Es m u ß sein . . . Energie!

        R e i m e r.

Ich zweifle nicht daß deine Entscheidung . . .

        W a l l y.

Einen Augenblick lieber Onkel!

       M a t h i l d e (bei Seite).

Was wird sie sagen!

      W a l l y (zu Edmund).

Mein Herr, Sie kommen soeben aus Brasilien, wie ich
höre, und haben wahrscheinlich vergessen, daß man in Deutsch=
land — unter solchen Umständen — gewöhnlich damit anfängt,
sich erst näher kennen zu lernen!

        E d m u n d.

Sie waren mir nicht mehr unbekannt, mein Fräulein, und
Ihr Oheim hat mir so viel Gutes, so viel Schönes gesagt . . .

        W a l l y.

Ach, mein Onkel, ist auch so ein alter Geschäftsmann und

ich glaube er betrachtet mich als einen kleinen Exportartikel, den er nicht böse wäre rasch abzuladen — — —

Reimer.

Was? weil ich voll Lobes über Dich bin — — ?

Wally (schelmisch).

Ehemals haben Sie wohl auch die Waaren sehr herausgestrichen ..., die Sie los werden wollten!

Reimer.

Hör 'mal, Du machst Bemerkungen ...

Wally.

Uebrigens glaube ich kaum, daß Herr Feldern auf ein „veni vidi, vici," ausgegangen ist und sich einbildet ich würde schon bei der ersten Begegnung eine unbezwingbare Leidenschaft für ihn fühlen?! —

Edmund.

Gewiß nicht, mein Fräulein, aber gestatten Sie mir wenigstens zu hoffen daß mit der Zeit — — —

Reimer (wieder längs dem Kamin zu Mathilden tretend).

Und Du, Mathilde, Du sagst gar nichts? Du solltest meinen Wunsch doch unterstützen und mir beistehen Wally zur Vernunft zu bringen.

Edmund (sich leicht verneigend).

Darf ich mir Ihre Fürsprache erbitten, gnädige Frau?

(Reimer stellt sich wieder zwischen Wally und Edmund.)

Mathilde

Das kann ich Ihnen nicht versprechen, Herr Feldern; denn in Heiratsangelegenheiten sich zu mischen, ist eine sehr delikate Sache.

Wally (aufstehend).

Und würde überdieß nichts an meinem Entschlusse ändern. (Reimer nähert sich erschrocken Wally.) Ich bedauere, Herr Feldern Ihren Antrag, so schmeichelhaft er auch für mich ist, nicht annehmen zu können. (Sie geht vor Edmund vorüber, nach dem Vordergrund links.)

Reimer (starr).

Eine Zurückweisung?

Edmund (bei Seite einen Blick auf Mathilde werfend).

Auf Commando?!

Mathilde (bei Seite).

Gottlob — sie hat Wort gehalten!

Reimer (streng).

Wally, wie soll ich Dein Betragen mir erklären? Vor einer halben Stunde, als ich Dir Edmund's Bewerbung mittheilte, willigtest Du mit Freuden in dieselbe — — —

Wally (bei Seite).

Da haben wir's.

Reimer.

Woher diese plötzliche und mir unerklärliche Aenderung Deiner Ansichten?

Edmund (bei Seite).

Ich glaube es zu errathen!

Wally.

Du lieber Himmel, Onkelchen, . . . ich wußte nicht, daß Herr Feldern bis jetzt . . . unter den Wilden gelebt hat . . . und da fürcht' ich mich!

Reimer.

Das kann doch kein vernünftiger Grund sein?

Wally.

Ob vernünftig oder nicht . . . mein Entschluß steht fest und keine weitere Einwendung wird ihn wankend machen.

Reimer (losbrechend).

Was? So ein rücksichtsloses Betragen mir gegenüber? — Geh', Du bist eine Undankbare!

Wally.

Onkel!

Reimer.

Ja, eine Undankbare, und seit langer Zeit gibst Du mir täglich den Beweis davon, indem Du nur Unfrieden in meinem Hause stiftest! Ich nahm Dich oft in Schutz gegen Mathilde, wenn sie über Dein störrisches Betragen empört war, aber jetzt begreife ich ihren Haß gegen Dich! (geht zu Mathilden).

Mathilde.

Meinen Haß? . . . Du übertreibst!

Reimer.

Hast Du mir's nicht hundertmal gesagt! (setzt sich ärgerlich auf's Sopha).

Edmund (vorkommend).

Ich bedaure die . . . unschuldige Ursache so ernster Zwistigkeiten zu sein ... aber es gibt Zeichen, die nicht trügen, und ich, der ich ziemlich abergläubig bin, ich hätte das plötzliche Unwohlsein Ihrer Frau Gemalin, bei meinem Eintritte in Ihr Haus, als schlimme Vorbedeutung ansehen sollen, als warnende Stimme, die mir zurief: „Geh nicht weiter ... Du gelangst hier nicht zum Ziele!"

Reimer (ärgerlich).

Lieber Freund ... das sind Kindereien ...

Mathilde.

Ich bin ganz der Meinung des Herrn Feldern ... man thut oft am Besten, einer ersten Eingebung zu folgen! (geht wieder an den Spiegel und richtet ihren Haarputz).

Reimer (bei Seite).

Sie auch? (steht auf).

Edmund.

Die gnädige Frau und ich ... wir verstehen uns! und ich glaube das Beste, was ich thun kann, ist ... wieder nach Brasilien zurückzukehren! (Er geht in den Vordergrund links).

Wally (halb träumerisch).

Und ich ... wieder in mein Dörfchen!

Reimer.

Nein, Fräulein Eigensinn! Ich bin Dein Vormund ... und ich allein habe über Dich zu verfügen! In meinem Hause bleibst Du aber nicht länger ... (Bewegung Wally's.) Du sollst in strengere Zucht ... Heute noch übergebe ich Dich meiner Schwester!

Wally (erschrickt).

Taute Therese? Onkel!

Mathilde (bei Seite).

Armes Kind ... und ich bin daran Schuld!

Reimer.

Packe Deine Sachen zusammen ... und von nun an kenne ich Dich nicht mehr!

Wally (mit verstellter Trauer).

Ach!! ——— (nach kurzer Pause, schelmisch.) Willst Du mir einen Abschiedskuß geben?

Reimer (mit seiner natürlichen Gutmüthigkeit kämpfend).

Nein ... später vielleicht ... (gedehnt, mit Beziehung auf

Edmund) wenn Du geneigter sein wirst, mir zu folgen! (Er dreht ihr den Rücken und bleibt, gegen das Publicum gewendet, stehen.)

Wally (bei Seite).

Ach! . . . wenn ich nur könnte!

Reimer.

Aber heute war Dein Betragen so . . . empörend . . .

Wally (bei Seite, seinen Entschluß fassend).

Einerlei! — (Läuft an die Mittelthür und dreht sich dort um.) Ohne Groll, Onkelchen!

Reimer (rasch).

Was?!

Wally.

Ohne Groll . . . allerseits! (Durch die Mitte ab.)

Edmund (bei Seite).

Ich werde Sie wiedersehen! — (Grüßt und folgt Wally, Mathilde tritt schwermüthig an's Fenster, Reimer wirft sich wüthend in den Fauteuil rechts vorne und streckt die Füße auf das Camingitter).

Der Vorhang fällt.

Ende des ersten Aktes.

———

Zweiter Akt.

(Zimmer bei Frau Müllner, jedoch etwas einfacher möblirt wie jenes bei Reimer. Links erste Coulisse ein runder Tisch mit drei Stühlen. Zweite Coulisse ein großer Kleiderschrank, daneben ein Tisch. — Rechts erste Coulisse eine kleine, elegante Commode; über derselben ein Spiegel. Zweite Coulisse ein Piano, auf demselben Armleuchter mit Kerzen. Nicht weit vom Piano ein ovaler, mit einem bunten, bis auf den Boden herabreichenden Teppich bedeckter Tisch; rechts von demselben ein Stuhl, links ein Fauteuil. Dritte Coulisse: eine kleine Tapetenthür. In der Mitte des Hintergrundes ein Balcon mit Glasthüren, welche sich nach außen öffnen und die Aussicht auf die Wipfel der Bäume gewähren. Rechts und links vom Balcon je ein kleines Sopha. In den beiden Ecken des Hintergrundes schräge Seitenthüren. Auf den Sopha's, Fauteuil's und Stühlen kleine weiße Schutzdeckchen. Das Ganze muß den Eindruck größter Ordnung und Reinlichkeit ohne jedweden Luxus machen.)

Erste Szene.

Wally (einfacher als im erster Akt gekleidet).

(Beim Aufziehen des Vorhanges sitzt sie auf dem Fauteuil am Tische rechts und säumt eine Serviette. Auf dem Tische steht ein Arbeitskörbchen und ein Päckchen neuer, noch ungesäumter Servietten.)

Wally.

Die eine Serviette wird bald fertig sein, es bleiben mir also nur mehr 23 zu säumen! . . . Seit den acht Tagen, die ich hier im Staatsgefängnisse bei der Brummtante bin, habe ich schon zehn Strafen bekommen . . . und heute bin ich schon wieder im Arrest! Dreimal weil ich die Thür zu heftig zuschlug, fünfmal weil ich widersprochen habe, gestern weil ich ohne Per-

miſſion zum Fenſter hinausſah, und heute ... weil ich geſungen
habe! „Wie, unverbeſſerliches Mädchen, Du erlaubſt Dir
ohne Erlaubniß zu ſingen? Aus Strafe wirſt Du zwei Dutzend
Servietten einſäumen!" ... Und ich ſäume ... während die
Andern bei Clärchen's Prüfung ſind! Aber das hindert mich
doch nicht zu ſingen!

(ſingt:) Blühe Blümlein auf der Haiden,
　　　Blühe Röslein an der Bruſt,
　　　Mag die Blumen gerne leiden,
　　　Hab' an Blumen meine Luſt.

(ſteht auf und kommt nähend und ſingend vor:)

　　　Und kommt einſt die frohe Stunde,
　　　Daß es ſich im Herzen regt,
　　　Geb' ein Röslein ihm die Kunde,
　　　Daß mein Herz für ihn nur ſchlägt!

(Sie bleibt plötzlich, über ihre Gedanken erſchreckend, ſtehen, denkt einen
Augenblick nach und ſagt dann naiv:) Ich kann mich doch ein Bis=
chen zerſtreuen ...? (Geht nähend im Vordergrunde auf und ab.)
Um ſo mehr, als meine neue Behauſung ohnehin nicht ſehr luſtig
iſt! ... Und Herr Edmund, aus dem die Brummtante jetzt
zwangsweiſe ihren Schwiegerſohn machen will, kommt auch täg=
lich ... nicht daß mir das unangenehm wäre, aber aufrichtig
geſagt, das iſt ein ſchlechtes Mittel, um ihn mir aus ... dem
Gedächtniß zu bringen! (Schreit leicht auf.) Ach! ... ich habe
mich geſtochen! ... Die Brummtante würde das eine gerechte
Strafe des Himmels nennen! ... aber leider iſt Mathilde noch
ſchwerer geſtraft als ich ... und das neue Heiratsproject bringt
ſie wieder in die alte Gefahr ... ich habe mich eigentlich ganz
umſonſt geopfert ... ach! — (Die Seitenthür links öffnet ſich.) Ah!
feierliche Rückkehr von der Prüfung!

Zweite Szene.

**Wally, Frau Müllner, Madame Pariſer, Clärchen,
Mathilde und Reimer** (alle feſtlich gekleidet, von links).

(Frau Müllner trägt einen Prämiantenkranz von Roſen in der Hand,
Clärchen hat einige andere Kränze am Arm und drei Prämienbücher
mit bunten Deckeln und Goldſchnitt in der Hand; ſie trägt ein ge=

schlossenes (hohes) weißes Kleid, breite Achselträger von rosa oder
blauem Seidenband, das sich vorne kreuzt und rückwärts an der
Taille in großen, langen Schleifen endigt. Mutter und Tochter sind
freudestrahlend; Madame Parifer ist in höchst feierlicher Stimmung,
Mathilde ist zerstreut und Reimer sieht sehr gelangweilt aus.)

Reimer (zuerst eintretend).

Triumph! Triumph! (Bei Seite) und schrecklich viel Lang=
weile.

Wally (zu Clärchen).

Ach, welch ein Glück! Du bist ja ganz beladen mit Schä=
tzen und Auszeichnungen! Empfange meine Huldigungen, Clärchen.
(Um für die Kränze und Bücher Platz zu machen, welche Clärchen
auf den Tisch rechts legt, nimmt Wally rasch Servietten 2c. und legt
sie auf die Commode, nur die Serviette, an welcher sie eben nähte,
bleibt auf dem Tische neben dem Arbeitskörbchen liegen.)

Clärchen.

Die bringst Du besser bei Madame Parifer an (deutet auf
dieselbe), meiner würdigen Pensionsvorsteherin, der ich meine
Kenntnisse und Auszeichnungen allein verdanke!

Mad. Parifer (immer sehr steif und aufgeblasen).

Sie verdanken sie Ihrem Fleiße und Ihren natürlichen An=
lagen, mein Kind.

Frau Müllner.

Ja, das ist wahr, meine Tochter ist von der Natur sehr
begabt!

Mad. Parifer.

Ich stelle sie auch allenthalben als Muster auf. Es ist frei=
lich kein Wunder ... wenn man aus solcher Familie stammt!
(Sie blickt, sich halb vorbeugend, auf Frau Müllner, Mathilden und
Reimer. Mathilde setzt sich nachdenklich an den Tisch links.)

Reimer (zu Wally).

Sie hat sechs Prämien bekommen! Ein halbes Dutzend!
(An den Fingern herzählend.) Prämium für's Clavierspielen, Prä=
mium für's Tanzen, Prämium für's Singen ...

Wally (lächelnd, leise).

Ich habe für's Singen eine Strafe bekommen!

Reimer (rasch, leise).

Schweig still! (Laut.) Prämium für Aquarellmalerei; Prä=
mium für Gymnastik.

Fr. Müllner.

Uns das werthvollste von Allen, dasjenige, das ein Mutterherz am meisten erfreut: Prämium für gute Sitten! (Sie zeigt stolz den Kranz von Rosen und setzt ihn Clärchen auf's Haupt.)

Mad. Pariser.

Und da sie ihn erhielt, so hat sie ihn auch verdient, denn bei mir gibt es keine Parteilichkeit, keine Bevorzugung ... (Bei Seite.) Zwar, wenn die Mutter mir kein so generöses Geschenk gemacht hätte ....

Wally.

Also nochmals meine herzlichsten Glückwünsche, Clärchen! — Prämium für Piano, Tanzen, Gymnastik ....! Du bist wohl auch sehr fest in der Orthographie?

Clärchen.

Na, das ist gerade nicht meine stärkste Seite.

Wally (ohne Ironie).

Und im Nähen?

Mad. Pariser (stolz).

Mademoiselle, Derartiges wird in meinem Institute nicht gelehrt.

Fr. Müllner (zu Wally tretend).

Apropos, nähen! Wie weit bist Du mit der Aufgabe, die ich Dir gegeben?

Wally (naiv).

Bei der ersten Serviette.

Fr. Müller.

Was? noch bei der ersten?

Wally.

Nun, da es eine Strafe ist ... je länger sie währt, desto nützlicher wird sie mir sein! (setzt sich links und näht wieder).

Fr. Müllner (streng).

Du wirst um ein Dutzend mehr säumen.

(Mad. Pariser, welche ebenfalls an dem Tische links steht, nickt Frau Müllner beistimmend zu.)

Reimer (zu Wally tretend).

Schön! Also noch eine Strafe! Recht hübsch!

Fr. Müllner.

Schämen sollte sie sich, ... heute ... in Gegenwart der Triumphe ihrer Cousine ...

Reimer.

Und wo Du doch eine ebenso gute Erziehung erhalten haft,
wie fie ...

Mad. Parifer (aufgeblasen).

Oh! — eine ebenso gute ....

Reimer.

Gewiß; fie ift die Schülerin meiner Gattin, deren Tugen=
den und fonftige trefflichen Eigenschaften fie fich zum Vorbild
nehmen follte! (Setzt fich an den Tifch links, Mathilden gegenüber.)

Wally (vorkommend bei Seite).

Armer Onkel!

Fr. Müllner (bei Seite).

Ift der Menfch dumm!

Wally.

Lieber Onkel, haben Sie nur noch ein Bischen Geduld; Sie
gaben mich in die Correctionsanftalt zu Tante Müllner, damit
ich mit der Zeit alle meine Sünden abbüße...

Fr. Müllner (wüthend).

Mädchen, wenn Du nicht ftille bift....

Clärchen (den Kranz abnehmend).

Mama,... laß mich heute Wally's Fürsprecherin fein ..

Fr. Müllner.

Fräulein Clärchen, wenn auch Deine Schulprüfung gut
ausgefallen ift, fo berechtigt Dich das noch nicht, ohne Erlaubniß
hier zu fprechen.

Clärchen.

Ich dächte doch, heute, wo Du mit mir fo zufrieden
bift...

Wally (drollig).

Clärchen hat recht, Tante; heute, wo Du mit ihr fo zu=
frieden bift, kannft Du mit mir fchon ein wenig unzu=
frieden fein, ohne daß das Gleichgewicht verloren geht!

Fr. Müllner (wüthend zu Reimer).

Hörft Du?!

Reimer.

Das Mädchen ift unverbefferlich!

Mad. Parifer (zu Reimer tretend).

Wer weiß, Herr Reimer? Und wenn Sie fie mir anver=
trauen wollten, fie würde in zwei, drei Jahren — —

Reimer (einfallend).

Auch bei Ihnen das Unterste zu Oberst kehren!

Mad. Pariser (mit bitter-süßem Lächeln zu Wally).

Das fürcht' ich nicht! Ich habe schon ganz Andere gezähmt! He? kleiner Eisenkopf? (Zum Publikum mit Selbstbewußtsein.) Mein Institut ist allbekannt! Das Wohl des Leibes wird bei mir ebenso gepflegt wie das des Geistes! Strenge Disciplin... unausgesetzte Beaufsichtigung ... keine Ueberanstrengung ... zweckentsprechende Hausordnung ... gute und reichliche Beköstigung ...! (Sie nähert sich wieder Reimer.)

Clärchen (leise zu Wally).

Täglich hartes Fleisch und trockenes Gemüse!

Mad. Pariser.

Sehen Sie, was ich aus Clärchen gemacht habe! Und ich bin stolz darauf ... ich werde sie sehr vermissen! (Weinerlich.) Es wird mir sehr schwer, mich von einer so vorzüglichen Schülerin zu trennen. ... (Umarmt Clärchen.)

Wally (bei Seite).

Die verdient sich ihr heutiges Mittagessen sauer!

Mad. Pariser (wieder zu Frau Müllner gehend).

Wenn Sie mir Ihr Töchterchen noch ein, zwei Jährchen, lassen wollten ...

Fr. Müllner.

Unmöglich, liebe Madame Pariser ... meine Tochter hat jetzt einer andern Bestimmung zu folgen....ich gedenke sie zu verheiraten!

Reimer (aufstehend).

Also wird es Ernst?

Fr. Müllner (trocken).

Ja wohl.... es ist fast so gut wie abgemacht!

Mathilde (ängstlich bei Seite).

Himmel!

Wally (welche allein Mathilde beobachtet und deren Aufregung merkt, wieder nähend).

Nun, zum Glück, ist diese Heirat noch nicht geschlossen... und wenn Clärchen meinem Rathe folgt...

Fr. Müllner (verächtlich).

Deinem Rathe?

W a l l y (fortfahrend).

Einen schönen Gatten geben Sie ihr da! . . . Einen Mann, den ich abgewiesen habe!

Fr. Müllner.

Das war ein Glück für ihn!

W a l l y (ihre Arbeit unterbrechend).

Und vielleicht wäre es auch ein Glück für Clärchen, wenn sie meinem Beispiele folgte.

Fr. Müllner (drohend).

Wally!

C l ä r c h e n.

Ich bitte Dich, Wally . . .

W a l l y (Frau Müllner nachahmend).

Fräulein Clärchen, wenn auch Deine Schulprüfung gut ausgefallen ist, so berechtigt Dich das noch nicht, ohne Erlaubniß hier zu sprechen!

Fr. Müllner (außer sich).

Ah!! — — (wendet sich entrüstet gegen die Uebrigen, welche mit Ausnahme Mathildens, sich ein wenig nach rückwärts gezogen hatten und ebenfalls entsetzt sind über die Kühnheit Wally's.) Gott straf mich — — sie verhöhnt mich! —

R e i m e r.

Diese Ungezogenheit . . .

Fr. Müllner.

Nun hat meine Geduld ein Ende, und da die Güte bei Dir nichts hilft, wollen wir's mit der Strenge versuchen! Du wirst heute nicht bei Tische speisen, sondern hier — — allein!

W a l l y.

Allein?

Fr. Müllner.

Und schläfst heute nicht im Kabinet neben meinem Zimmer — — das verdienst Du nicht mehr . . . sondern hier, auf dem Sopha!

M a t h i l d e (welche dieser ganzen Scene mit peinlicher Erregung zuhörte, aufstehend).

Aber, Frau Schwägerin, das ist zu hart. —

R e i m e r (zu Mathilde tretend).

Nein, nein, Mathilde, Dein Herz ist zu weich!

(Eine Magd öffnet die rechte Seitenthür.)

Wally (aufstehend und nach derselben deutend).

Das Festmal ist eben bereit! Es ist ohnehin schon spät geworden, da die Prüfung so lange gedauert hat! Bitte sich nicht länger stören zu lassen!

Fr. Müllner.

Ja, gehen wir, denn ich bin außer mir!

Reimer.

Und ich erst!

Fr. Müllner (nimmt den Kranz aus Clärchen's Händen und sagt mit einem bissigen Blick auf Wally, stolz).

Mein Kind, Du wirst heute bei Tische diesen Kranz auf= behalten.

Alle (mit Ausnahme von Mathilde und Wally, welche spöttisch, verstohlen lächeln, zunickend).

Ganz in der Ordnung!

(Alle gehen nach und nach rechts ab.)

Wally (zu Reimer, welcher zuletzt abgehen will).

Onkelchen! (Reimer wendet sich an der Thüre um; Wally knixt schelmisch.) Guten Appetit!

Reimer.

Du hast kein Herz! (Ab.)

Dritte Szene.

Wally.

Wally (allein, sinnend).

Kein Herz?! (Nach kurzer Pause lustig.) Ist die Welt ko= misch und wie trügerisch ist vieles was man so hört und sieht. (Ernst.) Wenn man alt geworden ist, muß man sie wohl recht hassen! — (Wieder heiter.) Aber Gott sei Dank, ich bin noch nicht so weit! (Geht an den Tisch rechts und besieht die Bücher Clärchens.) Clärchen hat da schon einen ganz hübschen Bibliothekfond! (Nimmt ein Buch und liest das Titelblatt.) „Paul und Virgine." (Lächelnd.) Eine Liebesgeschichte! (Wiederholt dasselbe Spiel mit einem andern Buche.) „Telemach." Wieder eine Liebesgeschichte! (Sie nimmt die Bücher und Kränze und trägt sie nach dem Tisch= chen neben dem Kleiderschrank, im Gehen die ersten Zeilen des „Tele=

mach" lefend.) „Calypfo kounte fich nicht tröften über die Abreife Ulyffes . . ." (Schelmifch.) Was fie aber nicht hinderte fich in Telemach zu verlieben, der feinerfeits wieder in die fchöne Nymphe Eucharis verliebt ift . . . ! (Hat während dem Bücher und Kränze auf das Tifchchen gelegt und kommt in den Vordergrund.) Man ift fehr moralifch in dem Mädchen=Inftitut!! —

Vierte Szene.

Wally, Reimer (von rechts).

Reimer (den Strengeu fpielend).

Wally, da haft Du dein Mittageffen! (er bringt ein großes Stück Brod und eine Flafche Waffer, auf welche ein leeres Glas ge- ftülpt ift, und gibt Beides auf den Tifch rechts.) Waffer und Brod!!

Wally.

Was?!

Reimer.

Sonft nichts! Meine Schwefter ift wüthend; . . . fie be= hauptet nur die härteften Strafen könnten hier eine Befferung erzielen . . . und obwohl ich im Prinzip ihr ganz beipflichte, kann ich mich doch mit einer folchen Diät nicht einverftanden erklären, . . . deßhalb beftand ich darauf Dir das felbft zu brin- gen . . . (im natürlichen Tone) und ging rafch in die Küche um ein Bischen Obft und Kuchen beizufügen! (er zieht aus feinen verfchiedenen Rocktafchen Obft und Kuchen, von dem Einiges in Papier gewickelt ift).

Wally.

Onkel, das haft Du für mich gethan?

Reimer (wieder ftreng).

Mathilde wollte es durchaus, denn ich . . . ich bin auch wüthend! . . . (wieder gutmüthig halblaut) Ich habe auch ein Fläfchchen Wein geftohlen. (Zieht daffelbe aus der Rocktafche und ftellt es ebenfalls auf den Tifch.)

Wally.

Auch Wein?! Ach, bift Du gut, Onkelchen!

Reimer.

Ich wollte Dir auch ein Stückchen Braten beingen, aber der fteckt noch am Spieß . . . da kount' ich nichts erwifchen!

Wally.

Siehst Du, Onkelchen, daß Du mich lieber haſt, als Du gestehen willſt.

Reimer (wieder strenge).

O nein ... durchaus nicht ... im Gegentheil ... ich bin ſehr unzufrieden mit Dir! (ſich vergeſſend.) Wirſt Du von dem kalten Zeug denn ſatt werden?

Wally.

Ohne Sorge, Onkelchen, mein Magen iſt nicht ſo heikel! Aber Du geh, laß nicht länger auf Dich warten, ſonſt ſetzen ſie Dich auch: „zu Waſſer und Brod!"

Reimer.

Spitzbübin! (Er will ſie umarmen, beſinnt ſich jedoch.) Nein ... keine Schwäche!

Wally.

Ach was! Die Brummtante ſieht es ja nicht!

Reimer.

Iſt auch wahr! (er küßt ſie.) Aber daß du ihr nichts ſagſt!

Wally.

Gott bewahre! (Zum Publikum.) Gutes, altes Haus!

Reimer (iſt unterdeß an die rechte Seitenthür gegangen, öffnet dieſelbe und ſagt laut und strenge um von Frau Müllner gehört zu werden).

Es bleibt dabei ... ich bin ſehr unzufrieden mit Dir! — (ab).

Fünfte Szene.

Wally dann Edmund.

Wally.

Dieſe Tante Müllner ... fangt an mir fürchterlich zu werben! Mich wie ein kleines Kind zu behandeln. Waſſer und Brod! Sie geht zu weit! Ich werbe revoltiren und gleich wieder auf der äußerſten Linken ſein! Wenn ich das Loos, das ſie mir hier bereitet, mit jenem vergleiche, das ich vor acht Tagen ausſchlug ...! — Glück und Freiheit ... mit ihm! Ah! Mathilde, Deine Ruhe koſtet mich viel! ... Aber ... er benkt wohl gar nicht mehr an mich! — Machen wir's ebenſo ... und geh'n wir eſſen! Ich habe Hunger! (ſetzt ſich an den Tiſch rechts.)

Edmund (im Jagdanzug, mit Flinte und einer wohlgefüllten Jagdtasche, tritt durch die linke Seitenthür ein).

Ei, Fräulein Wally, Sie hier?

Wally (erregt bei Seite).

Er!! (steht auf).

Edmund.

Ich kehre eben von der Jagd zurück, und bringe im Vor-
beigehen Frau Müllner das Resultat meiner Streifereien durch
Wald und Feld!

Wally.

Sie machen sich ja fast zu ihrem täglichen Gratis-Lieferan-
ten. Ihre gestrige Provision wird eben drinnen verzehrt.

Edmund.

Warum speisen Sie denn nicht mit den Andern?

Wally (zögernd).

Weil ich . . . (schelmisch) Strafe habe?

Edmund.

Was? Strafe? Sie?

Wally.

Ja, bei Wasser und Brot . . . und hätte nicht Onkelchen
mir einige Extra's auf unerlaubtem Wege verschafft . . .

Edmund.

Wasser und Brod — Sie? Und die schönen Repphühner
die ich gestern eigends für Sie brachte?

Wally.

O — — für mich?!

Edmund.

Gewiß!

Wally.

Nun . . . dann thut es mir doppelt leid, darauf verzichten
zu müssen. Aber Sie sind nicht zu gleicher Entsagung verurtheilt
. . . man hat sich eben erst zu Tische gesetzt und Brummtantchen
. . . (knixend) Tante Müllner, wollt' ich sagen, wird gewiß sehr
erfreut sein, Sie als Tischgenossen zu besitzen . . . selbst in
Ihrem Jagdanzuge . . . (bei Seite) der ihn übrigens ganz gut
kleidet!

Edmund (heiter).

Gott bewahre; statt mit Brummtantchen . . . Tante Müllner
wollt' ich sagen, Repphühner zu essen, zöge ich es vor, das

Stückchen Brod mit Ihnen theilen zu dürfen . . . Wenn Sie mir gestatten wollten mich selbst hiezu einzuladen!

Wally.

Wasser und Brod wollen Sie?

Edmund (verliebt).

In Ihrer liebenswürdigen Gesellschaft!

Wally (ohne darauf zu achten).

Nun — wenn Ihnen die schmale Kost Vergnügen macht . . . (sie bricht das Stück Brod entzwei und gibt ihm die Hälfte).

Edmund.

Danke — und jetzt wollen wir zusammen diniren!

Wally (immer ungezwungen und fröhlich).

Ja wohl! Die Brummtante soll grün und gelb vor Aerger werden! Wir Zwei wollen uns hier viel besser unterhalten, als die ganze hohe Gesellschaft da drinnen! Kommen Sie, Herr Edmund, rasch den Tisch gedeckt! Da habe ich gerade „feines Linnen" das ich selbst gesäumt habe! (sie nimmt die Serviette und deckt sie auf den Tisch links vorne).

Edmund.

Reizend! Ich werde Ihnen helfen! (er legt sein Stück Brod auf die Mitte des Tisches).

Wally (nimmt ihre Hälfte Brod vom Tische rechts und legt sie zu jener Edmunds). Das arme Sünder=Brod in die Mitte!

Edmund.

Wasserflasche und Glas! (holt Beides und stellt es ebenfalls auf den Tisch links).

Wally (die Weinflasche hochhaltend, mit komischer Grandezza).

Und Wein . . .! wenn Sie erlauben! Und Obst! und Ku=chen! (Hat Alles vom Tische rechts genommen und trägt es nach jenem links.)

Edmund (lachend).

Ah wenn Sie so verschwenderisch sind . . .!

Wally (mit erheuchelter Wichtigkeit).

Ja, ich habe selten Gäste bei Tische . . . aber wenn ich ein=mal anfange zu traktiren . . .! (Entfernt das Papier von Obst und Kuchen.)

Edmund.

Hahaha! . . . Fehlt sonst noch etwas?

Wally.

Richtig ... wir haben kein Messer!

Edmund.

Hier! (Zieht ein großes Jagdmesser hervor und legt es auf den Tisch.)

Wally.

Hilfe ...! Ein Säbel!

Edmund.

Aber es ist nur ein Glas da!

Wally.

Eigentlich brauchten wir zwei!

Edmund.

Thut nichts — ich werde zuletzt trinken.

Wally.

Haben Sie denn nicht einen kleinen Jagdbecher?

Edmund.

Natürlich! (Zieht ein ledernes Trinkschiffchen aus der Rock= tasche.) Hier ist der zweite Pokal! (Stellt es vor sich auf den Tisch.)

Wally.

Bravo! Da können wir bei Toasten die „Becher" klirren lassen! ... Haha! es wird immer lustiger! (Beide entfernen sich vom Tische.)

Edmund.

So! Jetzt ist der Tisch gedeckt! (Sehr ceremoniell Wally den Arm reichend.) Mein gnädiges Fräulein, darf ich es wagen?

Wally (die große Dame affektirend).

Sie sind sehr freundlich, mein Herr! ... (Edmund führt Wally zu Tische, dort machen sie sich gegenseitig eine tiefe Verbeugung; Edmund setzt sich der Coulisse zunächst, Wally ihm gegenüber; sobald sie sitzen und das frugale Mal einen Augenblick betrachtet haben, lachen Beide laut auf.)

Edmund.

Welch' ein köstliches Mal! (Sie beginnen zu essen und zu trinken, während der Dialog ununterbrochen fortgeht.)

Wally (harmlos).

Sie wissen gar nicht, was Sie verlieren ... da drinnen hätte man Sie neben meine Cousine Clärchen gesetzt ...!

Edmund.

Glauben Sie denn, daß ich Clärchen halber... so oft hieher komme?

Wally.

Ei, Brummtantchen glaubt, Sie wollten Sie heiraten

Edmund.

Dieser Aberglaube ist mein Glück, er ist der Schlüssel, welcher mir die Pforten dieses Hauses öffnet... sonst könnte ich Sie ja nicht täglich sehen.

Wally (stutzt).

Mich?

Edmund.

Sie, Wally, ja... denn nur Sie allein liebe ich!

Wally (ihn freudig aber ruhig anblickend).

Sie... lieben mich?

Edmund.

Seit dem Augenblicke, da ich Sie zum ersten Male sah.

Wally (wie oben).

Trotz meiner... abweisenden Antwort?

Edmund.

Vielleicht gerade wegen dieser! Ich erwartete ein kleines geziertes Fräulein zu finden, das auf Commando erröthet und die Augen niederschlägt, brei verschiedene Sprachen produziren und mir gleich in der ersten Viertelstunde ein Clavier=Concert mit Variationen an den Kopf schleudern wird...! Nichts von alledem! — Ich fand ein reizendes, junges Mädchen, ein Bischen hochmüthig, ein Bischen schelmisch... ich trug meinen Korb ruhig nach Hause... (mit losbrechender Glut.) Aber ich schwur mir's, bei allem Zauber, den Sie über mich besitzen, die Partie doch noch zu gewinnen!

Wally (nach ganz kurzer Pause, lächelnd).

Welches Feuer! (Nimmt die Wasserflasche.) Rasch, frisches Wasser, Herr Tischgenosse,.... um Sie ein wenig abzukühlen! (Edmund hält lächelnd sein Trinkschiffchen hin; Wally gießt Wasser ein.)

Edmund.

Tausend Dank, göttliche Hebe!

Wally (stellt erschrocken die Wasserflasche auf den Tisch).

Um Gotteswillen! wenn meine moralische Brummtante Sie hörte!

Edmund (sein Trinkschifflein ergreifend).

Stoßen wir an!

Wally (nimmt ihr Glas).

Gerne!

Edmund.

Ein Pereat der Brummtante!

Wally.

Mit Wonne! (Sie stoßen an und trinken.)

Edmund.

Oh, diese Frau...! diese Frau...! Seitdem ich sehe, wie schändlich sie Sie behandelt... Wahrhaftig, Fräulein Wally, i ch leide mehr dabei als S i e!

Wally (gefühlvoll, bei Seite).

Er liebt mich! —

Edmund.

Denn man erniedrigt Sie... man verfolgt Sie förmlich...

Wally (will, immer verlegener, dem Gespräche eine andere Wendung geben).

Ein wenig Kuchen? (Gibt ihm ein Stück.)

Edmund.

Diese Thrannei geht zu weit;... ein Mädchen wie Sie, braucht dieselbe nicht zu dulden!

Wally.

Ich muß es doch! Das einzige Mittel, mich aus derselben zu befreien, wäre eine Heirat gewesen... ich weigerte mich...

Edmund.

Diese Weigerung kam nicht von Ihnen!

Wally (erschrickt).

Wie?... Ein Pfirsich! (Gibt ihm einen.)

Edmund.

Ich habe Mathilden's Einfluß wohl errathen...

Wally (immer ängstlicher).

Oder diese Trauben... (legt sie vor Edmund hin).

Edmund (ihre Hand festhaltend).

Sie hindert Sie, jetzt meine Gattin zu werben... ja aber sie kann Ihnen nicht verbieten, mich zu lieben!

Wally.

Sie zu lieben?

Edmund (immer inniger).

Ja...! Bei Gott, Wally, Sie finden kein treueres, ergebeneres Herz, als das meinige! Vertrauen Sie mir... und fern von diesem Hause... (Wally entzieht ihm ihre Hand), befreit von diesen Qualen und Demüthigungen, sollen Sie die Glücklichste Ihres Geschlechtes werden...!

Wally (bei Seite).

Was wagt er mir zu sagen?

Edmund.

Bald werden wir Ihre herzlose Familie gezwungen haben, Ihnen die freie Verfügung über Ihre Hand zu gestatten, und dann...

Wally (aufspringend).

Kein Wort weiter, Herr Feldner!

Edmund.

Wally!

Wally (stolz).

Eine Entführung?

Edmund.

Vertrauen Sie meiner Ehre, meiner Liebe...!

Wally.

Genug, mein Herr! (Stolz nach rechts deutend.) Sie haben mich ausgestoßen aus dem Kreise, in dem Sie heute ein Prämium für gute Sitten feiern... gleichviel, ich weiß dennoch, was ich mir selbst schuldig bin! — —

Sechste Szene.

Vorige. **Frau Müllner** (von rechts).

Frau Müllner (ohne Edmund zu sehen).

Nun zu uns zwei, Mamsell Wally!

4

Edmund (stellt sich rasch vor den Tisch, um denselben zu verstecken,
bei Seite).

Die Tante!

Wally (wickelt rasch Alles, was auf dem Tische ist, in die Serviette
und schleicht damit nach dem Tischchen neben dem Kleiderschrank, wo sie
es versteckt; der Dialog geht unterdessen fort).

Frau Müllner (Edmund erblickend).

Ei, Herr Feldern!

Edmund.

Ich komme soeben, gnädige Frau.

Frau Müllner.

Weshalb so spät? Meine Gäste sind bereits fortgegangen...
Warum kamen Sie nicht zum Speisen?

Edmund (lächelnd).

Ich war... anderswo geladen!

Frau Müllner.

Einerlei..! (Barsch zu Wally.) Wally hätte immerhin so
vernünftig sein können, mich von Ihrer Ankunft zu benachrich=
tigen.

Edmund.

Verzeihung, gnädige Frau, ich wiedersetzte mich dem lie=
benswürdigen Anerbieten des Fräuleins... ich kam nur auf
einen Augenblick, um Ihnen mein heutiges Jagdergebniß zu
Füßen zu legen. (Er holt seine Jagdtasche, legt sie auf einen Stuhl
links vorne und überreicht nach und nach den Inhalt derselben Frau
Müllner.)

Frau Müllner (sich zierend).

Schon wieder!

Edmund.

Ein Perlhuhn...

Frau Müllner.

Wie aufmerksam! Schade, daß Clärchen nicht ihren Dank
mit dem meinigen vereinen kann...

Edmund.

Eine Wachtel!

Frau Müllner.

Aber die arme Kleine ist so ermüdet von der Aufregung
des heutigen Tages...

Edmund.
Ein Haase...

Frau Müllner.
Denken Sie sich, sie hat sechs Preise bekommen!

Edmund.
Und eine Wildente!

Frau Müllner (welche schwer beladen, etwas unbeholfen dasteht).

Sechs Preise... darunter auch den für **gute Sitten**!
(Durch die offene Balconthür gewahrt man den Beginn der Abend-
röthe; es wird nach nach ganz dunkel auf der Bühne, Wally zündet die
Lichter am Piano an.)

Edmund.
Seien Sie stolz darauf, gnädige Frau, und sobald ich das
Vergnügen haben werde, Fräulein Clärchen zu sehen...

Frau Müllner.
Morgen, lieber Edmund, morgen... es wird schon spät...
und meine Tochter wollte sich durchaus bereits zur Ruhe
begeben... (Mit Emphase.) Glückliches Alter, in welchem noch
nichts den Schlummer der Unschuld stört!

Wally (bei Seite).
Die gibt sich Mühe, (lächelnd) und er heiratet sie doch nicht!

Frau Müllner (gibt Wally Alles was sie in der Hand hält,
barsch).

Wally..! trage das Alles nach der Küche! — Und dann
wirst Du dem Mädchen helfen den Tisch drinnen abzuräumen.

Edmund.
Diese Mühe — —

Frau Müllner (kurz).
Wird ihr sehr wohlthätig sein!

Wally (ironisch).
Um Herz und Geist zu bilden!

Edmund (leise zu Wally).
Aber dieses Haus ist ja eine Galeere!

Wally.
Na, ob! (Rechts ab.)

Siebente Szene.

Frau Müllner, Edmund.

Frau Müllner (setzt sich links vorne und weist Edmund ebenfalls einen Stuhl an).

Mein werther Herr Feldern, ihre regelmäßigen Besuche sind mir zwar sehr angenehm, — — allein das empfängliche Herz meiner Tochter — — die Welt — — ich glaube Ihre redlichen Absichten errathen zu haben und bin nicht abgeneigt, Clärchen so bald als möglich zu verheiraten — — um sie dem gefährlichen Treiben Wally's zu entziehen.

Edmund.

Dem gefährlichen Treiben — — ?

Frau Müllner.

Dieses Mädchen ist ein Satan!

Edmund (aufstehend, ernst).

Wally — — ein Satan?

Frau Müllner.

Von der schlimmsten Sorte!

Edmund (lächelnd).

Ich habe noch nichts Diabolisches an ihr bemerkt!

Frau Müllner.

Sie kennen sie nicht! — — Aber ich habe sie sogar in einem Verdacht, der — —

Edmund.

In welchem Verdacht?

Frau Müllner.

Mir fehlt zwar noch die Gewißheit, allein — — der Gärtner hat mir gemeldet, daß er seit einigen Tagen im Sande Spuren von Männertritten findet — —

Edmund (etwas ungeduldig werdend).

Es werden wohl seine eigenen sein.

Frau Müllner.

Durchaus nicht. Er ist überzeugt, daß sich des Nachts Jemand hier einschleicht. Ist's ein Dieb? ist es ein — — ich will gar nicht sagen was?!

Edmund.

Und Sie haben Wally in Verdacht?

Frau Müllner.

Ich habe Wally überhaupt immer und bei jeder Gelegenheit in Verdacht — — das schadet nicht — — und einmal werde ich sie doch bei irgend Etwas ertappen! Aber in diesem Falle begreifen Sie meine Angst ... drei Frauen allein — — ohne Mann — — ohne Vertheidigung — — ich weiß nicht wozu ich mich entschließen soll — ich wollte schon zum Polizeikommissär gehen — —

Edmund.

Was fällt Ihnen ein — — wie leicht könnte hiedurch Jemand compromittirt werden — — Ueberlassen Sie die Sache mir; ich werde heute Wache halten — — und — —

Frau Müllner.

Wie, Sie wollten Sich diese Mühe geben?

Edmund.

Ich habe gerade mein Jagdgewehr bei mir — — Sie können sich also furchtlos zur Ruhe begeben.

Frau Müllner.

Meine Tochter wird Ihnen ewig dankbar sein!

Edmund (bei Seite).

Und wenn Wally wirklich — — ?! Oh unmöglich!

Frau Müllner (nach der linken Seitenthür zeigend).

Sie wissen, hier über den Gang gelangen Sie zum Garten. — —

Edmund.

Ich will gleich auf meinen Posten! (Nimmt Jagdtasche und Flinte).

Achte Szene.

Vorige, Wally (von rechts).

Wally.

Frau Tante, es ist Alles wieder in Ordnung, Alles aufgeräumt, ich habe nichts zerbrochen.

Frau Müllner.

Das ist ein Wunder — — bei Deiner gewöhnlichen Ungeschicklichkeit — !

Wally (bei Seite).

So, das habe ich für meine Mühe!

Edmund.

Gnädige Frau, ich will nicht länger stören!

Frau Müllner.

Also auf morgen, lieber Edmund!

Edmund.

Mein Fräulein!

Wally.

Auf Wiedersehen, Herr Feldern.

Edmund (betonend).

Ich gehe durch den Garten! — — (Bei Seite.) Nein, nein — ich kann es nicht glauben! (Links ab.)

Neunte Szene.

Frau Müllner, Wally.

Wally (bei Seite).

Wie er mich ansah?

Frau Müllner.

Und jetzt . . . (sie schließt die linke Seitenthür und steckt den Schlüssel zu sich.)

Wally (bei Seite).

Was hat er denn? Sollte diese boshafte Frau mich bei ihm angeschwärzt haben?

Frau Müllner (hat auch die Tapetenthür rechts abgeschlossen und den Schlüssel zu sich gesteckt).

So, das wäre in der Ordnung!

Wally.

Sie schließen mich ein?

Frau Müllner.

Ich treffe die zweckentsprechendsten Vorsichtsmaßregeln. (Sie löscht das eine Licht am Piano aus und nimmt das andere.) Und jetzt schlafe — — oder schlafe nicht, das ist mir einerlei! (Geht an die rechte Seitenthür und wendet sich dort noch einmal gegen Wally) Ein anders Mal wirst Du respektvoller gegen mich sein!

(Geht ab, man hört von außen die Thüre verschließen, es ist ganz finster auf der Bühne.)

Zehnte Szene.

Wally (allein).

Diese Behandlung! . . . (Sinnend.) Ja wohl, Edmund hat recht, ihre Tirannei geht zu weit! — Und als er mir mit beredten Worten Mittel und Wege zeigte, derselben ein rasches, vielleicht ein glückliches Ende zu machen . . . einen Augenblick schnürte es mir das Herz zusammen . . . ich glaubte seinen lockenden Einflüsterungen folgen zu sollen . . .! (Rüttelt sich) Doch, Gott sei Dank! das dauerte nur einen Augenblick . . . es ging vorüber . . . (Sie hat in Gedanken den Stuhl links gegen sich gelehnt; kniet nun halb auf demselben, während sie ihre Arme auf die Stuhllehne stützt und die Hände faltet). Lieber Gott! Du bist mein einziger Schutz und Schirm! Ich danke Dir, daß Du meinen Muth, mein Herz bewacht und in der Gefahr mich beschützt hast! Hilf mir auch ferner . . . und gib, daß ich ihn vergesse!!! (Sie steht auf und fährt sich mit der Hand über die Augen.) Und jetzt will ich versuchen zu schlafen! . . . (Legt sich auf das Sopha links vom Balcon.) Ja, es wird wohl das Beste sein, nicht mehr an ihn zu denken! . . . ich muß ihn zu vergessen trachten . . . (Kleine Pause; einschlummernd.) Ach, Edmund! Edmund!

Eilfte Szene.

Wally, Clärchen.

(Man hört nach einer kleinen Pause die Tapetenthür rechts von außen aufschließen.)

Wally (durch das Geräusch ermuntert, erhebt sich halb).
Wer kommt? Sollte die Tante . . .? Clärchen . . .?!
(Die Tapetenthür öffnet sich nach der Bühne zu und Clärchen erscheint auf der Schwelle derselben; sie hat die farbigen Schleifen abgelegt, ist ganz weiß gekleidet und trägt eine kleine Blendlaterne in der Hand; die Bühne bleibt dunkel.)
Clärchen (vorsichtig auf den Fußspitzen eintretend, will nach der linken Seitenthüre gehen; Wally legt sich horchend rasch wieder nieder und stellt sich schlafend).
Alles schläft! (Sieht Wally.) Himmel! (Wendet die Blendlaterne gegen das Sopha und erkennt Wally.) Wally? Hier in die=

sem Zimmer? Wie kommt das? (Betrachtet sie näher.) Dem Himmel sei Dank, sie schläft fest! . . . Rasch, eh' sie erwacht! . . . (Sie
öffnet den Kleiderschrank und nimmt eine Mantille aus demselben.) Er
wird wohl schon im Garten sein . . . Die Nacht ist kühl . . .

   Wally (die Alles leise beobachtet hat, bei Seite).

Sie nimmt eine Mantille? Wo will sie hin?

   Clärchen (zieht einen Schlüssel ans ihrer Tasche).

Und jetzt hinab! (Sie geht an die linke Seitenthür und öffnet
dieselbe.)

Wally (springt auf, faßt Clärchen an beiden Händen und dreht sie
      gegen sich).

  Wohin?

     Clärchen (erschrocken).

Wally?! . . . Du schliefst nicht?

     Wally (herrisch).

Antworte! Wohin willst Du? (Führt sie in den Vordergrund.)

     Clärchen.

Laß mich! (Will fort.)

    Wally (ihr den Weg vertretend).

Nein! . . . Wie kamst Du hieher? Ich war doch einge-
schlossen!

     Clärchen.

Mama hat von allen Thüren doppelte Schlüssel . . . ich
wußte, wo sie liegen . . .

     Wally.

Und Du nahmst sie?

     Clärchen.

Das war ja das einzige Mittel . . .! Jetzt laß mich gehen.

    Wally (sie abermals zurückhaltend).

Was hast Du vor?

     Clärchen.

Ich werde Dir Alles sagen . . . später . . . jetzt habe ich
keine Zeit!

    Wally (entreißt ihr die Blendlaterne).

Ich lasse Dich keinen Schritt weiter, eh' ich nicht weiß . . .

     Clärchen.

Wally, Du hast kein Recht . . .

     Wally.

Nicht? Dann werde ich Deine Mutter rufen.

Clärchen (erschrickt).

Meine Mutter?

Wally (stellt die Laterne auf den Tisch rechts).

Wähle!

Clärchen.

Du bist sehr neugierig ... aber um fortzukommen ... es erwartet mich Jemand im Garten.

Wally (ängstlicher).

Wer?

Clärchen.

Du erräthst es nicht?

Wally (sich an's Herz fassend).

Edmund?

Clärchen (achselzuckend).

Ah! ... Edmund ...!

Wally (starr).

Ein Anderer?

Clärchen (ungeduldig).

Jetzt laß mich. (Will fort).

Wally (sie wieder zurückhaltend).

Und ... woher kennst Du diesen Andern?

Clärchen.

Aus der Pension.

Wally.

Aus der Pension?

Clärchen.

Er wohnte dicht nebenan. Sein Garten war von dem unsern nur durch eine niedere Mauer getrennt ... Eines Tages sehe ich seinen Kopf über die Mauer hervorragen ... unsere Blicke begegneten sich ... und er verschwand ... Am andern Morgen trafen wir uns wieder ... er grüßte mich ... (stockt).

Wally.

Weiter!

Clärchen.

Ich dankte ihm natürlich! „Es ist heute sehr schönes Wetter, mein Fräulein," sagte er ... „Ja wohl", erwiederte ich ... „Madame geht deßhalb auch heute Nachmittag mit uns nach dem Stadtwäldchen." . . . Denke Dir, er verfolgte uns während der ganzen Promenade!

Wally.

Das war kein Wunder, da Du ihm ein förmliches Rendez-vous gegeben hast!

Clärchen (die Unschuldige spielend).

Ach, daran dachte ich gar nicht!

Wally.

So?! Doch, wie es scheint, seid ihr dabei nicht stehen geblieben?

Clärchen.

Ich kann wahrhaftig nichts dafür! Er beklagte sich, nicht mehr und öfter mit mir sprechen zu können; da sagte ich ihm, er möge sich nicht unterstehen über die Mauer zu klettern und in unseren Garten zu kommen, besonders des Abends, da ich da gewöhnlich allein spazieren gehe . . . und mich sehr fürchte!

Wally (ärgerlich).

Weßhalb hast Du ihm denn das gesagt? Das war ja wieder eine Aufforderung!

Clärchen.

Du glaubst?

Wally.

Und da kam er natürlich?

Clärchen.

Gegen meinen Willen . . . und . . . bald erklärte er mir, daß er mich anbete und heiraten wolle.

Wally.

Dich heiraten?! — Schön! . . . Aber seit den acht Tagen, daß Du wieder hier im Hause Deiner Mutter wohnst?

Clärchen.

Da ging's noch einfacher . . . denn unser Garten ist nur durch ein kleines Gesträuch von der Straße getrennt . . . (verliebt) und da er sehr leicht ist . . .

Wally.

Ah, er ist sehr . . . (nickt) hmhm! — Also kam er auch schon hieher?!

Clärchen.

Ja, des Abends! Ich mußte ihm doch mittheilen, daß

mich Mama zwingen will, diesen abscheulichen Edmund zu heiraten, von dem Du mir so viel Uebles sagtest und den ich hasse ... und heute wollen wir nun berathschlagen, was zu thun sei, um diese Heirat zu verhindern.

Wally.

Daß Du Edmund nicht heiratest, damit bin ganz ein=verstanden ... aber diese abendlichen Zusammenkünfte ...

Clärchen.

Oh, sei unbesorgt, ich bin sehr vorsichtig!

Wally.

Ja, es hat ganz den Anschein ... Redenz-vous im Mon=denschein!

Clärchen.

Der Mond scheint jetzt nicht!

Wally.

Desto schlimmer ... Da ist's noch finsterer ... (Einen Entschluß fassend.) Und kurz und gut, als Deine Verwandte, als Deine Freundin ... widersetze ich mich dieser ferneren Zu=sammenkünfte.

Clärchen.

Sei nicht kindisch, Wally ... laß mich ... er wartet auf mich ... die Nacht ist so kühl ... er kann den Schnupfen be=ommen.

Wally.

Wär' er zu Hause geblieben! Marsch auf Dein Zimmer ... Die Tante könnte uns überraschen!

Clärchen (immer ungeduldiger).

Du bist unausstehlich ... ich wette er steht schon unterm Balcon und ... friert! (Hat sich dem Balcon genähert und blickt verstohlen hinaus.) Richtig da ist er!

Wally (ebenso erstaunt).

Nein, das ist Edmund!

Clärchen.

Edmund?

Wally.

Ich erkenne ihn deutlich ... er hat sein Jagdgewehr ...

Clärchen (zitternd).

Wie kommt der hieher? (Eilt nach rechts vorne).

Wally (ihr folgend).

Vielleicht hat die Tante ihn . . .

Clärchen.

Sollte sie Verdacht schöpfen?

(A tempo fällt hinter der Szene ein Schuß. Die beiden Mäd=
chen schreien erschrocken auf, und kauern sich, die Ohren einen Augenblick
zuhaltend, auf den Boden).

Clärchen.

Ich sterbe!

Clärchen.

Rasch! (Eilt zum Balkon.) Ich sehe Niemand mehr!

Clärchen.

Was beginnen?

Clärchen (zitternd vorkommend).

Am Ende ist Dein Geliebter erschossen?

Clärchen.

Oder wenn Mama von dem Schuß erwacht . . . schnell
zurück in mein Zimmer! (Sie wirft die Mantille auf den Tisch
rechts, nimmt die Blendlaterne und entflieht mit derselben durch die
Tapetenthür).

Wally (starr).

Was? Sie geht? und kümmert sich nicht ob ihr Liebhaber
noch lebend oder todt ist?! Ah! ist das ein herzloses Geschöpf!

Zwölfte Szene.

Wally, Julius Kleinlich (sehr jugendliche etwas linkische
Erscheinung).

Julius (sich über den Balcon schwingend).

Retten Sie mich . . . retten Sie mich! (Er kommt tappend vor).

Wally (bei Seite).

Da ist er!

(Diese und die folgende Szene werden nun sehr rasch und leise
gesprochen).

Julius.

Sind Sie da, Clärchen?

Wally (bei Seite).

Lassen wir ihn in dem Glauben! (laut) Ja! . . . sind Sie
nicht verwundet?

Julius.

Ich weiß noch nicht ... warten Sie ... (er befühlt sich).

Wally (die sich ihm genähert hat).

Sie zittern ja?

Julius.

Und wie! ... Ich kann mich kaum auf den Beinen halten! ... Man hat ja nach mir geschossen ... ich fürchte sogar man wird mich noch verfolgen!

Wally.

Ich will gleich die Balconthür schließen! (thut es rasch).

Dreizehnte Szene.

Vorige, Edmund (einen Paletot am Arme, das Jagdgewehr in der Hand und den runden Hut am Kopfe tritt ungesehen durch die linke Seitenthür ein).

Edmund (bei Seite).

Er ist über den Balcon entwischt! (lehnt das Gewehr gegen die Thüre, und wirft Hut und Paletot auf einen Stuhl).

Julius.

Verwundet bin ich nicht ... aber meinen Paletot habe ich verloren!

Edmund (bei Seite, auf Julius horchend).

Ha! (bleibt horchend stehen).

Wally (vorkommend).

Aber was nun?

Edmund (wo).

Und Wally mit ihm?! (geht leise nach dem rechten Hintergrunde).

Wally (horchend).

Ich höre Schritte! ... man kommt!

Julius.

Herrgott! ... wo verstecke ich mich?

Wally.

Da unter diesen Tisch ... rasch! — (Edmund kriecht unter den Tisch rechts; Wally gibt ihm, um ihn zur Eile anzutreiben, einen kleinen Schlag auf den runden Hut; unwillig bei Seite). Leichtsinniger Mensch!

Julius.

Sie sind ein Engel! (verschwindet hinter dem Teppich).

Edmund (höhnisch bei Seite).

Ein Engel!

Wally (eilt wieder nach dem Sopha links).

Lassen wir die Gefahr zuerst vorübergehen! (legt sich nieder).

Vierzehnte Szene.

Vorige, Frau Müllner, (im Nachtkleide, die Haare in Papil-
loten u. dgl. ein Licht in der Hand von rechts.)

Frau Müllner.

Man hat geschossen!! (Sie hält die Hand hinter das Licht um
den Schein desselben auf Wally fallen zu lassen). Und dieser kleine
Faulpelz schläft auf beiden Ohren!

Julius (steckt den Kopf unter dem Teppich hervor und erblickt
Wally deren Gesicht jetzt hell beleuchtet ist; bei Seite). Sapperlott!
das ist ja nicht Clärchen!

Frau Müllner (wendet sich um und erblickt Edmund welcher sich
ihr genähert hat. Aufschreiend.) Zu Hülfe!

Edmund.

Beruhigen Sie sich ... ich bins!

Frau Müllner.

Ach so ... ich glaubte ... (sie wankt zu dem Fauteuil am
Tische rechts und setzt sich).

Edmund.

Der Schuß hat sie wahrscheinlich aus ihrer Ruhe geweckt?

Frau Müllner.

Ja wohl ... nun ... und ... haben Sie Jemanden
entdeckt ...

Edmund (betonend).

Er ist mir leider entwischt!

Frau Müllner (jammernd).

Sie haben ihn nicht gleich todtgeschossen?

Edmund.

Ich fehlte ihn ... allein ich fand seinen Paletot, den er bei
der Flucht verlor!

Julius (den Kopf unter dem Teppich hervorsteckend bei Seite).
Mein Paletot! (Verschwindet wieder.)

Frau Müllner.
Und wer glauben Sie . . . ?

Edmund (mit Absicht).
So viel ich in der Dunkelheit erspähen konnte, hatte er das Aussehen eines Diebes!

Julius (wie oben).
Ist das ein Grobian!

Frau Müllner (aufstehend und nach der linken Seitenthür gehend).
Aber wie kam der Mensch herein? . . . Ich schloß doch alle Thüren ab?

Edmund.
Ich fand sie offen.

Frau Müllner.
Also hat er falsche Schlüssel?

Edmund.
Wahrscheinlich!

Frau Müllner.
Die Angst tödtet mich . . . wenn er noch hier wäre . . .

Edmund (mit Absicht).
Vielleicht in jenem Kleiderschrank?

Frau Müllner (sehr ängstlich den Blick auf den Kleiderschrank gerichtet nach der rechten Seitenthür retirirend). Sehen Sie nach, lieber Edmund, aber behutsam!

Edmund (hat den Schrank geöffnet).
Niemand!

Frau Müllner (vorkommend).
Wie kann er nur entkommen sein?

Edmund (ebenso).
Wahrscheinlich auf demselben Weg, auf welchen er kam . . . und so wird er die andere Treppe erreicht haben . . .

Frau Müllner (immer ängstlicher nach rechts deutend).
Die nach jenen Zimmern führt? In der That, ich hörte Schritte im Corridor . . .

Edmund (rasch).
Das wird er wohl gewesen sein!

Frau Müllner (außer sich vor Angst).

Ha! (Sie sinkt fast ohnmächtig um, Edmund fängt sie in seinen Armen auf.)

Edmund.

Kommen Sie, gnädige Frau, ich will gleich Sie und Ihre Zimmer in Sicherheit bringen.

Frau Müllner (geht einige Schritte gegen Wally).

Aber diese Kleine!

Edmund.

Laffen wir Sie schlafen ... wozu sie erschrecken und ängstigen!

Frau Müllner (nach rechts gehend).

Nun so kommen Sie!

Edmund (bei Seite nicht ohne Bitterkeit).

So gewinnt sie Zeit ihn entschlüpfen zu laffen.

Frau Müllner (hat auch das zweite Licht am Piano angezündet).

Gehen wir ...

Edmund.

Ich folge Ihnen!

Frau Müllner (bebend).

Nein — nein — gehen Sie voraus.

Edmund.

Richtig ... als Avantgarde!

(Beide rechts ab; Frau Müllner nimmt das eine Licht mit, das andere bleibt am Piano stehen).

Fünfzehnte Szene.

Wally, Julius.

Wally (auffspringend).

Endlich sind sie fort!

Julius (ein wenig hervorkriechend).

Ach, ist das unbequem, so unter'm Tisch!

Wally (den Teppich emporhebend).

Schnell, mein Herr, fliehen Sie!

Julius (kriecht ganz hervor und bleibt vor dem Tische auf den Knien).

Verzeihen Sie, daß ich Sie früher für Fräulein Clärchen hielt.

Wally (böse).

Wenn ich jetzt Zeit hätte, möchte ich Ihnen wohl sagen, was ich von Ihrem Betragen halte!

Julius (aufstehend).

Aber weßhalb kam sie denn nicht in den Garten? Weßhalb ist sie nicht hier?

Wally (stolz).

Weil ich es verhinderte!

Julius.

Sie? . . . Ich bin zwar gar nicht böse Sie bei dieser Gelegenheit kennen zu lernen . . . ein so schönes Fräulein —

Wally.

Was unterstehen Sie sich! . . . Sehen Sie lieber, daß Sie fortkommen . . . und zwar so schnell als möglich!

Julius.

Wie Sie befehlen . . . aber . . . wo komme ich hier hinaus?

Wally (immer kurz angebunden).

Ich werde Sie führen . . . auf der Treppe ist es stockfinster . . . geben Sie mir Ihre Hand . . .

Julius (ihr seine Hand gebend).

Sie sind sehr freundlich! (Beide gehen einige Schritte nach links.)

Wally (bleibt stehen und horcht).

Still! . . . Ich höre Schritte auf der Treppe!

Julius (läßt Wally's Hand los und flüchtet in den Vordergrund).

Heiliger Gott!

Wally.

Der Gärtner wird durch den Schuß aufgewacht sein . . .!

Julius (fast weinerlich).

Das ganze Haus macht Jagd auf mich . . . wenn sie mich finden . . .!

Wally (unruhig).

Die Tante wird auch gleich wieder zurückkommen . . .

Julius (erschrickt).

Der Mann mit der Flinte auch?

Wally.

Sie müssen sich abermals verstecken.

Julius (kleinlaut).

Wieder unter'm Tisch?

Wally.

Nein ... in den Kleiderschrank ... den haben sie schon
durchsucht ... da sind Sie sicherer! (Sie führt Julius zu dem
Schranke).

Julius.

Gott, ist das eine Nacht ... wenn ich je wieder so unvor=
sichtig bin ...

Wally (stößt ihn ungeduldig in den Schrank).

So gehen Sie doch! (Julius stolpert hinein, Wally schlägt
rasch die Schrankthüren zu). Es war die höchste Zeit! —

Sechzehnte Szene.

Vorige, Frau Müllner (das Licht in der Hand, kommt mit)
Edmund (von rechts).

Frau Müllner (Wally erblickend).

Nun, bist Du endlich wach?

Wally (sich verschlafen stellend und die Unschuldige spielend).

Was geht denn hier vor?

Frau Müllner (stellt das Licht auf den Tisch rechts).

Hast Du denn nichts gehört.

Wally.

Nein ... ich schlief.

Frau Müllner.

Sehr fest, wie es scheint!

Edmund (bei Seite).

Wie sie sich verstellen kann!

Frau Müllner (Wally immer scharf ansehend).

Es hat sich ein fremder Mann bei uns eingeschlichen ...
weißt Du nichts Näheres darüber?

Wally.

Wie sollte ich etwas wissen!

Frau Müllner.

Wir durchsuchten schon das ganze Haus konnten aber Nie=
mand finden ...

Edmund.

Der Schuldige wird dasselbe, durch den Lärm verscheucht,
wohl bereits verlassen haben.

Wally.

Wahrscheinlich!

Edmund (wüthend bei Seite).

Diese Ruhe . . .!

Frau Müllner.

Aber da fällt mir ein . . . Sie haben ja seinen Paletot gefunden — vielleicht gibt der Aufklärung. (Geht nach hinten und holt den Paletot, dessen Taschen sie durchsucht.)

Edmund (rasch, leise zu Wally).

Ist er fort?

Wally (erschrickt).

Sie wissen?

Edmund.

Vorsicht!

Wally (starr bei Seite).

Glaubt er am Ende, daß i ch — — ?

Frau Müllner (hat einen Brief aus dem Paletot gezogen, wirft den Letzteren wieder auf einen Stuhl und kommt vor).

Ein Brief! (Nähert sich dem Lichte und liest.) „Kommen Sie heute Abend zur gewöhnlichen Stunde, wir müssen einen Entschluß fassen, um mich zu b e f r e i e n!"... Keine Unterschrift . . .! Also war es d o ch k e i n Dieb?

Edmund (unruhig).

Von wem kann der Brief sein?

Frau Müllner.

Von wem? Sie fragen noch? (Wüthend auf Wally deutend.) Da steht die Verbrecherin, die von mir b e f r e i t sein will!

Wally.

Ich?! — — ist das m e i n e Handschrift?!

Frau Müllner (höhnisch).

Spaß! — — die ist geschickt verstellt — —

Wally (empört).

Ich verbiete mir — — —

Frau Müllner (herrisch).

Schweig! (Bemerkt die Mantille auf dem Tische rechts.) Und die Mantille, die ich selbst im Schranke aufbewahrte? Wie kommt diese Mantille hieher? He? Willst Du noch läugnen?

Wally (bei Seite).

Auch das noch! — — Was wird er von mir denken?!

Frau Müllner.

Und wie sie sich ruhig schlafend stellte! Oh! Oh!

Edmund (bei Seite).

Sie erwiedert nichts!

Frau Müllner.

Heraus mit der Sprache — — wer ist jener Mensch — — irgend ein Bruder Leichtsinn — — ein Taugenichts?!

Wally (die Fäuste ballend, bei Seite).

Und schweigen zu müssen — — !

Edmund.

Erlauben Sie, gnädige Frau, vielleicht ist er von guter Familie — — vielleicht läßt sich Alles noch auf eine a n st ä n d i g e Weise repariren — —!

Wally (bei Seite).

Auch er?! ... Schändlich!

Frau Müllner.

Nein — — ich mische mich nicht weiter in diese Angelegenheit — — der Ruf meines Hauses muß, meiner Tochter halber, gewahrt bleiben — — aber mein Bruder hat keine Kinder — — er ist ihr Onkel, er soll mit seiner Nichte, dieser Schande unserer Familie, machen was er will!

Wally (vor Wuth fast weinend, bei Seite).

Oh, Clärchen! — — Oh, Mathilde! — —

Frau Müllner.

Für heute Nacht werde ich sie unter die Aufsicht ihrer ehrbaren, sittsamen Cousine stellen. — —

Wally (losbrechend).

Nein — — (sie geht einen Schritt gegen Frau Müllner — bleibt jedoch stehen, faßt sich an's Herz und sagt bei Seite.) Nein, ich darf sie jetzt nicht verrathen!

Frau Müllner (ängstlich zu Edmund).

Und Sie, Herr Edmund — — ?

Edmund.

Gehen Sie ganz beruhigt wieder nach ihrem Zimmer, gnädige Frau, ich will nochmals Alles genau durchsuchen und erst, wenn jede Gefahr vorüber ist, werde ich das Haus verlassen.

Frau Müllner.

Oh! tausend Dank! — (Zu Wally auf die Tapetenthür zeigend.)

Und Du — da hinein! (Zieht einen Schlüssel aus der Tasche und öffnet die Tapetenthür.)

Wally (bei Seite).

Ich muß ihn noch sprechen! (Ab durch die Tapetenthür.)

Frau Müllner (schließt zu und steckt den Schlüssel wieder zu sich).

So! — Gute Nacht, lieber Edmund, und auf Wiedersehen morgen! (Ab durch die rechte Seitenthür.)

Siebenzehnte Szene.

Edmund, Julius, dann Wally.

Edmund (sich umsehend.)

Ob dieser kühne Jüngling noch hier ist? — Ach ich hätte eine große Lust ein paar Worte mit demjenigen zu wechseln, dem .... sie heimliche Rendezvous gibt! ... Und ich Thor, der ich einen Augenblick glaubte ... sie liebe mich! — Ich Narr! — Ob er noch hier ist? — (Sieht unter den Tisch.) Nein! (Sieht mit dem Licht unter den Sopha's.) Auch nicht. — (Bemerkt, daß sich die Thüren des Schrankes bewegen, leise.) Ha! dort! — (Der Schrank öffnet sich ein wenig, jedoch so, daß Edmund Julius noch nicht sehen kann.)

Julius (den Kopf ein wenig aus dem Schrank steckend).

Ach, ist das unbequem in so 'nem Schrank.

Edmund.

Er ist's! (Geht gegen den Schrank.)

Julius (hört das Geräusch und schließt hastig die Schrankthür.)

Edmund.

Jetzt hab' ich ihn! (Stellt das Licht auf den Tisch, versucht dann den Schrank zu öffnen, Julius zieht jedoch die Thür stets wieder zu, wodurch dieselbe einige Male auf und zugezogen wird, endlich reißt Edmund beide Thüren gewaltsam auf und man gewahrt Julius in einer komischen Attitüde im Schranke.) Heraus, mein Herr!

Julius (bebend).

Gnade — ich —

Edmund.

Heraus!

Julius (stürzt zitternd und bebend aus dem Schrank, stößt an einen Stuhl, den er umwirft, flieht, das Gesicht immer gegen Edmund gekehrt quer über die Bühne und fällt dort rücklings auf das offene Piano, dessen Claviatur durch den Fall sehr stark ertönt).
Keine Thätlichkeiten, wenn ich bitten darf!

Edmund (ärgerlich bei Seite).
Er ist nicht einmal häßlich!

Julius (ängstlich aufstehend).
Mein Herr — — wenn es Ihnen einerlei wäre — — zöge ich es vor wieder zu g e h e n — —

Edmund.
Danken Sie Gott, daß ich nicht zur Familie gehöre und jeden Skandal vermeiden will, sonst . . .

Julius (erschrocken durch Edmunds drohende Geberden, fällt wieder rücklings auf das Piano, das abermals ertönt).
Keine Thätlichkeiten, mein Herr — — ich habe redliche Absichten — —

Edmund.
Ihre Handlungsweise spricht nicht dafür!

Julius.
Ich werde sie heiraten!

Edmund.
Heiraten?! — Das wollen wir erst sehen.

Julius.
Papa wird wohl einwilligen.

Edmund.
Ah, wir haben einen Papa — — ? Ich werde seine Bekanntschaft machen.

Julius (erschrickt).
Wie? Sie wollten ihm sagen — — ?

Edmund.
Wo ist er? wo wohnt er?

Julius.
Wo er wohnt?

Edmund.
Keine Ausflüchte . . . ! Die volle Wahrheit!

Julius (zieht eilig eine Visitenkarte aus der Brusttasche; ruhig).
Hier haben Sie meine Karte, . . . Name . . . Adresse . . . Alles d'rauf . . .

Edmund (liest).

„Freiburg ... Rosengasse **11** ...“ Sie heißen Freiburg?

Julius (achselzuckend).

Ja wohl!

Edmund (die Karte einsteckend).

Das genügt!

Julius (bei Seite).

Die Adresse meines Schneiders!

Edmund.

Und jetzt fort!

Julius (erblickt seinen Paletot).

Ah, mein Paletot! (Nimmt denselben.)

Edmund.

Der muß hier liegen bleiben ... Frau Müllner braucht nicht zu wissen, daß ich Sie noch hier fand ...

Julius.

Recht schön ... aber ...

Edmund (wüthend).

Lassen Sie ihn liegen, sag ich ... (Nimmt seine Jagdtasche um und setzt seinen Hut auf.)

Julius (den Paletot rasch wieder auf den Stuhl werfend, kleinlaut).

Ich habe ihn mir erst gekauft ...!

Edmund.

Und nun vorwärts!

Julius.

Mit Vergnügen! (Geht einige Schritte gegen die linke Seiten= thür und horcht.) Es ist schon wieder Jemand auf der Treppe! (Man hört die Tapetenthür leise von Außen aufschließen.)

Edmund (horcht).

Frau Müllner scheint auch zurückzukommen! Rasch fliehen Sie über den Balkon, Sie sind ja über denselben hereingekom= men! (Die Tapetenthür öffnet sich ein wenig, Wally erscheint, unge= sehen von den beiden Andern, horchend an der Schwelle.)

Julius.

Ueber den Balkon? Da brech' ich mir ja Hals und Beine!

Edmund (hat indessen sein Jagdgewehr genommen und die Bal= konthüren geöffnet, drohend).

Wollen Sie, oder wollen Sie nicht?! —

Julius (flieht auf den Balkon).

Keine Thätlichkeiten! ... (Bei Seite.) Er hat 'ne Flinte ... (Die Fauſt ballend.) Wenn er keine hätte ... (Kleinlaut.) Aber er hat eine!

Edmund.

Wird's?! —

Julius.

Empfehle mich beſtens! — Angenehme Ruhe! (Schwingt ſich über den Balkon und verſchwindet.)

Achtzehnte Szene.

Edmund. Wally (tritt ganz aus der Thüre).

Edmund (ohne Wally zu ſehen).

Und dieſen Menſchen zieht ſie mir vor ...! Einen kleinen feigen Laffen ...? Ach Wally! Wally! Welche Enttäuſchung! (Stürzt links ab.)

Wally (einen Augenblick ſtarr).

Was?! Er glaubt mich wirklich ſchuldig?! — (Will Edmund nachſtürzen, bleibt jedoch in der Bühne ſtehen und richtet ſich hoch auf.) Nein! Wenn er ſo wenig Vertrauen zu mir, zu meiner Ehre hat, dann liebt er mich nicht ... und dann ... iſt ja doch Alles verloren! (Sie ſinkt weinend auf's Sopha.)

Der Vorhang fällt.

Ende des zweiten Aktes.

Dritter Akt.

(Garten bei Reimer. Rechts erste Coulisse eine kleine Laube, in derselben zwei Gartenstühle und ein kleines Tischchen. Zweite Coulisse der Anfang einer Allee. Dritte Coulisse ein Pavillon, zu dessen Eingangsthüren mehrere Stufen führen. An den Pavillon anschließend eine niedere Mauer, welche quer über den Hintergrund der Bühne geht, und in deren Mitte ein großes Gitter sich befindet. — Auf jeder Seite des Gitters eine hohe Pappel. Links an der ersten und zweiten Coulisse Reimer's Wohnhaus, theils mit geöffneten Marquisen, Blumentöpfen, Statuen u. dgl. geschmückt. Zur Eingangsthür des Hauses führen ebenfalls Stufen. In der dritten Coulisse gleichfalls der Beginn einer Allee. Links im Vordergrunde ein großer freistehender Weidenbaum, rings um denselben eine kleine, weiße, runde Bank. Der Prospekt zeigt eine große Stadt. — Alles wieder sehr elegant und luxuriös.)

Erste Szene.

Mathilde, dann Reimer.

Mathilde (sitzt auf der Bank unter der Weide, liest in einem Buch und läßt dasselbe dann in den Schooß sinken).

Ich kann nicht lesen! Mir flimmert's vor den Augen... und meine Gedanken beschäftigen sich nur mit der drohenden Gefahr! Wenn Edmund wirklich Clärchen heiratet... wenn ein Wort, ein Blick uns verriethe... ach, welche Qualen leide ich!! — Und Wally, ist sie wirklich schuldig? Ich kann es nicht glauben... Ha, mein Mann!

Reimer (Mit Hut und Stock aus dem Hause links).

Schon im Garten, Mathilde?

Mathilde.

Ja, ich wollte die frische Morgenluft ein wenig genießen. Doch Du, willst Du schon ausgehen?

Reimer.

Ja, ... ich habe eine schrecklich unruhige Nacht verbracht... Diese Wally wird mich noch zur Verzweiflung bringen... Seit den wenigen Tagen, die sie wieder in meinem Hause ist, habe ich Alles versucht, sie zu einem Geständnisse zu bringen... um endlich die Wahrheit über jene mysteriöse Geschichte zu erfahren, deren meine Schwester das Mädchen anklagt... vergebens! Sie beharrt in ihrem eigensinnigen Schweigen, sie begründet hierdurch den Verdacht ihrer Schuld nur noch mehr und ich bin daher entschlossen, dem Rathe Theresens zu folgen und Wally auf einige Zeit in ein Kloster zu geben!

Mathilde.

In ein Kloster? Conrad, was fällt Dir ein? Das hieße ja der Welt noch mehr die Augen öffnen... Hüte Dich vor Uebereilung! Eine solche Strenge scheint mir gefährlich... gegen ein junges Mädchen... das vielleicht nur das Opfer eines unbegründeten Verdachtes... eines bösen Scheines ist!

Reimer.

Eines bösen Scheines? Und das nächtliche Rendezvous? Ist ein Mann in dem Zimmer eines jungen Mädchens ein böser Schein?... Ist ein vorgefundener Liebesbrief ein böser Schein? — Jetzt begreife ich freilich, weshalb sie die Bewerbung Edmund's zurückwies...! Weil sie bereits einen andern Liebhaber hatte!

Mathilbe (beschwichtigend).

Lieber Freund... höchstens einen verliebten Waghals, der...

Reimer.

Der ein unverschämter Abenteurer ist, und sich dadurch aus der Affaire zog, daß er Edmund eine falsche Adresse gab! Schickt ihn zu einen Schneider! Es ist niederträchtig!... Ich seh' es ein, ich war zu schwach, zu nachsichtig gegen Wally... die Folgen haben es traurig genug bewiesen! Die Erziehungsmethode meiner Schwester ist die richtige! Sieh ihre Tochter an, Clärchen, was ist aus der geworden? (Frau Müllner erscheint hinter dem Gitter und schellt unaufhaltsam und mit größter Gewalt an der Thorglocke.)

Reimer.

Was ist denn das für ein Spektakel?

Zweite Szene.

Vorige. Frau Müllner.

Frau Müllner (noch hinter dem Gitter).

Macht auf! Macht auf! (Ein Diener in Livree kommt eiligst aus dem Hause links, öffnet das Gitter und geht dann in die Allee links ab. Das Gitter bleibt bis zum Schlusse halb geöffnet. Frau Müllner stürzt athemlos auf die Bühne.) Ach, mein Bruder, mein Bruder!

Reimer.

Großer Gott, was hast Du denn? Du bist ja ganz außer Dir!

Frau Müllner.

Laß mich an Deine Brust stürzen! (Umarmt Reimer heftig.)

Reimer.

Diese Zärtlichkeit?

Frau Müllner (auffahrend).

Ich bin wüthend!

Reimer.

Ach so! Also deshalb!

Frau Müllner.

Ich fühle mich sterbend!

Reimer.

So setz' Dich nur! (führt Frau Müllner unter die Weide).

Frau Müllner (sich auf die Bank setzend).

Conrad! Conrad! Wenn Du wüßtest!

Reimer (ohne sich aufzuregen).

Was denn? (Setzt sich zu ihr, während Mathilde rechts von Müllner stehen bleibt.)

Frau Müllner.

Ich habe gar nicht die Kraft, zu sprechen ... die Worte bleiben mir im Halse stecken!

Reimer (wie oben).

An dem Uebel leidest Du doch sonst nicht!

Frau Müllner.

Ein Ereigniß ... das unglaublichste, das nichtswürdigste, das exorbitanteste, das monstruöseste ....

Reimer (bei Seite).

Na also ... nun stecken sie nicht mehr! (zu Frau Müllner.) Was gibt es denn eigentlich?

Frau Müllner.

Meine Tochter.... mein Clärchen...

Reimer.

Ist sie krank?

Frau Müllner.

Ah ... wenn es nur das wäre ....

Reimer.

Am Ende von einem Wagen überfahren worden? — Das geschieht jetzt so häufig!

Frau Müllner (ungeduldig).

Conrad, Du machst mich nervös!

Reimer.

J, so sprich doch!

Frau Müllner.

Diesen Morgen sag' ich zu dem Dienstmädchen: „Rufen Sie meine Tochter zum Frühstück." Da antwortet sie: „Das wäre schwer möglich!" und geht rasch hinaus ... Ich, erstaunt, beunruhigt im höchsten Grade, eile in das Zimmer Clärchens und finde ...

Reimer (etwas beunruhigt).

Ich errathe, sie wird einen Roman gelesen haben, ... ist dabei eingeschlafen ... das Licht blieb brennen... der Bettvor= hang fing Feuer ...

Frau Müllner (aufspringend, grob).

Du bist ein Strohkopf!

Reimer (verletzt, ebenfalls aufstehend).

Erlaube...

Frau Müllner.

Einen Roman... Sie liest keine Romane ... sie spielt sie selber!

Mathilde und Reimer.

Was?

Frau Müllner.

Aber den Gärtner jag' ich fort ... die Köchin jag' ich fort .. denn sie stecken Alle mit im Complott ...!

Mathilde.

In welchem Complott?

Frau Müllner.

Das die Flucht begünstigte!

Mathilde und Reimer.

Eine Flucht?

Reimer.

Was? Clärchen?

Frau Müllner.

Ja, Conrad! Deiner Schwester mußte das geschehen!! Meine Tochter, trotz meiner Strenge, mit der ich sie bewacht und gehütet habe ... meine Tochter ... ist aus dem mütterlichen Hause entflohen!!! —

Mathilde.

Entflohen?! (Bei Seite, aufathmend.) Edmund wird sie nicht heiraten!

Reimer (starr).

Durchgegangen? Clärchen? Die ein Prämium für gute Sitten bekommen hat?

Frau Müller (drohend).

Aber wenn ich sie erst wieder habe ... wenn ich erst weiß, wohin ihr Räuber sie gebracht hat ... denn ein Räuber ist dabei im Spiele ... deßhalb komme ich, Bruder, Du mußt mit mir zur Polizei ...!

Reimer.

Therese, um Gotteswillen keine Ueberstürzung ... vielleicht ist Clärchen's Ehre ... ihr Ruf noch zu retten ... aber ist einmal der Skandal öffentlich ...

Frau Müller.

Aber was nun thun? Denn geschehen muß etwas ... jeder Augenblick Zögerung bringt Gefahr ...!

Dritte Szene.

Vorige, Wally.

Wally (singt hinter der Scene das Liedchen aus dem zweiten Akte).

Blühe Blümlein auf der Haiden,
Blühe Röslein an der Brust,
Mag die Blumen gerne leiden,
Hab' an Blumen meine Lust.
u. s. w.

(Der Dialog geht ununterbrochen während des Liedes fort.)

Frau Müllner (nach links horchend).

Ist das nicht Wally?

Reimer.

Jawohl!

Frau Müllner (von einem Gedanken ergriffen).

Sie wird wissen, wo ihre Cousine ist! Ich habe sie sehr in Verdacht ...

Reimer.

Du glaubst?

Frau Müllner.

Ich bin sogar überzeugt, daß sie an Allem Schuld ist ... deßhalb singt sie wohl auch so lustig ... weil ihre schlechten Rathschläge befolgt wurden, weil ... oh, dieses Mädchen!

Wally (in einem hübschen Morgenkleidchen kommt singend aus der Allee links).

Ah, guten Morgen, Onkelchen! (Sieht Fr. Müllner, bei Seite.) Die Brummtante? Halb links! (Will wieder ab.)

Reimer.

Halt! weßhalb fliehst Du meine Schwester?

Wally (achselzuckend).

Unwillkürlich! Ich fürchte immer, sie will mich wieder mit= nehmen!

Reimer.

Ist das der einzige Grund?

Wally.

Ich habe keinen andern.

Reimer.

Wer weiß! Jedenfalls bleibe und beantworte unsere Fragen.

Wally.

Welche Fragen!

Frau Müllner.

Und hüte Dich zu lügen . . . sonst werden die Gerichte Dich zur Wahrheit zwingen.

Wally.

Die Gerichte? Hu! das klingt ja schauerlich!

Frau Müllner (sich hoch aufrichtend).

Wo ist meine Tochter?

Wally (geht einen Schritt näher).

Was sagen Sie?

Frau Müllner.

Wo ist meine Tochter? Du weißt es, läugne nicht.

(Reimer geht einige Schritte zurück zwischen Frau Müllner und Wally, welche auf diese Weise die äußerste Linke einnimmt.)

Wally.

Sie fragen, wo Clärchen ist?

Frau Müllner.

Spiele nicht die Unschuldige . . . Dein schlechtes Beispiel allein hat sie verleitet!

Wally.

Verleitet? Wozu?

Frau Müllner.

Ohne Deine elenden Rathschläge wäre es ihr niemals in den Sinn gekommen ihre Mutter zu verlassen.

Wally (starr).

Sie hat Sie verlassen?

Frau Müllner.

Noch einmal: wo ist sie?

Wally.

Ich wollte, ich wüßte es. Clärchen ist meine Muhme, ich bin ihre Freundin . . . und es schmerzt mich tief, so etwas von ihr erfahren zu müssen.

Frau Müllner.

Heuchlerin!

Wally.

Weßhalb hatte sie sich nicht mir anvertraut! Ich hätte alle Ueberredungskunst, alle Liebe angewandt, um sie von solcher Schande abzuhalten.

Frau Müllner.

Keine Flausen! Mich täuscht Deine Heuchelei nicht. Du bist ihre Mitschuldige!

Reimer (zu Mathilde).

Ihre Worte klingen allerdings so aufrichtig . . .

Mathilde.

Ich bin überzeugt, daß sie die Wahrheit spricht!

Frau Müllner.

Glaubt in Eurer Gutmüthigkeit, was Ihr wollt . . . ich
weiß bestimmt, daß sie Clärchens Aufenthalt kennt!

Wally.

Wenn das der Fall wäre, würde ich hineilen und, ich stehe
Ihnen dafür, ich brächte Clärchen zurück!

Mathilde.

Aber da fällt mir, sie hatte ja intime Freundinnen in der
Pension . . . . vielleicht weiß dort Jemand um das Geheimniß?

Reimer.

Das ist eine Idee . . .

Frau Müllner.

Die zu gar keinem Resultate führen wird.

Mathilde.

Ich will jedenfalls rasch hinfahren!

Frau Müllner.

Und ich gehe directe auf die Polizei! Komm!

Reimer.

Wäre es nicht besser abzuwarten?

Frau Müllner.

Komm' — oder ich geh' allein!

Reimer.

Wenn Du durchaus willst . . .

Frau Müllner (zu Wally).

Und dieser Mamsell da wollen wir die Zunge schon lösen.

Reimer (mit Fr. Müllner durch das Gitter abgehend).

So beruhige Dich nur, Schwester.

Wally (bei Seite).

Jetzt wird sie ganz verrückt!

Mathilde (zu Wally).

Fürchte nichts, Wally — und warte hier, bis ich zurück= komme! (Ab ins Haus links.)

Vierte Szene.
Wally, dann Clärchen.

Wally (geht ganz in den Vordergrund links).

Clärchen von ihrer Mutter entflohen . . der Spaß ist ein Bischen stark, aber . . . es mußte so kommen!

Clärchen (die Thür des Pavillons öffnend, leise).

Wally!

Wally. —

Was seh' ich?

Clärchen.

Bist Du allein?

Wally.

Ja! komm!

Clärchen (aus dem Pavillon tretend).

Gottlob, daß ich Dich endlich sprechen kann!

Wally.

Hör' mal, Du scheinst Ueberraschungen zu lieben, aber diese übersteigt denn doch alle Grenzen! Wie kamst Du denn in un= sern Pavillon?

Clärchen.

Ach, Wally! ich hielt es nicht länger bei der Mama aus! Dieses Leben ward mir unerträglich . . . ihre Strenge, ihre Härte . . .

Wally.

Ja, die kenne ich!

Clärchen.

Das Haus wurde mir ein Kerker! Und wenn Mama aus= ging, bewachte mich wieder ein alter Drache, den sie in ihre Dienste nahm, folgte mir auf Schritt und Tritt, spionirte nach jedem Blick, um ihn zu rapportiren . . . !

Wally (lächelnd).

Aha! eine Duenna, ein Kerkermeister! Spanisches Genre!

6

Clärchen.

Und dann erfuhr ich nichts mehr von Julius! Ich lebte in einer Todesangst, konnte ihm nicht schreiben, denn man bewachte mich ja Tag und Nacht ... kurz, ich verlor den Verstand und lief endlich gestern spät Abend auf und davon!

Wally.

Das war sehr unrecht von Dir! Deine Mutter zu verlassen ...! Doch jetzt ist keine Zeit zum Predigen! Sag mir nur, wie Du in diesen Pavillon kommst?

Clärchen.

Durch einen Zufall; ich wollte Anfangs ...

Wally.

Doch nicht zu Deinem Monsieur Julius?

Clärchen.

Gott bewahre! Wie kannst Du das glauben? Nein! ... zu einer Freundin, welche schon vergangenes Jahr aus der Pension trat, aber mich dort fast täglich besuchte. Ich wußte, daß sie seit einiger Zeit heimlich verlobt sei ... ihre Eltern jedoch die Partie nicht zugeben wollen. Ich dachte mir: sie würde meine Leiden verstehen, sie würde mir rathen können ... ich eilte also zu ihr ... dieses Unglück ...!

Wally.

Sie war auf einem Balle?

Clärchen.

Nein, ... ihr Bräutigam hatte sie Abends entführt!

Wally.

Entführt? ... Hatte die auch ein Prämium für gute Sitten bekommen?

Clärchen.

Nun verlor ich allen Muth und alle Ruhe! Nach Hause zurückkehren konnt' ich nicht mehr — — und so faßte ich den Entschluß mich Onkel Conrad anzuvertrauen, ihm alles zu gestehen und seine Hilfe anzuflehen. Allein als ich hier ankam, schlich sich eben Sabine aus dem Hause — —

Wally.

Ja, die läuft immer herum.

Clärchen.

Sie sagte, sie müsse heimlich zu einem Polterabend, sie käme erst am Morgen wieder — im Hause schliefe schon Alles — und da versteckte sie mich dort im Pavillon.

Wally.

Jetzt begreife ich.

Clärchen.

Ich schloß die ganze Nacht kein Auge — — Früh Morgens übermannte mich die Müdigkeit — und als ich eben erwachte und aus meinem Versteck wollte — — hörte ich die Stimme meiner Mutter!

Wally.

Genug! Wir müssen ihre Abwesenheit rasch benützen und einen Entschluß fassen.

Clärchen.

Aber welchen? Rathe mir Wally!

Wally.

Das ist sehr schwierig! Ich möchte gerne Deine Für= sprecherin bei Onkel Conrad sein, aber man hält mich für Deine Mitschuldige — sie werden mir nicht glauben —! Wenn nun Julius —! Das einzige Mittel ist eine schnelle Heirat!

Clärchen.

Du glaubst!

Wally.

Ja! — schreib ihm rasch!

Clärchen.

Ich dachte schon daran .... und dort im Pavillon ...

Wally (geht mit Clärchen einige Schritte gegen den Pavillon).
Nur schnell ... bevor Deine Mutter wieder zurückkehrt.

Clärchen.

Ach, nimm mir nicht das Restchen Muth ...!

Wally (welche eilig durch das Gitter sah).
Ha!

Clärchen (erschrickt).

Die Mama?

Wally (vorkommend).
Nein — — Herr Julius!

Clärchen.

Was will der hier?

Wally.

Das werden wir gleich erfahren.

Clärchen.

Ich möchte nicht, daß er mich gleich sieht ...

6*

Wally.

Weßhalb?

Clärchen (immer verlegener).

Ihm zu gestehen, daß ich Mama verlassen habe — daß ich
seinethalben — —

Wally.

Nun, da es die Wahrheit ist...

Clärchen.

Aber das — wäre gegen den Anstand!

Wally (sarkastisch).

Und Dein „Durchgehen" ist nicht gegen den Anstand?
Komische Ansichten lernt Ihr in Euren Mädchen=Instituten!

Clärchen (ausweichend).

Erforsche erst, was ihn hieher führt — und ich — dort!
(Deutet auf die Laube rechts.)

Wally.

Wie du willst — ich aber an Deiner Stelle...

Clärchen.

Er kommt — thue, wie ich Dir sage! — (Verbirgt sich in
der Laube.)

Fünfte Szene.

Vorige, Julius (erscheint am Gitter).

Wally (bei Seite).

Den sendet der Himmel, vielleicht kommt es jetzt zu einer
Aufklärung.

Julius (hat forschend umhergeblickt, steht endlich Wally und tritt
schüchtern ein).

Ach, Fräulein Wally! Wie glücklich bin ich, Sie endlich
u finden! Sie suchte ich...

Wally (setzt sich unter die Weide und weist Julius einen Platz
neben sich an).

Mich? Woher wußten Sie denn, daß ich wieder bei Onkel
Reimer bin?

Julius (setzt sich).

Durch den Gärtner der Frau Müllner — ich habe ihm

gute Worte und — etwas Geld gegeben und da gestand er mir gestern — —

Wally.

Also mich suchten Sie — schön! Was wünschen Sie von mir?

Julius

Oh viel —! Zuerst möchte ich Ihnen meinen Dank sagen. —

Wally.

Wofür?

Julius.

Wofür? Ei, Sie haben mich ja beschützt — gerettet vor der Wuth des — jungen Mannes mit der Flinte! Denn Ihre Schuld ist es nicht, daß er mich schließlich dennoch fand. —

Wally (etwas ängstlich).

Herr Edmund fand Sie?

Julius.

Ja, im Kleiderschrank — aber er war ziemlich artig — er verlangte nur meine Adresse — (Naiv lächelnd.) Ich gab ihm die meines Schneiders.

Wally (ironisch).

Das war sehr schlau!

Julius.

Ja — ich mußte es sein — wegen Papa!

Wally.

Aha! Weiter!

Julius.

Nun aber erfuhr ich durch den Gärtner, daß Sie, Fräulein Wally, die Sie eigentlich an Allem ganz unschuldig sind, allein für die Schuldige gehalten werden. — daß man Alles auf Ihre Rechnung schob. —

Wally.

Das ist wahr — und bis jetzt hält man mich auch noch für schuldig!

Julius.

Wie? Also alle Vorwürfe alle Beleidigungen, alle Verfolgungen haben Sie schweigsam, geduldig ertragen —? Aus Freundschaft für Clärchen? Oh, das war edel, das war große müthig von Ihnen, das verdient Bewunderung. — (Steht auf und verbeugt sich.) Ich bewundere Sie, mein Fräulein!

Wally (steht ebenfalls auf).

Der Zufall fügte es so — und ich möchte meine Cousine nicht verrathen!

Julius.

Aber sie — sie hätte sprechen, die Wahrheit bekennen sollen. (Beide kommen vor.)

Clärchen (bei Seite).

Er hat recht!

Wally.

Sie wagte es nicht. — Die Furcht vor der Strenge ihrer Mutter —

Julius (entschlossen).

Desto schlimmer! — Ich werde es wagen — und ich bereue, nicht früher gekommen zu sein —! Aber sehen Sie, liebes Fräulein, bei mir dauert es immer sehr lange bis ich zu einem Entschluß komme — und dann — der Mann mit der Flinte — Apropos, kommt er auch hieher?

Wally (nicht ohne Bitterkeit).

Seitdem ich wieder hier zurück bin, war er noch nicht da!

Julius.

Das ist mir sehr angenehm! Herr Reimer soll jetzt die ganze Wahrheit erfahren! Ich will nicht, daß Ihre Familie glaube, Sie... während Sie im Gegentheil doch gar nicht... Ach! warum bin ich nicht früher hiehergekommen!

Wally.

Nun, es ist noch nicht zu spät... rechtfertigen Sie mich, das wird eine gute, edle Handlung von Ihnen sein! (Lustig.) Brennen Sie mich so weiß wie möglich! Auf diese Weise wird man erfahren, daß Sie Clärchen lieben und die Heirat macht sich von selbst!

Julius (kratzt sich hinterm Ohr).

Die Heirat?

Wally (stutzt).

Ist das nicht etwa Ihre Absicht?

Julius (zögernd).

Das heißt... Clärchen ist allerdings sehr hübsch und liebenswürdig...

Wally.

Und für sie haben Sie fast Ihr Leben gewagt.

Julius.

Das war ein Fehler!

Wally.

Wie?

Julius.

Ja, eine Unvorsichtigkeit, und wenn ich gewußt hätte, daß es so gefährlich wird?

Wally.

So hätten Sie gezögert?

Julius.

Nein, ich hätte mich gar nicht riskirt!

Wally (etwas heftiger).

Ich denke, wenn man leidenschaftlich liebt ... Sie lieben Clärchen doch ...?

Julius.

Ich will nicht das Gegentheil behaupten ... aber ich glaube kaum, daß sie mich so innig liebt.

Clärchen (bei Seite).

Was sagt er?

Wally.

Sie zweifeln?

Julius.

Bedeutend! Als ich damals in Gefahr war, wer kam mir zu Hilfe? Nicht Clärchen — Sie, Fräulein Wally!

Clärchen (bei Seite, immer erregter).

Das ist wahr!

Julius.

Weil Sie gut sind, weil Sie ein edles Herz haben!

Wally.

Nun, so wende ich mich jetzt an das Ihrige! Lassen auch Sie Ihr Herz sprechen; es wird Sie mahnen daß Sie die Schwäche eines Mädchens nicht länger mißbrauchen dürfen ...

Julius.

Oh — mißbrauchen ... mein Gott, wir sprachen uns öfters ... ganz unschuldige Rendez-vous ...

Wally.

Einerlei! Clärchen's Ruf, ihre Zukunft liegt dessen ungeachtet einzig und allein in Ihrer Hand... Es gibt nur ein Mittel, Alles wieder gut zu machen und ich hoffe, Sie werden damit nicht zögern. Tante Müllner wird gleich hier sein... erwarten Sie sie und werben Sie um Clärchen's Hand!

Clärchen (bei Seite).

Was wird er sagen?!

Julius (verlegen seinen Hut mit dem Aermel streichend).

Ja — wenn Clärchen Ihnen gliche — aber mit ihr... bin ich eben nicht sehr beruhigt..! In der Pension nahm sie meine Liebeserklärungen sehr bald und sehr freundlich auf... wer weiß, wie das in der Ehe würde... denn als meine Frau könnte sie, während ich sanft schlummere, auch des Nachts in den Garten gehen... und...

Clärchen (entsetzt aufschreiend).

Ha! (sinkt fast ohnmächtig auf den Stuhl in der Laube).

Wally.

Armes Mädchen! (Eilt in die Laube und kniet vor Clärchen nieder.)

Julius (starr, bei Seite).

Sie war hier? — Sie hörte Alles?

Wally.

Clärchen! Komm doch zu Dir!

Julius (bei Seite).

Ich glaube, das Gescheidteste ist, so rasch als möglich... (Er ist mit langen Schritten gegen das Gitter geschlichen und stößt dort auf den eben eintretenden Edmund.) Ha!

Sechste Szene.

Vorige. Edmund.

Edmund.

Das junge Herrchen aus dem Schrank!

Julius (bei Seite).

Der Mann mit der Flinte!

Edmund (Julius fest am Arme fassend).

Habe ich Sie endlich wieder, Herr Freiburg? (Kommt mit ihm links vor.)

Julius.

Keine Thätlichkeiten, wenn ich bitten darf!

Edmund.

Was suchen Sie hier? Wohl Fräulein Wally?

Julius.

Ja wohl! Allerdings! Ich kam hieher, um Fräulein Wally zu . . .

Edmund.

Wann werden Sie sie heiraten?

Julius (dumm).

Was? Die soll ich heiraten?

Edmund.

Hoffentlich haben Sie doch nicht die Frechheit . . . Aber nein, (verächtlich) ich will ein solches Kinderspiel nicht tragisch nehmen . . . ! Doch merken Sie sich eines: ich weiche nicht von Ihrer Seite, bis Sie sich erklärt und Alles ehrenvoll in Ordnung gebracht haben! (Er schüttelt ihm krampfhaft die Hand.)

Julius.

Drücken Sie nicht so!

Edmund (zieht Julius nach dem Gitter).

Kommen Sie zu Ihrem Vater!

Julius (bebend).

Zu meinem Vater!

Edmund.

Vorwärts!

Clärchen (mit Wally aus der Laube tretend).

Halt!

Edmund (bei Seite).

Die beiden Mädchen!

Clärchen.

Lassen Sie den Herrn seiner Wege ziehen.

Edmund.

Wie? Ich soll . . . ? Oh nein, erst hat er hier seine Pflicht zu thun!

Wally.

Das ist auch meine Meinung! Halten Sie ihn nur fest!

Julius (zu Wally).

Er will ja, daß ich Sie heirate!

Wally (ernst).

Mich nicht ... sondern meine Cousine!

Edmund (stutzt).

Ihre Cousine?

Clärchen (fast tonlos).

Der Schein hat Sie betrogen, Herr Feldern ... ich hatte nicht den Muth, meine Schuld zu gestehen ...

Edmund (Wally anblickend).

Was sagt Sie? (Wally sieht ihn ernst und vorwurfsvoll an).

Clärchen.

Aber jetzt muß die Wahrheit an's Licht ...! Ich bin allein die Schuldige ... jenes Stelldichein ... galt mir!

Edmund.

Ihnen?

Julius.

Natürlich! Wir kennen uns ja schon aus der Pension ... wo wir uns täglich sprachen ... über die Mauer ... (Bei Seite.) Ist der Mensch begriffsstützig!

Edmund.

Also Wally?

Clärchen.

Ist die beste, aufopferndste Freundin, die sich lieber unschuldig anklagen ließ als mich zu verrathen! O Wally, Wally ... Du weißt nicht, wie tief beschämt ich bin! Vergib mir ... und entziehe mir Deine Freundschaft nicht ... die einzige, die mir wohl auf Erden mehr bleiben wird!

Wally (herzlich).

Meine Freundschaft? Thörin! Ich habe nie aufgehört Dich zu lieben und ... zu achten!

Edmund (zu Clärchen).

Ach Fräulein, ... Ihr Geständniß macht mich unendlich glücklich ... (zu Julius) Sie doch auch?

Julius (zieht ein Taschentuch und wischt sich die Augen).

Ja wohl ... ich bin gerührt! Clärchen, Sie haben mich gerührt! Sie haben auch ein gutes Herz ... nur ich, ich habe keines ... oder ein miserables ... denn wenn ich bedenke ... (nähert sich Clärchen immer mehr und spricht immer leiser) daß ich vorhin hier ... so häßliche Worte ... aber ich nehme sie zurück ... vergessen auch Sie ... und verzeihen Sie mir ...

denn ... (fällt auf beide Knie vor Klärchen) ich liebe Sie, Clärchen!

Clärchen (traurig).

Nein, nein Julius, Sie lieben mich nicht!

Julius (steckt sein Taschentuch wieder ein und springt auf).

Ich Sie nicht lieben? Clärchen wie können Sie so sprechen? Ich liebe Sie wahnsinnig, ewig, bis zu meinem letzten Athem= zuge ... und noch länger ... wie der Dichter sagt: „über's Grab"! Doch vorläufig wollen wir an's Grab noch nicht den= ken, sondern wie's Lorle sagt: „erscht recht lebe — lang' lebe"! Ja? Mein Clärchen! (Er küßt ihr feurig die Hand.)

Wally (drollig).

Na also! es löst sich ja Alles wieder in allgemeines Wohl= gefallen auf!

Julius.

Heute spreche ich noch mit meinem Vater ... ich bin beinahe volljährig und keine Macht der Erde wird mich länger hindern Sie zum Altar zu führen!

Wally.

Bravo!

Edmund.

Das heißt gesprochen!

Julius (trocknet sich den Schweiß von der Stirne).

Und jetzt zu Frau Müllner! Wo ist sie? Ich will sie sofort sprechen!

(Man hört das Rollen eines Wagens.)

Wally (nach dem Hintergrunde blickend).

Da kommt sie eben mit dem Onkel.

Clärchen.

Ach, wenn sie mich hier findet ...

Wally.

Geh' ins Haus ... Mathilde ist vielleicht noch da ... laß mich den ersten Sturm pariren! — (Schiebt Clärchen in das Haus links.)

Siebente Szene.

Wally, Edmund, Julius, Frau Müllner, Reimer.

Frau Müllner (zu Wally.)

Der Polizei=Commissär ist von Allem unterrichtet!

Wally.

Schade um die Mühe!

Frau Müllner (auffahrend).

Wie?

Wally (hänselnd).

Bitten Sie doch diese beiden Herren um Auskunft! (Deutet auf Edmund und Julius.)

Reimer,

Edmund mit einem Fremden? Wer ist der Herr?

Edmund.

Er wird sich Ihnen gleich selbst vorstellen. (Zu Julius.) Vorwärts, junger Mann, und muthig den Sturm gewagt.

Julius (sehr ängstlich).

Gnädige Frau! ... Ich fühle mich sehr glücklich Ihnen anzeigen zu können, daß Papa einwilligt ... das heißt ... er wird wohl einwilligen ...

Frau Müllner.

Papa?

Reimer.

Papa?

Frau Müllner (wüthend und ungeduldig).

Mit wem habe ich das Vergnügen, mein Herr?!

Julius.

Gnädige Frau ... ich bin der junge Mann ... Sie wissen ja ... der des Nachts in Ihrem Garten ...

Reimer und Frau Müllner.

Sie?!

Julius.

Ja und ... ich bitte ... um meinen Paletot!!!

Frau Müllner (außer sich).

Sie kleiner Unglücksmensch ...

Edmund (Frau Müllner zurückhaltend).

Schüchtern Sie ihn nicht ein!

Julius.

Um so mehr, als Papa sicher einwilligen wird! ...

Frau Müllner.

Vor allem Andern wer sind Sie?

Julius.

Ganz richtig! Julius Kleinlich, 23 Jahr alt ... zu Mi=

chaeli . . . ich könnte beinahe schon Wahlmann sein . . . wenn überhaupt Wahlen ausgeschrieben wären . . .

Reimer.

Bleiben wir bei der Sache! — Es gibt leider zu viele Spekulanten, welche leichtgläubigen Eltern eine reiche Mitgift entlocken . . .

Julius.

O, ich bitte — wir sind selbst wohlhabend. — Mein Vater liebt die Mechanik, er macht Locomotive!

Reimer.

Sie sind der einzige Sohn?

Julius.

Ja, Herr Reimer, ich habe nur zwei Schwestern, die noch im Pensionat sind.

Wally (ironisch).

Gratuliere!

Julius.

Und deßhalb nehme ich mir die Freiheit und werbe hiemit . . .

Frau Müllner.

Um meine Nichte?

Julius.

Ihre Nichte?

Wally (bei Seite).

So, jetzt fangt die Geschichte von Anfang an!

Julius.

Ich glaubte immer sie wäre Ihre Tochter?

Frau Müllner.

Nur meine Nichte . . . ich habe an diesem Verwandtschaftsgrad schon genug.

Wally (bei Seite lächelnd).

Es verwickelt sich immer mehr!

Frau Müllner.

Mein Bruder ist der Vormund — wenden Sie sich an ihn.

Wally (leise zu Edmund, der heimlich mit ihr gesprochen hat).

Lassen wir sie ruhig gehen . . . warum sollen wir uns nicht auch ein wenig amüsiren?!

Julius (zu Reimer tretend).

Ah! Herr Reimer ist . . .? Ich glaubte, Sie wären der

Vormund von ... und nun sind Sie auch der Vormund von ...
so, so! — (grüßend) darf ich mir also schmeicheln?

Reimer.

Ich werde mit Ihrem Vater sprechen, und so unangenehm
diese Partie mir auch ist, ich werde meine Einwilligung geben!

Julius.

Sehr schmeichelhaft! (Geht zu Wally und Edmund.) Nun wä=
ren wir ja also glücklich heraus!

Wally (schalkhaft).

Glauben Sie?

Edmund (zu Julius).

Geben Sie 'mal Acht! (Wendet sich zu Reimer und Frau
Müllner.) Meine Herrschaften! auch ich erlaube mir als Freier
aufzutreten ...

Frau Müllner (bei Seite).

Himmel! Jetzt wird er meine unglückselige Tochter begeh=
ren, und ich weiß nicht, wo sie ist?

Edmund.

Ich bitte Sie hiemit um die Hand des Fräulein Wally.

Reimer.

Wally? Sie hörten doch, daß ich sie eben diesem Herrn
zusagte!

Julius.

Entschuldigen Sie ...! Keinen derartigen gefährlichen
Irrthum ... ich warb um Fräulein Clärchen.

Frau Müllner.

Um meine Tochter? Sie?

Edmund.

Um derentwillen er über Mauern und Balcone kletterte ...
sich unter Tischteppichen und in Kleiderschränken versteckte ...

Frau Müllner.

Dieser Milchbart?!

Wally.

Und seinethalben hat Clärchen Ihr Haus verlassen.

Frau Müllner (stürzt auf Julius los).

Zum Polizei-Commissär!

Julius (ausweichend).

Keine Thätlichkeiten ...

Reimer (zu Wally).

Und ich beschuldigte Dich, meine arme Wally! (Umarmt sie.)

Frau Müllner (zu Julius).

Aber meine Tochter? Was haben Sie mit ihr angefangen, Sie schändlicher Lovelace?! (Fast weinerlich.) Soll ich denn mein Kind nie wiedersehen?!

Eilfte Szene.

Vorige, Mathilde und Clärchen (sind schon bei den letzten Worten aus dem Hause getreten).

Mathilde (leise zu Clärchen).

Das ist der günstigste Augenblick.

Clärchen (ihrer Mutter zu Füßen fallend).

Mutter ... Verzeihung!

Frau Müllner (wendet sich, erblickt Clärchen und stürzt wüthend zu ihr).

Ha, endlich! Unwürdige Tochter! Du wagst es vor meine Augen ...

Reimer (dazwischen tretend).

Liebe Schwester ... fange nicht wieder von vorne an!

Julius (bei Seite).

Mir scheint, bei der Schwiegermutter werd' ich schlechte Zeiten haben!

Reimer (hebt Clärchen auf).

Steh' auf, Clärchen! Deine Mutter schreit zwar gerne ... aber im Grunde hat sie doch ein gutes Herz und wird in Deine Verheiratung mit Herrn Kleinlich willigen! Was nun Edmund betrifft ... (zu Mathilde) denn er hat seine Werbung um Wally's Hand wiederholt ...

Mathilde (bei Seite).

Himmel!

Wally (Mathilden's Schrecken bemerkend, mit Festigkeit).

Und ich wiederhole meine Abweisung.

Reimer.

Abermals? Das scheint eine Antipathie zu sein?

Edmund.

Nein, Herr Reimer, ich kenne den Grund dieses Entschlusses, Fräulein Wally hat ihn mir selbst mitgetheilt.

Mathilde (unruhig, bei Seite).

Sie?

Edmund (lächelnd).

Fräulein Wally ist eine schlechte Patriotin, sie liebt ihr deutsches Vaterland nicht ... hat den Wunsch, die weite Welt kennen zu lernen ... und wenn ich ihr den Vorschlag machte, uns in England oder Amerika anzusiedeln ...

Wally (rasch, freudig).

Für immer?! Sie versprechen mir das?

Edmund.

Ich schwör' es Ihnen bei meiner Liebe!

Wally.

Das ist etwas Anderes! — (Reicht Edmund die Hand.) Meine Herrschaften, ich habe die Ehre, Ihnen hier meinen Bräutigam vorzustellen. (Allgemeine freudige Erregung, nur Frau Müllner seufzt laut auf und schleudert wüthende Blicke auf Julius und Clärchen.)

Mathilde (bei Seite).

Gottlob! Ich werde ihn nicht mehr sehen!

Reimer (zu Frau Müllner).

Nun, liebe Schwester, begreifst Du endlich ...

Frau Müllner (einfallend).

Ja wohl ... ich begreife, daß ich noch nicht wachsam genug war, da meine Tochter, die ich so strenge hütete und be-wachte ...

Wally.

Der Strenge und der Aufsicht gar manches Mädchen lacht,
Nur jenes ist gehütet, das selbst sich streng bewacht.

(Sie reicht Edmund die Hand, Reimer umfaßt Mathilde, Julius will Frau Müllner umarmen, diese gibt ihm einen leichten, abweisenden Stoß; Julius geht ängstlich, auf Frau Müllner blickend, zu Clärchen und küßt ihr die Hand, während Frau Müllner in der Mitte des Vordergrundes mit gekreuzten Armen starr dasteht, und wüthende Blicke auf Julius wirft.)

Der Vorhang fällt.

Ende.

CPSIA information can be obtained
at www.ICGtesting.com
Printed in the USA
BVHW04*1416200918
528044BV00007B/95/P

Louisa Heaton lives on Hay
Hampshire, with her husban
a small zoo. She has worked
the health industry—most re
as a Community First Responder, answering
999 calls. When not writing Louisa enjoys other
creative pursuits, including reading, quilting and
patchwork—usually instead of the things she
ought to be doing!

Also by Louisa Heaton

Risking Her Heart on the Trauma Doc
A Baby to Rescue Their Hearts
Twins for the Neurosurgeon
A GP Worth Staying For
Their Marriage Meant To Be
Their Marriage Worth Fighting For
A Date with Her Best Friend
Miracle Twins for the Midwife

Discover more at millsandboon.co.uk.

THE BROODING DOC AND THE SINGLE MUM

LOUISA HEATON

SECOND CHANCE FOR THE VILLAGE NURSE

LOUISA HEATON

MILLS & BOON

First published in Great Britain 2023
by Mills & Boon, an imprint of HarperCollins*Publishers* Ltd,
1 London Bridge Street, London, SE1 9GF

www.harpercollins.co.uk

HarperCollins*Publishers* Macken House, 39/40 Mayor Street Upper, Dublin 1, D01 C9W8, Ireland

The Brooding Doc and the Single Mum © 2023 Louisa Heaton

Second Chance for the Village Nurse © 2023 Louisa Heaton

ISBN: 978-0-263-30606-4

05/23

This book is produced from independently certified FSC™ paper to ensure responsible forest management.
For more information visit: www.harpercollins.co.uk/green.

Printed and Bound in the UK using 100% Renewable Electricity at CPI Group (UK) Ltd, Croydon, CR0 4YY

THE BROODING DOC AND THE SINGLE MUM

LOUISA HEATON

MILLS & BOON

To Sheila H and Sheila C

CHAPTER ONE

Greenbeck Village Welcomes Careful Drivers
Twinned with Vebnice, Croatia

DR STACEY EMERY smiled as she drove past the sign, glancing briefly into the rear-view mirror. Her son, Jack, was looking out of the window at a field filled with sheep and new lambs. 'We're here!' she beamed, hoping to see him smile and fill him with some excitement about their move. But he didn't even meet her eyes.

She did worry about him. This move to Greenbeck was meant to be the answer to all their problems and worries. Their fresh start. Their reset button. All her hopes and dreams were pinned on Greenbeck working its extraordinary magic and bringing back the fun-filled, happy boy she'd used to know.

Greenbeck had been her childhood home and she had many wonderful memories here. She couldn't remember a time when she hadn't been happy. It had always seemed to be summer. Sunshine…warmth on her face. Flowers. Playing with her friends. Feeding the ducks at the duckpond. Watching the canal barges drift beneath the Wishing Bridge. Calling to the people on the boats and waving.

She'd grown up on Blossom Lane, where the only traffic she'd had to be careful of was the horses being led out through the gate of High Field Farm. Whenever they'd come she'd run inside to tell her grandad to bring his shovel, because said horses had left some helpful, steaming piles of manure on the road he could acquire for his rose bushes and vegetable patch.

She'd picked blackberries and gooseberries from wild bushes. Scrumped apples from Merryman's Orchard. Swung on a swing above the brook. Paddled barefoot in the water, looking for sticklebacks with a bright neon-yellow net on the end of a bamboo cane. There'd been the fun of the village fete. Skipping to school. Sports days with egg and spoon races...

Apart from when she'd lost her parents, Stacey couldn't remember a time here when she hadn't smiled. And she needed that for Jack.

She couldn't remember the last time he'd truly been happy. Truly laughed. Truly enjoyed being a little boy.

She needed, desperately, for Greenbeck and her grandparents to work their magic all over again.

But she'd been away for so long. She hoped and prayed that the village had somehow ignored the passage of time and was still exactly as she remembered it.

The road after the sign would lead her down into the valley where Greenbeck nestled. She drove past the ancient ruins of Castle Merrick, a place she'd often looked up at and dreamed was filled with the ghosts of lords and ladies from centuries past. It was now a heritage site and she could see tourists gathering. Its one last turret stood formidably high, defiant against the years, casting a shadow over the road that suddenly began to twist and turn as it took her through the woods.

The green canopy of trees high above flickered with the snippets of sun breaking through, dotting the road and her windscreen with a dazzling array of strobing light. Then the car broke free from the woods and opened up into bordering fields, where she saw more sheep. Cows… Horses… And was that an alpaca?

A road sign declared that the upper speed limit for driving through Greenbeck was twenty miles per hour, so she slowed down, glad of the chance to look around and re-familiarise herself with a place that she hadn't seen for a long time.

The few visits she'd managed had been way too short. Weekends here and there. Once to introduce her grandparents to her now ex-husband Jerry. Another after Jack had first been born. Her grandparents would have loved to keep their great-grandson in their lives, but it hadn't been possible. Her job had been in Scotland. She'd done what she could…maintaining video calls once a month. But being a single mother didn't often leave her with much time on her hands and so they'd not visited in person as often she would have liked.

Her grandparents, Genevieve and William Clancy, were so proud of her, though. For doing well at school, despite the trauma of losing both her parents in a tragic accident so early on in life. They'd supported her and cheered her on when she'd applied to study medicine at university, waving her off as she'd driven her ancient car away from Greenbeck to travel all the way to Edinburgh.

They'd managed to come up for her graduation ceremony, which had been nice, and had listened to her on the phone each week as she'd described to them what it was like on her hospital placements and then her GP training. And then how it had felt to fall in love.

They'd taken the news in a non-judgemental, wonderful way when she'd told them she'd eloped to Gretna Green to marry a GP she'd met and not invited anyone to the wedding. They'd listened in the same way when her marriage had crumbled after she fell pregnant with Jack...

So much had passed since she'd been away. So much heartache. So much pain. And not once had they admonished her. Their love for her was eternal and something that could never be broken, it seemed.

Which was what they both needed. Her grandparents knew of Jack's troubles. Knew of Stacey's despair. And when they'd told her, *'Come home. There's a place for Jack at Greenbeck Juniors. We've already checked...'* she had known in her heart it was the right thing to do. It was time to come back home and be healed, despite the memories that impeded the thought of doing so. She'd lost her parents here.

The road took her through the heart of Greenbeck, past the village green, where small families stood by the pond, feeding the ducks and a pair of resident swans. She smiled, remembering the many hours she'd spent doing exactly the same thing.

'Look at all the ducks, Jack!'

He made a non-committal sound in his throat and tightened his grip on his teddy bear, Grover, the stuffed toy he'd become attached to since he was a baby. Grover was a little bedraggled now. Stacey had lost count of the amount of times she'd stitched him up, repairing his paws and ears, because Jack never let him go when he was at home.

Stacey noticed a new building next to the church. Single-storey. Built in the same grey stone that most of the buildings here were constructed with, but with a large, modern glass frontage. *Greenbeck Village Surgery.*

So that's where I'll be working...

When Stacey had been a little girl the doctor had operated out of his own house. Dr Pickwick had been a dour-faced old man. A bit gruff, with steel-rimmed spectacles. But every time her grandma had taken her to see him, either because of illness or for an inoculation, Dr Pickwick had opened up his desk drawer and let her choose from a box of sweeties or lollipops if she'd been a good patient. And sometimes when she'd sat in the waiting room, ready to be seen—actually the front parlour of his home—Stacey had been able to smell whatever Mrs Pickwick was baking.

For a long time she'd associated going to the doctor's with the delicious aroma of apple pie. One of Mrs Pickwick's favourites... But that was for later. And even though she was also keen to call in on her grandparents, whom she hadn't seen in person for a few years, she was very much aware that she'd been driving for hours and what she wanted most was something to eat and drink and maybe to take a shower, so that she could see them when she was feeling refreshed.

There was a parking space over by The Buttered Bun Café and she slid into it, pulling on the handbrake. 'Here we are! Let's grab a quick bite to eat. I don't know about you, but I'm starved.'

She helped Jack clamber from his seat and then she held his hand as they entered The Buttered Bun. Above their heads a bell rang to announce their entrance and, spotting a seat by the window, she parked Jack and gave him one of the complementary colouring sheets and pots of crayons whilst she went to give their order.

There were plenty of delicious-looking treats on display. Sausage rolls, pies, sandwiches, cake slices, cream cakes, gingerbread men... She ordered two hot sausage rolls, one hot chocolate and a pot of tea for herself, paid, then went to sit down. Jack was busy studiously colouring in a dragon in bright purple crayon.

'Wow, that looks amazing,' she said.

'Thanks.'

It was only one word, but it was the most she'd had out of him in hours. It warmed her heart. Made her feel hopeful. She sat and watched him for a few minutes, noting the way his eyebrows were arched in concentration, the way he worried at his bottom lip. Then the waitress, a pretty young woman with red hair almost the same shade as Stacey's, brought over their order.

'Hey, great dragon!' she said.

Stacey saw her name tag: Jade. She smiled, then walked away, went behind her counter, busying herself with making coffee for an elderly gentleman who had come in after Stacey. Who *was* that? He looked familiar. But it had been so long her mind struggled for names from the past.

The sausage roll was perfect. Buttery, crisp pastry with warm, spiced meat inside. She needed a napkin afterwards to wipe her fingers.

Jack ate most of his, and was just finishing his hot chocolate when the bell sounded above the door again and in rushed the most handsome man Stacey had ever seen in her entire life.

She tried not to stare. But it was hard not to at a man like that!

Already her heart rate had increased, and she sucked in a breath to try and steady it, pretending to take a renewed interest in Jack's colouring, in the hope that he wouldn't notice her.

She'd fallen for a handsome man before and he'd been nothing but trouble. Men like that got noticed everywhere they went. By other women. Other men. They got hit on. Flirted with. And that was often an irresistible thing. It certainly had been to Jerry, her ex-husband. Meaning Stacey had been burned by love. Left as a single mother. And

Jack was fatherless. His father wasn't dead. Just absent. Being burdened with a child was not something Jerry had ever wanted.

Why didn't I see it?

So Stacey would quite happily stay away from men who turned heads wherever they went.

She noticed the waitress—Jade—had perked up considerably at the man's entrance. She was beaming a smile at him, eyes gleaming, chest thrust out, fluttering her eyelashes.

'Hi. Can I help you?'

'I've pre-ordered six of your finest white chocolate chip cookies.'

Stacey couldn't help but notice that he was a fine figure of a man. Flat stomach. A hint of muscle beneath his shirt-sleeves. Nicely shaped thighs and butt in tailored trousers. He didn't look the sort to gorge on chocolate chip cookies. He looked like an avocado on toast kind of man. A man who knew exactly how much protein he consumed each day. Who could bench-press a considerable weight. Who she would no doubt see jogging around the village most days, looking all hot and sweaty and delicious...

He turned. Glanced her way.

Immediately she turned to Jack, leaning over the table to grab a crayon and help her son complete his picture. Stacey concentrated hard, until she heard the man finish his transaction and the ring of the bell behind her as he left.

She let out a breath and Jack looked up.

'What is it?'

'Oh. Nothing...'

She glanced at the waitress, who was twirling her necklace in her fingers as she looked longingly out through the café's front window, clearly tracking the man's progress.

Stacey shook her head slightly, feeling that she could easily give some wise, womanly advice to Jade about watching out for men like that. But she had enough on her plate and it was time to go.

'Finished?' she asked Jack.

He nodded.

'Good.' Stacey gathered their things, then thanked Jade. 'Actually, could you help me?' she added. 'I'm looking for Blacksmith's Cottage, Honeysuckle Lane. Could you direct me? I'm not familiar with that road.'

Stacey had assumed it was a new road, built in the intervening years since she'd been here last.

Jade looked at her curiously. 'Sure. You turn right, then head to the end of the High Street. First left, then second right. It's on the edge of the new development site there.'

Where the old blacksmith used to be, Stacey thought. On the edge of the village. Made sense, considering the name of the cottage. 'Thanks,' she said.

'Welcome to Greenbeck.' Jade smiled.

'Thanks,' she said again.

They headed back out to the car. Stacey was keen to get settled in. Offload their belongings. It was a shame they couldn't stay with her grandparents, but there simply wasn't room for both her and Jack. Jack was a growing boy. Her grandparents had offered, but no, it wouldn't have been right. Jack needed his own space, and it would have been unfair to him for them both to squeeze into her old childhood bedroom. Her gran and grandad were getting on in years, too, and it would have been unreasonable to expect them to cope with a noisy young boy—much though she knew they would love having Jack in their lives.

'Come on, Jack. Let's find home.'

* * *

Dr Daniel Prior stood by the mantelpiece, staring at the picture of his wife Penny and his son Mason. It was something he did a lot. Often when he felt alone, or when he had a decision to make in life. As if staring at the image would somehow tell him what to do.

In the picture, Penny and Mason had just released lanterns into the night sky during a holiday in Oahu, Hawaii. Like them, he had stood and watched the lanterns float upwards with hundreds of others, during the lantern festival, and he'd pulled out his mobile to take pictures. The first picture had been of the sky, lit by the multitude of lanterns, and the second picture—the one he was looking at now—was Penny standing behind Mason, her hands on his shoulders, as they'd both turned to look at him, smiling—no, *beaming* in delight.

It had perfectly captured their delight and joy, and in that moment he had loved them both so much he'd thought to himself, *Even if I never get another day it doesn't matter, because right now is perfect.*

'But I was wrong,' he said sadly to the empty room. 'I'd give anything for another day with you two.'

His wife and son smiled back at him, unaware that their lives would both be cruelly cut short just one day later. The guilt of that thought tortured him even now.

Daniel rubbed at his hip. It still ached. Two years since the accident. If he'd lived, Mason would be six now—in junior school. Penny would be thirty. She'd always had such big plans for her thirtieth birthday party…

Sighing, he turned from the mantelpiece and went to the kitchen to pick up the bag of chocolate chip cookies he'd collected earlier from The Buttered Bun. It wasn't much.

Just a little housewarming gift for the new doctor. Or rather an annexe-warming gift.

When the senior partner, Dr Zach Fletcher, had told Daniel he'd hired someone new for their expanding practice he'd offered to put them up until they could find somewhere more permanent. His annexe was empty—it might as well be put to use. The rent would be nice, too. But most of all he knew how hard it was to find a place to buy in Greenbeck.

Since its arrival on the list of the UK's top ten best villages to live in, places to rent and buy here had become extortionate in price. Not many people left the village, and properties tended to stay within families. An incoming GP would struggle to find a place, so Daniel had kindly offered his annexe as part of the job, for as long as the new doctor needed it.

Zach had told him the new GP, the Clancys' granddaughter, had lots of experience in her old practice. Apparently, she'd been instrumental in putting together a variety of support groups for her patients: a diabetes support group. A 'Knit and Natter' group for some of her more elderly patients. A 'Men's Shed' for widowers to get together and make new friends. A volunteer support group, and even a group for anxiety sufferers, who apparently took it in turns to meet at each other's houses.

It certainly sounded as if she was a proactive person, and he was looking forward to meeting her. But even though she'd be in his annexe, and they would be colleagues, he hoped that she would respect his boundaries. Colleagues, friends and neighbours they might be, but he wouldn't want them popping in every five minutes. Daniel liked his solitude now that he'd got used to it, and when he went home for the day he treasured his alone-time. It allowed him to recharge his batteries and let go of the stresses of the day.

His doorbell rang and he knew it would be her. She was early. He hadn't had time to leave the cookies in the annexe yet, with the welcome note he'd been going to write.

Oh, well.

He put the cookies down and went to answer his front door. He pulled it open and stood there for a minute, absolutely stupefied at the sight of the young redheaded woman before him, her hands resting on the shoulders of a child who was clearly her son. He was the spitting image of his mother. Red-haired. Freckled. Pale, creamy skin.

There'd beenphotographs on the Clancys' hearth, but he'd never looked at them up close.

'Yes?'

He couldn't help but notice her green eyes. The soft, gentle waves of the long red hair hanging below her shoulders. She was pretty…

No. She's beautiful.

'I'm Dr Stacey Emery. And this is my son, Jack.'

She was looking at him with uncertainty.

Daniel looked down at the boy, who was looking up at him with curiosity.

'Erm…' His brain scrambled madly for something sensible and welcoming to say, but all he could feel was fear and apprehension. Was he ready for this? A young boy? A child who could be the age Mason would be now?

I'll just keep my distance.

'I…er…wasn't expecting you this early. You made good time?'

'Not bad.'

'You must be tired. Let me grab the keys and I'll show you around.'

He grabbed the annexe keys off the hook, and the bag

of cookies, and closed his front door behind him, intending to show her the annexe quickly and then leave her to it.

This was the woman that he'd spotted in the café! It had been a quick glance, but enough for him to hope that she wasn't the person he was waiting for. He'd thought for a second that she was someone who looked a bit like Stacey Emery, but hoped it wasn't.

He led the way around the side of his cottage to the annexe that he'd had built at the bottom of his garden. Originally he'd built it as a project in his spare time, intending to use it as a place for his parents to move into. But his mum and dad had begun to require nursing care as they'd got older, and they'd recently moved into a facility in Guildford instead, leaving the new annexe free.

He'd contemplated making it into some kind of studio. He'd had grand plans for making videos about what it was like to be a GP…maybe doing a podcast? Interviewing people with interesting medical stories and posting them online? But all that required that he be quite the extrovert, and he wasn't ready just yet. Renting out the annexe had seemed like a good substitution.

He unlocked the door and pushed it open, stepping back so Dr Emery and her son could go in first.

She gave him a slight smile as she passed, and he couldn't help but inhale the scent of her perfume. Floral. Light. Not overpowering in any way. The kind of scent that made you want to close your eyes and savour it for as long as you could.

But of course he wasn't going to do that, so he just waited a moment or two for them to be in the heart of the living space and then followed them in.

'This is the living area. Kitchen's through there. It's got

everything you should need. Dishwasher, cooker, micro-wave. Cookies.'

He awkwardly placed the brown paper bag on her counter. Not wanting to draw too much focus to the gesture. Hoping she'd let it pass and just accept it as a run-of-the-mill housewarming gift.

'There's a separate utility room out the back. Down there are the two bedrooms and a bathroom, complete with shower.'

He wanted to hand over the keys and get out of there, even if it seemed rude. He was still scrabbling to accept that this was the Clancys' granddaughter, incredibly beautiful, and that she had a son the same age Mason would be, had he not died...

He let out a breath as she turned this way and that, perusing everything. 'You can make any changes you want in regard to furniture,' he said. 'But I'd appreciate it if you could store anything original in the attic space.'

'It all looks wonderful. And bringing the cookies was thoughtful. Thank you.' She smiled, then knelt down to face her son. 'Jack? Want to go choose a bedroom?'

The little boy nodded and sped off down the corridor, clutching a manky-looking teddy bear that had clearly seen better days. It needed to go in the washing machine, but Daniel wasn't sure it would be in one piece after a wash.

The annexe had two double rooms. Both the same size. He'd kept decorations quite minimal, thinking of his parents. White walls. Lots of stained wood. Lots of greenery. He imagined it would all seem a little too grown-up for a young boy.

'If he wants to put up posters and things, that's fine.'

'That's great. I appreciate you letting us stay here for a

while. Hopefully it won't be for too long.' She smiled again, lighting up her green eyes.

He nodded. 'You're the Clancys' granddaughter?'

She seemed surprised that he knew this. 'Yes. You know them?'

'Kind of.'

He couldn't say any more. His mouth didn't seem connected to his brain right now.

He couldn't think of anything else to say to her, so reached out a hand to pass her the keys.

'Here you go. Do you need help with your bags, or...?'

Please don't need help with your bags.

'We'll be fine. Just a couple of cases in the car.'

'Right. Well, I'll leave you to it, then.'

He turned and walked out of the annexe, breathing a huge sigh of relief once he was back in the fresh air.

What a complication! He'd fervently hoped Dr Emery would keep her distance and respect his boundaries before she got here, but now he knew that he would have to keep her at arm's length as much as possible. Because, as much as he'd loved his wife and vowed never to look at another woman ever again, he'd felt an instant *something* when he'd opened the door to Dr Emery.

In his experience that *something*...that *spark*...always led to something more, and he wasn't ready for it.

Dr Emery and her young son Jack were a threat. A danger.

And he knew he had to protect himself at all costs.

Oh, no.

That had been her first thought when Dr Prior had opened the door, and the second one that had come tumbling right after it was, *Don't let anything show on your face.*

Dr Prior—the man she was renting her home from, living next-door to, becoming his tenant—was exactly the same man she'd seen rush into The Buttered Bun to collect a bag of cookies. That stunner of a man who now, up close, she could see was even more handsome than she'd realised whilst at the café. Dark-haired, with a well-groomed beard, chocolatey brown eyes, a jawline that was square and proud. And since he'd been in the café he'd removed his tie and opened the neck of his shirt. She'd been able to see the slight hint of a hairy chest upon well-developed muscle.

Her mouth had instantly dried, even as her heart rate had rocketed. Thank God for Jack, who'd stood in front of her like a human shield.

For a brief moment she'd hoped it was a mistake. He'd certainly looked confused by her arrival, as if he'd not been expecting her, and she'd hoped that maybe she'd stopped at the wrong cottage and the address she really needed was next door, or something. But no. She wasn't in the wrong place and this man was going to be her landlord and her new colleague...

Oh, dear God, he's going to be hard not to look at.

That was the problem with beautiful things. You looked at them. Admired them. And admiration turned to wanting, and wanting led to...

It's best I don't think about what that leads to. Dr Prior is off-limits. I'm off-limits.

Her grandparents had said that her new landlord was a nice man. A very good doctor whom they'd known for a few years. So she'd expected someone *older*.

But the annexe was perfect for her and Jack, and Jack looked keen to explore.

Now Dr Prior had handed her the keys and left she was able to take in its features better—without the distraction of an Adonis at her side. It had a large living area, with soft leather sofas, a low coffee table, and bookshelves filled with a selection of mixed fiction, mostly crime and thrillers. The kitchen was modern and sleek, with soft-close drawers and cupboards. The utility room was functional, with both a washer and a dryer, and the bathroom had black marbled tiles with both a shower and a bath.

The bedrooms were very modern-looking, with a Swedish feel to them. Jack chose the room that looked out onto the garden and she took the other, leaving the suitcases that she'd heaved from the car waiting to be opened by the side of their beds. With nothing in the fridge or the cupboards, she figured it was time they went to see her grandparents and finally let them meet Jack for real—though she would have loved to relax in the shower first...

The drive from Blacksmith Cottage to Blossom Lane barely took ten minutes, and as she pulled into the road where her grandparents lived she thought it was a lot smaller than she'd remembered. The road seemed more narrow, the cottages were closer together, the gardens filled with more flowers.

Her grandparents' place, Gable Cottage, had recently been rethatched, and the purple jasmine around the door was in full bloom. Once upon a time she would have just walked straight in, but she'd been away for so many years she felt awkward, and she knocked instead.

When her grandmother opened the door Stacey beamed a smile at the woman who had raised her after her parents' death. Genevieve Clancy had not changed one bit. Okay, maybe there were one or two more lines upon her face, maybe she'd got a little plumper, and maybe her hair was a fine silver, but the woman herself was just as wonderful and warm.

'Stacey! My darling girl!' Genevieve threw her arms around her and gave her a big squeeze. Then she turned her attention to her great-grandson. 'And my mighty Jack! Haven't you grown?' She stooped down and threw open her arms, and Jack stepped into them for a hug. 'William? Will! they're here!'

Stacey looked up to see her grandad making his way down the hall. He walked with a stick now, it seemed, but that was his only nod towards the fact that the pair of them were now well into their eighties and he was still going strong.

'You're looking pale, Stacey. Have you been eating?' he asked.

'Oh, you know what it's like… It's been a long drive. And the stress of moving—that's all it is.'

'You're sure?'

'Absolutely.'

She stepped towards him and gave him a hug, inhaling the scent of his usual soap and aftershave. It was like coming home. So familiar and yet also poignant. She'd forgotten it, having been away so long…

'Let's get you both in and I'll make some tea. Jack, I've made a cherry pie, if you'd like a slice?'

Jack nodded.

'He needs to eat some dinner first, Gran.'

'Oh, right… Well, let me see… I've got some shepherd's pie in the fridge. Shall I heat that up for the both of you?'

'That'd be great, thanks.'

Her gran beamed. She always had liked feeding people. Mothering them. She and her grandfather were forever taking in waifs and strays who needed help. Even if they saw a homeless person when they were out and about they'd buy them something hot to eat or drink.

Her grandad led them into the living area and it was like stepping back in time. There was the old three-piece suite, still with the pure white antimacassars on the backs and arms. The cabinets were still filled with trinkets and knick-knacks. The circular rug was in front of the gas fire. The horse brasses hung on either side.

And on every conceivable surface family photos took pride of place. Stacey. Jack. Her parents. Gran and Grandad on their own wedding day, holding each other's hands and gazing into each other's eyes with so much love. it almost made you want to weep.

Gran's bag of knitting lay at the side of the sofa. There was Grandad's pile of papers and TV guides. A book on World War II with his reading glasses perched on top.

Stacey might have gone away and changed her life, but here in Gable Cottage time, it seemed, had stood still.

'Hey, Jack. We got you some things to play with so you wouldn't be bored.'

Her grandad pulled out a box from his side of the sofa, and pushed it towards her son. It was filled with books, toys, cars and jigsaws and Jack dived into it with glee.

Stacey smiled to see him happy. She'd missed that.

She settled onto one of the sofas. 'Can I help with anything, Gran?'

'Oh, no, dear! You sit down and rest. I've got it all in hand.' Gran bustled in from the kitchen, wiping her hands on her flowery apron and beaming at Jack, who was playing on the floor. 'We picked up a few bits from the local charity shops. It's not much, but we didn't want him to be bored.'

'It's great. You've gone to a lot of trouble.'

'Oh, no trouble at all! It's what you do for family. Have you moved in yet? Have you looked around the annexe? What did you think?'

'Oh, it's very modern. Very nice.'

'Daniel has worked very hard on it.'

'Daniel?'

'Dr Prior. Your landlord.'

At the mention of his name she felt her cheeks glow. 'Oh, right. Yes. Him.' Stacey gazed down at Jack, who'd emptied a jigsaw puzzle onto the floor. The picture he was trying to make was of a whole lot of cartoon characters. 'You never mentioned he was my age. Or so good-looking,' she admonished kindly.

Her gran looked at her, innocently. 'Didn't I? Must have slipped my mind. Can I get you some tea, Stacey? Coffee?'

'Tea would be great, thanks. We've not had time to go food shopping, so there's nothing in.'

'Oh, we've got plenty in our cupboards! You must take something home with you until you can make it to the shops.'

'That's all right. I'd hate to take food away from you.'

'It's no problem at all. I'll put a little bag together right now.' And her gran bustled back into the kitchen, glad to have a project.

Stacey looked up at her grandad. 'Nothing changes.'

He smiled and nodded. 'No, nothing changes. Your gran likes to make sure people are all right. It feeds a need in her.'

'She's always been the same.'

'Like that doctor of yours. She—'

At that moment her gran came in again and her grandad stopped talking as Genevieve got down on the floor to help her grandson with his jigsaw.

Stacey wondered what her grandad had meant. *That doctor of yours*? Did he mean Dr Prior? The Adonis of Greenbeck? How had her gran been helping him? And why? He seemed a man strapping enough to take care of himself.

He'd also seemed a little standoffish, and not the kind to accept help. Especially from an elderly lady.

I must have misunderstood what he was getting at.

'Oh, I *have* missed this! Having a little one around the place!' said Gran.

'Well, get used to it—he's going to be here a lot!'

'When is his first day at the school? Monday?'

Stacey nodded, suddenly full of apprehension. 'Yeah. Same as me. My first day at the surgery.'

'He'll be all right. You explained everything to them? They know what happened at his last place?'

Memories of that time filled her with the darkness and fear that she'd begun to hate. 'They know.'

Gran reached out to touch her knee. 'He'll be fine at Greenbeck Juniors. They're good there. Nice kiddies. Small classes. He'll fit right in…you'll see. They'll keep an eye on him.'

'I hope so.'

The bullying Jack had received at his last school had sunk her son into a vast depression. His difference—a large, bright red birthmark that covered most of his stomach—had made him a target for bullies, and Jack had become school avoidant. He'd begun complaining of illness most days, growing more quiet every day, and the day he'd stated that he wished he were dead had struck fear into her heart like a knife.

Only recently there'd been an article on the news about a boy who'd killed himself due to online bullying. There was no way that Stacey was going to let a bunch of bullies ruin her son's life. He'd already lost his father, due to no fault of his own, and now his childhood was being stolen from him. She'd not wanted to run away from the problem, but she'd been so scared, and so alone, she'd longed for the warmth and protection that family gave. So she'd returned home for good, hoping that the magic of Greenbeck Juniors— the school that she herself had attended, and in which she'd been so very happy—would somehow work its magic and bring back the boy she'd once known.

'There's never been an issue at that school. He'll be happy there. Won't you?' Gran asked her great-grandson.

Jack just looked at her uncertainly and shrugged.

'It's okay to be nervous on your first day. I'm sure your mum will be, too.'

'First days are the hardest,' Stacey agreed. 'But once they're done and out of the way all the other days are much easier.'

Jack didn't look sure, and she couldn't blame him. He probably thought the new kids he'd meet would be fine until they saw him get changed for PE and then the bullying would begin. If it did she had no idea what she'd do. Home-school him? How would she do that? With her job? They couldn't live on thin air…she needed to be working.

'No word from…?' Her grandad nodded towards Jack and she knew he was asking about Jack's dad—Jerry.

'No. I thought he might get in touch when I informed him we were moving, but I haven't heard a peep.'

Grandad shook his head, totally disgusted at Jerry's behaviour. 'Shocking.'

Gran and Grandad had never been big fans of Jerry after meeting him, but they'd kept their doubts to themselves when she'd announced that they were getting married. They had supported her, believed in her own ability to make the choices that were right for her. And when it had all come crashing down around her ears months later, after Stacey fell pregnant, they'd been there again, to support her. Even making a rare trip up to Edinburgh on the train to stay with her for a week or two. They'd never blamed her. It was always Jerry.

'That's all in the past now, though. This is our new start and we're going to be fine!' she said, trying to convince herself as much as them.

'Of course you are, love,' said Grandad. 'It's going to be all right.'

She smiled at them both, overwhelmed by the love she felt for them and wishing that all her dreams for her and Jack's future would come true.

CHAPTER TWO

'THIS MUST BE JACK?'

A young woman with golden blonde hair tied up in a high ponytail approached Stacey as she and Jack stood in Greenbeck Juniors' playground, waiting for the bell to go.

'My name is Miss Dale and I'm going to be your teacher. I thought I'd take you in and show you around the classroom before all the other kids get in—what do you think?' She held out her hand for him.

Jack looked up at Stacey in question. She smiled and nodded. Jack took his teacher's hand.

'I believe his grandparents are collecting him at home time—is that right?'

'Yes.'

'Perfect. I'll bring Jack out to them and feed back on his first day, but it's all going to be fine!'

Miss Dale was bright and perky, and she had even Stacey feeling more confident that Jack was going to be well looked after in his new school. They were taking her comments about what Jack had faced in the past seriously, and she appreciated that.

'Say goodbye to Mum, Jack. You'll see her later.'

'Bye, Mum.' Jack gave her a little wave.

She could see he was still nervous—but of course he would be! No doubt he was expecting the bullying to start all over again! He had no other frame of reference. He'd always been bullied in school.

'Bye,' she said.

She wanted to say so much more. *Have fun! Make lots of new friends! Don't be scared!* But she remained quiet and watched her son being led away, her heart filling with fear and worry.

If it didn't work out at this school…

Fighting the urge to run after him and snatch him away from Miss Dale, take him home, where she could keep him safe, Stacey turned around and walked slowly from the playground, determined not to look back. She had her own first day to start. She was due at the surgery in less than fifteen minutes and she didn't want to be late. No matter how much she wanted to stand outside this school and watch out for her son, she had to go.

Please let his first day go well.

She got back into her car and drove the short distance to Greenbeck Surgery, parking in an allocated doctor's bay. She looked up at the modern building and wondered again if she'd done the right thing. Coming back home again after all this time. It had seemed the best thing to do when she'd been stuck so far away, with her whole world collapsing around her, but was running away ever the best thing? Was going back ever the right thing?

I'll soon find out.

If Jack could face his challenges, then so could she. Inside awaited a new team that would soon, she hoped, become like a family. Dr Zach Fletcher, who'd interviewed her for the post over video calls. And Dr Prior. Both men who, quite frankly, were far too attractive and looked like the kind of doctor you'd see in a primetime medical drama rather than in real life.

Stacey checked her reflection in the rear-view mirror, applied lip balm, then gathered her things. She sucked in a deep breath and got out of her car, ready to go into the surgery. Patients were already arriving. An old lady was currently pushing a wheeled shopping bag in front of her, and the doors were sliding open at her approach.

Get a grip.

This shouldn't be so hard. She'd done plenty of first days before. First day at uni. First day on placement. First exam. First GP placement. First job. She knew how to do this! But for some reason it seemed more imperative than ever that *this* first day go right.

Squaring her shoulders, she walked towards the sliding doors, her eyes falling on the posters reminding patients to wear a face mask if they weren't exempt from doing so. Inside the small foyer there was a machine that patients could use to test their blood pressure, a collection box for samples, and then there was the reception desk—a broad sweep of what looked like genuine oak, behind which sat three ladies of various ages. One was at the front, admitting patients, one was answering the phone, and another looked to be sorting through prescriptions.

Stacey stood in line, waiting her turn so she could announce herself, but then she was spotted by the man who'd interviewed her. Dr Zach Fletcher.

'Dr Emery! Pleased to meet you at last!' He stepped forward, all tousled brown hair, broad grin and twinkling eyes, his hand outstretched in greeting.

'Dr Fletcher! Likewise.' She shook his hand.

'Come through. I'll introduce you to the medical team first.'

She nodded, following him down a corridor into a staff room that was small, but perfect. Usually in staff rooms she saw chairs with dubious stains, furniture cobbled together from donations. But this staff room was bright and modern, with soft and squishy lime-green chairs, cream scatter cushions, and a low coffee table topped with a bowl of fresh fruit and a large jug of water. There was a small kitchenette with a dishwasher, microwave and—most important item of all—a kettle.

She also saw a beautiful young woman in a dark blue nurse's uniform, a healthcare assistant in a pale grey uniform, a young lady in a pale blue uniform, and last, but most definitely not least, Dr Prior.

He was standing over by the window, holding a magazine in his hand, and he gave her a simple nod of greeting. She nodded back, suddenly nervous again.

'Daniel you already know. Our HCA is Rachel, our resident vampire is Shelby, and this is our new advanced nurse practitioner Hannah—it's her first day, too.'

Stacey smiled at them all—especially Hannah. Maybe they could share their first day nerves together later?

'Let's get you a drink. Tea? Coffee?' asked Zach.

'Er…tea, please.'

'Milk and sugar?'

'Just milk, thanks.'

Once the drinks were made, and Zach had shown her the consulting rooms, he took her through to the back office, where he reintroduced her to the practice manager, who'd been in on the video job interviews, and then the admin team. Finally they went back through the building and he introduced her to the reception team.

Everyone seemed lovely and welcoming, and she was beginning to feel more at ease. Her own consulting room was in the middle, between Zach's and Daniel's. The nurse's and the phlebotomist's rooms were at the far end of the corridor.

Zach escorted her back to her consulting room, which she noticed already had her name plaque on. 'You're familiar with the operating system,' he said. 'So you shouldn't have any problems with that. But because you're still getting to know everyone we've allocated you twenty minutes per patient this first week—just until you find your feet a bit more.'

'That's perfect, thanks.'

'Any questions…anything you're not sure of…just come and grab me or Daniel.'

Stacey nodded and then he was gone, after one last dazzling smile. She blew out a long breath and sat on her chair, booting up the computer. She'd done it. She'd walked in here and seen Daniel Prior again and it had been fine. It hadn't been awkward, and it hadn't been difficult. There'd been so much information to take in, along with learning everyone's names, she'd not had any time to find her gaze wandering to her new colleague and landlord.

But he's right next door if I need him.

Stacey took out her stethoscope, checked the batteries on the BP machine, inspected her otoscope, then looked at her patient list. She had eight patients for the morning and four in the afternoon. There was a staff meeting right after lunch, and she had no home visits on her schedule for today. It looked as if Zach had had her blocked off from visits for this week, but next week her calendar for those was open. She appreciated that he was allowing her time to settle in before a full workload would be allocated to her.

She looked at the name of her first patient. Mr Elgin. Eighty-six. She thought she recognised the name but couldn't remember where from. She checked his medical history, and his current medication, and then she pressed the button that would ask Mr Elgin to come through from the waiting room.

Now she felt confident. This was the part she knew.

She could only hope that Jack was feeling just as confident, too...

Her last patient of the morning was a young woman called Sarah Glazer. She'd booked an appointment that morning, telling the receptionist who'd answered the phone that she was having bad stomach cramps that were worse than her normal irritable bowel syndrome symptoms.

Stacey had received a screen message from the team on Reception to say that Sarah had been given a glass of water and put in a side room, as she really didn't look well and was struggling even to just sit in Reception as the cramps were so bad.

Stacey went to fetch her and saw instantly that Sarah was grimacing and leaning against a wall, rubbing at her lower tummy.

Period pains, perhaps?

Sarah's medical history showed nothing remarkable. No history of menstrual problems...no endometriosis. No surgeries or injuries. The only times she'd been into the surgery had been for some travel jabs two years ago, when she'd flown to Africa, a late bout of chicken pox, one case of the flu and her diagnosis of IBS. There'd been nothing else. Could it be Crohn's? Diverticulitis?

'Let's get you through to my consulting room, Sarah. Do you need a hand?'

She reached out to help Sarah walk the few steps from the side room to Stacey's room. She got her seated, even though Sarah didn't look as if she wanted to be sat down, and kept shifting and grimacing.

'Okay, why don't you tell me what's happening?'

Sarah nodded. 'I started in the early hours of this morning with what I thought were just period pains. I am due on. But I've never had them like this. They come in waves and they're getting worse.'

'There's no chance you could be pregnant?'

Sarah laughed. 'No. I don't think so.'

'But you're sexually active?'

'Yes. I have a boyfriend. We live together at his parents' place.' Sarah grimaced again. 'Oh, God, here comes another one.' She groaned and rubbed at her lower abdomen.

There was a possibility that there could be kidney stones, or some sort of bad infection, but Stacey needed more information. 'Do you think you could do a urine sample for me?'

'I don't know... Maybe.'

'Any stinging or burning on urination?'

'No. But I passed this weird *thing* a few hours ago.'

'You're going to need to be more specific.'

'It was... I don't know. Like phlegm? But there was blood in it?'

It sounded like the mucus plug discharged from the cervix before a woman delivered her baby. But Sarah had no visible bump... *Could* she be pregnant? About to give birth to a baby?

'I'm going to need to examine you, Sarah. Can you get up on the bed for me, so I can feel your tummy?'

'I'll try...'

Sarah groaned as she got to her feet, then stopped to breathe through another pain, and Stacey began to feel more and more that what she was observing was a woman in labour. Maybe an ectopic pregnancy?

With Sarah on the examination bed, Stacey felt her tummy, and she was able to feel, for sure, the shape of a fully grown baby tucked neatly away within Sarah's abdomen. She'd heard of these cases before but had never come across one. A woman with no idea or visible sign that she was pregnant!

'Have you been having regular periods?'

'Yes, but they've been lighter for a while.'

'Any weird sensations in your tummy?'

'No. Well…maybe… A lot of gas.'

'I'm going to need to perform an internal examination—is that okay?'

'What do you think's wrong?'

'I think, Sarah—and this is going to come as a shock—that what you're experiencing is labour and you're about to give birth.'

'*What?*' gasped Sarah, immediately going into another contraction and breathing heavily through it. 'No, it's not possible!'

'I assure you it *is* possible. Can I examine you?'

Sarah nodded, undoing her jeans and removing them with great difficulty, before taking off her underwear.

Stacey washed her hands and donned gloves, then adjusted the light she used for intimate examinations—and instantly discovered the baby's head in Sarah's birth canal.

Sarah was about to give birth imminently!

Her mind raced. Was there time to call for an ambulance?

'I can feel the baby's head, Sarah. You're fully dilated.'

'What? No!'

'I'm afraid so. Just stay there for a moment.'

Stacey ripped off her gloves and bent over her computer, sending an instant screen message to Daniel and Zach saying that she needed assistance. Then she went back over to Sarah.

'I've got nothing I can give you for pain relief, so you're going to need to breathe through the contractions.'

'Contractions? You're serious? I'm *pregnant*?'

Stacey nodded, almost as much in shock as Sarah was. 'I'm serious!' She gave Sarah her hand to hold.

Behind them, there was a brief knock on her door and then someone was behind her. Zach.

'What can I do?'

'Call an ambulance.'

'I'll get Reception on it.'

He dashed away, but as he left Daniel arrived.

'Hey, Sarah.'

'Doc.'

'Big news, huh?'

'You're telling me!'

Daniel smiled at her. 'Want me to call Luke?'

Sarah nodded.

'Is that the baby's father?' Stacey asked.

'Yeah... Oh, God, here comes another one!'

Stacey gripped Sarah's hand tightly as another contraction came. 'Take a deep breath and push hard into your bottom. Believe me—pushing helps.'

Sarah grimaced as she concentrated hard on giving birth to a baby she hadn't known anything about until moments ago.

Stacey couldn't imagine the shock and surprise she must be feeling. This young woman had come to the doctor thinking she was just having some really bad period pains—had no doubt thought that she might prescribe her some painkillers or something. And instead she'd discovered she was about to become a mother!

Daniel got off the phone.

'What did you tell him?' asked Sarah.

'I just told him to get here as quickly as he could.'

'Did you mention the baby?'

'No, I didn't.'

'Oh, God!' Sarah began to push again.

Daniel donned gloves, and behind him Zach appeared again. 'Ambulance is en route. Daniel? I'll take your last patient, so we can clear the surgery.'

'Thanks.'

With Zach gone again, it was just Stacey and Daniel and their patient.

'You had no idea at all?' Stacey asked her.

Sarah shook her head. 'No. I've been having periods all this time! I've been a little bloated, but I thought it was gas. I'd been on a keto diet and someone told me that could happen!' She sucked in another breath to bear down on another contraction.

'I can see the baby's head, Sarah,' said Daniel.

How long had it been since Stacey had last helped deliver a baby? Two years? Three? You didn't get to deliver many babies whilst being a GP.

She'd heard of cases like this, but had never before met anyone who'd gone through it. All the pregnancies she'd dealt with had been standard. The mums had all known they were pregnant, they'd mostly enjoyed their months of pregnancy. Their bellies had swelled, their periods had stopped, they'd experienced kicks and babies having hiccups and eventually birth, either at home or in a hospital.

Not this. Never like this.

She was glad and grateful that Daniel was helping her. He was a reassuring presence at her side. A calm, cool and collected individual who didn't appear to be flustered in the slightest. It was as if he faced amazing and unexpected surprises every day. Just the sort of person you needed in a crisis.

'Oh, God, it hurts!'

'You're doing brilliantly, Sarah. Just keep breathing.'

'Little pushes now…little push again… That's it…one more… Brilliant…and pant! Pant for me!'

Sarah began huffing like a train, and Stacey looked down to see the head being born. The baby had a thick head of hair and looked to be full term. Of course they wouldn't know for sure until they reached the hospital and got the baby weighed and measured, but everything looked good for now.

'Perfect! Now, one last big push!'

The baby—a boy—slithered out into Daniel's waiting hands and he delivered the baby onto Sarah's belly.

Stacey draped a spare blanket over the baby, to keep it warm, and Sarah burst into happy tears. 'Oh, my God, it's real! An actual baby! What is it?'

'Take a look.' Daniel smiled.

Sarah lifted up one of the baby's legs. 'A boy?' She laughed with sheer happiness and joy, just as the baby burst into a cry, as if joining in with his mama.

Stacey looked at Daniel and he smiled back at her. She felt as if someone had smacked her in the gut. Daniel's smile was not only the most friendly he'd given her since she'd arrived, it also made her accept the fact that she was clearly attracted to him. Because her pulse had begun to race more from his smile than it had from the birth!

She glanced away, rubbing the baby, to keep him warm and to give herself something other to think about than Daniel's warm smile. Had he realised he'd smiled at her in such a way? Did he know the effect he was having on her? She hoped not. Stacey was not looking for a relationship—and even if she was, she would not have another relationship with someone she worked with! Look at what had happened the last time, with Jerry. It had been impossible to deal with when they broke up. It had made being in the workplace truly difficult.

There was a knock at the door and Stacey went to answer it, pulling the door open slightly. A young man stood there, confusion writ large across his face.

'I'm looking for Sarah?'

'Are you Luke?'

He nodded.

'Take a deep breath, Luke.'

Stacey stepped back so he could see into the room. His eyes fell on Sarah straight away and a half-smile filled his face—until he realised there was a mewling bundle in her arms.

'What…what's happening?'

'Sarah's had a baby,' Daniel explained. 'You've both had a baby.'

'It's a boy, Luke. A son!'

Stacey watched Luke carefully, ready in case it looked as if he might pass out. But kudos to him—he handled it perfectly. No sign of fainting, no denial…he just stepped right up and seemed as fascinated by the baby as Sarah was.

'Wow! Oh, babe…'

Stacey risked one more glance at Daniel now, because she knew he was watching the young couple realise they'd become parents. His soft smile was heart-warming, full of genuine happiness, warmth and contentment—and then he met her gaze and his face changed.

It was as if she'd caught him out.

He stopped smiling, looked down and away, an then checked Sarah's bleeding levels, all business again. It was as if he felt embarrassed that she'd caught him out experiencing genuine happiness and somehow it bothered him.

Odd. But okay. It was none of her business what he did. Not really. So why was she so captured by the dark chocolate of his eyes? Why did she feel that when she looked at him she was looking at a hurt soul? Why did that hurt call out to her? Pulling her, making her gravitate towards him uncontrollably?

Why can't I stop myself from sneaking looks at him?

The sound of sirens could be heard. Keen to escape his orbit, Stacey volunteered to go and meet it.

The two paramedics were young women, who were thrilled to hear the baby had been born safely, but sad that they'd missed what was usually the highlight of their day.

It felt odd to lead them through the surgery to her room as if it was something she did every day. This was her *first* day! And what a start it had been! Not something she'd ever forget, that was for sure.

'Still awaiting delivery of the placenta,' Daniel said, allowing the paramedics to take over and move Sarah from the examining bed to a trolley, so she could be wheeled out to the ambulance.

'Thank you, Dr Emery... Dr Prior,' said Sarah.

'No thanks necessary. You did all the work.'

'Have you picked a name?' asked one of the paramedics.

'I don't know...it's all still a shock.' Sarah glanced up at her boyfriend, Luke, who squeezed her shoulder in reassurance.

'Take care of yourselves,' said Stacey.

The paramedics wheeled away their patient and she watched them go, knowing she not only had a lot of notes to write up, but also a bed to clean!

Once the ambulance doors were closed, and the vehicle had begun to drive away, Stacey went back inside.

'You certainly know how to mark your first day!' said Francesca on Reception.

'I know!'

She let out a huge breath—one she hadn't realised she'd been holding—and went back into her room. Daniel was still in there, cleaning up her examining bed.

'Oh! Thanks. You didn't need to do that.'

'That's okay.'

'You're very kind. Thank you. And thank you for your help.'

He seemed unaccustomed to thanks. Or compliments. And he looked awkward.

'It was no problem. I'd better let you get on with your notes.'

And then he was gone.

She stood staring at the doorway after his disappearance, frowning. He was clearly a very confusing man. From the moment she'd first seen him in The Buttered Bun she'd sensed he was trouble, and now she felt she knew it as surely as she knew the sky was blue.

He blew hot and cold. One moment awkward, keen to get away from her, the next a compassionate doctor—calm and confident and reassuring. And all that smiling at Stacey when the baby was born and then stopping when she noticed.

Daniel had to be a man with baggage—and Stacey did not need anyone else's baggage to contend with. She already felt as if she was dealing with enough problems between herself and Jack. Whatever Dr Prior had going on could remain his problem. Because she was going to stay away.

But those eyes of his... Dark. Chocolatey. Intense. The kind of eyes that invited you to stare into them. The kind of eyes that hooked your attention. The kind of eyes that pulled at you and made you want to look within them.

Dangerous eyes.

He clearly found being in a room with her uncomfortable. Perhaps he didn't actually *like* her? Or maybe he was just one of those people who took their time to warm to someone new?

No. There's something else going on there.

Stacey had never had people not liking her. Not that she was bragging, or anything, but she'd been told how easy it was for people to talk to her. It was part of what made her a great doctor. Patients felt able to confide their problems to her.

He'd been so great at helping deliver that baby, though.

She found herself smiling as she sat down at her computer, her fingers hovering over the keyboard, ready to write up her notes on Sarah Glazer.

The way he'd calmly rolled up his sleeves, donned gloves and taken the birth of a baby in his stride... He'd kept a damned cool head on his shoulders. And what shoulders they were, too! Broad. Muscled.

He looks after himself.

There had to be a Mrs Prior. Or one waiting in the wings. Just because Stacey hadn't met her at the cottage, it didn't mean she didn't exist. A man like Daniel would never be single—she'd seen the way that waitress in the café had watched him, and the appraising looks of those two female paramedics, the blushing cheeks of the young HCA whenever he passed her by.

Women noticed men like Daniel Prior.

He'd be taken already.

No need for her to worry about him at all.

CHAPTER THREE

IT HAD BEEN a long but exciting first day. The adrenaline rush of helping Sarah give birth had lasted all afternoon, but she was keen to get to her grandparents' place on Blossom Lane to collect Jack and hear if his day had been just as good.

She packed up, and as she left popped her head around the door to Dr Zach Fletcher's room. 'Hey. Just thought I'd say goodbye and thanks for all your help today.'

'How did you find it?'

Zach was another handsome man, with a twinkle in his eye, but she didn't feel a reaction when she looked at him—not the way she felt something when she spoke to Daniel. Also, although she might be imagining things, she thought she could hear a little Scottish twang in Zach's voice. Or maybe she was just used to hearing it and so had picked up on it?

'Great! Crazy morning with that delivery,' she said, 'but...yeah, all good. Have you nearly finished?'

'I've got about ten more prescriptions to do, then I think I'm done. Got any interesting plans for the evening or are you going home to put your feet up?'

'I'm picking up my son from my grandparents.'

'Oh, yes, you mentioned them before. Genevieve and William Clancy, right? I know them well!'

She beamed. 'All good things, I hope?'

Zach laughed. 'Absolutely. They're a great couple. They really look out for people who need an extra hand or just someone to talk to.'

'Gran does collect a lot of strays.'

'Yes, she does,' he said, almost knowingly. 'Well, it's good to have you finally here, Stacey. I'll look forward to seeing you tomorrow.'

'You too.'

She closed his door, then turned, sucking in a breath, hoping that maybe Daniel had already left so she wouldn't have to have an awkward conversation with him. She paused outside his door, hoping to hear nothing, but she could hear him typing inside.

Stacey let out a heavy sigh and rolled her head on her shoulders, then gently knocked and pushed open the door. 'Just thought I'd say goodnight...'

He looked up from his desk, dark eyes meeting hers.

She noticed he had a nice-looking room. Pictures on the walls drawn by kids in crayon. Lots of framed photos on his windowsill. Stacey noted that they were mostly of a woman and a young boy. Clearly his wife and son. Odd that he'd never mentioned them when they'd first met. Daniel's wife was very beautiful. Long blonde hair, with honey tones. Large blue eyes. A bright, wide smile. His son had Daniel's dark hair, but his mother's blue eyes. He looked cheeky and full of fun. Stacey wondered if he was at the same school as Jack?

'Goodnight.'

She waited for him to say more, but clearly he wasn't one for over-sharing. Either that, or he just liked to focus on his work when he was here.

'Thanks again for your help today,' she said.

He looked up again. Nodded.

'I'm just off to collect my son—Jack. See how his first day went.'

'Of course.'

She felt as if she was floundering. He wasn't giving her much to go on. 'Does your son go to Greenbeck Juniors too?' She indicated towards the photo on the windowsill.

Daniel opened his mouth to answer, then seemed to think better of it. He smiled. 'I'm sorry, I don't mean to be rude, but I don't really talk about my family, and I have an engagement this evening that I really need to get to.'

She nodded, feeling chastised. 'Oh! Sorry. Well, don't let me hold you up.'

She glanced at the photos again, confused. If he didn't like to speak about his family, then why did he have their photos on display? Surely he expected people to mention them? If he was a private man, why have their photos on show at all?

'Something nice, I hope?'

'Dinner with a couple of friends.'

'Excellent. Well, thanks again, and I'll see you tomorrow.'

'You will. Take care.'

And so she left, feeling even more confused about this man who blew hot and cold. Those smiles of his were amazing. Warm. Inviting. Those dark cocoa eyes shone with genuine pleasure. Yet he was also abrupt and stand-offish and clearly had some barriers up. She knew she would respect them, but why did it bother her so whether he responded to her or not?

It only took her a few minutes to drive to Blossom Lane. It was a beautiful day. The sun was still out and all the flowers in her grandparents' garden were in full bloom. Bursts of pink and purple and red. Peonies, camellias, tall foxgloves. And hollyhocks at the back. There were even a few sunflowers standing proud.

She couldn't wait to see Jack. She was hoping that it had all gone well—because surely if it hadn't someone would have rung her?

She briefly knocked, then pushed the door open. 'Anyone home?'

She'd hoped that Jack would rush into her arms, a huge smile upon his face, but that didn't happen.

'We're in the kitchen!' called her gran.

Stacey hung her bag and jacket on the row of hooks by the front door and headed down the hall towards the kitchen, from where delicious smells were emanating.

'Something smells good.'

Her gran turned, wearing a different apron from the one she'd worn yesterday. This one had a picture on the pocket of chickens swinging in a hammock and sipping cocktails. She smiled. 'I thought you'd like to stay for dinner after such a big day the both of you've had!'

'Thanks. What's on the menu?' That was so kind of her! But Gran was always thinking of others.

'Chicken chasseur, served with my world-famous butter-mashed potatoes and baby vegetables.'

'Sounds great!'

'Want some tea, love?' asked her grandad, coming in from the garden, leaning heavily on his stick.

'Perfect, thanks. Where's Jack? How did it go?'

'He's in the garden. In the treehouse. Why don't you pop out there? I'm sure he'd love that.'

'But his first day went well?'

'As well as could be expected. Go on, he's waiting for you.' Gran smiled.

Stacey felt a little apprehensive as she set foot into the

back garden. It was so familiar—the winding pathway of stepping stones across the neatly trimmed lawn, the cornucopia of bushes and plants and ornamental grasses. And Grandad's garden shed, newly painted blue, with the bird house and bee station on one side. His greenhouse was filled with his beloved tomato plants, and beyond was the willow tree, and beside it the oak, in which her grandad had built her a treehouse when she was seven years old.

She had a lot of memories of that place. The hours she'd spent up there as a child. Sitting among the branches, listening to the birds and the bees as she sat upon a beanbag with her book, trying hard to concentrate on the words and not on the pain in her heart at the loss of her parents.

The treehouse had become a sanctuary of sorts. A place that was just hers. Was it still safe up there? It had been a long time...

'Permission to come aboard?' she called out from the bottom of the ladder.

She noticed that the old pieces of wood hammered into the trunk of the sprawling oak to make steps had been replaced by a new metal ladder. Her grandad must have done it.

'Permission granted!' said Jack, poking his head out from the treehouse window. 'Hey, Mum.'

She looked up at him, smiling. 'Hey, you.'

Why was she suddenly afraid to climb this tree? She could have done it blindfolded as a child, without a single change in her heart rate, but suddenly the treehouse seemed much farther away from the ground than she remembered.

And I don't like heights.

Her heart thudded in her chest as she looked down at her black pencil skirt and white blouse. She'd do better in jeans and a tee shirt, but this would have to do. Her son was up there and she needed to know he was okay.

There were just eight rungs on the ladder, and she took each one with grim determination, finally reaching the tree-house platform and hauling herself in. She looked about her and realised that somehow her grandfather had done more updates. There were shelves, a small table, a blanket and some cushions. The beanbag was gone, but there were a couple of stools over in the corner. And there was the black knot still in the wall to the eastern side. There were her initials still etched into the wood. There were the scuff marks and gouges in the floor that her grandad had made when he'd put the roof on.

'Wow. This is great, huh? You like it?'

Jack nodded. 'Gramps said it used to be yours when you were little.'

'He's right. He built it for me. But I guess it can be yours now.'

Jack smiled. 'Thanks.'

'So? How did it go?'

He shrugged. 'It was okay.'

'Okay good? Or okay bad?'

'Just okay.'

'Uh-huh. Did you make any new friends, or…?'

'They told me to sit next to this boy called Sam.'

'Oh, right. And what was Sam like?'

'Nice.'

'That's great!'

'He's deaf. Wears a hearing aid. And the teacher, Miss Dale, has to wear a microphone so that he can hear her when she speaks.'

'Oh. That sounds interesting. What did the two of you talk about?'

'Sam likes spaceships, so we talked about space. He wants to be an astronaut.'

'Well, why not? That sounds like it could be an amazing adventure.'

'He says sound doesn't exist in space. Is that true?'

'Erm... I guess it is.'

Jack seemed to think about this for a while. 'I told him I wanted to be a doctor, like you.'

She smiled. 'You can be anything you want to be. So, it was an okay day, then? And things can only get better, remember?'

'What was your first day like?'

Stacey thought of Sarah and her baby. Of Daniel. She nodded. 'It was great.'

'Did you make people better?'

'I hope so.'

'Dinner in ten minutes!' called Gran from the cottage.

Stacey ruffled her son's hair. 'What say you and I climb down and go and wash our hands and then see if Gran needs help in the kitchen?'

'Sure.'

'Okay.'

Stacey crawled across the floor of the treehouse, noting that a plank had come loose in the floor. She made Jack climb down first, then positioned herself on the edge of the treehouse platform and tried to shift herself off onto the ladder. She feared she'd snagged her skirt when she heard a tearing noise, and looked down to see there was now a split in the seam going up to her mid-thigh, where it had caught on a nail. At the bottom of the steps, she awkwardly tried to hold it closed.

'Maybe Gran has a sewing kit stashed away somewhere? Come on, squirt.'

They headed up the garden. Stacey was feeling good about things. Jack seemed fine, and it sounded like he'd had a good start, even if he thought it was only 'okay'. It sounded as if Sam could be a good friend for her son.

They wandered into the kitchen just as Gran was straining the water from her potatoes. 'We'll just wash our hands, then give you some help.'

'No need. I have everything under control,' Gran answered in her usual way.

Stacey and Jack washed their hands in the small downstairs bathroom. There was no safety pin or anything similar in the bathroom cabinet, so she headed back into the kitchen—and stopped dead at the sight of the tall, perfectly built and now casually dressed Daniel Prior, who was in the kitchen next to her gran, helping her mash the potatoes.

'Dr Prior?' she said in confusion.

Gran turned, beaming. 'I invited Daniel to join us!'

Stacey stood staring at him in absolute shock.

He was the last person she'd expected to see.

Daniel hadn't expected her to be there when he got to their cottage. Once a week, on a Monday evening, he had a standing reservation for dinner with the old couple who had been there for him since the loss of his wife and son.

Most people in Greenbeck—especially his patients—had been so kind and so patient, waiting for him to come back to work. And when he had there'd been an outpouring of love and concern.

Genevieve had called round to his cottage the first day he'd been back from the holiday that had turned into a nightmare. She'd brought him a casserole and a rhubarb crumble and told him that she would pop by the next day, and the day after that. And she had. Checking on him every day long after everyone else had stopped. She'd kept inviting him to go to their house for a meal, but he'd always politely refused. And then one day he'd felt so low, he'd accepted. Just glad not to be sitting in the cottage alone for yet another night.

Since then it had become a weekly Monday evening date. Something he looked forward to. He enjoyed Genevieve and William's company immensely, despite their age difference. He found comfort in being with them. They made no demands of him. He didn't have to talk if he didn't want to, and often they would sit in companionable silence, or play a board game or two. It was simply company. The hand of friendship. And he knew he owed them big-time for helping him go on.

Of course they'd spoken about their granddaughter. Why wouldn't they? They were proud of her. He knew she'd had a difficult time of it, with a relationship breakdown, but Genevieve and William hadn't gone into huge detail. And he knew they'd always wished she were closer. That they could have the relationship with their great-grandson Jack that they craved. That the little boy had been the victim of bullying.

Daniel had been bullied himself, as a young boy, so he knew how that felt. It was isolating. Horrendous. His heart had ached to hear of his troubles. His healing was going to be painful, and it didn't always happen easily.

In some way, he felt he already knew them. Only in reality he didn't. Not at all. And he felt bad having doubts about having them as tenants.

But he'd lost his wife and son, and now a single mother and her son had moved into the property at the bottom of his garden. He doubted the wisdom of it. Doubted whether he was ready to have another boy of Mason's age so close and involved in his life. He didn't know how to deal with that, and he knew that maybe he'd been a little standoff-ish towards Stacey. But how could he tell her it was out of self-preservation?

'Hello,' he said, looking at Stacey uncertainly, then glancing down at her son.

'You said you had a dinner to get to—I didn't realise it was with my grandparents.' She seemed puzzled.

'I should have said. I just didn't think you'd be here when I arrived.' He felt uncomfortable. He didn't like to impose. 'If you'd rather I leave, then—'

'Nonsense!' interrupted Genevieve. 'Sit yourself down, Daniel. I'll finish those potatoes. Stacey, we have a guest. Why don't you fetch him a drink?'

Stacey nodded quickly. Apologetically. 'What can I get you?'

'Juice is fine.'

He indicated the large jug in the centre of the table, filled with orange juice, ice and slices of orange. He pulled out a chair for her when she'd finished pouring out drinks for everyone, and noticed she gave him a cautious glance as she sat down.

He hoped this wasn't going to be too awkward, but he was feeling shocked, too. He really hadn't expected Stacey to be here. He'd thought she'd collect Jack and be on her way home by the time he arrived. William and Genevieve certainly hadn't mentioned that they'd asked Stacey to stay for dinner, but what business of it was his? This was *her* family. Not his. *He* was the interloper. The stranger. The waif and stray they'd adopted.

Genevieve placed the pot of chicken chasseur on the table, along with trays of buttered mash, vegetables, and some tiny bread rolls heaped in a bowl.

'Tuck in, everyone!' she said, with a huge smile on her face.

Nothing made Genevieve happier than to have a full table. Not full of food, but of family and friends. That was what was important to her, and Daniel always went home feeling like part of her family. Would that feeling remain now that Stacey and Jack were back?

'So…how was your first day, Stacey? I do hope our Daniel, here, didn't work you too hard?'

Our Daniel. He wondered how she'd react to that.

'It went great. We delivered a baby together.'

Genevieve beamed. 'You did? How exciting!'

He glanced at Stacey, caught her looking at him and quickly looked away. She had intense eyes. The green of emeralds. Darkened now by the shadow of her long red hair that he noticed was loose. She'd worn it up at work. Now it fell down her shoulders and her back in gentle waves, like ripples of flame, contrasting beautifully with the pale creamy nature of her skin.

I'm staring.

He reached for the vegetables to offer them to her before taking any himself.

'Thanks.'

'You're welcome.'

Her fingers brushed against his as he handed over the dish and he told himself the spark he felt was simply due to the awkwardness he felt being around her. He was meant to be keeping his distance. Letting Stacey and Jack find their feet in Greenbeck without interference. Not allowing himself to be pulled into their orbit. But he was now beginning to suspect that Genevieve wouldn't let him get away with that. She seemed more determined than ever to include him.

'So, Daniel, I hear on the village grapevine that you've been asked to be a judge at the village fete this summer?' she asked.

He looked at Genevieve. 'I haven't decided if I'm going to do it yet.'

'Oh, but you must! You remember last year, don't you? The wrong contestant won. That Robin Hood costume was truly awful!' Stacey looked confused, so her grandmother explained. 'Every year they have a competition for the best dressed up baby. I think they call it costume play, or something silly like that?'

'Cosplay?' Stacey clarified.

'That's it! Well, the Becker baby won last year, and the costume wasn't even green! I tell you! Don't even ask me what I thought the judge was on to pick *that one* as a winner.'

Stacey ladled some chicken chasseur onto her plate and Jack's, then passed the dish to Daniel. He accepted with a quiet thank-you.

'Sounds awful,' she said. 'I'd hate to choose. Won't a lot of parents be disappointed?'

'Well, then, they shouldn't enter if they're worried about losing!' said William.

'They've asked Zach to judge, too,' added Daniel.

'Stacey should judge it with you!' suggested Genevieve with a beaming smile. 'Then all the doctors will judge the show. That makes sense, doesn't it?'

'I've not been asked, Gran,' Stacey said, glancing quickly at Daniel.

He saw that she didn't want to do it. And most certainly not with him. Well, that was fine by him. The less time he spent in her company the better.

'She's right,' he said. 'I think you have to be asked. Not just volunteer.'

'Nonsense! I'll have a word with Walter. He organises everything. I'm sure we can get you on the judging panel.'

Stacey managed a smile that was neither happy nor genuine. Daniel covered it with one of his own, and changed the subject. 'This is wonderful, Mrs C. As always.'

She beamed. 'I know it's one of your favourites. It's one of Stacey's, too.'

Daniel met Stacey's eyes, then looked away. 'So, Jack, how has your first day been?'

Jack was pushing peas around his plate. 'It was okay.'

'He made a friend—Sam,' Stacey interjected.

'That's fantastic. I'm sure you'll make many more.'

Jack shrugged, and Daniel saw the look of concern and worry on Stacey's face that she tried to hide by taking a drink from her glass. Was her hand trembling? A pang of awareness shot through him and he realised he wanted to make her feel better. Make her feel more relaxed.

'There's a great Scout group in the village that a lot of the local kids go to. Jack might find that interesting.'

She nodded. 'Maybe. One thing at a time, huh, Jack?'

Daniel took that as meaning she didn't need him telling them how to live. That he knew nothing of their situation and maybe should keep his nose out of it and let her look after her son. Fair enough. But he really did think it would be a good idea for Jack to join in with the Scouts. There were a lot of team-building exercises, and it would help Jack to widen his circle of friends and develop his interests.

The rest of the evening went fairly well. Genevieve talked about the next speaker they'd got coming up at her book club—some local author that she was excited about, as apparently she'd read all her books. Will chatted about his plans for the garden and the progress of the vegetables he was growing to compete at the fete. Stacey, Daniel and Jack mainly sat and listened, and when dinner was over Daniel offered to wash the dishes.

'Oh, would you? You are sweet,' said Genevieve. 'My legs are playing me up today. Stacey, dear, would you dry for him? You know where everything gets put away. Jack? You can help me with my jigsaw. Come along, dear!'

Daniel began to see what Genevieve was doing. Maybe she wasn't trying to matchmake, exactly—because she knew what he felt about people trying to interfere in his life—but she was certainly trying to make him and Stacey friends, at least. The atmosphere around the dinner table had quite clearly shown that they weren't yet comfortable in each other's company, but maybe they ought to be? They were landlord and tenant. Work colleagues. They ought to be friends. He would try to manage that.

'I'm...er...sorry about earlier,' he said. 'If I came across as a bit...' He shook his head, as if struggling to find the right words. 'I've not been in the greatest headspace lately.'

She nodded, acknowledging his apology. 'I get it. We've all been there.'

'Your grandparents are really lovely people. I owe them a lot,' he said, passing soapy dishes onto the drainer for Stacey to pick up and dry with her tea towel.

She nodded, smiling. 'They *are* lovely. They have big hearts and they like to see people happy.'

He agreed. 'They do. They talked about you a lot when you lived in Scotland. They missed seeing you. I almost felt like I knew you and Jack.'

'Can you ever really know someone?'

He thought about it deeply. 'I hope so.'

'They never told me about you... *Our Daniel*,' she said with amusement, as if trying to lighten the conversation.

'You picked up on that, huh?'

She smiled. 'It was quite a familiar term.'

'What do you want to know?' He turned to look at her,

placed another plate on the draining rack. 'I'm not taking advantage of them. I consider them good friends. Maybe more than that. They picked me up and helped me when I was struggling, and for that I will be grateful to them for ever.'

'I don't need to know anything. I trust their judgement, and they're old enough to know what they're doing. If they want to help someone, then so be it. They helped me when I had no one. It's something they've always done.'

She was right. They had. 'You lost your parents quite young, I understand?'

Stacey nodded. 'Yes.'

'How old were you when it happened?'

'Five. I'd just started school.'

'I'm sorry. That must have been tough?'

She sighed and paused. 'Imagine being blissfully happy. Every day is a summer's day. You're loved. You have a great little family. And then *boom*. It's all gone. In an instant. The people who love you and adore you the most are brutally taken away.'

He knew. He didn't have to imagine. And he could hear the pain in her voice so clearly he felt an almost physical ache in his heart that someone else had been through such a horrible experience as he had. Her pain was old. It had happened when she was five. His pain was much more recent. But the grief was the same, he had no doubt.

He began to consider Stacey Emery in a new light, now that they had actually met.

She met his gaze. Gave a sad smile. Picked up a saucepan to dry.

'My grandparents lost their daughter and son-in-law in a freak accident at a music venue. Crush injuries in a fire. They must have felt awful themselves, and yet they opened their hearts and their home to me. And ever since then, whenever someone has been in need, they've reached out to help them, too.'

'I'm sure that having you, a piece of their daughter, gave them comfort.'

'I'm sure that I probably caused them a few hair-raising moments.'

'But they loved you. That's what's important. You had someone you could come home to.'

'They wanted me to come home after Jerry left.'

'Jerry?'

'Jack's father. If I can use that word for someone who's had nothing to do with him since he was born?'

'He didn't want to know?'

It was the kind of behaviour that intrigued Daniel. He couldn't imagine not wanting to know his own child. It was something that puzzled him greatly. Children were amazing. And your own kids? Your own baby? That was something special, and he couldn't imagine giving up that opportunity. Did they not realise how valuable and amazing they were?

'No, he didn't. We had a whirlwind relationship. I thought he was a general practice prodigy. His mind…his way of thinking about his patients was astonishing. I fell in love with the way he thought and the way he made me feel.' She gave a short, bitter laugh. 'I thought he felt as strongly about me as I did him. I began planning our future. The kind of life we'd live. Our home. I thought he felt the same way when we eloped to Gretna Green. It was fun, and I got completely carried away—which was something I used to do all too easily—and when I fell pregnant I thought our lives were starting a brand-new chapter. That he'd be as ecstatic about the baby as I was.' She gave another short laugh. 'Boy, can I be wrong about people!'

'So you broke up?' He was trying to picture this Jerry, but struggling. Amazed that anyone could treat someone he was meant to care about in such a manner.

'Yes. And it was awkward. We both worked at the same GP practice. He'd been there longer than me…people took sides. There was gossip. It all became quite ugly. Jerry was happy to give me money for Jack—to pay for him and anything he needed—but he never wanted to be a father. The man I'd thought I knew had never been there after all. So we divorced, and I moved to another practice.'

She smiled at him, her eyes blurred with tears, and although he wanted to smile back, maybe rest his hand on her arm to let her know he was there, as he would with any good friend, he felt he didn't know her well enough and it would be awkward.

He reached for a piece of paper towel, tearing it from the roll and passing it to her.

'Thank you. Look at me! Crying on my first day in front of a new colleague!'

Now he smiled. 'No. In front of a new friend.'

Stacey tucked Jack into bed, read him a story, and then turned out the lights. She left his door slightly ajar, knowing he liked to have a strip of light showing from the hall, and then she went downstairs to sit and watch some mindless television.

She'd learned a lot tonight. The biggest thing being that Daniel, her landlord, was her grandparents' latest waif and stray. She'd heard them mention a Daniel, of course, but hadn't remembered any specifics, wrapped up as she'd been in her own dramas, and she'd certainly never thought that the Daniel her grandparents had taken an interest in was the same Daniel she'd be working with.

How she wished she'd listened! Remembered. Then perhaps she might understand him more. He'd been so standoffish to begin with. Clearly not comfortable in her presence. And yet now, after spending some time with her at her grandparents' place, they were talking. She felt a little closer to him. As if they had a new understanding of each other.

And that was nice.

Scary still, but nice.

It would be so easy to let her mind get carried away with the idea that his smiles meant something. With a man that good-looking it would be hard not to. He had those easy good looks that were so pleasing to the eye. He was a flame and she could be a moth. Drawn to him instinctually.

But his natural good-looks were coupled with the fact that there was a mystery about him. A tragedy somewhere in his past. Why had her grandparents been inviting him for meals week after week?

'They picked me up and helped me when I was struggling.' He'd said that himself, when they'd been doing the dishes together. *'I've not been in the best headspace lately.'*

She supposed she could ask her gran, but then her gran would read too much into that, and she was clearly already trying her best to push the two of them together. Oh, she hadn't missed that! Pretending her legs were bad so the two single people could spend some time alone.

Typical Gran!

She smiled to herself at the thought of her gran trying to be a matchmaker. She'd never stopped trying to fix Stacey up. Ever since the breakdown of her marriage to Jerry, her gran had told her that she ought to get herself back out there. Not give up on finding the right man for herself.

Gran wants me to be happy, I know.

But the truth of the matter was she was terrified by the

idea of a relationship with another man. Her heart was scarred. Burned by love. She'd lost her parents, and she'd lost Jerry, the man she'd thought she would be with for ever. She couldn't keep going through that pain. That loss. That grief. How many times could a heart stand it before it permanently broke into two?

Stacey stared at the flickering television screen, not really seeing the two chefs competing to be the winning finalist, thinking instead of how it had felt to stand beside Daniel doing something as normal and boring as drying the dishes.

She'd felt nervous at first, but then, after his apology, as they'd talked about her parents, about Jerry and her family, she'd begun to feel something else. Something other than nerves. Something that had surprised her. Especially when he'd passed her that paper towel and told her it was okay for her to cry because now they were friends.

Something...

She'd dabbed at her eyes, sniffed and laughed, met his gaze with her own. And he'd looked away, almost shyly... almost as if...

As if what?

But no, she told herself, dismissing the feelings. Hadn't she done this before? Got carried away, imagining things and feelings that weren't actually there? She could never look at Daniel in that way. See him as something he wasn't. Because she could not fall for another man. She had Jack to think about. And she most certainly could not fall for another colleague! Imagine the mess they'd get into when it all broke down again.

When she and Daniel had gone back into the living room Jack had begun to yawn, and she'd made excuses about getting him back early as it was a school night and said goodbye to everyone. She'd hugged her grandad. Gran. And then, unexpectedly and impulsively, she'd hugged Daniel.

He'd felt solid. Strong. He'd smelt *amazing*.

And he'd hugged her back.

CHAPTER FOUR

THEIR KITCHENS FACED one another. It was something she'd noticed earlier, and now, when she was standing at the sink, washing a few breakfast things, she looked out of her window, across the lawns and flowerbeds, towards Daniel's house.

He had herbs on his kitchen windowsill. At least, they looked like herbs. And to one side there was a small green watering can.

She found herself wondering if he cooked much. And if he was any good. She liked a man who could cook. There was something intriguing about a man who knew his way around a kitchen, and she could clearly imagine Daniel in her head, standing by a chopping board, showing his skills with a knife, whizzing through an onion or some peppers and whipping up an exotic dish that would send her to heaven and…

What am I doing? This is ridiculous! I've got to stop thinking about Daniel Prior.

And then she saw movement. A shadow moving further back in the kitchen. Was it him?

Her heart quickened, she felt herself tense in anticipation, and then, yes, it was him, also standing at his sink, also washing up. She found herself staring at him. Wondering about this man who intrigued her so. Wishing she could be in his kitchen and just talking to him. Finding out more about him. Asking him questions whilst watching him work.

They would chat and laugh. They'd have a mug of coffee each and it would be comfortable. Pleasant...

He looked up. Met her gaze.

Stacey sucked in a breath, looking down and away, embarrassed to have been caught staring.

She quickly grabbed a towel, dried her hands and walked away.

The washing up would have to wait until later.

Her next patient was a young mother—Helena Farrow. She came bustling through Stacey's door, not only pushing a double buggy, containing twins, but also holding the hand of a much older child—perhaps around four years of age? And she was pregnant. She looked pale. Exhausted. Her hair was unwashed, and there were large dark circles beneath her eyes.

She sank into the chair set aside for patients with relief. 'Hi.'

'Hello, there,' Stacey replied. 'You've got a handful.'

'Tell me about it. No! Stanley! Put that down!'

Stanley had made a beeline for the multi-coloured pot on the desk that held the strips for testing urine samples. He scowled and put it back.

'How can I help you today?' asked Stacey.

Helena let out a huff of breath. 'I've been feeling exhausted. Absolutely exhausted! I'm not sleeping, because the twins have me up all night, every night. I'm run ragged every day, and I just don't seem to have the energy I used to have.'

'Looking after three small children can be exhausting— and you're pregnant, too. How far along are you?'

'Six months.' Helena leaned in and whispered, 'If I'm being honest with you, I didn't want a fourth, but my husband did, and I guess my big belly shows he got his way.'

Stacey smiled sympathetically. 'Does he work?'

'Yes. Up at the distillery.'

'So he's not able to help you with the children during the day?'

'No. He works full time.'

'So do you! Does he help in the night?'

'He tries, but he doesn't often hear the babies crying, so it's usually me who gets up to see them.'

Stacey checked Helena's last bloodwork. She'd been close to having low iron levels before, but it hadn't actually been out of the normal range. Maybe it was time to give her some extra help?

'What about any other family to help?'

'My parents live in France. They haven't been over since the pandemic. Dad's got long Covid. It's difficult.'

'You're eating and drinking the right things?'

Her patient grimaced. 'I try, but sometimes I just pick at the kid's leftovers. I snack a lot. It just seems easier than trying to eat a meal whilst it's still hot.'

'I think we should check your iron levels. Maybe your thyroid. And we'll do a full blood count. But in the meantime I'm going to give you a prescription for iron tablets. You're very pale. Start taking them straight away, and when I get the blood results I'll call you to let you know whether you need to continue. I'll just take your BP and temperature now…'

Stacey carried out her examinations as best she could with a rampaging toddler in the room, who kept getting himself into trouble taking things from Stacey's desk that he shouldn't.

Helena's temperature was fine, and her BP was only slightly raised. Nothing too worrying.

'Try and make sure you eat healthily,' Stacey told her. 'And I'll contact you as soon as I get the bloods back, okay?'

She nodded. 'Thank you, Doctor.'

'And maybe ask at Reception to see if they know of any local children's clubs that you could take Stanley to. Just to give yourself a little break and allow him to burn off some energy.'

'I will. Thank you.' She got to her feet again, and shepherded Stanley out before her.

When she was gone, the room seemed incredibly quiet again, and Stacey found herself really empathising with Helena. It must be hard. All alone and without much family around. A lot of families with young children had struggled during the pandemic, and she'd seen more than one young couple who'd ended up having more children than they'd expected!

Stacey herself had been alone in Scotland with Jack during the pandemic, and it had been incredibly difficult. Especially as a keyworker. She'd had to continue working as a doctor and keep Jack in nursery—a place he hadn't wanted to be—as well as an after-school club. Each day she would come home weary and tired. Oftentimes made distraught by what she'd had to deal with. And then she'd have to deal with a very upset young boy who was being picked on.

She'd gone into the school so many times to get them to deal with it, and she knew they'd done what they could, but without physically being by Jack's side twenty-four-seven there had been no way she could protect him. Watching Jack's slide into withdrawal and then depression, she had found her fears for her son's health and wellbeing magnified, and had known she'd have to take extra steps.

She had eventually withdrawn him from school and re-turned home to Greenbeck, where there would be love and family and support and the small community school where she herself had so many happy memories. She could only hope and pray that it was still as wonderful as she'd re-membered it.

Stacey went to refill her water bottle and found the staff room empty. She'd just filled the bottle, and was wiping the excess water from the lid, when Daniel came in.

He smiled at her. 'Good morning.'

'Morning.'

She hoped her face wasn't flushing red. She felt her heart-beat accelerate and couldn't help but notice how wonderful he looked this morning. He wore dark trousers and a pink shirt, his sleeves rolled back to mid-forearm, revealing a nice amount of dark hair and muscle, and a chunky watch.

Would he mention the kitchen thing?

'How are you?'

'I'm good. How about you?'

'Very good. I've got an interesting case coming in later.'

'Oh…?'

'A patient who had necrotising fasciitis in hospital. She lost a lot of leg muscle because of it. She's coming in for a general check-up and to have some stitches removed. I'm sure if you were free and wanted to pop in to have a look Pauline wouldn't mind. You'd be more than welcome.'

'Oh, sounds intriguing. I don't think I've ever seen a case of that first-hand.'

'Well, if you're free…?'

'I'll try to be. Thanks.'

'You're very welcome.'

Did he just wink?

She headed back to her room, glad that the pair of them

were past the awkward greetings they'd initially exchanged and were now on a more friendly and less formal basis. But which was better? When Daniel had been standoffish she hadn't had to worry about getting too close to him, but now... Ever since last night at her gran's something had changed, and now her whole body reacted to his presence and she knew she would have to fight her attraction to him.

She really didn't want an awkward situation like she'd had before, after Jerry. Everyone looking at her. Gossiping. Pitying her. It had been such a relief to hand in her notice.

But that wink... Maybe it had been an involuntary reaction? Or perhaps just a blink. But she thought it had only been with one eye...

Whatever it had been, it was just friendly. It had to be. He was acknowledging that they had a connection now. Not just because she lived in his annexe and they worked together, but because he'd practically become a part of her grandmother's family.

Our Daniel.

She got back to her room and saw the rest of her morning patients, finishing early and noting that Mrs Pauline Ronson was in with Daniel now. The necrotising fasciitis case.

Should I go in? Or stay here?

She looked at the clock, then looked back at the computer screen. She didn't want to impose. Wouldn't it seem odd if she just went in unannounced and said that Daniel had invited her? Wouldn't the patient wonder if she'd been talked about? Stacey bit her lip, and then an instant message appeared on her screen.

Pauline's here. She says you're most welcome, if you want to pop your head around the door.

Instantly she got to her feet and stepped out of her room. She hovered outside Daniel's, not wanting to seem too keen, but she was intrigued by the case and didn't want to miss out. And, of course, it meant spending more time with Daniel.

She rapped her knuckles against his door.

'Come in!'

She pushed the door open and saw a lady in her seventies seated on a chair opposite Daniel's desk.

'You must be Dr Emery? I've heard so much about you,' she said.

'All good, I hope?' Stacey smiled, entering the room blushing.

'Of course. Daniel here never says anything bad about anyone.' Pauline winked at Daniel. 'I'm kidding! He hasn't said a word. It's the villagers! The grapevine is rife with rumours of your arrival. You're Genevieve's granddaughter, aren't you? You probably don't remember me, but you once visited my house with your mother. I was so sorry to hear of her passing. You had a tea party in my garden with your teddy bears.'

There was so much information to process in that short introduction that Stacey felt bewildered.

'I'm about to have my stitches out. Shall I hop up onto the couch?' she asked Daniel.

'Please do. Need a hand?'

'No need. I'm not that old yet.' And she clambered up onto the couch and lay down. Turning back to Stacey, she said, 'I hear you've got a young one yourself?'

Stacey nodded. 'Yes. Jack.'

'And you're on your own?'

Another nod.

'Pretty girl like you'll be snapped up quickly—you mark my words. Look at that hair of yours! And those eyes!'

Stacey blushed. 'What about you, Pauline? Are you married?'

'Three times! Divorced. Died. The current one is on his last legs, too. Which is why it was so important the hospital saved mine.'

Daniel was slowly removing the wrappings around her leg. Stacey could see that a lot of the muscle had been removed as even under bandages it was clear that the right leg was considerably thinner than the other. Almost all of the calf muscle was gone, and she'd had some skin grafts placed. She also had about four stitches to the side of the lower leg.

'It wouldn't heal,' Pauline explained. 'Damn thing kept popping open. But it looks okay now, don't you think?'

Stacey nodded, glancing at Daniel, who soon agreed. 'It looks very good. No sign of infection…no redness. You're healing very well.'

'So they can come out finally? Thank goodness! It's all very well being a special case, but sometimes you do just want to get back to pottering around in your garden.'

'Would you like to do the honours?' Daniel asked Stacey, wheeling an equipment trolley beside her. Upon it were placed some sterile gloves, tweezers and a stitch cutter.

'I would.' She smiled at him, grateful, and tried not to imagine too much of what was going on behind his eyes. He was being quite gentlemanly, and she liked that.

Stacey washed her hands, dried them on paper towels, then donned the gloves and picked up the stitch cutter and tweezers. The four stitches came out easily enough, and she and Daniel worked together to redress the leg with lighter dressings.

'So, when can I go back to my dancing lessons?' Pauline asked.

'I don't see why you can't do that now. But take it easy. You don't have as much muscle in that leg any more, so you may find your balance is off, or you get tired quicker.'

'Oh, it's just a slow waltz. I'll be fine. Me and Walter were doddery to begin with! What about your leg, Daniel? Still stiff?'

Daniel smiled at his patient, before glancing awkwardly at Stacey.

He had a problem with his leg? She hadn't noticed. What would have caused that?

I really should have listened to my gran when she rattled on about the villagers.

Stacey smiled. 'I'll…er…leave you to it, then. Thank you for letting me see you today, Mrs Ronson.'

'Call me Pauline, dear.'

Stacey left the room, returning to her own, and sat down behind her desk. It was lunchtime. She was starving. It was such a lovely day outside, she decided to take her packed lunch with her and walk over to the duckpond and one of the benches beside the Wishing Bridge.

It really was beautiful out. The perfect British summer day, where the skies were clear and blue and the sun shone, bathing the world in a warm embrace. She walked across the village green and noted that the benches she'd wanted were already filled. So she found a quiet spot beneath a tree, sat down and got out her sandwiches.

She closed her eyes, enjoying the feel of the warm breeze and the soft caress of the sun upon her skin. She could hear birds singing high in the branches above her, as well as the occasional quack from one of the ducks. There was splashing and wing-flapping and the occasional giggle of a young child throwing them some treats.

She hoped it wasn't bread. Bread was bad for ducks. It had no nutritional value and filled up their small tummies, so they wouldn't forage and receive what they needed. It could cause them to be malnourished...

'You're in my spot.'

She opened her eyes and looked up to see Daniel standing there, holding his own packed lunch in one hand and a bottle of water in the other. The sun lit him from behind, so she couldn't see his face clearly as it was so bright, but she felt that he was smiling.

'You're welcome to join me,' she answered, indicating that he could sit alongside her.

'Thanks.' He settled onto the grass beside her.

'No home visits for you?'

'No. Zach's got that duty today.'

She nodded, watching as he carefully adjusted his position. She thought of Pauline's comment about his leg. 'You okay?'

'Just a little stiff. It's a good day today, though. It usually gets worse when it's cold or damp. The sun actually helps.'

'Is it arthritis?' She was genuinely interested, but then realised she might be probing too much. 'You don't have to tell me if you don't want to.'

'No, it's fine. I was in an accident a couple of years back. Broke my hip. It's not been right ever since.'

'Oh. I'm sorry to hear that.'

Stacey looked out across the green towards the pond. Two swans were pushing their way through the ducks to get to the offerings being thrown into the water by the young child. She wondered about the kind of accident he'd had. Was now the right time to ask him about it? Or would that be considered pushy? She got the impression that Daniel was quite a private person...

So instead she decided to change the subject. Pick something that she assumed would be safer to talk about. 'I couldn't help but notice those pictures in your room. A woman and a child. Your wife? Girlfriend? Your son?'

And just like that it was as if a cloud had passed over him, even though the sun was still shining bright and unobscured in the azure blue sky. His eyes became downcast and he looked away.

I've said something wrong.

'They're not here any more.'

'Oh. I'm sorry.'

And she meant it. Clearly he'd been part of some relationship break-up and the woman he'd loved had taken his son from him—possibly far away.

'They died. Two years ago.'

Her heart almost stopped and suddenly she ached to hold him and protect him, throw her arms around him and say *I'm so sorry!* She couldn't imagine surviving an ordeal like that. Were their deaths connected to the accident he'd mentioned? No wonder he acted the way he did! He isolated himself to protect himself. She got that. She did.

She didn't feel close enough to him yet to throw her arms around him, so instead she reached out and placed her hand on his as it lay upon the grass. Hoping he wouldn't pull away. She knew it had been right to do so when he clasped her fingers with his own.

'I'm so sorry, Daniel. I didn't mean to push.'

'You were bound to find out sooner or later.'

She nodded. This was a small village after all. Gran and Grandad obviously knew, and that was why they'd taken him in. Because he was alone. Knowing Gran, she wouldn't have been able to leave him on his own like that. Her heart ached. She wanted to make him feel better, but knew that any small thing she did would mean nothing against the weight of such pain.

'We were on holiday in Oahu, Hawaii. Paradise on earth. Amazing place. Have you ever been?'

She shook her head.

'It's unlike anywhere else. The people are so friendly, the nature's so bountiful, and every corner you turn there seems to be another amazing beach, or forest, or waterfall. We'd got up really early that day, to drive to this particular beach and watch baby turtles make their way to the water after hatching. It was the most wonderful thing I'd ever seen. Second, of course, to seeing my son Mason. born.'

He smiled in remembrance. Paused. Sucked in a breath.

'We spent hours there, seeing the sunrise and watching these tiny creatures waddle and flip their way down to the water, off to begin their lives, their adventures, knowing that in years to come they'd return to the beach to lay their own eggs. We were hungry, so we got back in the car to find a café that served breakfast. Another driver, who'd been drinking the night before, was speeding on one of the turns and lost control of his car, ploughing into us.'

'Oh, my God, Daniel…' she whispered, her heart in her mouth.

'He sent our vehicle down a small ravine. The car turned over a few times. We kept hitting trees and bushes and rocks, and then we crashed into a large boulder, which stopped us.'

She almost couldn't listen, but the sheer horror of his story kept her rapt.

'Penny—my wife—was trapped. As was Mason. Their side of the car was badly damaged. Crumpled in like a concertina. I'd sustained injuries to my hip and leg, and my right arm was broken too. I tried to help them, but my seat-belt had jammed so I couldn't move. I tried to get them to open their eyes. I kept pleading with them not to sleep...' He looked down at their hands entwined on the grass. 'It was too late.'

She closed her eyes at his pain. Trying to imagine being in the same situation, but thankfully unable to conjure the image.

'I was trapped in the vehicle for two hours with their bodies beside me. When the rescue team arrived I almost didn't want them to free me. I wanted to stay with them. But of course I couldn't. They wanted to get me medical attention. I needed surgery. I never saw them again.'

'So your last image of them is...?'

She almost felt sick. She pushed her lunch away and scrambled towards him, etiquette be damned, so she could give him a solid hug. She yearned to find Jack and hold him tight, but he wasn't here, so she held Daniel in her arms instead, not caring who might see, or whether it was inappropriate.

Daniel had just shared his private pain with her. He had exposed himself to her, shared with her, and that *meant* something, dammit. And she would show him that she'd heard him. That she empathised with him. That she wished she could change it for him.

'I'm so sorry. I'm so sorry...' she whispered, over and over again.

Just for a moment, they held each other in silence beneath the tree, with the sun shining and the birds singing and the quacking noises going on in the background. It felt right to be holding him. He held her back. She could feel his hands on her and it was comfortable, and normal. She couldn't actually remember the last time she'd held some-one like this, apart from Jack.

Daniel was broad and strong, and he felt good in her arms. But when she realised she was still holding him, her hands softly stroking his back, she froze, knowing she had to let go, that maybe she'd overstepped some mark, that she shouldn't be hugging him as if she'd known him her entire life.

She let go. Sat back on her haunches and gave him an awkward smile. 'I'm sorry. I get carried away sometimes. I'm a physical person.'

'It was fine. It was nice,' he said softly, looking into her eyes.

'It was nice.'

Hardly an overwhelming description, but somehow it meant everything, and Stacey didn't know what to do with that. She felt embarrassed, and awkward, and she felt her cheeks colour as she looked around to see who might have witnessed her hugging Daniel in the middle of the village green!

She glanced at her watch. 'We ought to be getting back.'

He checked his own watch. 'Yeah. Listen… Thanks for… you know…just being there. I don't like telling that story. I don't tell it at all, usually. But you made it easy.'

They both got to their feet, brushing themselves down to remove any loose blades of grass that might have adhered to their clothes.

She smiled at him, waving away his compliment. 'I guess it's easier when you know the other person has been through trauma, too.'

He nodded. 'Your parents?'

'Yeah.' She nodded. Looked at him. Wondering what to do next?

They made their way across the village green, avoiding the crowds around the duckpond, and walked up onto the Wishing Bridge. It was a small arched stone bridge that spanned the Beck Canal. A barge was drifting towards it, one man at the helm.

'My gran told me that my parents got engaged on this very spot.'

She reached out to touch the stone. Tried to imagine her mother and father here in the moonlight after having been to a local dance. Her father down on one knee.

'Really? Did they make a wish?'

'Yes. To be together for ever.'

Daniel smiled, watching as the barge drifted below them, emerging on the other side. The captain of the barge gave them a wave and a smile.

'Do you think love was easier back then?' he asked.

'In my parents' time? I don't know... I think love is complicated and difficult no matter what the era. Relationships are hard work, and there will always be a million things to tear you apart.'

Daniel nodded. 'Do you think our hearts are destined to be broken?'

She looked at him, considering his question. She'd loved her parents and lost them to a tragic accident at a music concert, when they should have been having fun and enjoying themselves. She'd loved Jerry, but he hadn't wanted the same things in life as her, so she'd lost him, too. Her grandparents weren't getting any younger, and though she loved them intensely she knew she would soon face losing them, too. Daniel had loved his wife and child and had lost them at a time in their lives when they should have been at their happiest.

No matter who you were, life and death took your loved

ones from you. Was the pain worth having known them at all?

'Yes, they are,' she said. 'So we need to know how to take our happiness when we can.'

CHAPTER FIVE

'WHAT ARE YOU DOING?'

Daniel looked up from his weeding to see Stacey's son Jack standing beside him, watching him. 'I'm getting rid of this bindweed. Can you see?'

He pointed out the dreaded weed to the young boy, then looked over his shoulder to see if Stacey was around. She didn't appear to be. Perhaps she was busy in the annexe?

'Why?' Jack asked.

'Because if I don't get rid of it, it'll choke the plants that I *do* want in the garden.'

'Why?'

Daniel smiled. He'd forgotten that kids could do this. Ask why? Why? Why? 'Because that's what bindweed does. It has a pretty flower itself. You see that white bloom just there?'

Jack nodded.

'It may look pretty, but it chokes the other plants. If you look here… Can you see how it's bound itself around the stems of these?'

'Yes.'

'Well, we need to get rid of it or it'll kill them off.'

'Can I help?'

Daniel looked at the boy. He was wearing shorts and a

tee shirt. He didn't look to be wearing anything special, so perhaps his mum wouldn't be too cross if he got a little dirty.

'Sure. Let me show you how.'

And so he showed Jack how to tackle the bindweed. How to pull at the bindweed that was on its own and how to be more delicate with those bits wrapped around other plants.

The little boy knelt beside him and began to help, and they worked together pleasantly for a time.

'How are you getting on with school?' asked Daniel. 'Still good?'

'It's okay.'

'You know, I was picked on when I was little.'

'You were?'

'Oh, yeah. There was this kid called Billy Granger, and he was the biggest kid in the year. Terrifying. And me? I was the smallest. The youngest. And I wore these thick glasses... Billy made my life a misery, but then I learned that he had a really bad home life. He didn't have the greatest background, and bullying me and some of the other kids was just his way to feel powerful for a little while. I'm not excusing his behaviour—what he did was wrong. But as an adult I can see why he did it. So, you know, those bullies you faced before... They might have something similar going on in their lives.'

Jack was silent for a moment. 'So the bully is like this weed? Bigger and stronger, but it can't help what it does?'

Daniel sat back on his haunches and looked at Jack. Such a profound conclusion for someone so young! 'Absolutely. And we have to do what we can to stop it. Use the tools we have in our power and one day we'll beat it.'

Jack nodded and smiled, pulling out one particularly long length of bindweed. 'Got you, you stupid weed!'

Daniel smiled, then became aware of a figure behind them.

'Working hard?'

He turned. Stacey.

Jack grinned. 'I'm helping Daniel!'

'I can see that.' She smiled.

Daniel liked her smile. Also liked it that it had been easier than he'd expected to talk to Jack and be around him. In fact, it hadn't been scary at all.

The next Monday evening Daniel felt much more relaxed about going to Genevieve and William Clancy's house for dinner. For one thing, he felt a lot more comfortable around Stacey now, having got to know her a little better, and he felt good that he'd shared with her his pain about Penny and Mason. There would be no more walking on eggshells... no more having that story hanging over him, knowing she would find out about it sooner or later.

He'd thought maybe her grandparents might have told her, but she'd seemed to be quite unaware of it, obviously hearing it for the first time under that tree on the village green. That was good, though. It meant that Genevieve and William hadn't talked about him to others. What he had said to them, the way he had talked to them about losing his wife and child, had remained between them.

They were good people, and so was their granddaughter Stacey. And Jack? He was a great kid, too.

He opened the door to their cottage. 'Hello?'

Genevieve appeared in the doorway to the kitchen. 'Daniel! What brilliant timing. How was your day, dear?'

He thought of his lunch at midday, sitting in the sun with Stacey, looking into her eyes. 'It was great, thanks.'

'Marvellous! Now, I know you've only just walked in, but Jack's said there's a wobbly floorboard in his treehouse, and as William can't get up there any more, and you did all those other repairs for us, I wondered if...'

'Say no more. I'll happily sort it out. Is his shed unlocked?'

She beamed. 'He's already out there, waiting for you.'

He hung up his jacket and walked through the cottage towards the back door. William Clancy was pottering about in his shed, leaning heavily on his stick, but had propped the door open with his toolbox, upon which sat a hammer and nails. Jack was trying to do keepy-uppy on the lawn.

He smiled, feeling comfortable now. 'Hey, Jack.'

'Daniel! Want to play football?'

He smiled, but inside his heart ached. Mason had loved nothing more than to have a bit of a kickabout with his dad. 'Sure. But I'm just going to fix your treehouse first.'

'Can I help?'

'I don't see why not.'

It was strange. At first he'd been so determined to stay away from Stacey and Jack. Keep his distance. But there was something just so damned easy about being with them! Both of them. He'd thought he'd feel awkward. Thought he'd find it difficult.

His first reaction had been to stay as far away as possible. They were the embodiment of everything he'd lost. But there was something peaceful about being with them. Something that soothed his troubled soul. And he was kind of happy that he was getting to spend some time with Jack without Stacey there.

When they'd first met, last week, Jack had been quiet and reserved at the dinner table. And after dinner Genevieve had monopolised Jack until home-time. When they'd been weeding and working in the garden together it had been great. They'd got a little more one on one time. At least until his mother had come out.

He climbed up into the treehouse first, then helped Jack. 'Which board is loose?' he asked.

'That one.'

Jack pointed to the centre board, which had a piece of material attached to it, as if someone had caught their clothing on it.

Daniel sat down beside it, laying the hammer and nails to one side. Jack was right. The board was quite loose and two of the nails were missing.

'We'll fix this in a jiffy.'

'What can I do?' asked Jack.

'Well, we need to get this nailed down. Are you any good with a hammer?'

'I've never used one.'

Of course not. From what he'd heard, from Jack's grandparents and Stacey, the little boy hadn't ever had a father figure in his life to teach him stuff like this. And although Stacey was pretty hands-on, he couldn't say for certain whether she was any good at DIY.

'Okay. See these holes here?'

Jack nodded.

'That's where we want to put the new nails. We'll need two of them. Pick the longest ones in that packet.'

He watched as the young lad did so.

'Perfect. Now, how about I get them in to begin with and then you can finish them off?'

Jack smiled and nodded.

'Okay.'

Daniel put a nail in one end of the floorboard and tapped it easily with the hammer, until it was halfway in. Then he did the same with the second nail, before passing the hammer to Jack.

'Tap gently to begin with. Try and make sure the hammer hits the nail square-on. We don't want them to go wonky.'

Jack took the hammer and followed his instructions well. His first hit was a little off, and his second missed entirely. But then he began to get the hang of it, and although the nail had begun to go in a little diagonally, Daniel straightened it for him with a couple of taps from the hammer and passed the tool back to Jack for him to finish off.

'We did it!' yelled Jack in delight.

'We did. A job well done! Put it there.' Daniel held out his hand for a high five and Jack returned it with an enthusiastic slap.

They both stood on the previously wobbly board and it was perfect. A little creak, but no movement. The treehouse was safe and secure once more.

'Boys? Dinner's ready!' called Genevieve from the back doorstep.

'Let's go,' said Daniel, leading the way down the ladder and waiting for Jack to follow.

'After we've eaten, can we play football?'

'Sure. We'll let our food go down a bit first, but I promise you a kickabout. Did you play at school today?'

'We played rounders.'

'How'd that go?'

'I got caught out,' Jack said sadly.

'That's a shame. But you had fun, yes?'

Jack nodded.

'Your mum will be pleased to hear that.'

'I told Sam he could come to ours to play, but Mum said we'd have to ask you if that was okay first.'

'Why wouldn't it be okay? It's your place.'

'Mum says you own it, and because Sam might want to bring his dog with him she said we'd have to ask permission.'

'Oh. What type of dog?'

'A small one.'

Daniel smiled as Jack reached the ground. 'I'm fine with it. I'll tell your Mum for you, if you like?'

The young boy nodded and raced inside. Daniel heard William tell Jack to go and wash his hands, and as he went inside his mouth watered at the aroma of the chicken biryani that Genevieve had cooked.

He saw the table was laid for five as he went to wash his hands at the sink, and as soon as he'd got the water running he heard the front door open and Stacey's voice calling out, 'Anyone home? Something smells good.' He felt his heart lift at hearing her voice. And a smile even crept across his face.

He looked up and saw Genevieve smiling back at him. 'What?' he asked.

'Nothing,' she answered, trying to sound as innocent as she could.

He smiled ruefully. He hoped the older woman wasn't thinking that he was having romantic thoughts about Stacey. He liked her, but that was all. He was in no place to begin a romantic entanglement. Certainly not with a colleague, and most definitely not with a woman and child who'd already been let down by a man. Not that he was the type to let anyone down, but he wasn't ready. Even though he liked Stacey as a friend, and had felt able to share his personal grief with her earlier today, that was as far as it could go. Good friends. She had a child to think about. And he must think of him too. Jack was a good kid who'd had a tough time of it lately. He didn't need some guy messing around with his mother.

Not that I would. Not that I am.

He watched Stacey surreptitiously as he came out of the kitchen, hoping that Genevieve wouldn't notice or think anything of it. He just wanted to see how she was after work. They did work together after all.

'All done?' he asked, placing a plate of poppadoms down on the table.

'Yes! A patient rang just after you left, worried about a rash on her baby, so I stayed a little later to check it out.'

'Was it okay?'

'Yes. Just a little eczema.'

He smiled. That was common enough. Both the last-minute call from a patient just before the surgery closed as well as the eczema.

'Where's Jack?' she asked, looking around her.

'Just washing his hands,' said Stacey's gran, as she added a jar of mango chutney to the table. 'He's been helping Daniel fix the treehouse.'

'Oh. Did he have a good day today?'

'He said he did. He played rounders,' answered Daniel.

'That's good to hear,' she said, her shoulders relaxing.

He knew how worried she was about her son. He would be too, considering all that Genevieve and William had told him about the young boy. He could only imagine the stress that Stacey and her son had been through.

'Mum!' Jack barrelled into his mother's legs and gave her a hug. 'Did Daniel tell you we fixed the treehouse? I used the hammer!'

'Did you, now?'

Stacey hugged him back, looking up at Daniel and smiling so happily he felt a little shift inside. A warmth spreading through him. He'd helped to bring this moment of happiness for them both. He'd missed that. Missed being able to bring a smile to a child. To its mother. It made him feel part of something. No longer alone.

William came in and kissed his granddaughter on the cheek in greeting, then settled himself at the head of the table. Genevieve sat at the other end. Between them on one side sat Stacey and Jack, and Daniel sat opposite Stacey.

The biryani smelt wonderful! Spicy and aromatic. Along with the poppadoms were some garlic and coriander naans, a mix of chutneys, and for Jack a bottle of tomato sauce. It went on everything, Stacey explained. Even biryani.

He smiled. Mason had been the same. He'd often said to him at the dinner table. *'Do you want some dinner with your ketchup?'* The memory hit him hard, out of nowhere, and for a moment he felt briefly winded. He'd forgotten that simple thing. And now, as he watched Jack pour the red sauce all over his rice and chicken, he was seeing in his mind's eye Mason doing the same.

'I noticed in the local paper that there's a flat up for rent. The Stowell place,' said William conversationally. 'I've circled it for you, Stacey, in case you're interested. Two bedrooms.'

'The Stowell place?' asked Stacey.

'Above the newsagents.'

'Oh. Right…'

Daniel was startled out of his reverie by William's suggestion. He knew his annexe was only meant to be a temporary measure for Stacey and Jack, but were they moving out already?

Maybe that's a good thing. I wanted distance, remember?

But distance seemed like a bad thing now that he'd met them. Now that he knew them. Now that he had begun to feel a part of them and their family.

'Above the newsagents?' answered Genevieve with distaste. 'They'd be woken every morning with the delivery of the newspapers before the sun's up! I don't think that's a good idea!'

Daniel watched Stacey's face to see how she reacted to this. Was she keen to move out? Would she prefer to stay? Was she worried about being woken early every morning? She seemed interested, and why wouldn't she be? She probably thought she was imposing on Daniel by staying in his annexe.

'Hmm… Gran's probably right. But maybe I ought to look at it?'

'You're welcome to stay at the annexe as long as you need,' said Daniel, wanting to make his position clear.

But everyone looked at him, and he felt his face colour, and Genevieve's knowing smile was rather embarrassing.

'That's kind of you, Daniel. Thank you,' Stacey said.

Jack smiled, with ketchup around his mouth.

'It's very kind,' agreed Genevieve. 'We don't need Stacey and Jack rushing into anything, William!'

William held up his hands in surrender. 'I only thought to mention it!'

'Well, maybe run things past me first,' his wife said, with an undertone that implied he shouldn't have mentioned anything at all. 'Springing things like that on people at the dinner table…'

Daniel met Stacey's amused gaze and he smiled back, reaching for a poppadom and passing her the plate.

She took it from him, taking one, breaking it into two and giving half to Jack. 'Thank you.'

'You're welcome.'

Daniel hadn't enjoyed himself like this for ages. All this time he'd secluded himself away from others, believing that was what he needed. What other people would prefer. Who wanted to hang around someone who was suffering from grief? But being with people, people who felt like family, being a part of a group again, made him feel so much more alive than he had in years.

The Clancys, Stacey and Jack had welcomed him in, and right in that moment, sharing a secret smile with Stacey that said they were both amused by the polite spat between the older couple, made him feel whole again.

He had shared his intimate pain with Stacey today and she hadn't treated him like some kind of leper that needed to be avoided—as a lot of people did when they didn't know what to say. In fact, she had reached out to him, hugged him, held him, softened his hurt with her comfort and empathy. Holding her had felt wonderful. He hadn't wanted it to end. But good things always did.

When had he last had a hug like that?

It was two years ago. The day Penny died. They'd watched each and every turtle shuffle down the sandy beach, the sun had risen, and his wife had walked over to him and wrapped her arms around him, squeezing him tight as she said, *'Thank you for bringing us to Hawaii.'*

It had been a surprise trip, for their anniversary. He'd got time off from work, arranged for a locum to cover his list whilst they'd left to spend two weeks in paradise. It had been Mason's first time flying. His first big adventure. Daniel had wanted it to be a holiday of a lifetime. A fantastic family memory that they would look back on and smile.

Instead, he'd gone through the worst tragedy in his entire life. Losing everyone he held dear.

Stacey's hug and spending some time with Jack had reached across the years, bridged his grief and his memory and reminded him that he could still feel comfort and joy, despite all that had happened.

'Jack. Slow down. It's not a competition,' said Stacey, clearly noticing how fast Jack was shovelling food into his mouth.

Jack stopped mid-chew and smiled, and then exaggeratedly did the slowest chew in the whole wide world.

Daniel smiled. That was exactly the kind of thing Mason would have done, too. 'You should listen to your mum,' he said. 'You don't want tummy ache stopping you from playing football with me later.'

'I won't get tummy ache. And if I did, you and Mummy could make me better.'

Daniel glanced at Stacey, one eyebrow raised.

She laughed, shaking her head.

And he revelled in how her bright laughter made him feel.

Stacey was wiping down the kitchen counters when movement outside in the back garden caught her eye. Daniel and Jack were playing football together.

Daniel was being so kind and so gentle with her son. Allowing him to tackle him softly and take the ball, get it past him and kick it into the goal, which had been created from two flower pots they'd moved into the centre of the lawn.

Jack yelled with delight, hands in the air. 'Goal!'

She smiled.

'They're good together, aren't they?' said her gran, who'd somehow silently crept up behind her.

Stacey nodded, blushing at being caught watching with a smile on her face. 'They are.'

'It's nice for Jack to have a male influence in his life.'

'It is.'

'Not that I'm saying you haven't done a marvellous job on your own! You have. That boy is the sweetest little boy I've ever met and, yes, I'm biased, but I think it's true.'

'Have I protected him enough, though? All that bullying he went through… He'll always remember it. How it made him feel. Could I have stopped it earlier?'

'You did everything you could. Don't beat yourself up about that. Now, then, why don't you go out there and join in the fun? I'll bring you out some home-made lemonade.'

'I'm not sure I want to spoil their fun.'

'How would you be doing that? Jack would love to have you both out there, you mark my words.'

Stacey looked at her gran, who nodded vehemently. 'Okay…' She passed her gran the cloth she'd been using to wipe up, and opened the back door to head outside.

'Mum's coming!' yelled Jack excitedly, and she felt a beaming smile break across her face.

'Couldn't let you boys have all the fun on your own!' she said.

Daniel smiled at her approach. 'Want to go in goal?'

'I do!'

She settled herself between the flowerpots as Jack tackled Daniel for control of the ball once again. He managed to take it and began to dribble the ball towards her, glancing up to check her position before he took aim. Stacey paused, giving the ball just enough time to get past her.

'Goal!'

Jack lifted his hands into the air and ran at Daniel in triumph. Daniel scooped him up and swung him around in the air and Stacey couldn't remember the last time she'd smiled so much. Felt so carefree.

Soon Daniel got the ball, dodged around Jack and shot the ball in her direction. She blocked it with her foot, sending it back in the direction of the two boys.

'Mum! You come and tackle, too!' encouraged Jack.

'All right. But I'm not very good.'

She ran out of the goal towards Daniel and Jack, who were both vying for the ball. She didn't want to get in their way, and thought she'd let Jack get the ball first and then let him go past her. But as they both edged towards her the spirit of adventure got the better of her and she suddenly wanted to try and tackle for the ball too. So she went in. Feet and ankles wrestling for the ball with Daniel and Jack.

They were laughing, yelping, giggling, and then Jack made a surge for the ball at the same time as Stacey and Daniel, and somehow their legs got entangled and they all fell down in a heap, Stacey falling on her back and Daniel practically on top of her, Jack at their side.

She lay there for a moment, breathing heavily, a smile still on her face as she looked up at Daniel, who lay over her, propped up by his hands, staring down into her eyes, just inches away.

Awareness shot through her at the feel of him, the *proximity* of him, in a position that was actually quite intimate! His body against hers. The length of him. The weight of him. His solidness. Her breathing was heavy and she looked up into his face with uncertainty, aware that her son was still at the side of them, laughing with mirth and struggling to his feet, because the ball was free and he was going to get an open shot at goal.

Daniel got to his feet and held out a hand to help her up. She took it and he pulled her to a standing position.

'Okay?' he asked.

Stacey nodded, still holding his hand. 'Yes. I'm fine, thank you.'

Awareness was rushing through her again, and she blushed, letting go of his hand and looking down to brush grass off her clothes, in case he should see the heat filling her cheeks.

'Goal!' Jack cried behind them.

Daniel couldn't stand still. He tried to. But his mind wouldn't let him settle. He felt as if his body was flooded with adrenaline and this was either a fight, flight or freeze response.

Most likely flight.

I thought about kissing her.

That was what he couldn't get out of his head. He'd been having such a fun time. A relaxing time. Playing football with Jack. He'd used to play football with Mason all the time, so the opportunity to play with Jack and remember what it had been like had been awesome! In a way, it had been almost as if Jack was his son. He'd been helping to guide him. Showing the little boy that he was interested in him. That he wanted to spend time with him. That he was important.

And then Stacey had joined them.

Penny had never joined in their football games. She'd always watched, or used the time that Daniel was with their son to get a few jobs done around the house. Daniel hadn't minded that. It had given them a little father-son bonding moment.

So when Stacey had joined in he'd been amazed, and then delighted. They'd had a fun time. It had been relaxing, the three of them together. Nice. Easy. *So* easy! He'd almost not been able to believe how easy it was for him to be with them.

And then the tackle.

They'd all gone for the ball at once and somehow tumbled into a tangle of arms and legs. And he'd landed on top of Stacey. Not fully. His hands had broken the fall, and he'd tried to avoid squashing her. But she'd been lying beneath him, red hair splayed out against the green grass. Her laughter-filled eyes had looked up at him, there'd been a smile on her face and he'd been so close to her!

He'd felt her breathing, her chest rising and falling. Her softness. Her legs entwined with his. Their faces had been so close. Mere inches away from each other! And the thought had risen unbidden to his mind.

What would it be like to kiss her?

He'd been so startled, so alarmed, he'd instantly got to his feet and pulled her up to hers. Behind them, Jack had scored an open goal. Stacey had started brushing loose bits of grass from her clothing and he'd simply not known where to look. Towards the house?

Genevieve had been in the back doorway, leaning against the jamb, arms folded, a knowing smile upon her face, before she'd turned away and gone back inside.

'Sorry. Did I hurt you?' he'd asked.

'No! No, I'm fine,' she'd replied, nodding, looking anywhere than at him.

And it was then that he'd realised she must have felt it too. That moment when their bodies had been pressed close together...

'I'm winning!' Jack yelled in delight.

Stacey turned and laughed, ruffling her son's hair. 'Yes, you've won. But I think that's enough for tonight. Let's get you home and bathed. School tomorrow.'

Jack nodded and ran inside, still clutching the ball.

'He seems much brighter,' Daniel stated.

'Yes, he is. He's making friends and...well, I guess you help, too. He likes spending time with you.'

She turned away to bend down and lift one of the flowerpots, but he knew it was heavier than she imagined.

'Let me do that.'

'You're sure?' She looked at him uncertainly.

'Of course.'

He lifted the pots easily. Placed them back in their original position and then stood looking at her as if he didn't know what to say or do next. It was a similar feeling to the end of a date, when you don't know whether to just say goodbye, or whether you should give the person a kiss?

'Well, I'll see you at work tomorrow...'

She nodded. 'Yes. Yes, you will.'

'And if Jack ever needs anyone for a quick kickabout I'm happy to oblige.'

'That's kind of you.'

He shrugged. He wanted to. Being with Jack fuelled a need that he had. A need he hadn't realised had been gnawing at him for some time. Spending time with Jack eased the pain inside his heart.

'Well, I'd better go. See you tomorrow,' she said.

'See you.'

He watched her disappear inside the house and then he turned away and walked down to the bottom of the garden, breathing heavily, hands on his hips, blown away by what a close call that had been.

Imagine if he had kissed her! With Genevieve watching! Or Jack!

He couldn't do that. Besides, he wasn't ready for what would come after that if he did!

It was a close call.

Running his hands through his hair, he tried not to think of her soft lips, gently curved in laughter. Tried not to remember the look in her eyes when she'd lain on the grass and looked up at him as if she was expecting him to press his mouth to hers. Tried not to think how close their lips had been. Tried not to think about how that had made him feel...

The very fact that he'd wanted to kiss her perturbed him.

He didn't think he was ready for that. Because he was no fly-by-night guy. He'd never been into casual relationships or flings. He was a long-term guy. A steady relationship guy.

And there would be so much at risk, being with Stacey! She was a colleague. A friend. A mother! It would make being at work extremely uncomfortable. And this wasn't just about him, or them, it was about a little boy who had already had so much trauma in his life. He didn't need him entering his life and potentially ruining it when the relationship didn't work out.

No. I can't let that happen.

CHAPTER SIX

'HEY, HAVE YOU got a minute?'

Stacey popped her head around Daniel's door in between patients. She had something important to ask him. It was quite a big ask, but she didn't have any other choice.

'Sure. What's up?' He smiled as she came into the room and sat down in a chair.

'I've had an email this morning from the practice manager. She wants me to go on a dementia training day next Wednesday, to become the practice's dementia ambassador, but it's in Southampton and I won't get back until seven-ish that night. Unfortunately, my grandparents have chosen that day to go on a day trip to Brighton, so I don't have anyone to look after Jack.'

She looked at him, hoping he'd get the message before she had to ask outright.

He did. 'And you need me to babysit?'

She let out a breath. 'I know it's a big favour, and I wouldn't ask if I had any choice in the matter, but I saw you're not on call that night, and he doesn't know anyone else, and... Well, I trust you with him.'

He smiled. 'Of course I can.'

'You're sure?'

'Absolutely. We'll play footie...order a pizza. Have a boys' night.'

What a relief! She was thrilled. She'd known she could rely on him.

'Thank you! You have no idea how grateful I am!'

'Hey, I like Jack. He's a good lad. It'll be good for us both.'

'Thank you.' She stood, not knowing whether to shake his hand, or give him a hug, or…

Or what? Kiss him?

She'd thought about kissing him ever since they'd fallen in a tangle on her grandparents' back lawn and he'd landed on top of her. Seriously, it was as if her mind wouldn't stop putting it on replay! And then it would helpfully provide an image of what it would have been like if they *had* kissed…

It would be easier if he wasn't so damned good-looking and if she herself didn't feel so damned lonely. It had been hard since Jerry's desertion. Going through her pregnancy alone. Giving birth alone. Raising a child alone. All the time she questioned herself and her decisions, and she missed having someone to talk to. Someone to discuss things with.

Someone to snuggle up with.

Someone to hold her at night.

Having Daniel fall on top of her had been the closest she'd come to having any physical male attention since Jerry had left—and boy, oh, boy, had it woken up her dormant desires to be wanted!

'Is there anything else?' he asked, looking at her expectantly.

Hold me. Kiss me.

'No. No, that's it. That's all.' She began to back away towards his door, smiling, blushing, feeling awkward.

I'm acting like all the other women who have probably got a crush on Dr Daniel Prior!

'Well, have a good morning,' he told her.

'You too.'

And then she was out of the room, standing in the corridor, breathing a huge sigh of relief, feeling hot and sweaty and keen to sit in front of a fan to help her cool down.

Her next patient was a middle-aged woman called Daisy Goodman, who came in, sat down, and burst into tears.

Stacey passed her some tissues and waited until she'd got control of her breathing again.

'Sorry! I just get so anxious in the waiting room.'

'It's okay. I'm here to help. What seems to be the problem?'

'I think I've hit the menopause. I'm all over the place hormone-wise. My husband says it's like living with Jekyll and Hyde. One minute I'm fine—the next I'm weepy or angry. I lose my temper with the kids if they leave a mess or don't tidy up after themselves.'

'Have you noticed any change in your periods?'

Daisy nodded, dabbing at her nose with a tissue. 'They're all over the place. And I've always been so regular. Sometimes they're really heavy, too. It's almost frightening how much blood comes out.'

'What other symptoms have you been experiencing?'

'I don't sleep! And I keep having these night sweats. This bloom of heat starts in my chest and rises up into my face. I have to throw everything off and wait to cool down. Paul, my husband, he's just snoring away, which irritates me, because I can't get back to sleep, and then I'm tired and grumpy during the day, and I'm just... I'm just a mess!'

She began to cry again, and whilst she did so Stacey waited.

'Let's have a look at your blood pressure,' she said eventually, and wrapped the cuff around her patient's arm and let the small machine do its thing. Daisy's BP was only slightly raised, and that was probably down to her being so upset.

'Any headaches?' she asked.

Daisy nodded, dabbing at her eyes. 'Yes.'

'Any other problems down below? Dryness? Soreness during intercourse?'

'Yes. Will I have to have a blood test to check my hormones? Only, I'm terrified of needles.'

'No. We don't routinely check for menopause with a blood tests any more. We go on patient history and symptoms, and it certainly sounds like what you're experiencing is menopause. You're fifty-one years of age, so it all fits. Have you thought about what you'd like to do to try and tackle these symptoms?'

'I'm no good at taking tablets, but I'd like to try HRT if I can.'

'Well, we can prescribe it in a gel or as a patch.'

'A patch sounds good.'

Stacey smiled. 'Okay. Any history of blood clots in the family?'

'No.'

'Breast cancer? Anything like that?'

'No.'

'And there's no chance that you could be pregnant?'

Daisy laughed. 'Not a chance.'

'Okay. Well, I can prescribe you a low-dose patch—say twenty-five milligrams to begin with. You'll see how you go with that, then come back in three months for a review with the HRT nurse, and we'll go from there. If you need a stronger dose we can increase it.' She printed out the prescription and signed it before handing it over. 'Is there anything else I can help you with today?'

'No. Thank you, Doctor. I really appreciate you listening to me today. Hearing me.'

'Of course. It's no problem. It's what I'm here for.'

'I just have difficulty sometimes in believing any doctor will listen to me.'

'Why's that?' Stacey was genuinely interested.

Daisy shrugged. 'I wasn't listened to as a child. I was very thin, and a picky eater, because food used to make me sick. My mother—a very overbearing woman—told everyone I was anorexic, even though I told the doctors I wasn't! But they wouldn't listen! It wasn't until I was thirty-five years of age, when I moved here, that Dr Fletcher listened to me and ran a few blood tests. They proved I was coeliac, not anorexic, so coming to the doctor always makes me nervous.'

Stacey let out a breath. How awful for this poor woman! 'I'm so sorry you had that experience.'

'I stayed away from doctors for all those years. I only came in to see Dr Fletcher because I'd moved to the area and he wanted to do that new patient check. He's a good doctor. You're all good doctors here.' She smiled.

'Well, it's very nice of you to say so. Thank you. And please know that you can come here for anything and we *will* listen.'

'I know you will. Thank you, Dr Emery.'

'No problem at all.'

Daisy got up and left the room, and Stacey began to write up her notes in the patient records.

She knew what it felt like not to be listened to. For people not to hear you. Her pleas to Jerry had fallen on deaf ears from the second she'd announced her pregnancy. She'd never have believed he could be like that. He was a doctor! He cared for people. She'd thought he'd be a natural at being a father—would be thrilled at her news!

Only he hadn't been. And he'd refused to talk to her about it.

She knew he'd had a difficult relationship with his parents and his siblings, but to completely blank her... To make work difficult for her, so that she'd had to move...

She'd tried to build a new life for herself in Edinburgh, only then she'd begun to feel that Jack's schoolteachers weren't hearing her concerns. They'd told her that they did, and that they were doing their best to put an end to her son's bullying problems, but each day had just got worse and worse. Bullies were clever, and teachers couldn't watch Jack all six hours of the day.

So she'd taken matters into her own hands.

It hurt not to be heard.

'Are you missing your mum?'

Daniel crouched down in front of Jack. They were in Daniel's back garden. Between his house and the annexe. And Jack didn't seem himself.

He nodded.

'Was it a bad day today at school?' he asked softly.

'No. It was okay.'

'No one upset you?'

A shake of his head.

'You didn't eat much for dinner either.' He pressed the back of his hand to Jack's forehead. He felt a little warm and he *was* pale. 'You feeling okay?' he asked.

'My tummy hurts.'

Ah... Children often complained of a tummy ache. It could be a number of things, and most of them were not serious, but Daniel had to admit to feeling his heart race a little. He was supposed to be looking after Jack. Stacey had said she trusted him with her son, and he wanted to prove that her belief in him was solid. It wouldn't do for Jack to be ill by the time she got home.

'Where does it hurt?'

'Here.' Jack pointed to his belly button.

'Want me to take a look?'

Jack looked at him then, with uncertainty in his eyes, and said in a small voice, 'I don't show people my tummy.'

Daniel smiled. 'Let me tell you a secret. I don't show people my tummy either.'

'Do you have a birthmark on yours, too?'

'I do. But just a small one.'

'I have a big one.'

'Well, I'm a doctor. So I've probably seen every kind of birthmark you can imagine.'

Jack thought for a moment. 'Okay. But in the house.'

Daniel nodded and followed the young boy back into the annexe, where he suggested that Jack lay on the couch.

'We'll do this only when you're ready. Just one question. And it's my favourite question to ask patients! Have you pooped today?'

Jack smiled at the word. 'Mummy says we shouldn't talk about poop at the dinner table.'

'Well, we're not at the dinner table. So, have you?'

Jack shook his head.

'Gone pee-pee?'

Jack nodded, and then slowly reached down to clasp the tee shirt that he had tucked into the top of his shorts and lift it.

Daniel was careful not to change his facial expression. He wasn't shocked by what he saw, but he fully understood why Jack would feel he needed to hide his stomach. The birthmark stretched across one side of it, from his right hip bone to just under his left nipple. It was like a paint splash.

It wasn't raised, or red, but it was large, and his heart went out to this little boy who'd had his life made miserable by other little kids who didn't like anyone different.

He rubbed his hands together to make them warmer. 'Can I press on your tummy?'

Jack nodded.

'If anything hurts, you tell me—okay?'

Another nod.

Jack's tummy was soft and palpable, and he didn't grimace or show any signs of anything serious.

Daniel wondered if Jack was simply missing his mum. He didn't know this area, even if Stacey did, and he was still getting used to knowing his grandparents in person, a new school, new classmates. And now he had been left with his mother's work friend.

He checked his watch. 'Want to call your mum? She should be driving home by now, but I know she's connected her phone to the car's system, so she can talk hands-free.'

Jack seemed to brighten.

'Okay. Let's do it!'

Stacey pressed the speaker button on her steering wheel when the phone rang from her home. 'Hello?'

'Hey, I've got a bit of a poorly boy here, who wants to speak to his mum.'

Jack was poorly? Her instincts flared. At his previous school Jack had often stated he was poorly before school to get the day off, as well as saying the same *after* school, in the hope of getting the next day off as well. If he was doing that again...

'Has he had a bad day at school?'

'He says not. Want to speak to him? I've got you on speaker.'

'Sure. Hey, Jack? How are you doing, buddy?'

'Okay. My tummy hurts.'

'So I heard. Have you pooped today?'

She heard him laugh a little.

'Daniel asked that, too.'

She smiled. 'And what was the answer?'

'No.'

He sounded embarrassed, but of course he would. He was only little, and poop was either incredibly embarrassing or incredibly hilarious.

'Okay. Do you feel sick?' she asked.

'A bit.'

'Does he have a temperature?' She addressed Daniel.

'He is a little hot to the touch.'

'There's some infant paracetamol in one of the cupboards in the kitchen. The one above the kettle.'

'Okay.'

She heard Daniel move, and then in the background the sound of the cupboard door being closed.

'When will you be home?' Jack asked.

'Soon. I'm stuck in traffic at the moment. The M27 is jammed. But I'm trying my hardest, okay? Do whatever Daniel says, and maybe try and go to sleep. Or watch a movie. But you need to be in bed by eight at the latest.'

'Okay, Mummy.'

'I love you, squirt.'

'I love you, too.'

'I'll see you soon.'

'Bye.'

'Bye.'

She switched off the phone and stared at the rear of the vehicle in front of her. It was covered with amusing car stickers and she tried to allow herself to find the humour contained upon them, but her mind was on Jack.

What if he was lying? What if there was a problem at school? What if Jack felt as if he couldn't say what was truly happening because he knew how much she'd wanted to move back home?

She worried at her lip until she felt a pain, and then re-alised she'd torn off a small sliver of skin. She looked at her raw red lip in the rear-view mirror.

'Damn…'

Daniel was getting worried. It had been over an hour since their call to Stacey and she still wasn't home. And Jack wasn't getting any better. Instead, he'd said he felt worse, and Daniel was now taking a bowl to him because he said he was beginning to feel really sick.

'Here you go. How's that pain doing? Any better since the paracetamol?'

'No. It hurts more.'

'Show me where.'

Jack pulled back the duvet and pointed to the midpoint between his belly button and his right hipbone.

Uh-oh. 'Can I have a feel?'

Jack nodded miserably. He looked pale. More clammy. And his hair was getting sweaty.

Daniel began to palpate Jack's abdomen, and when he got over McBurney's Point, Jack groaned and grimaced.

'Does it hurt more when I press down or when I let go?'

'When you stop.'

This was beginning to seem like appendicitis, but Daniel didn't want to overreact. Nor did he want to wait too long. If this *was* his appendix it might burst, and he would never forgive himself if something happened to Jack. He was a doctor. And Stacey had left Jack in his care. He might have been unable to help his wife or his own son, but he could help Jack. Maybe it was better to be safe than sorry?

'I think you might need a different doctor, Jack.'

'Why?'

'Because there's this thing in your tummy called an appendix and I think that's what's bothering you. I could be wrong, but I don't want to take any chances, okay? I'm going to call for an ambulance, but I don't want you to be scared.'

'I need Grover.'

Daniel passed him the teddy bear. It was a tatty old thing, but Jack loved it. Mason had had a bear. Butters, he'd called it. Daniel still had it in his bedroom. It sat in the middle of his bookshelf, next to a picture of the boy who had loved him so much.

He pulled out his mobile and made the call, his heart racing in his chest.

Stacey received the call from Daniel telling her that he'd called an ambulance for Jack and her whole world fell apart once again. What was worse was that she was still stuck in traffic, even though she was incredibly close to her turn-off. She could see it! It was right there! About four car lengths away!

But she couldn't get to it. There was no hard shoulder on this part of the road, no way she could swing around the cars in front of her and bypass them quickly. So she had to sit there and sit there.

Finally, when they got moving again, she knew she had to drive carefully. No need for her to come off the road by being stupid.

Jack's in the best place. He's in the best place!

Her grandparents had called too, to say they were back home and were making their way to the hospital. Gran had sounded incredibly brave, but her voice had been wavery and trembly and Stacey knew that they were just as scared as she was.

'I'm coming, squirt. I'm coming,' she said to herself, over and over again.

She got stuck behind a learner driver who was travelling at least eight miles below the speed limit, but managed to pass him after a quarter of a mile, and then she was on the open road, speeding towards the hospital, where her son might or might not be having an appendectomy!

Her brain was helpfully providing her with all the things that might go wrong. Infection. Peritonitis. Sepsis… It took her a huge effort of concentration to run through the stats she knew in her head. Thousands of people had surgery for appendicitis each year and they recovered just fine. No complications.

But when has my life ever been uncomplicated?

She managed to find a parking spot, then ran into A&E and tried not to burst with frustration as she stood in a queue waiting to get to the reception desk.

'Stacey?'

She turned, and there was her grandad, over by the vending machine, waiting for it to deliver a cup of what would no doubt be questionable tea.

'I thought it was you, love. Your gran's in a state. I thought a tea might calm her nerves, and I said I'd pop down to see if you were here.'

'How's Jack?'

'He's been taken for surgery.'

'What? Why didn't anyone call me?'

'There wasn't time, love. They thought his appendix might have burst, so they just rushed him in. Terrifying, it is.' He took her arm. 'Let me take you up to the ward.'

She nodded, and walked patiently beside her grandfather, wishing he would walk faster, but knowing his limitations. If Jack was in surgery already there was no point in rushing anyway. Whether she arrived on the surgical ward in the next five minutes or twenty-five minutes would make no difference to Jack. He wouldn't be there.

She tried not to think of him in surgery. Her poor little boy all alone on the table.

Up on Shelley Ward, in a family waiting room, her gran was pacing the floor, and seated on a green plastic chair, staring forlornly at the floor, was Daniel.

'Look who I found,' said her grandad.

They both looked up. She saw tears form in her grandmother's eyes and a huge look of relief on Daniel's face.

'Any news from Theatre?'

'No, nothing,' said her gran, gratefully accepting the cup of tea from her husband, taking a sip and wincing at the heat.

Daniel had got up. He was by her side, his hand on her arm. 'Are you okay?' he asked.

She was grateful for his concern. 'Yes. Scared, though.'

'Of course. I know exactly how you feel,' he answered quietly, his eyes clouding over.

'Did they say how long it might be?'

'No. But a very nice nurse said she'll come out to update us when she can,' said her gran.

'Here, take a seat,' suggested Daniel, and she sank into one of the ugly green seats beside him.

It felt wrong to just be sitting there. Doing nothing. This was her son, and he needed help, and she had to rely on other doctors, people she didn't know, to save his life. It was the most impotent she'd ever felt in her whole life. Tears began to fall, and her gran passed her a tissue from the depths of her handbag.

'We've had such a wonderful day in Brighton,' said her gran. 'To come back to this…' She shook her head, almost in disbelief.

'I know…' said Stacey. 'I feel so useless.'

Daniel reached out and took her hand. Squeezing it. Holding it. Just letting her know that he was there. That he understood.

Of course he did. He'd been stuck in a car, unable to move, unable to help his wife and child. He'd watched them die!

I could never be that strong.

She leant into him, rested her head on his shoulder without thinking. It felt right. It felt like what she needed. Just a moment of support from someone whom she knew was probably as terrified as she was. He knew how scared she must be. How lost she felt.

'This tea is terrible!' Her gran winced after taking another sip. 'And now I need the loo. Where are the toilets?'

'There are some just outside the ward. Want me to show you? I could do with a tinkle as well,' said her grandad, and he took his wife's hand and they ambled off, leaving Daniel and Stacey alone.

'I feel I should be doing more. Should I be calling someone?' she asked, her mind whizzing with thoughts.

'Like who? All his family is here.'

She was silent for a moment. Thinking of Jerry. 'Not all of them.'

She felt Daniel reach for his mobile. He handed it to her. 'If you need to call him, then do.'

She lifted her head to look at him. 'No, he's never wanted anything to do with Jack.'

She swallowed hard, suddenly immensely sad for her son. Guilty that she hadn't managed to give him a father.

Hadn't managed to hold on to her husband. Hadn't managed to keep Jack safe.

Her heart ached.

She looked up into Daniel's face, searching for answers, for clues as to how he'd got himself through such an ordeal. How she was meant to deal with this! But instead she found herself getting lost in those deep brown eyes of his. Daniel was looking down at her with such concern, with such intensity, with such…longing…

She felt it too. That need to reach out and find comfort from another human being. That need to feel that you had a soft place to fall when all around you the world was sharp with shards of brittle glass.

His face was so close to hers. They were so close to each other. Her hand was still in his. Her body was turned to his. Her heart was racing. Her breathing much faster as she contemplated accepting the comfort she would find in him.

All it would take would be for her to edge closer.

She looked down at his lips. Saw that they were parted. Expectant. Waiting. Longing. She yearned to press her mouth to his, to give in to the attraction she felt, the need she wanted to feed, to embrace Daniel…

'Are you Jack's parents?'

The voice intruded, breaking the fantasy she had begun to believe might finally come true and thrusting reality back into her face.

They broke apart as Stacey turned and stood, releasing Daniel's hand. 'I'm Jack's mother.'

'The surgery went well. He's in Recovery. Would you like to come and see him?'

Oh, the relief!

'Thank you! Thank you so much!'

Stacey turned to Daniel, but it was like looking at a different man. He'd stepped back, looking guilty, and now he could barely meet her gaze.

She wanted to tell him that it was okay.

But she needed to see Jack more.

Jack lay in his hospital bed holding his tatty teddy. A drip was attached to his arm, and although he still looked pale, he looked a lot better. Seeing his pain increase had made Daniel feel awful.

Stacey had hurried to her son's side and Jack's face lit up at seeing her.

'Hey, squirt!' she said, taking hold of his hand as she bent over the bed to press a kiss to his forehead. 'How are you feeling?'

'I'm okay.'

'Any pain?' Stacey looked Jack up and down.

'No. Not any more.'

'That's good.'

'Where's Daniel?'

Stacey turned to look at him and Daniel gave her an awkward smile and stepped forward, so that Jack could see him too. 'I'm here.'

The little boy smiled and closed his eyes, drifting off again into the land of nod.

Daniel stood opposite Stacey, still trying to figure out what had just happened out in the waiting area of Shelley Ward.

There'd been a moment.

That was the only way he could describe it.

Stacey had been resting her head on his shoulder and she'd looked up at him and...

He swallowed. 'Do you think we should talk about what happened out there?' he asked in a low voice.

Stacey blushed and turned to look at Jack, but he was fast asleep. 'Nothing happened.'

'But it nearly did. You were going to… I mean, I was going to… And then that nurse arrived.'

'This isn't the place, Daniel,' she whispered.

He looked at Jack, still sleeping. 'No. Maybe not.'

Behind them, Stacey's grandparents suddenly arrived, masked and gowned. 'The nurses said we could have five minutes. Just to see him. And then we've got to come back out.'

'He's okay. Still sleepy,' Stacey said, glancing over at Daniel.

She looked angry. But what did she have to be angry about? Was she angry with him? Or herself? Clearly she thought that whatever *hadn't* happened between them had been a mistake.

And maybe she was right.

'I'll go,' he volunteered. 'You and William stay, Genevieve.'

Mrs Clancy looked over at him in gratitude and surprise. 'Are you sure?'

'Of course. He's your grandson. I'll wait outside.'

And he strode away from the bed and went back out into the corridor, sighing heavily, still feeling distraught. He'd been so scared, watching Jack deteriorate. He'd witnessed that before. Trapped in a car with his wife and son, unable to help either of them, he'd watched the life slowly leave their eyes, screaming in frustration and grief. To witness it again, with Stacey's little boy, whom he'd been left in charge of…he couldn't let it happen.

He'd done the right thing.

But that moment…

He couldn't get the image out of his head. How Stacey had looked up into his eyes. How it had made him feel!

Excited. Terrified. Wanting. Doubt. Fear.

Adrenaline had rushed through him and he'd debated whether to press his lips to hers or not. This was a stressful situation…they were only in it because of Jack. Would it have happened anywhere else? In any other situation?

Maybe.

He'd been fighting his attraction to her ever since she'd arrived, and he'd got the feeling that maybe she was doing the same thing, too.

They needed to talk.

Daniel paced the corridor, back and forth, back and forth, so much so that he thought he'd wear a rut in the floor. Suddenly the doors opened and William and Genevieve came out, smiling.

'He's asking for you.'

He looked from one old friend to another. 'Oh, I'm not sure I should interfere—'

'Nonsense! He wants to see you. You go on in.'

He nodded, then used the hand gel on the wall and cleaned his hands once again before going back in and moving towards Jack's bed.

Stacey was where she'd been before. Sitting by her son's bed, still holding his hand. But this time, Jack looked a little more awake. The boy even smiled.

'Daniel!'

'Hey…you're looking much better.'

'Thank you.'

'No problem.'

'Thank you for looking after me when I got poorly.'

'My pleasure.'

'When I get out of here, maybe we can play football again?'

'Daniel might be busy,' Stacey said, not looking at him.

Was she trying to tell him to stay away? Maybe he should. He didn't need to be getting involved with these two. He should have stuck to his first impression and stayed away. Not got involved.

'We'll see. When you're better.'

He glanced at Stacey, but she refused to meet his eyes. Okay. That was fine. He got the message.

'I'd better let you rest.'

'Stay? Please?' Jack whined, letting go of Grover to hold up his left hand for Daniel to take.

How could he refuse?

So Daniel stepped forward, sat down on the other chair and took Jack's hand.

The little boy smiled and drifted off to sleep again.

Stacey kept her gaze fixed on her son.

Daniel decided to stay quiet and do exactly the same thing.

It was fine.

He didn't want to go to dinner the following Monday evening. Anyway, it was his turn to be the duty doctor, and he also had a home visit booked in. So he called the Clancy house and Will picked up.

'Hello?'

'Hey, it's Daniel.'

'Ah! Our hero! How are you?'

He didn't feel like a hero, but he skipped over that. 'I'm great. Listen, I thought I'd better give you a quick call. I've got a home visit to do tonight after surgery, and then I'm on call, so I won't be popping round for dinner.'

'Oh! That's a shame! I know Gen was hoping to cook

you something special—you know, as a thank-you for what you did with Jack.'

'There's no need.'

'Nonsense! What will you do for food tonight? Probably grab a sandwich from the store, I'm guessing. Look, I'll get Gen to do you a plate and you can pop in your way home and take it back with you…heat it up in the microwave.'

'Oh, I really don't want her to go to any trouble…'

'You're family, Daniel, it's no trouble. You know she likes to keep you well fed! Do me a favour and give me a night off from her worrying and fretting about you not looking after yourself properly. Accept the meal.'

He smiled. 'All right. But it'll be a flash visit.'

'Perfect.'

When he arrived at the Clancy house that evening he sat in the car for a brief while, just breathing in and out, trying to psych himself up for seeing Stacey. She'd not been at work since last week, when Jack had got his appendicitis, because she was looking after him, but he assumed she'd be at her grandparents' place today—as she had been the last few Monday evenings.

Once he felt ready, he made his way up the garden path, ready with a mouthful of excuses as to why he couldn't stay so that he didn't make it awkward for Stacey. Or himself! But when he made it inside he discovered only William and Genevieve at the kitchen table.

'They're not here, if you're wondering,' said Genevieve.

'Jack's still resting at home,' said William, closing his newspaper and getting up to reach for a tray upon which sat a covered plate of food. 'It's still hot, if you've got time to eat it here?'

'No. Thank you. My patient is expecting me.' Daniel accepted the plate, wrapped in a towel to keep it warm.

'Everything all right between you and Stacey?' asked Genevieve, curiosity soaking her words.

He nodded, smiling. 'Fine!'

'You don't seem fine. She doesn't blame you, you know.'

'Blame me?'

'For Jack getting appendicitis. She knows it would have happened whether she was there or not.'

'I know, and everything's fine.'

'Hmm… That's what she said.' Genevieve pursed her lips, clearly not believing either one of them. 'You know you can talk to us about anything, Daniel. We're here for you. We always have been.'

'I know, and I'm very grateful for how you've looked after me since…since I lost Penny and Mason.'

She nodded and got up to give him a quick hug. 'All right. Well, you'd better be off, if you're in a rush.'

'I am.'

He thanked them once again and went back out to his car, laying the plate down in the footwell of the vehicle and hating himself for lying to them. But what could he have said?

Your granddaughter and I nearly kissed. Only we didn't, and then it got awkward.

Daniel started the engine and set off to see his home visit patient.

CHAPTER SEVEN

STACEY RETURNED TO work the same day Jack returned to school. She'd enjoyed having time with him at home.

Just as she'd been getting ready, pulling on a navy skirt, her gran had rung to tell her that she'd seen Walter, who was in charge of the village fete, and he'd agreed that Stacey could judge the baby fancy dress competition, alongside Zach and Daniel.

Her heart had sunk. That would mean pasting a smile on her face and hoping that everyone thought she was having a whale of a time!

Maybe I could stick close to Zach? Interact with him?

It had been easy to avoid Daniel over the last few days. He'd been at work for most of them, except the weekend, and she'd kept the curtains of the annexe closed, lowered the blinds at the kitchen window and enjoyed movie marathon days with her son and a few bowls of popcorn.

Jack was recovering brilliantly. He'd been a bit scared of getting up and walking around at first, but when he'd realised that there wasn't any pain—due to the strong painkillers he'd been given—his recovery had come on much faster, and a few nights ago—much to her intense surprise—he'd started asking about when he could return to school?

'I miss Sam. And George. And Toby!'

She'd laughed, delighted at this turn of events. Despite

the drama with Daniel, perhaps moving here *had* been the best thing for her son?

When she got to the surgery, after dropping Jack off at school, she hurried straight to her room and closed the door behind her. She was hoping to just get on with her morning list and go and eat her lunch somewhere, without being spotted by Daniel, then finish her afternoon list and go home.

Only she wasn't that lucky.

Knuckles rapped on her door.

'Come in,' she said, hoping fervently that it was Hannah, or Zach, or a member of staff from Reception.

But it was Daniel.

Her heart began to thud painfully in her chest so she sat behind her desk, logging into the system after inserting her NHS card into the computer.

'We need to talk,' he said.

'Do we?' She kept her eyes fixed on the screen.

'Yes. We do. Talk about what happened.'

'Now isn't the time, Daniel.'

'Then when is? Because you wouldn't let me talk at the hospital, and you've avoided me all the time whilst Jack has been recovering. I knocked on your door at the weekend. I knew you were in there, but you didn't answer.'

She'd heard it. Wondered if it had been him and guiltily ignored it. 'I'm sorry. I didn't hear you.'

Daniel sank into the patient's chair beside her desk. 'We're adults. Let's deal with this. Nothing happened between us—there's no reason we can't just be friends.'

She looked up at him then. Not believing him. 'It's that easy?'

'Yes!' he said, exasperated. 'It has to be. Listen, I was just as shocked as you at what nearly happened, and it freaked me out too. Believe me, I don't need to develop feelings for you and Jack, because all I can think of is what will happen when it ends. I'm so scared of how I'll feel if it all goes wrong that I can't even contemplate letting it *start*. So... friends only. Okay?'

She listened to his words. Shocked. Surprised. She wasn't used to guys telling her the truth up-front. She was used to awkward silences, refusals even to discuss anything important, and then eventual desertion. This frankness and honesty was surprising! And actually quite nice. She really ought not to have suspected he'd be like Jerry.

'You're right. I've been feeling the same way.'

'You have?' He sounded unsure.

She nodded. 'I've been in a relationship with another GP in the same practice and it didn't work out well for me when it ended—so, yes, I kept thinking that my life would end up the same. And I'd have to leave here. Leave just as everything is getting good! Maybe I'm pessimistic, but when you've had your entire life turned upside down by a romantic relationship, it makes you terrified of the next one!'

He stared at her. 'I don't ever want you to feel that you would have to leave.'

'Well, you haven't. Not yet.' She smiled at him, trying to inject a bit of humour into a fraught moment.

'So, we continue as we are? Just friends?'

'Just friends.' She held out her hand so that they could shake on it.

He took her hand in his.

She kept the smile on her face, ignoring the thrill that ran up her arm and ignoring the way her body still reacted to him. She would teach it. Teach it to expect nothing from this man. They had established clear parameters for their relationship. It was the most grown-up she'd felt in ages.

He let go. 'Okay. I'll see you later?'

'You will.' She watched him go, letting out a huge breath of relief once he was out of earshot.

Daniel initially felt much better, having spoken to Stacey, and was glad that he'd taken Zach's advice on the matter. He'd met Zach first thing that morning, asked if he could have a quick word, and Zach had invited him to share. His best friend had listened well and told him just to be honest with Stacey.

It turned out that Zach—whom Daniel knew had secret feelings for Hannah, the new advanced nurse practitioner—wanted to tell Hannah how he felt, but knew how much pressure that would put on her after what had happened to her in a past relationship. He didn't want to scare her off. But he thought that because Daniel and Stacey weren't even involved yet, they should talk. Set the record straight.

Which he'd done.

He'd been terrified, but he'd done it. Even if it wasn't exactly true about them not being involved yet. He *felt* involved, and that was why he had to pull away. He was becoming entwined with her family and her history. He'd practically been adopted by her grandparents. He'd babysat Jack. Cared for him when he was sick. Worked with Stacey. Sat and told her of his painful past on the village green. And she'd sat and listened to him, her eyes full of empathy and support. They'd eaten meals together. Washed dishes together. Laughed. Joked. Rolled on the grass together. Been happy.

And then, at the hospital, had come that moment in which they'd almost kissed...

He had to pull free of her. It was the only way to secure the safety of his heart.

So why do I feel so rubbish?

He told himself the bad feeling would pass. That it was a feeling he could deal with. This disappointment. This sadness. It would be easy enough. It wasn't the heart-stopping brutality of utter grief and loss. That was what he was trying to avoid.

I'm doing the right thing.

His first patient of the day was Brooke Miller, a young woman of twenty-six, who sat down in front of him with a nervous smile.

'Morning,' he said. 'How can I help you today?'

'I want to quit smoking. I've tried before. Tried doing it on my own. But I wasn't strong enough so I think I need some proper advice.'

'Well, usually I ask a patient what their motivation is. If the motivation is strong, then that's a good foundation to start.'

'I want a baby. Me and my partner Jacob…we want to start a family. But I'm worried about the effect of smoking on my pregnancy.'

'Okay. That's a great reason!' Daniel smiled, diving into his desk drawer to pick out the stop smoking literature he had in there, which listed support groups and their telephone numbers, as well as helpful websites that Brooke could visit. 'How many do you smoke a day?'

'About twenty.'

'And what did you try before? Just willpower?'

'Yeah.' She nodded. 'And chomping on mints and sweets. But then I just got fat and broke out in spots. And that would be okay for me if I was pregnant, but not when I was actually trying to seduce my partner, you know?' She giggled and blushed.

Daniel smiled. 'How about we prescribe you some nicotine patches and gum? The gum is sugarless, and it really helps in conjunction with the patches.'

She nodded. 'Sounds great. I think I have an addictive personality. My willpower isn't that great either, so I need all the help I can get.'

'Well, give these a try and come back and see me in about a month.'

'Thanks.' She took the prescription. 'It's just so hard, you know? When you want something so bad and you know what you have to do to achieve it, but you just can't bring yourself to do it… It seems so big. Too hard. Scary. It's easy to give in and not try, right? The easier road?'

He stared at her and nodded. 'Maybe everything that's worth having is worth fighting for?'

Brooke smiled. 'It is. It truly is. Thanks, Dr Prior.'

And she was gone.

Daniel thought of her words and then his own.

He knew staying away from Stacey and Jack was the easier road. The safer road. But he also knew that they were the type of people worth fighting for.

He just knew he didn't have it in him to do the fighting.

It was Hannah, the advanced nurse practitioner, who told Stacey about the house for sale.

She knew she had to find somewhere. There was definitely no way she could stay at the annexe—it was too distracting. Just the other night she'd been standing at the kitchen sink, washing a few dishes, and hadn't been able to help but notice Daniel doing the same thing. She'd begun to stare at him. Aware of the vast space between them that she felt unable to cross. Wondering what he was thinking. Whether he was struggling with this just as much as she was.

She had begun to dream of him now, and it was frustrating to have him so near and yet so far.

And then later, after she'd put Jack to bed, she'd grabbed herself a nice glass of wine and happened to notice Daniel in his garden, on his patio, head down, reading a book. How long he'd been there she didn't know, but wouldn't you know it? He glanced up and looked at the annexe right at that moment. She'd jumped back out of view, in case he caught her looking, and then frantically worried about whether he'd seen her watching him or not!

So, no, staying at the annexe was too difficult. But now that she was looking around the completed show home at the new development being built on the outskirts of Greenbeck, she wasn't sure how she'd feel about leaving it either.

The show home was beautiful. As all the houses obviously would be. The best interior decorators had clearly played their hands here. Everything was tasteful, yet somehow decadent, and the agent had allowed her to look around by herself, after he'd given her a detailed tour.

It would make someone a lovely home, but was it the right sort of place for her and Jack?

She sucked in a breath as she stood in one of the bedrooms of the house and looked out across the building site. The houses were in various states of construction and there were workmen everywhere. She tried to imagine it as a new estate. With all the families that would eventually move in. All the new patients who would ask to be taken on at the surgery.

Could she live here?

There were designs in the plans showing a community park in the centre, with a playground for little ones, which would be nice. And the developers were clearly trying to keep it as green as they could as they intended to plant lots of new trees, too, and create a rewilding centre to encourage butterflies and bees and local wildlife, which was excellent.

But was it home?

She was biting her lip, worrying about what to do, when the agent came running up the stairs shouting for her.

'Dr Emery?'

'Yes?'

'I'm sorry to bother you, but we might be in need of your expertise.'

She frowned. 'How do you mean?'

'One of the carpenters has had an accident. There's a hand injury, I believe. Any chance you could take a look?'

She nodded, smiled. 'Sure. Of course.'

This happened a lot when she went out. If people knew she was a doctor, and there was an incident, she was often called. She had no equipment with her, and she wasn't at the surgery, so she wasn't sure how much help she'd be, but...

She followed the agent through the front doors and he led her to a Portakabin to the left of the new estate, where a young man sat with his hand wrapped in a towel.

'What happened?'

'I tripped over some lumber and put my hands out to stop the fall. I landed on a saw. I'm sure it's superficial. Looks a lot worse than it is. I've told these guys I'm fine.'

She smiled. 'Let me be the judge of that. Can I have a look?'

He nodded and she unwrapped the towel and found quite an injury across the base of the man's palm. Another inch or two and the serrated edge of the saw would have cut into his wrist, where all the delicate and important nerves and arteries ran. As it was, he'd need the wound to be cleaned and he would require stitches.

'You can feel me touching you here?' she asked. 'And here?' She lightly grazed his palm and fingers with her own.

'Yeah.'

She checked his capillary refill. That looked fine. 'I'm not sure you'll need plastic surgery or a hand surgeon, but you do need to go to hospital for stitches.'

He frowned. 'You sure?'

'The wound needs to be cleaned properly, for a start. Are you up on your tetanus shots?'

'I don't know.'

'Well, you'll need that to be checked too.'

'You can't do it for me at the surgery?'

'We're not a minor injuries unit, I'm afraid. We don't do walk-ins. We're not equipped for that.'

'Okay. All right. Thanks, Doc.'

'You're welcome.'

She headed for home, armed with a brochure for the new houses, and as she walked down the side of Daniel's house to head to the annexe, where her gran was looking after Jack, she met Daniel, who was just bringing a bag of rubbish out to his bin.

She smiled awkwardly. 'Hi.'

'Hi.'

She saw his gaze drop down to the brochure and for a brief moment he looked puzzled, hurt. But then he brightened and forced a smile. 'House-hunting?'

She shrugged. 'Oh, you know… Keeping my options open. We can't impose on you for ever.'

'It's not a problem. I've told you—stay for as long as you need.'

'That's kind of you.'

'See anything you like?'

What?

She blushed, then realised he was talking about the houses on the new estate. 'Oh…erm…you know what these places are like. Expensive. Perfect. But are they home? I don't know. I think I'm looking for a place with a bit more…heart.'

He nodded. 'I get that.'

She stood looking at him a moment more, realising she couldn't think of one more word to say to him. But then she said, 'I'll be helping you judge that baby fancy dress competition at the village fete, after all.'

'Oh?'

'Yes.' She laughed self-consciously. 'Gran twisted that guy's arm. Walter?'

He nodded. 'Great. I look forward to it. How's Jack?'

'Doing well still. Back at school.'

'That's great. It's good for him to be back to normal.'

'It is!'

Another awkward silence descended and Stacey simply didn't know what to do. Staying away from Daniel had been hard, and she'd missed their casual chats. Even Jack had noticed that he hadn't seen Daniel for a while, and had asked her when they could next play football. And it was also hard standing there, looking at this man she felt so many things for, pretending that everything was fine and that they were just friends, when there was an underlying tension between them.

'You've remembered it's Shelby's birthday tomorrow?' he said.

Shelby…the phlebotomist at the practice. 'Yes.' She nodded.

'I've said I'll bring in a cake, but I'm not that great at baking and I only have a packet mix. Got any advice?'

Stacey laughed. 'Just add water, I think.'

Shelby's work friends were going to fit a small celebration for their work colleague during the lunch hour, when the surgery was closed. Pieces of paper with a selection of various food items written on them had been put into a hat and they'd each had to pull out one, telling them what they had to bring in. Stacey had got crisps and cheesy nibbles, packets of which were already in her cupboard. But she felt for Daniel, having drawn the duty of the cake. That was important—and was it fair to bring in a packet mix cake?

'I can help you,' she offered. 'You know...in the spirit of friendship. Because friends is what we are.' She smiled winningly.

Daniel nodded. 'You'd do that?'

She shrugged. 'Sure! Why not? Like you say, we're both adults. And it's just making a cake. It's not like we're getting engaged or anything.'

Daniel smiled and it warmed her heart. She liked making him smile. Liked to see the creases in the corners of his eyes, the way his eyes would light up.

'Well, I'd appreciate that. Thank you. Do you want to come over to mine, or should I come to yours?'

'I'll come to yours. Let me tell Gran and ask her to babysit Jack. Shall I come round at about eight? Is that okay?'

'Sure.'

'I'll bring what we'll need.'

Just after eight she stood at the French doors, holding a small bag, and she smiled as he let her in.

He'd changed his shirt, she noticed, and his hair was damp. Had he had a shower since seeing her? He certainly smelt good! A dazzling array of beautiful aromas was assailing her senses. Soap. Bodywash. Shampoo. Shaving balm? All wrapped up in the stunningly handsome parcel that was Dr Daniel Prior.

She swallowed, sensing suddenly that maybe this wasn't a great idea. But she'd promised to help, so she told herself to just soldier on. She had complete control of her body and she didn't have to do anything that would complicate matters.

They were friends.

Friends.

And friends were allowed to notice if someone had made an effort to smell nice. Friends were allowed to notice if another friend looked nice.

'So, what's in the bag?' he asked.

'Lots of cake-making goodies. What have *you* got?'

Daniel smiled. 'I had a good rummage in my cupboards. I found eggs, flour, some vanilla essence that's amazingly still in date—though how I come to have it, I can't remember—and some icing sugar.'

'Perfect! Come on, then! I've found a recipe I think we ought to try.'

She put her bag down on the counter and then picked up the recipe she'd printed off the internet earlier and showed it to him.

Daniel raised an eyebrow. 'That's…ambitious. A rainbow cake? Have you ever made one of those before?'

'Yes, I have. Let's amaze our work colleagues, shall we?'

They both washed their hands at the sink, drying them off on towels. Then Stacey set Daniel to work, weighing out ingredients, as she got out bowls and cake trays and the batch of food colourings she already had.

'You're sure about this? Can we really do six tiers?' Daniel asked.

'Of course we can? You afraid?' She smiled.

'A little.'

She laughed. 'We'll be fine.'

'Okay… Caster sugar, eggs, flour, milk—all in. Where's that vanilla extract?'

'Just here.' Stacey handed it to him as if she was passing him a scalpel and he was performing surgery.

He smiled at her and added a few drops.

'Mixer.'

She passed him the electric handheld mixer and he placed it in the mix and turned it on.

'Is your gran okay staying with Jack?'

'Yes. She's happy to wait for me to get back. He'll be fine.'

When he'd finished, she helped him pour the mixture into three bowls and then started playing alchemist, adding red, orange and yellow food colouring to each of and mixing well.

'This is fun!' Daniel said. 'Much better than me trying to half-ass my way through making a boring sponge and burning it.'

'You don't bake very often?'

'No. Not really. Penny always used to bake, though. She enjoyed it. She was always producing stuff for the village fete's bake sale.'

'Maybe we should do something for that, too, then? Join forces? Combine and conquer? I quite fancy winning a rosette.' She smiled as she added a little more yellow to the mix.

'You don't think it'll get tongues wagging if we enter a joint cake?'

'I live in your back garden. I work with you. We're both single. If you haven't realised that tongues are already wagging then there's no hope for you.'

He laughed. 'You're right.'

'Okay, let's get these three in the oven and make up another batch of mixture for the green, blue and purple layers.'

When all the cakes had been cooked, and were out cooling on racks, they began to make the icing, mixing sugar, cream cheese and butter until they had a nice thick consistency.

'We can layer them now?' asked Daniel.

'First we need to check the cakes are cool enough. If they're still hot, the icing mix will melt and we'll end up with a collapsed cake.'

'Okay. You're the boss.'

She smiled at him. 'In this kitchen, maybe.'

Stacey held the layers as Daniel began to ice them and stick them together. They worked well, laughing and giggling every time icing got smeared across their hands and fingertips. It was a messy business.

'Now I understand why I'm a doctor and not a plasterer,' he said.

'Interior decorators across the land are grateful.'

He turned and smiled at her, laughing. 'Just hold that bit still.'

They were close. Her arms almost entwined with his as he tried to get at all the curves of the cake. It was exciting being this close to him and she was enjoying it. They were involved in their task and had a focus, so being close was so much easier.

As the cake grew taller with each layer it became messier and more funny, and by the time they'd finished icing the cake they were both laughing so hard at how much mess they'd made, they'd completely forgotten their awkwardness of earlier.

Stacey put the cake in the fridge and turned to survey

the mess. 'Better get this place cleaned up, I suppose... I'd hate the landlord to think I didn't clean up after myself.'

'Let me help you.'

Within ten minutes the kitchen was clean again, and all the dishes and bowls were in the dishwasher.

Stacey finished wiping down a countertop, happy that it was all done.

She turned to look at Daniel. 'All done!'

'You've missed a bit.'

'Where?' she looked around, not seeing anything.

Daniel took a step forward and she turned back and met his gaze. And that was when she realised he was concentrating hard on her face.

'You have a bit of flour just here,' he said softly, raising his hand to touch the smear she had on her chin. He held her face gently and, using his thumb, gently wiped it off. His concentration was intense. So much so, she almost couldn't breathe.

He was standing so close...gazing down at her mouth, her lips, his thumb slowly stroking her skin, every brush a scintillating delight.

She looked up at his eyes and knew in that moment she was helpless before him. She wanted this man. She had been fighting her instincts over him since the first moment she'd seen him run into The Buttered Bun. She'd known then that he was a danger. A threat to her equilibrium. And yet here she stood in his kitchen. Having just made a birthday cake with him. Having just laughed and flirted her way through an hour with him.

And now? Now he was close, smelling delicious, looking intense and broody and dark-eyed. And by God she wanted to see if he tasted as good as he looked!

But maybe he didn't want to make a move? They'd almost

kissed before and look at what had happened. Maybe he didn't want that awkwardness again—because why would he? Maybe he was waiting for her permission before he made a move?

So, with her heart pounding, with her blood racing hot and needy through her veins, she reached up to him, resting her hands upon his chest, going onto tiptoe, and brought her lips to his.

It had been so long since she'd last kissed someone! Since she'd last been made to feel she was someone special. That she was important and someone other than a mother or a doctor. That she was a woman. A woman with needs and desires.

Daniel saw her. She knew he did. And the feel of his mouth upon hers was sending fireworks up into the sky between the two of them. Her nerve-endings were alight with need. Her body was pressing against the long, solid length of him. Now his hands were in her hair and he made a soft growling noise in the back of his throat... And, oh, that made her want him even more!

He pushed her back against the kitchen counter and she moaned with pleasure as his hands began to roam her body. Everywhere he touched lit up like a beacon, and then suddenly he was lifting her onto the counter and she was wrapping her legs around him, urging him closer.

It was as if time had slowed. As if the rest of the world had fallen away to nothing and all that existed was her and Daniel.

She felt him. Tasted him. Consumed him.

All she could think of in those moments was *him*.

Blood pounding. Heart thumping. Breath racing.

She was hungry for him after starving herself of his attention for so long. After being so close to him for so long, but not being allowed to touch. To enjoy. To explore.

Now she could.

Stacey moaned in delight as his hands moved over her body, as his tongue danced with hers, and she plummeted into a world of longing and desire.

It had been so long since she'd been with anyone. There'd been no one since she'd had Jack. One or two dates, but nothing had ever come of them. She'd been too afraid to allow anything to get that far. It had been dinners. Drinks. Maybe a peck on the cheek at the end of the date. Perhaps a quick kiss on the lips, if she'd really liked them. But she'd never let it get any further. She'd kept putting on the brakes. Telling them *It's me, not you* and letting them down gently. Her world had been turned upside down by the failure of a romantic relationship and she'd been so terrified of taking anything further.

But with Daniel…

She reached for his belt, struggling with the buckle, getting frustrated, laughing when Daniel had to help her. Their lips met again as she unzipped him and took him in her hand, thrilling at his low growl. And then he was reaching up beneath her skirt to remove her underwear, pulling it off in one swift move and pulling her towards him. And when he thrust himself into her she gasped aloud and clutched him tight, allowed herself to fall completely under his spell.

When had sex ever felt like this? This need to consume, to devour, to take everything a man had to offer?

Her breathing quickened. She arched against him, felt his lips at her throat, his hot breath on her neck as he nibbled and sucked and licked, and then his lips met hers once again. He breathed her name and it was the sexiest thing she had ever heard.

A small voice in the back of her head questioned what she was doing... If this was right... If this was sensible... But she quashed it in an instant because she really didn't want to hear it. It was nonsense. Of course it was right. How could something that felt so good, be wrong?

It was only afterwards, when he'd made her come spectacularly and reached his own climax, that she stilled and gathered her breath, and her senses and the little voice got louder.

She was still entangled in him, but her brain was clearing, sense and reality beginning to intrude.

And she was terrified of what she was thinking.

There was an awkward dressing moment. Almost as if neither of them could believe what they had done.

Daniel helped her find her underwear and helped her slide it back on in a gentlemanly manner, his fingertips grazing her calves and then her thighs, until his hands were on her hips and he was gazing into her eyes again.

Even now—because it was him—she felt that she could throw caution to the wind and go for it all over again. But her mind was not so completely overcome by lust, and she remembered that her gran was waiting for her to get back to the annexe.

'I'd better go. Gran's expecting me.'

He grazed her lips with his and sighed, nodding. 'I know. Are we...okay?'

She nodded, straightening her clothes, running her hands through her hair, hoping to make herself look less...ravished. 'Do I look presentable?'

Daniel smiled. 'Of course. Always.'

She looked at him for a moment. 'I'll see you at work tomorrow?'

'Yes.' His eyes darkened as she walked away.

At the door, she turned, faced him. 'Don't forget to bring the cake.'

'I won't.'

She was searching his face, trying to decipher what she saw on it, and she read guilt in his eyes. Of course he'd feel that way. She was probably the first woman he'd slept with since losing his wife. At least, she hoped she was. Because now that she thought about it she realised that in their desperate need for each other they hadn't used a condom. But he didn't look the type to sleep around. What she knew of him told her the same thing. He was a decent guy. No fly-by-night. No gigolo. No player.

He was a gentleman. A gentleman who could make her heart race so fast she thought it might explode.

I'm on the pill. It should be fine.

She said goodbye and made it back to the annexe, feeling guilty, as if she'd been out on the town past her bedtime.

Her gran was waiting for her by the front door. 'Oh! Stacey! I was beginning to get worried about you. Everything okay?'

'Yep! Good. All good.'

'The cake went well?'

'Perfectly. I think Shelby will be very pleased.'

'Well, you look happy—though I'm sure that's more to do with Daniel than any baking you might have done.'

She blushed. 'Whatever do you mean?'

Her gran tilted her head to one side. 'Oh, come on. I know you like him. Don't you think I haven't noticed how you change when you talk about him?'

'I don't change! What on earth are you going on about?'

'Your voice! Your voice changes when you say his name… *Daniel*. Like he's someone special.'

'He's my landlord! And a work colleague!'

'And…?' Gran grinned.

'And nothing! Now, I've kept you later than I should have, because we had to wait for the cakes to cool, but now I'm here you can get back to Grandad. Want me to order you a taxi?'

'Your grandad is already on his way to pick me up.'

'Okay. Well, thanks for babysitting Jack.'

'My pleasure. Now, what's that in your hair…?' Gran stepped forward to reach for something.

Stacey blushed and waited, nervous to see what it was.

It was a sprinkle. One of the many that she and Daniel had sprinkled on top of the cake when they'd finished icing it.

Her gran smiled knowingly.

It seemed to take an age before her grandad arrived, and Stacey was so happy when he did. Having her gran around, smiling at her as if she knew Stacey's secret, was getting to be a bit much.

When they'd gone, Stacey locked the door with a huge sigh, thinking over the last few hours.

She'd had active, vigorous, kitchen counter sex with Daniel! She'd never done anything like that before in her entire life! With Jerry, even at the beginning, they'd always been in a bedroom, but she'd considered her sex-life quite fine, thank you very much.

But with Daniel…

Stacey opened Jack's bedroom door to check on him quietly, and saw that he was sound asleep. She closed his door and headed for her own room. She brushed her teeth in the ensuite bathroom and then headed to bed, after getting into the tee shirt and shorts that she liked to wear to sleep in.

She opened her bedside drawer to take out the contraceptive pills that she took to help with her heavy periods and realised that the days didn't match up. If this packet was right, she'd not taken a pill last night, nor the night before that!

Feeling heat rise in her cheeks, she took the pill for today and told herself she'd be fine. There was no other choice. She couldn't take the morning-after pill as she was allergic to the main ingredient, levornogestrel. She'd found that out after a condom had broken early in her relationship with Jerry. Not a pleasant few days... Symptoms-wise or Jerry-wise...

Besides, loads of people had sex all the time and didn't get pregnant. She and Daniel hadn't been careful, but technically she was on the pill and...

I'll be fine. Anything else isn't worth thinking about.

Daniel lay in bed, unable to sleep, his gaze resting on his and Penny's wedding photo. In it, they stood within the arched doorway of the church, holding hands and looking at the photographer. They were both beaming with happiness, absolutely sure that their marriage was going to be for ever. That they were going to be different. That their marriage was going to make it until they were old and grey and giving interviews to the local paper on the secret of a successful marriage.

They'd even joked about it once. He'd told Penny how much he loved her and how, in the future, he'd tell anyone willing to listen that the secret to a good marriage was to be loyal and honest, no matter what. And he'd truly believed that. Loyalty and honesty mattered the most to him, and even after that drunk driver had run them off the road he'd believed he would always be loyal to his wife. Even after her death.

But it appeared that wasn't true at all.

And Daniel was struggling with that.

He'd never imagined himself with anyone else. He really hadn't. And then Stacey had come into his life. Working with him. Living in his annexe. And she was perfect and beautiful and, God damn it, she'd got under his skin!

And tonight... Neither of them had planned that. It had been unexpected and surprising and off-the-charts scorching hot! His senses, his logic—all had gone out of the window just from touching her and tasting her. He'd fought his attraction to her for so long... To finally be able to indulge himself in how she felt and tasted, how she moaned and gasped and hungered for him in turn, had been...

There were no words.

But all he could think about now was that he'd been with another woman. Something he'd never imagined when he'd wed Penny. They should have been together for ever, but death had parted them. She and Mason had been taken too soon and he'd been left behind. Unable to help them. Unable to protect them. And surely because of that he didn't deserve to find happiness with anyone else? Doing so would be a betrayal of his promise to his wife.

But did it matter that he'd broken his promise? Who knew about it, after all, except for himself and Stacey? Others might be thrilled for him to find happiness with someone else. Genevieve and William would be, that was for sure.

We didn't use protection.

In the heat of the moment he just hadn't thought. What he had been doing with Stacey had just felt so right, so normal, so *necessary*, that his brain hadn't been telling him to remember to take precautions!

I'll check with her in the morning. See if she's on the pill, or something.

They were both doctors. They'd be sensible about this. As much as they could be *after* the act…

Rolling over, he turned away from the photo and stared up at the ceiling.

So far that morning Stacey had treated a case of postnatal depression, a fungal toenail, dealt with a referral request for a knee issue and a case of scarlet fever. There was a knock at her door and Daniel slipped in.

Instantly, she blushed, then smiled, standing to greet him. 'Good morning.'

He came to her. Stopped. Seemed unsure as to how to greet her, then decided on a brief kiss on her cheek.

'Good morning. How are you today?'

She nodded. 'I'm good. You?'

'I'm fine.'

'Good.'

Having him in the room with her, standing this close, it was as if her fingers were inching forward to entwine with his…

'I…er…thought that after last night I ought to check that we're…covered.'

Was he blushing? She liked it that he was. It was endearing.

'I'm on the pill, if that's what you were asking?'

He gave a brief embarrassed laugh. 'Yeah. I was. Phew! Okay…'

Should she tell him that she'd missed a couple of tablets? What would that garner but his stress to deal with alongside her own? There was no point in stressing him out. Not unless there was something to stress about, anyway.

'I haven't been with anyone since my wife,' he said. 'So you don't have to worry about STDs.'

'That's good to know. And I've only ever been with Jerry, so...'

He nodded. Seemed happy with her answer, too. It was a minefield these days... STDs were on the rise, especially among younger people. Diseases like gonorrhoea and chlamydia were not worried about as much as they used to be because there were medications available to treat them.

It was not something she wanted to consider.

'I don't think either of us needs the complication of an unexpected pregnancy or an uncomfortable visitor,' he said.

'No! Absolutely not!' she agreed, smiling as he pressed his forehead against hers.

He looked deeply into her eyes and then, in an instant, they were kissing again.

Heat rose in her body as she reawakened to his touch and attention. Every touch, every stroke, every caress of his hands made her come alive. And the fact that they were doing this at work... In secret... As if it was forbidden... Made it even better!

She'd lain in bed last night, telling herself not to be so stupid as to think that it meant something. It was a fling—that was all. She couldn't stop herself when she was with Daniel. It was impossible! She was drawn to him like a moth to a flame. Like a bee to a flower. Like a sunflower to the sun. She had to go to him. Turn to him. Embrace him. It was as if she couldn't get enough of him.

It was only the knock on her door that made them suddenly break apart, guiltily and breathlessly, creating space between them. Stacey sat down behind her desk and Daniel stood on the opposite side, as if he'd just popped in for a chat.

'Come in?' she said.

It was Hannah, the advanced nurse practitioner. 'Oh, hi. Sorry… Am I interrupting?'

'No! Not at all!' Stacey hoped she wasn't blushing. 'How can I help?'

'I've got a patient who's come in with a rash on her chest, and I can feel a lump. Would you come and check it out for me?'

Stacey looked at her morning list. Her next patient hadn't arrived yet, so she had time. 'Sure!'

Daniel smiled. 'I'll catch you later? At lunch?'

Stacey nodded. 'You will.'

Shelby's birthday party went brilliantly. She'd clearly had no idea that the other staff had planned a celebration for her, and she cried some happy tears, when she saw the spread they'd put on for her.

'And that cake! Who made that? Was it you, Gayle?' Shelby asked one of the ladies on Reception, who was renowned for making cakes and bringing them in as treats for everyone.

'No, not me.'

'Then who?'

Daniel raised his hand. 'I made it. With help from Stacey.'

Shelby looked happily surprised. 'Who knew you had this in you?'

Daniel was pleased to have put a smile on Shelby's face. He glanced at Stacey and gave her a wink, before looking over at Zach, who had caught him winking.

Zach smiled knowingly and raised an eyebrow at Daniel.

He turned away from his friend's knowing look and passed Shelby the cake knife, leading the group in a rousing chorus of 'Happy Birthday'.

When it was over, she cut into the tower of cake and

squealed. 'A rainbow cake! Oh, my God, this is awesome!'
Shelby threw her arms around Daniel and gave him a huge
hug, before turning and hugging Stacey. 'You two are awesome!'

Stacey smiled.

Daniel was feeling great. He'd missed this. He'd not realised how much he'd withdrawn from everyone over the
last couple of years. It was as if his pain and grief had isolated him from everyone—but not because they'd turned
away from him. They'd tried to help. He was the one who
had kept everyone at arm's length.

Before, when there'd been birthday parties at work, or
other celebrations, he'd given muted congratulations, raised
his mug in a toast and then slipped quietly back into his consulting room to be by himself. Seeing others so happy when
he still hurt had been overwhelming. He hadn't hated it that
they were happy. It had just been that their happiness made
him sad, because he'd known he'd never be happy again.

And then he'd made a connection. Allowed himself to
get close to Stacey and Jack. And by doing so he'd started
doing other small things that were reintegrating him into
society. He'd made a cake for a work colleague. Done it with
Stacey. And seeing the joy of something he'd done showing on Shelby's face in absolute delight... Well, that made
him feel wonderful.

To begin with he had felt as if Stacey was a wrecking
ball. Breaking down his carefully constructed walls while
he kept trying to rapidly rebuild them and protect himself. But he couldn't protect himself from her, and that was
what made being with her so terrifying and exciting all at
the same time. Being with her had brought him back to life
again, making him feel he could partake in other people's
happiness again—because *he* was happy again.

All because of her.

And then there was Jack... Dear, wonderful Jack. A little boy who'd been through his own trauma and had begun to heal here.

He'd like to think he'd had a hand in that. That in some way he'd helped Jack feel he had another friend. He'd played football with him, fixed things with him, taught him to use a hammer. They'd gardened together, read stories together, and most of all they'd *talked*. And laughed. And enjoyed each other's company. Something Daniel himself had never thought he'd be able to do.

Yes, he felt guilty, but that was natural after all he'd been through. It didn't mean he didn't love Penny. Or that he would forget her and Mason. How could he? That could never happen.

But maybe now he was beginning to accept that perhaps he didn't have to be alone for the rest of his life?

He looked at Stacey across the room, chatting with Hannah. She was a beautiful person, inside and out. He was so glad he'd let out his annexe to her and Jack. He had been emboldened by doing so and it made his life better. All because of them.

He went to stand by her. 'The cake's a hit. Thank you very much.'

She gave him a secret nudge with her arm. 'You're very welcome.'

Shelby was handing out slices of cake to everyone and Daniel had to admit it did look great. All those colours! It was perfect. And he would never have managed it without Stacey. Without her, there might be a questionable Victoria Sponge sitting on the counter instead, most likely with burnt edges hidden under icing sugar. But because of what he and

Stacey had created everyone was so happy. So delighted. And he liked the feeling it engendered in him.

Maybe *everything* that he and Stacey did together would bring happiness?

'Only a couple more weeks until the village fete,' said Gran, as she and Stacey sat together at her grandparents' kitchen table having a cup of tea together the next weekend.

'I know! Are you entering any of the competitions?' Stacey asked.

'I've got a plum and ginger jam I might enter. And I know your grandad is going to enter one of his giant marrows. He came second place last year—do you remember me telling you?'

'I remember the newspaper cutting you sent, yes.'

Outside in the back garden Jack was playing football with Daniel on the lawn.

'Those two get along brilliantly, don't they?' said Gran, conversationally.

Stacey watched them. Jack was grinning—beaming—playing happily with Daniel, who at that moment in time was trying to dribble the ball past Jack to get towards the goal.

'They do. It's nice to see him so happy.'

'Do you mean Jack? Or Daniel?'

Stacey turned to look at her gran, who had one of those weird, happy but knowing looks on her face. 'What do you mean?'

'Oh, come now… I've told you before. It's perfectly obvious to me that you and Daniel have very strong feelings for one another.'

Stacey shook her head, laughing, and turned away. 'Don't be silly. We're just friends.'

'Don't think I haven't noticed how he looks at you. How he likes to stand close to you. How you touch each other when you think no one's looking.'

'Gran!'

Her gran smiled. 'It's *lovely*, darling. That poor man has been through hell in the last few years, and to see him smile the way you make him smile… That warms my heart…it really does. He deserves happiness and so do you. You've both been through the mill.'

Stacey wanted to protest, but what was the point? Gran saw everything. Maybe she ought to set herself up at the village fete with a crystal ball?

'I do like him, yes, but I've got to be cautious, too.'

'Because of Jack?'

She nodded.

'Daniel loves Jack. Look at them together. It's good for him to be around my great-grandson. It brings him to life again. I understand your caution, but don't let it hold you back, dear. Knowing Daniel, no matter what happened between the two of you, that man would be there for your boy for ever.'

'You think so?' Stacey asked wistfully, watching the two of them once again.

Gran was right. They *were* good together. But Stacey had had her life ruined once before by a romantic relationship in the workplace going wrong. She wouldn't be able to bear it if it happened again and she lost everything. Because she was the interloper here. Even though she'd grown up in Greenbeck, she'd left. Daniel had been here for years. This place felt like his. Her work colleagues were his. Her friends were his. If something were to go wrong, would she lose everything all over again and be forced to move away?

I couldn't. Jack is happy at school and his happiness has to come first.

'I do,' said her gran. 'He's an honourable man.'

Yes, she thought. *He is.*

Daniel was nothing like Jerry. If something bad were to happen between them she couldn't imagine Daniel trying to drive her out of the practice, the way Jerry had. And besides, she was sick of running. Greenbeck was where she wanted to start putting down roots.

Outside, Jack scored a goal and came running back towards Daniel, arms in the air, yelling with delight. Daniel gave him a high five, then whirled her son around in the air, celebrating with him.

She smiled. Seeing them together made her happy.

After their football, Jack and Daniel lay back on the grass, breathing heavily and staring at the white clouds drifting by overhead.

'That one looks like a dog,' Jack said, pointing.

'It does! A little terrier. What about that one?' It was Daniel's turn to point.

'A kite?'

'Yep! You know, I made a kite once…'

Jack turned to look at him. 'You *made* one? How did you do that? Could you teach me?'

'Sure! I got taught at my Scout group when I was your age.'

'What else do they do at Scouts?'

'Well…lots of things. They all work together and have fun earning different badges. First aid, cooking, sewing, woodwork, metalwork… Anything you can imagine. It's fun!'

'I like the sound of that.'

'Well, there's a local Beaver Scouts group here in Green-beck. Maybe you should ask your mum about it?'

'I'm not sure…'

'Are you worried about the other children?' he asked gently.

'A bit.'

'Believe you me, there's no bullying in Scouts. Everyone works together. The leaders work hard to create an atmosphere that is friendly and kind, and everyone looks out for one another. You're a group. A team. I think it'd be great for building up your confidence.'

'You think so?'

'I do! You've already made such huge strides here. I really think you could take on the world if you wanted! Do anything!'

Jack smiled, and Daniel liked seeing him do so. He truly was building his confidence and growing his friendship groups at school. Being involved in the Scouts could surely only help that.

'Want me to talk to your mum about it?' he asked.

Jack nodded.

'Okay. Ready for the second half?' He grabbed the football.

Jack laughed and got to his feet.

They all walked home together. It was a nice cool evening and perfect for a stroll. Jack was ahead of them, bouncing his football as he walked.

'You've done such a lot for Jack,' Stacey said. 'Being his friend…'

He smiled. 'Well, he's helped me, too.'

'He has?'

'Of course. Being around a kid his age again… I wasn't sure I'd be able to handle it, to tell you the truth.'

'Because of your son?'

He nodded, his eyes darkening.

'You must miss him terribly.'

'I do. Sometimes so much it hurts. And then I feel guilty, because being with you two makes me smile. And sometimes when I'm with you I forget about the heartache and the pain, but when you're gone again I remember and feel worse.'

She nodded in understanding. 'Life's a roller coaster. It's fine when you're on a high, but there are always those drops, reminding you that there's a long way to fall if you're not careful.'

'Are *we* being careful, do you think?'

'How do you mean?'

'In what we're doing? Are we taking a risk in thinking we can be happy?'

'We *are* happy, aren't we? When we're together?'

Daniel nodded in assent. 'We are. I know we are. But I also know I'm waiting for that fall you mentioned. Relationships are tough, and the longer you're in one, the more complications arrive.'

'Are you saying you want to take a step back?'

He stopped walking, turned to look at her. 'No. Most definitely not. Are you?'

She smiled. 'No.'

They began walking again, watching Jack up ahead, keeping an eye on him.

'I guess I'm saying I just don't want to get hurt. And I don't want to hurt either of you two.'

'Ditto. So, let's make a pact, then. If there's an issue we talk to one another about it. We don't brood. We don't fret.

We're open with one another. We face it. Talk it through like adults.'

Daniel nodded. 'Sounds good to me.'

'Shake on it?' She held out her hand.

He laughed and shook it.

Jack had been in bed for ages and Daniel was watching the end of a movie with Stacey. They were sitting together on the couch, and halfway through Daniel had reached out for her hand and taken it in his.

It had felt right, and the entire time he'd been sitting there, next to her, he'd wanted to hold her.

The movie was an action-adventure film, and although it was good, it wasn't as wonderful as it was just to sit there and be holding Stacey's hand, feeling as if he was part of something special. Something new and exciting and vibrant.

When the credits rolled, she laid her head upon his shoulder and relaxed into him.

He savoured the moment, closing his eyes and just enjoying it. Eventually she lifted her head and turned to look at him. Her green eyes bright and shining, she asked, 'Do you want to stay over?'

He did. Very much so.

'What about Jack?'

'If you leave before he wakes in the morning he'll never know.' she said enticingly, reaching up to pull his lips towards hers.

The kiss was electric. Even more so than it had been before. Full of promise and secrets and delights.

He pulled back for a breath, switched off the TV with the remote and then stood, leading her towards her bedroom, closing the bedroom door softly behind them.

For a moment he just looked at her. Taking her in. Those

tumbles of red hair, dark in the shadows. Her green eyes, looking up at him with so much want and anticipation. Suddenly he couldn't wait a moment longer and he was in her arms. Stumbling towards the bed. Falling backwards so that she lay atop him. Pulling her close, deepening the kiss, struggling to remove clothes and feel the heat of skin and intimate connection.

Barriers removed, he rolled her over onto her back and pinned her arms above her head as his lips went to her throat. She gasped, arching up to meet him, whispering his name.

He couldn't deny the heat between them. It was as if they were made for each other. The fire in his belly burned for her. The scorching furnace of his blood raged in its intensity to light up every single nerve-ending in his body. And where they connected, skin to skin, he imagined sparks of electricity between them.

He needed her so much! Had yearned for her so much these last couple of days, wondering if they'd get to be together again. Something so right could never be wrong.

Stacey was perfect, and even though he yearned to be within her he held off for as long as he could. Waiting. Teasing. Delighting in watching her urge him on.

They were as quiet as they could be, but her gasps and heavy breathing were enough, and finally, when he could wait no longer, he slid into her and thrust long, hard and slow. He watched her face, kissing her, building his pace, until she erupted beneath him and he rode her wave with his own.

His lips returned to hers. A kiss. A breath. Another kiss. It was as if he didn't want to let her go. Didn't want to be not touching her. But he rolled to her side and pulled her close, smiling with satisfaction as she cuddled into him. She draped her leg over his and let out a delicious sigh.

They didn't need to say anything.

Their bodies had said everything they needed to say to each other.

And once he was sure she was asleep he closed his eyes and drifted off into a dreamworld of his own.

Each night after that Daniel shared her bed, getting up at around six a.m. to creep from the annexe and return to his own home.

Those moments were agony for Stacey. Their nights were steamy, their dreams dreamy, but when her gentle alarm woke them in the early hours they had to leave the little fantasy world they'd built and part, returning to reality.

Daniel would groan at having to leave her bed, and sometimes, unable to bear him going, she would grab him and pull him back onto the bed, kiss him and hold him and stroke him in places that she knew would drive him wild.

But always he would stop her and tell her, 'I have to go. Jack will be awake soon.'

And then she'd let him go.

They were doing the right thing. Of course they were. She didn't want to give Jack any hopes about Daniel being a permanent fixture in their lives. It was bad enough as it was. Jack *adored* Daniel. They played football and badminton together all the time. Daniel made time for her son and she loved that. But sometimes she worried about what she was doing.

What if it all went wrong?

She couldn't help but be fatalistic. Every other relationship she'd had had gone bad. Why would this one be any different?

Only it *felt* different. She couldn't understand why, but did that difference mean that she could depend on it going well? She didn't know, and so she was scared all the time. Waiting for the ball to drop. Waiting for something awful to go wrong and ruin everything.

Sometimes Daniel caught her having those dark moments.

'What's wrong?' he'd ask.

'I'm waiting for the bubble to burst.'

And he'd kiss her forehead, or her cheeks, or her lips, and stroke her face and comfort her.

'I don't know what the future holds for us. Let's just try to enjoy what we have right now.'

And she'd smile back and kiss him back, because he was right. If she spent all her time worrying about the future she'd never enjoy the present. And these rare moments of happiness were too good to miss or not appreciate. He was her special secret right now. And it was amazing.

For too long she'd been so stressed and worried about Jack. About how to make his life better. Moving all the way down the country in the hopes of finding a new life. In a place where they could both thrive. Daniel was making her feel that right now she could. That joy and contentment were possible for her. And that was too valuable for her to throw away.

As she drove into work one morning, she began to see preparations for the village fete. Bunting was being hung up all over the place—all around the village green, in front of the shops and the pub, and even at the surgery. People were working hard on making their gardens look nice, and flowers were in abundance everywhere she looked. Pink and purple. Roses and clematis. Hollyhocks, foxgloves and lupins. All standing proud and pretty.

And everyone seemed to have a smile.

Her first patient was coming in for a coil insertion—a young woman who'd had her second baby just over two months ago.

Phoebe Harrow entered the room with her baby asleep in a pushchair. 'Sorry. I couldn't get anyone to watch him. But he should sleep for another hour anyway.'

Stacey smiled. 'It's no problem.'

She went over with Phoebe the procedure that would take place, what to expect, and how to check that the intrauterine device was still in place afterwards. She described the side effects she might notice and told her how to deal with any discomfort or bleeding afterwards.

When Phoebe was happy with everything, Stacey sent a screen message through to Rachel, their HCA, to say that they were ready.

Rachel wheeled a small trolley through, draped with blue paper to protect the sterile field, and positioned it next to the examination bed after Phoebe lay down.

Stacey opened up Phoebe's vagina to take a good look at the cervix, and nodded to Rachel to unseal the packet that contained the IUD.

'Okay, nice steady breaths and try to relax.'

The IUD went in smoothly, which Stacey was glad of—and no doubt Phoebe too. There was a minimum amount of blood. When Rachel had left the room, Stacey taught her patient how to feel for the IUD and check that it was still in place.

'All good?'

'Perfect! Thank God that's over! I thought it would be much more painful than that. Now I can relax a little bit. I love my kids…but I don't want any more!' she said, and laughed as she stood to get dressed.

Stacey smiled as she removed her gloves and washed her hands in the small sink. 'Two can be a handful. How old is your other one?'

'Seven. Quite a gap, I know. Just as I got my life back— bingo! I was pregnant again. My surprise baby. But...' she pulled back the curtain and emerged from behind it, smiling at her baby '...he's so perfect I can't imagine life without him. Isn't that odd? Because I was terrified when I found out I was expecting again.'

'It must have been quite a surprise if you weren't trying.'

She shook her head. 'We weren't. And we were using protection. But sometimes those suckers just get through no matter what, huh?' She laughed again, and gently rocked the pushchair as her little one snuffled a bit.

Stacey nodded. 'What's meant to be will be. Now, re-member—you can take paracetamol if you need it. Any cramps or bleeding should soon stop, but you can always call us if you think there's an issue. I'll book you in for a check-up in about...four weeks? Just to make sure it's still in place and you're not having any problems.'

Phoebe nodded. 'Sounds great!'

Stacey went through the calendar on the computer and brought up her appointments for those days, finding an empty spot just before lunchtime.

'Does that date work for you?'

'Yes.'

She waved Phoebe and her surprise baby away and began to type up her notes. She was glad the insertion had gone smoothly, because she was starting to feel a little bit of a headache. Bending over and twisting at weird angles to in-sert the coil certainly hadn't helped! She felt better sitting back at her desk, but she opened a drawer, found her own packet of paracetamol and took a couple, just to stave off anything worse. She felt peckish, too, so whilst she had a couple of minutes she ate half the ham salad sandwich that she'd picked up earlier.

She'd eat the rest outside and enjoy a bit of sunshine at lunchtime…

Daniel saw her sitting outside on a bench by the village green. She sat there, eyes closed, face turned upwards to the sun, just enjoying the warmth and the beautiful day. For a brief moment he stood and looked at her, realising how much he felt for her.

He loved to see her happy and content.

He loved spending time with her and Jack.

And he wanted to spend more.

So, smiling, he crossed the road, holding up his hand to thank the driver who let him skip across the road, and walked across the verdant green grass to settle himself down on the bench next to her.

She opened her eyes and smiled when she saw it was him.

'Hey,' he said.

'Hey…'

'You looked so perfectly relaxed. I had to join you.'

'Why not? It's gorgeous here. Feel that sun… I missed that in Scotland. Don't get me wrong. Sometimes we had the most beautiful days. Just not that many. And when I popped out for lunch there wasn't a park or a green near the surgery, so I'd drag a chair outside and sit in the car park.'

He smiled. 'It's not the same, is it?'

She laughed. 'No. It's not.'

She blinked and watched him open up his packed lunch. A delicious aroma emerged.

'What have you got there?' she asked.

'Coronation chicken. Want one?'

'Ooh, yes, please!' She sat up straighter and he proffered her half the sandwich, which she devoured in seconds.

'Wow? Did you not pack yourself any lunch?'

'I did, but I ate most of it earlier. I was starving.'

'Long morning?'

'No. Perfectly ordinary. I was just hungry.'

He smiled. It got that way sometimes. 'Is it okay to come round again later?'

'Sure! I could do us some dinner. What do you fancy?'

'Anything is great. But I do have an ulterior motive.'

She raised an eyebrow. 'If it's to take advantage of my body again, I may just let you!'

He smiled. 'Understood. Actually, I wanted to talk to you about Jack.'

Her smile disappeared. 'Why? What's wrong?'

'Nothing's wrong. It's just we were talking the other day about him being a Beaver Scout. I told him I used to be one and he seemed interested. He asked me to talk to you about it.'

'He asked *you*? He didn't feel he could tell me himself?'

He could see she was hurt by this. 'He's getting on great at school, and he heard my stories about camping and activities with the Beavers and he wanted to give it a try. I said I'd ask you if I could take him. They do introductory visits. You don't have to pay for the first couple…just see if he likes it or not.'

'Oh.' She stared out across the grass towards the duck-pond. 'I should be glad. I know he's happy. Why do I feel like he's suddenly growing up?'

'Because you've been his rock all this time. He's only ever needed you. Now he's spreading his wings, as all little boys do.'

She nodded, forcing a brave smile. 'Okay. You can take him. Or maybe we should take him together?'

Now it was his turn to feel surprised. 'You're happy to do that?'

'Yes.'

'Okay. Let's do it.'

CHAPTER EIGHT

STACEY WAS SO incredibly nervous that her stomach actually felt queasy! She couldn't remember the last time she'd been so nervous!

Actually, I can. Jack's first day at Greenbeck Juniors and my first day at the surgery.

She would be leaving him. Letting him walk away and knowing he was in someone else's hands. She had trusted that the school would protect him, and now that trust would be placed with the Beavers leaders and all the other children.

Most she recognised from Jack's school, so hopefully that was a good sign. There were kids here that he already knew.

They were meeting in the Scout hut, which was situated down the road from the church. At the back of the hut was a long row of wooden benches. Stacey and Daniel sat there and watched.

She felt anxiety building in her throat as her son stood alone, not sure what he ought to be doing. Her desire to go to him was strong, but just as she was about to get up out of her seat and go and take his hand, tell him they could go home, his friend Sam saw him and pulled him into the throng. She heard a chorus of cheers at his arrival.

'See? Nothing to worry about,' said Daniel.

She smiled at him. 'I can't help it.'

He placed his hand on hers reassuringly. 'I can see that.

Try to picture yourself sunning yourself on that bench again, as you were the other day. Pretend that you're not actually in a small hall filled with loud children armed with whistles.'

She nodded, looking for Jack again. She saw him instantly. The only one not in a blue Beavers polo shirt. Seeing him involved and happy should be making her feel better, but her stomach was still churning slightly.

Wow! I really have got myself worked up.

She searched in her handbag and found an old packet of mints. She sucked on one and hoped it would help.

I'm probably just hungry, too.

It had been a long day and she was still yet to cook.

Stacey had wanted to impress Daniel with her culinary prowess and create a meal that would leave him asking for seconds and thirds, but at this rate they'd be calling into the chippy on the way home and getting something fast. She wasn't sure she had the patience, or enough mints, to hold off the hunger and the nausea.

It was a long hour and a half, but Jack had a whale of a time, and afterwards he bounced over towards Stacey and Daniel and asked if he could join straight away?

'We'll do it next week. I promise. Come on—you must be starving!'

Jack nodded, and skipped ahead to find the car.

'See? Nothing to worry about,' said Daniel, his hand in the small of her back as he followed her out, being careful not to let Jack see him touching her.

She was grateful that he was sensitive to that.

They got into the car and Jack babbled non-stop all the way to the chip shop and all the way home. The smell of fish and chips with salt and vinegar permeated the car, and Stacey was practically salivating by the time they made it inside and served up.

'Let's eat in the garden,' suggested Daniel.

So they made their way to his patio and sat down on his outdoor chairs and began to eat.

The food was delicious and really hit the spot! Soft, fluffy chips and meaty, thick fish in crunchy batter. She hadn't been sure she'd eat it all, but she did—very quickly—and washed it down with some orange juice that Daniel had prepared earlier and left in his fridge.

'Are you looking forward to the village fete?' he asked.

'I am! I haven't been to one since I left the village, but I have fond memories of them. I'm sure Jack will like them too, now that his confidence has grown and he's got some friends.'

'And the baby-judging?'

She groaned. 'Hmm... I'm not so sure. I didn't ask to do it—Gran volunteered me. But how do you judge *babies*? Aren't we supposed to say they're all wonderful? How do we go about picking a winner?'

Daniel shrugged. 'I don't know... Judge the outfit and not the child?'

'But even so...' She really didn't like the idea of it at all, and just the thought of it made her feel incredibly uncomfortable. 'And what about the parents? They're the ones with all the hopes! They're the ones thinking that their child is adorable and bound to win. And when they don't... I hope we don't get hated!'

'I'm sure we won't. Everyone knows it's just a bit of fun.'

She must still look ill at ease. Fidgety, maybe. Because Daniel asked, 'Want to go for a walk?'

She looked at him and nodded.

They set off into the village, taking with them a bag of peas for Jack to feed the ducks and the pair of swans that had taken up residence at the pond. She and Daniel stood back, watching him, and Daniel took the moment to slip his hand into hers.

She turned to look at him and smiled.

'Are you happy?' he asked.

'I am. Are you?'

He nodded. 'I am. If you'd told me a few months ago that my whole life would change with the arrival of a new GP at the practice I would have laughed and told you not to be so ridiculous.'

'And if you'd told me I would come back home and fall for another GP at the same practice I worked at, I would have done the same!'

He smiled. 'You've fallen for me.'

The ducks had surrounded Jack, quacking and waddling. Some were floating on the water, but most had clambered onto the grass to get closer to the little boy with the food. But his throwing handful after handful of peas meant he was soon about to run out, and when he did the birds all quacked their annoyance and one even pecked at his trainer.

Jack giggled and ran back to Stacey, who had by then slipped her hand out of Daniel's.

'Come on, let's walk.'

There was a public footpath that led through the village. To the south it ran into the New Forest, and to the north, just behind the surgery, it took them up the hill towards the castle ruins. Because Jack was with them, they decided to take the north path.

What started off as a nice, meandering walk, soon turned into quite an uphill trek! But Jack seemingly hardly noticed. He ran here and there, clambering over fallen trees and investigating clumps of mushrooms, then finding himself a nice stick. Daniel seemed to be tackling it easily too, but Stacey was huffing and puffing as her leg muscles burned.

'I thought I was fitter than this!' she breathed.

'Come on, Mummy!' Jack laughed, skipping ahead to a tree with a hollow trunk and investigating.

Daniel turned back to grin at her and she made a 'time out' sign with her hands and sat down on a fallen log. 'I just need five minutes...'

She sat there, her hands on her knees, breathing heavily, quite unable to believe that a simple walk had her out of breath like this! Normally she considered herself quite fit, but actually, when was the last time she'd gone to the gym? Or the swimming pool? Or partaken in any exercise that didn't involve her being naked with Daniel?

'We'll have to get you doing a bit more cardio,' he joked.

'Looks like it. I guess this is what you get for sitting down at work all day.'

Daniel laughed and held out his hand for her to take. 'Come on. I think Jack would like to reach the castle before dark.'

She smiled ruefully and accepted his hand, and soon they were off again, heading up to Castle Merrick.

From what she remembered, the castle had stood for centuries, looking down over what had originally been a small hamlet called Greenbeck. It had grown into a village sometime around the eighteenth century.

The castle itself had been built for Lord Edwin Merrick, a man who'd had three wives, losing the first two in childbirth and outliving the third after she'd died of some sort of respiratory illness. Of his five children, four had been killed in battle and the fifth, the only girl, had entered a nunnery. So the Merrick line had ended. The castle had fallen into disrepair and was today a sightseeing attraction, with a nearby gift shop and coffee house.

These were both now closed, due to it being so late in the

evening, but the castle ruins were there for anyone to have a look around, at any time of the day or night.

Now that the uphill climb was over, Stacey's leg muscles were feeling a bit better. If only the same could be said for her body in general. She felt exhausted! The trek up the hill from the village had really done her in, and all she wanted to do was just lie down and take a nap!

But Jack was excitedly exploring the ruins, and Daniel still had her hand in his, so she allowed herself to be pulled along—even if she did keep yawning.

Daniel turned to her and grinned. 'Tired?'

'You bet. Must be all these nights you've kept me awake with your physical demands.' She smiled, stroking his face when she knew Jack wouldn't see.

'Complaining?' he asked, with mock hurt.

Stacey laughed. 'Not at all! It's one of the best ways to lose sleep, if we're going to rank reasons for a lack of it.'

'Agreed.'

He took a look around and then pulled her close. Her hips pressed to his as he took her face in his hands and moved in for a kiss.

It was illicit and exciting! And even though she knew she really ought to not be doing this, in case Jack saw them, she didn't have it in her to push him away. She wanted him. All of him! And a kiss would have to be enough.

When they broke apart, grinning at each other, they re-alised that Jack was standing next to them, looking up at them quizzically.

Stacey blushed and rapidly stepped away from Daniel, pasting a smile upon her face and trying to act innocent. 'Have you seen the portcullis gate, Jack?'

But Jack wasn't stupid, and he refused to be redirected. 'Are you my mummy's boyfriend?' he asked Daniel.

Daniel glanced at her. Clearly she was the one who needed to answer, but what to say? She didn't want to lie to Jack, now that he had caught them kissing like that.

'Well…erm…what would you say if he was?'

Jack just shrugged. 'I'd be fine with it.'

Stacey smiled at the nonchalant way in which he'd answered and then looked up at Daniel, who was letting out a breath of relief and smiling himself. *Wow.* That could have gone so many ways! And yet it didn't bother Jack as much as she'd thought the news of a man in her life would!

'Okay… Well, we're just seeing how it goes, all right?'

'Okay!' And he ran off to explore some more.

Stacey turned to Daniel. 'Well, that went better than I expected it would.'

'He does know me. It's not like I'm a stranger.'

'I guess… And you do spend an awful lot of time with him. I know he likes you a lot.'

'Well, that's important to me. Almost as much as it is that *you* like me a lot.'

She smiled at him. 'I do.'

'How much?'

She blushed and turned away, not really looking where she was going, not really aware of her surroundings, and tripped over a protruding rock.

Down she went, hands out to break her fall. She felt her head connect with the ground, felt a sharp pain to the front of her face, and when she felt Daniel's arms around her, helping her into a sitting position, blood began to drip down her forehead.

'You're bleeding!' Daniel squatted down in front of her, his face full of worry and concern.

A strong ache was blooming in her head and she winced, trying to stem the blood.

Daniel reached into his pocket for his phone.

'What are you doing?' she asked.

'Ringing for an ambulance.'

'I'm fine.'

'You hit your head on a rock and now you have a cut that needs stitches. There's no way you're walking all the way back to Greenbeck. Jack? *Jack!*' he called, turning around to look for her son.

Jack came into view, smiling, then frowned when he saw his mum sitting on the ground, holding her head. His little face was a mask of shock when he saw the blood. 'What happened to Mummy?'

'She tripped and fell. But she's going to be all right—okay, champ?'

Jack nodded and sank onto the grass next to her, taking her hand in his.

She smiled at him gratefully, trying to act as if this was nothing, because she didn't want him to be worried. 'We're going to get frequent flyer miles at the hospital at this rate.'

'Some people will do anything to get out of judging a baby competition,' Daniel joked as he tore a strip from the bottom of his shirt and used it to stem the bleeding. 'Press here.'

Stacey sat with her back against some stones, feeling an utter fool. She hurt, and she was tired, and honestly all she wanted to do was go to sleep and sort out the wound in the morning.

It took some time for the ambulance to get there, and the paramedics apologised and said they were swamped at the moment. They got them all into the back of the ambulance, applied a pressure dressing to Stacey's head, and then they were off, bumping over the potholes in the old castle lane before they reached the main road that would take them to the hospital.

Stacey spent as much of that time as she could smiling and laughing and joking with Jack, so that he would know that she was just fine, and when they wheeled her into A&E she loved how Jack held Daniel's hand—perhaps in lieu of not having Grover to hold.

They stood back, whilst a doctor examined her.

'It's an easy enough wound to fix. We'll clean it out and stitch it up for you—no problem. What caused the accident?'

Stacey explained.

'And you weren't feeling dizzy or anything before the fall? You just tripped?'

'That's right. I was tired from the uphill walk, but not dizzy.'

'Well, that seems straightforward. We might do an X-ray…just to confirm everything's okay. You've got quite a lump forming.'

Stacey winced. 'Great. Thanks.'

'An X-ray will mean radiation, so…any chance you could be pregnant?'

She blinked and looked at Jack and Daniel.

Daniel smiled. 'I'll take this one to get a drink. Come on, squirt.' And he led Jack away.

'I don't think so,' she told the doctor. 'I mean… I'm on the pill. But…' She frowned.

'But?' said the male doctor, smiling at her.

'But there was an incident when I missed a couple of pills. I started taking them again straight away, and I'm sure it's nothing, but I guess I ought to mention it.'

The doctor smiled. 'We'll do a pregnancy test, then—just to be on the safe side.'

She nodded, reassured. 'Okay.'

She didn't really think she would be. What were the chances? But a niggling voice at the back of her head told her that there was a chance, and she'd been right to mention it to the doctor. What must Daniel be thinking? Would he have seen that she thought it could be a possibility?

She hoped that he'd only thought she wanted him to take Jack away so that he wouldn't hear a conversation about her being on the pill. Little boys didn't need to know that kind of thing about their mothers—especially one who had just learned that his mother had a boyfriend now.

Poor Jack! He'd gone through so many changes and challenges recently and she really felt for him—even if he did seem to be taking everything in his stride. His confidence had soared since he'd come to live in Greenbeck, and she was so proud of him.

Just thinking about Jack made her feel as if she might cry, and she sniffed and wiped at her eyes just as the doctor came back and asked her if she would produce a urine sample for the test.

'Sure. No problem.'

She peed into a small bottle and returned to her cubicle, giving the sample to a nurse and settling back on the bed. For a moment she just lay there, trying to be conscious of relaxing. Lowering her shoulders. Not frowning. Loosening her jaw as if she was trying to get into a meditative state. And then she closed her eyes. For just a moment...

She was woken by the sound of the curtain being pulled back and she blinked awake to see Daniel at the side of her bed, with a sleeping Jack on his lap.

'How long have I been out?'

'About twenty minutes,' said Daniel quietly, and they both looked at the doctor who'd just come in.

'Dr Emery?' The doctor looked at Daniel. 'This is your husband?'

'No, we're not married.' She blushed.

'Would you prefer me to give you the results on your own, or…?'

She stared at the doctor. What was going on?

'No, we're both doctors. You can tell me in front of him.'

'You're sure?'

She nodded.

'The test shows that you're pregnant, Dr Emery. The levels of HCG in your blood indicate that you're in your first trimester.'

Stacey stared at the doctor who had just delivered the news, not quite believing what she was hearing. She glanced at Daniel, but he looked just as much in shock as she was!

'What? Could there be a mistake?'

'Of course there's always that possibility, but in my experience, no. We can take a blood sample to confirm, but I think we can probably accept the facts in this case. You say you're on the pill?'

She nodded. 'But I missed a couple…' she said numbly, the news sinking in, her head wound forgotten.

Pregnant! A baby!

'How have you been feeling lately?'

Her brain felt slow. Murky. But the doctor's question made her think back over the last few days and weeks and she remembered the tiredness, and the headaches, and feeling hungry all the time. She'd felt sick on occasion. And now that she thought about it a bit more she had felt some tenderness in her breasts, but had put it down to the new bra she'd been wearing. She'd kept fiddling with the straps to get the fit right as it had seemed a little small.

I blamed the manufacturer!

'What about the X-ray?' she asked, her mind fixing on the one thing she could deal with right now.

'Well, there is a small risk to the foetus from radiation. We could cover you with a protective apron, or you could decide not to have an X-ray and we could monitor you for a while, to make sure you're okay. On palpation no fractures were indicated, but due to the swelling it might be advisory to have the X-ray. It is, of course, up to you. I'll leave you for a moment to decide.'

And then the doctor was gone again, swishing the curtain closed behind him.

Stacey looked down at Jack. He was going to be a big brother!

CHAPTER NINE

'YOU MISSED A couple of pills?' Daniel asked, in shock.

'It was before we… I noticed after… I…' her voice trailed off.

Clearly she was just as much in shock as he was!

On his lap, Jack continued to sleep, completely unaware of the tension in the cubicle.

'Why didn't you get the morning-after pill?'

She looked at him. Suddenly defensive. 'I couldn't! I'm allergic to it!'

Stacey was pregnant. With his baby!

He couldn't compute this! It was so unexpected! So out of left field! He wanted to get up and pace, move about, go and get some fresh air. But he couldn't, because he held her sleeping son on his lap.

He'd practically become a father to the little boy. And he'd been enjoying it. Selfishly spending as much time with Jack as he could because it fed a need he had inside himself and it had felt safe to do so. He wasn't his own flesh and blood. He'd figured that he'd feel somehow removed from him if anything happened. But now he was going to be an actual father to his own actual child…

He felt guilt drowning him in wave after wave of recrimination. They should have been more careful. He should have checked with her afterwards, when they'd had that talk about contraception and other partners they'd been with. He should have been clearer!

I can't deal with this.

Without thinking, just reacting, he gently scooped Jack up and lay him down on the bed next to Stacey.

'Where are you going?' she asked. 'We need to talk about this.'

'I can't! I just… I'm not leaving. I just…need to think about this.'

And he left the cubicle, walked away, needing space, needing some time to wrap his head around the enormous news that had just descended and changed his entire world in a single second.

'Daniel!'

He heard the pain in her voice. Heard the fear. And if this had been any other time he would have gone to her. Taken her hand. Asked her if she was all right.

But it wasn't any other time. Things had changed and he needed some time alone to process. He told himself that she must need it too. He'd told her he wasn't leaving her. He wasn't abandoning her the way that jerk Jerry had. He just needed a moment.

They both needed some space.

Stacey stared after him, hoping he'd been honest with her and would come back. Miserable, with tears beginning to fall, she picked up her mobile phone and called her gran.

'Hello?'

'Gran, it's me.'

'Darling, whatever's the matter? Why are you crying?'

'I'm in the hospital.'

'The hospital! Are you all right? Is it Jack?'

'No. No, it's not Jack. I had a fall. Hit my head. I'm okay, but… Could you come?'

'Of course, darling. We're on our way. Who has Jack?'

'I do. He's here with me. Asleep. I need you to come and take him.'

'Fifteen minutes, darling, and we'll be there—okay?'

She nodded and ended the call, dropping her phone back onto the bed and snuggling into Jack for comfort.

Daniel had left. *Left!* In the one moment when she needed him the most. When she herself was reeling from the news that she was pregnant with his child.

Pregnant.

This was monumental. She'd never expected this. Yes, she'd missed a couple of pills, but…

She groaned and squeezed Jack tightly.

The last time she'd been in this situation it hadn't gone well. Jerry had very quickly deserted her—told her that being a father was not something he felt able to do. That he had a hard enough time looking after himself and had no time in his life to look after a baby. And then he'd offered to pay for an abortion. Was Daniel going to do the same? She couldn't face such desertion again. Would he do something like that to her? He knew what had happened to her in the past—surely he wouldn't be the same? He was different. Daniel was a much better man. Wasn't he?

Having her own child had meant the world to her. Especially having lost her parents! Yes, she'd had her grandparents, but they'd been miles away and she had been alone, craving love. There'd been no way she'd get rid of her baby back then.

And now?

Daniel had disappeared. For good? Who knew?

Knowing of his past, and what had happened to Mason

and Penny, she had no idea what was going through his head right now. Was he panicking? Was he terrified? Confused? Because if he was, then he could join the club! What did he think *she* was feeling? She hadn't planned this. She hadn't wanted another baby and set out to trap him, for crying out loud. This was a surprise to her, too!

When her grandparents arrived Daniel had still not returned. She told herself that he probably wouldn't now. She was trying to put on a brave face. Accept her fate. Accept that the same thing was happening again and she'd coped before and would do so again.

Her gran and grandad rushed into her cubicle, gasping when they saw her bandaged head and swollen face.

'Oh, my goodness!' Gran embraced her tightly, squeezing her, then pulling away. 'What happened?'

'I tripped on a rock. Up at the castle.'

'The castle?' said her grandad. 'What were you doing up there?'

'We went for a walk with Daniel.'

Her grandad looked around them. 'And where is he?'

She swallowed, feeling sad, but determined not to cry. 'He's gone.'

'Gone? I don't get it…' he said.

Her eyes welled with tears and she looked up at her gran, in the hope that she would find understanding.

She did.

Her gran took her hand. 'Will, why don't you take Jack out to the car and get him settled? I'll be there in a few minutes, okay?'

Her grandad nodded and gently woke Jack.

Jack kissed his mummy's bandage and smiled, then placed his hand in his great-grandad's and went with him.

When the boys were gone, her gran turned back to her and raised an eyebrow. 'What's going on?'

Stacey sucked in a breath. 'I'm pregnant.'

Genevieve Clancy gasped, but quickly controlled herself, clearly realising that now was not the time for dramatics. 'Daniel's baby?'

Stacey nodded.

'And he's not taken it very well?'

'No.'

'I can imagine... Where is he?'

'I don't know. He said he needed a moment to think, but that was ages ago. I think... I think the same thing is going to happen, Gran. I'm going to be on my own.'

'Hush, now. I don't believe that for a minute. Daniel is *not* Jerry. He's better than that. The two of you just need to talk. Sort things out. That's all. You've both had a shock.'

'You think he might come back?' she asked, hope filling her voice.

Gran smiled. 'I know he will. I know that man and he loves you—whether he realises it yet or not. You mark my words. He'll be back.'

Stacey tried to smile through her tears, but it was hard.

She wanted to believe that Daniel loved her. She really did. Because if he did it would solve everything.

But her hopes continued to fade with every second that her cubicle remained empty of him.

Daniel sat with his head in his hands in a small garden in the hospital grounds. It wasn't a huge garden. Just a circle lined with benches, a few shrubs, a couple of ornamental roses and in the centre a dwarf willow tree.

At the base of the tree was a small plaque.

This garden was built in memory of
Nurse Wendy Sinclair,
who served forty-two years here on the renal ward.
It is in recognition of her service and the care that
all our nurses provide to every patient
who walks through our doors.
Wendy knew the importance of having a space
to think and relax,
and it is our hope that this garden provides a
comfort and a haven to all who need it.

Well, he needed it. Space. Comfort. A place to think.

He'd not been able to think in that small cubicle. Not with the doctor there. Not with Jack on his lap—a big reminder that he was already in much too deep with Stacey and her family. And not after hearing the news that he'd got Stacey pregnant and was going to be a father again.

He'd accepted that his family had died with Penny and Mason, and he'd never, ever considered starting another with another woman. Maybe for a time there he'd allowed himself to play at being part of a family, and the time he'd spent with Stacey and Jack had been amazing. And not just with Stacey and Jack, but Genevieve and William. They had all embraced him wholeheartedly.

What was he doing? He'd run. He'd escaped when suddenly it had all got very real. He couldn't imagine what Stacey was feeling. Hadn't her last partner deserted her on finding out she was pregnant?

I haven't deserted her. I just need space.

Could he do it again?

I have no choice. It's already happened. That baby exists.

The question was, was he strong enough to be vulnerable again? Just seeing Stacey fall and bang her head had scared him. All that blood! When he'd been trapped in that car in Hawaii with Penny and Mason, the blood had dripped down Penny's face too, and seeing Stacey like that had catapulted him back in time, filling him with the sensation that he was helpless and useless and the whole world was going to implode.

I thought that I was going to lose her.

The waiting for the ambulance had been terrible. He'd sat there, dabbing at her head, checking her vitals, thinking that with every minute they were waiting a big haematoma could be forming. At any second she would pass out, or start to seize, and there'd be no help for her. He'd be alone again. Helpless.

It had all been too much.

But the head wound had been the least of it! He was going to be a father again, and in Stacey's womb the baby they had made was already growing. It was innocent. This new life that they had created!

Am I strong enough to lay my heart on the line again? What if something happens to the baby? To Stacey? To Jack? What if I can't protect them?

He stared at Wendy Sinclair's plaque, reading the words over and over again. She'd been a nurse. He was a doctor. Same as Stacey. They all cared. That was what they did. They cared and they tried to make people better, sometimes despite the odds, and they would continue to fight for their patients.

If he could do it for them, surely he could do it for his own family?

The idea of walking away was impossible. He knew that deep inside. Being a father was the most wonderful thing a man could do. Being present, raising a child, was a gift. One that he would never ignore. Nor would he want to.

Daniel got to his feet and turned to look at the hospital. He'd been gone long enough.

CHAPTER TEN

'HERE'S A LEAFLET on head wounds and what to look out for,' said the doctor. 'Rest easy for a couple of days, and in about ten days you can get those stitches removed by your GP.'

Stacey nodded, accepting the leaflet, smiling, trying to be brave. Gran had gone with Jack and Grandad to take Jack home to bed. Gran had told her they would stay, so they could take her home, too, but Stacey had wanted to be alone for a while and Jack needed his sleep. Nor did she need her gran and grandad hanging around the hospital. She knew it gave them bad memories they didn't want to experience all over again.

'Thank you,' she said now.

'You're welcome. Take care—and watch your step from now on.'

She smiled. 'I will.'

When the doctor had left Stacey stood up, sliding her mobile back into her pocket. She looked up when the curtain swished open again, expecting a nurse.

Only it wasn't.

It was Daniel.

Her heart thudded in her chest and she felt herself grow hot, her cheeks flushing. The need to cry again was so strong she had to dab at her eyes.

'If you're coming back to tell me it's all over, there's no need.'

'That's not what I've come to tell you,' he said, stepping forward.

And that was when she realised he was holding a carrier bag. She looked up into his eyes in question.

'This is for you.' He passed her the bag.

Frowning, confused, she opened it and looked inside, gasping as she saw a little white baby onesie. It was tiny. Newborn to three months—that was the sizing. Pure white, with an embroidered teddy on the front.

'I got something unisex…seeing as we don't know what it is yet.'

The onesie was so cute she wanted to cry, but still she held back her tears. 'I don't understand.'

He stepped forward, took her hand in his. 'I needed a moment.' He smiled ruefully. 'It took longer than I expected.'

'A moment for what?'

'To realise what I have. What a gift you are. You. Jack.' He looked down at her belly. 'The baby.'

Stacey sniffed, looking into his eyes with love. She couldn't help herself. 'Tell me more.'

'I panicked. I thought that I wouldn't be able to protect you. I failed before, and I knew I couldn't feel like that again. But then I realised, sitting out there, that I most certainly couldn't protect you if I wasn't around. If I was at a distance. Hiding. Thinking I was doing the right thing for me. But it's not just about me. And I promise you that I will not panic any more. I will not leave you. Any of you. You've brought so much to my life in these last few weeks and I can't imagine you not being there. I need you. *All* of you. If you'll have me.'

He reached up to stroke her face, wiped her tears away with his thumb, smiling at her with such love.

She hiccupped a laugh. Gave a smile. 'I'm scared, Daniel. Scared of what all this means. The changes that are about to happen. I never planned this. Never expected it. But… I know I can do it. I'm strong enough. And what makes me happy is having you by my side.' She laughed. 'I knew you were trouble the moment I laid eyes on you! But you're the best kind of trouble. The only kind of trouble.'

She leaned forward. Dropped a kiss onto his lips.

'I love you. And Jack does, too. We can do this, you and I. We can do anything together.'

He smiled and nodded. 'We can. I love you, too.'

And they kissed.

There was a huge turn-out for the fete. The whole village had shown up, and as an added bonus the sun was shining, making everyone doubly happy. There were food stands filling the air with the aroma of hot dogs and burgers and candy floss, a doughnut van and a juice bar. There were clowns and jugglers—even one who was walking around on stilts!

Stacey could hear a voice speaking through a megaphone. She couldn't make out the words, but she felt she knew the voice. Was it Zach? No. It couldn't be. What would he be doing on a megaphone?

Everywhere she looked she saw smiling faces. People were looking as happy as she felt.

Walking hand in hand with Daniel, she leaned in and whispered to him, 'You're sure I look okay?'

She touched her fingertips to where she'd hit her head a couple of weeks ago. The stitches were out, and the swelling was down, but there was still some lingering green-yellow bruising, and she'd looked in the mirror that morning to hide it with make-up.

'You're the most beautiful woman here.' He smiled and planted a brief kiss on her lips as Jack ran on ahead to try his luck at the football game.

They passed the cake marquee and Stacey waved at her gran and grandad, who were inside. Her gran was fussing over a three-dimensional cake that she'd made to look like a lighthouse. It looked amazing, and she hoped that Gran would win. Next to the cake stand was the vegetable stall, and she peered inside to see if she could see her grandfather's cabbage and the marrow that he'd entered. But there were so many items of a giant nature it was hard to know which were his.

Their destination was the baby cosplay marquee. They were due to judge there, along with Zach, and they could already see him standing there, holding on to a clipboard. Beside him stood Hannah, their advanced nurse practitioner, who was all smiles and playing with her necklace.

'How are those two getting along?' Stacey asked Daniel.

'I don't know,' Daniel replied. 'But they look good right now, don't you think?'

Stacey nodded. 'You should ask Zach.'

'I will. Later.'

At that moment they reached the marquee and there were a lot of hellos. Zach clapped Daniel on the back and then leaned forward to kiss Stacey on the cheek. They both smiled at Hannah.

'Ready to judge?' Zach asked.

'Not really.'

Zach grinned and nodded towards Stacey's belly. 'Just think. Next year, you can enter *your* little one!'

Stacey cradled her belly protectively. 'Er…we'll think about it!' she said, and laughed.

Walter came up to them and gave her and Daniel a clipboard each. Each entrant had their name, age and character written down, and a space for them to enter a mark out of ten. Inside the marquee they saw lots of frantic parents trying to present their babies. Some were blissfully asleep in their costumes, others were crying, whilst some just looked bemused.

'Off you go,' said Walter. 'You give each entrant a mark out of ten and at the end we'll tally the scores. In the case of a draw, it's down to the head judge to decide on the winner—that's you, Dr Fletcher.'

Zach nodded and let go of Hannah's hand.

Stacey and Daniel followed them into the marquee and began judging. There were lots of amazing costumes. Dragons, a mermaid, Robin Hood… Their eyes were assaulted by such a wide breadth of imagination.

Stacey looked at all the babies, wanting to give them all ten out of ten, but she knew she couldn't, so tried to be as fair as she could. She spoke to each parent, and each child if it was awake, and when she was done headed into the judges' tent to tally up the scores and hand their marking sheets to Walter, who would officiate.

'I'm so nervous!' Stacey said. 'And hungry!'

'Want me to fetch you something?' asked Daniel.

'No, I'm fine. I can wait.'

'Nonsense. I'll get you something.'

Daniel had headed off in an instant.

Zach turned to her. 'You've made him a very happy man again, you know. It's good to see him like this.'

'Well, he's made me very happy, too,' Stacey replied, smiling. 'Ecstatic, even. And Jack adores Daniel. I could never have hoped for this much happiness when I came back to Greenbeck. I'd hoped for *some*, but all of this... It's magical.'

Daniel returned with a glazed doughnut. Her favourite. He kissed her on the lips after he'd passed it to her.

'I'll be huge at this rate!' She laughed, biting into the doughnut.

The prize for the best costume went to a one-year-old dressed up as a spider, and now their judging duties were done she and Daniel headed away from the village green over to the Wishing Bridge. On the way Daniel waved to Jack and gave him a nod, and her son joined them.

Standing there, arm in arm, they looked down at the water beneath them for a brief moment, and then Daniel was turning her to face him, smiling, looking deeply into her eyes.

'I have something to ask you.'

'Oh?' Stacey glanced at Jack, who was grinning broadly.

Daniel looked nervous suddenly. And then he got down on one knee.

She gasped, stepping back, looking at the two people she loved most in the world.

Daniel nodded at Jack, smiled, and then reached into his pocket and produced a small box.

'I've already asked Jack for his permission. He gave it. But I need to ask *you*, Stacey Emery, love of my life, if you will marry me?'

He opened the small box and inside was a gorgeous diamond and sapphire ring.

She almost couldn't believe it! He'd proposed!

'Yes! Yes! Oh, my God, yes!'

Daniel got to his feet and slipped the ring onto her finger, and then he was kissing her, and she was laughing and crying, and Jack was hugging them both. Daniel lifted Jack up and they all held one another, and loved one another, and Stacey knew without a shadow of a doubt that she would never be alone ever again. That she had found her happiness here in Greenbeck. That Daniel would be there for them all.

She was loved. Protected. Adored.

Taking a step back into her past had propelled her into a wonderful future.

She kissed her son, then she kissed Daniel, and with a hand on her belly she knew that wishes did come true.

* * * * *

SECOND CHANCE FOR THE VILLAGE NURSE

LOUISA HEATON

MILLS & BOON

To all my friends at LWS x

CHAPTER ONE

Three months ago

'WOW. YOU CAN really be wrong about some people, huh?' Dr Zachary Fletcher said after the interviewee had left the room. He stood, stretched out his back muscles and let out a sigh. 'Tea?' he asked Lucy, the practice manager.

It had been a long, exhausting day, interviewing potential candidates not only for the new GP spot they were opening up, but also to replace their advanced nurse practitioner, who had left after moving closer to family.

Both he and Lucy had agreed on the new GP—Dr Stacey Emery, whom they had interviewed via video call, was the perfect candidate for their team. But they were struggling with finding the right nurse practitioner.

Their surgery was a small practice at the heart of the Greenbeck community, and Zach had worked hard to choose staff who fitted in with the type of practice he was trying to create. Warm, approachable, team players... He'd seen some great nurse practitioners today. But were any of them the right fit for Greenbeck?

The last one had had a great CV, that was for sure, but her personality wasn't what he was looking for. In the interview she'd come across as a little abrupt, a little sharp, and had responded to their questions in a prickly manner—almost as if she'd thought they were being nosy. But a job interview demanded that the employer ask questions. It wasn't just about qualifications. It was about finding the right person.

'It's a shame we can't make it Irish tea. But plain old boring tea will have to recharge us so we can get through this last one.' Lucy picked up the application form with a heavy sigh. 'Hannah Gladstone. Happy to relocate if offered the job.'

Zach switched on the kettle. 'Where does she live now?'

Lucy perused Hannah's letter of application. 'Epsom.'

'Okay. Well, let's hope she's amazing—because we've run out of applicants.'

He made the tea, and offered Lucy biscuits from the tin, before he sat down and sipped at his own drink and scanned the application. It all looked good, but so had the last one, so…

'Ready?' he asked.

Lucy smiled. 'As I'll ever be.'

'Okay. Let's go.'

It was a nice waiting room. Modern. Brightly decorated. In one corner there was a large bookcase filled with children's books that had a sign above it informing parents that children could borrow books and take them home.

Like a kids' library, Hannah thought, smiling.

There were the usual noticeboards, filled with posters informing patients of both sexes of the value of checking themselves for lumps and/or anything different from usual. And a sign stating that breastfeeding was welcome in the waiting area or, if the mother preferred, a private room could be supplied, which was nice. Behind the reception desk were photographs of the surgery during its rebuild—doctors and nurses, office staff and receptionists. Everyone was smiling.

Would her face end up on the wall? Hannah wondered. She doubted it. Clearly she was the last interview of the day.

The interviewers would be tired, or just ready to get home. They would have heard all the clever answers to their questions already.

What are your strengths?

What are your weaknesses?

Why should we hire you and not one of the other candidates for the job?

The reception team were less busy now than they had been when she'd first arrived. Appointments were being wrapped up. There was only Hannah and a young mother still waiting. The mum was on her phone while her infant lay back in her buggy, mouthing a rusk. The young woman looked up and over at Hannah.

She smiled politely, her stomach churning with nerves. She wasn't good at job interviews. Not any more. They'd never used to bother her, but since the accident and everything that had happened with Edward, her ex-fiancé, her self-confidence had taken a bit of a dive. To sit in front of people assessing her, judging her, reminded her too much of the past. Put under pressure, she stuttered, or said the wrong thing as she waited for the other person to realise that she wasn't worth their trouble. Or worse...they pitied her.

But I need this job! I need to get away from where I am.

There was a caught thread puckering her dark trousers, midway down her right thigh. She'd never noticed it before. Frowning, she tried to smooth it out, but her nail caught on it and pulled it more instead. It looked awful, suddenly. Exposing a small hole the size of a pea that revealed her thigh. She looked as if she couldn't afford a decent pair of trousers, and she hated to think that the interviewers' eyes would be drawn there.

'Shannon Glossop?'

The young mum got up and wheeled her baby down the

corridor towards a woman in uniform. A nurse? An HCA? She couldn't tell.

Now Hannah was alone in the waiting room, feeling sweat forming in her armpits and running down her back. Her mouth was dry. Was there a water fountain? She looked about her and saw one in the far corner. She put her bag down and went over to pour herself a drink of cold water.

She was just about to take a sip when a deep, slightly accented voice said, 'Miss Gladstone?' and she jumped, spilling the water down her white silk top.

Hannah looked down at herself in dismay.

Damp top. Hole in trousers. Perfect.

'Are you all right?'

She turned, cheeks flushing wildly, knowing she must look a mess, to see a man standing before her.

Tall. Dark-hair, slightly tousled. Cheeky blue eyes and a great smile. He was looking at her strangely.

Probably he's hoping that I'm not his interviewee!

Hannah brushed her top down, trying to wipe off the excess water. 'Y-yes. I'm f-fine. I'm sorry I spilt all that…maybe if there's a mop I could…? Sorry. Hannah Gladstone.'

She held out her hand for him to shake, realised the cup was still in it and hurriedly swapped it over, spilling more, forcing a smile, and hoping he couldn't feel her trembling as he shook her hand.

He was simply the most remarkable-looking man she'd ever seen in her life. Was he for real? The temptation to pinch him and check that he wasn't wearing some sort of mask was overwhelming.

'Don't worry about that. We'll get it sorted. Put up a sign…'

He smiled at her, which she almost didn't notice, so lost was she in listening to his soft Scottish burr. Which part of Scotland was he from? Glasgow? Edinburgh? She suddenly wished she knew everything there was to know about Scotland, just so she could talk to him about it and listen to him speak. There was something so mesmerising about the lilt and flow of his speech she almost forgot what she was there for.

Job interview. Come on, now. Snap to it!

'Oh, r-right. Thank you. If you're sure?'

He nodded and smiled again. His smile revealed a row of lovely white teeth and his eyes gleamed with amusement.

It was something she was familiar with, having received a fair amount of amused looks over the last year or so. She'd become a figure of ridicule back home. At least that was how it felt, and although she knew she shouldn't care so much about what others thought of her she couldn't help it. She was too sensitive.

'We're just in here.'

He stood back and indicated that she should go into the room ahead of him. Inside, a woman sat behind a desk with a pile of papers, upon which sat Hannah's application. Next to that was a mug of tea and a plate of fruit shortcake biscuits.

The woman stood. 'Miss Gladstone?' She smiled.

'Hannah. Yes.' She shook the woman's hand.

'Please take a seat. My name is Lucy Dent and I'm the practice manager here in Greenbeck, and this is Dr Zachary Fletcher, the senior partner.'

Zachary... Zach... It suited him, she thought, turning and smiling even harder as he closed the door behind her, slipped past, and indicated that she should sit before he settled into his chair opposite her.

'I hope you found us all right?' asked Dr Fletcher.

'Eventually! I followed your instructions, but still somehow got lost.' She laughed, assuming they'd laugh with her, but then realised she was on a job interview and needed to seem competent. 'I mean, I know how to follow directions, of course...

I'm just not very… I struggle with…' She laughed nervously. 'I'm just not that good with maps.' She blushed madly and leaned in. 'Good thing I'm not a pirate! Not that pirates are…'

She bit her lip. Knew she was babbling. She glanced at Zach and saw that he was staring at her with a confused smile. She sucked in a breath. Gathered herself.

Stop panicking.

'I got here just fine—thank you.'

'I'm glad to hear it.'

He glanced at Lucy and they shared a look.

Hannah felt her heart drop like a stone.

I'm ruining it!

'So, why don't you tell us about yourself, Miss Gladstone?' suggested the practice manager.

She nodded. She could do that, right?

'Erm…well… I'm Hannah, and I've been working as an advanced nurse practitioner for about ten years now. I've been at the same GP practice all that time—it was my first job—and now I'm looking for a change.'

'And that's full-time?' asked Dr Fletcher, looking down at her application form.

'Yes. Full-time. Well, mostly… I…er…had an accident and was off work for a while, and when I came back I had a phased return, but then I went back to full-time.'

He nodded. 'I'm sorry to hear that. How long ago was that?'

'Two years ago.'

'You're fit and well now?'

'Absolutely! One hundred percent. Tip-top.'

Why the hell did I say tip-top? When have I ever, in my entire life, said tip-top?

Lucy smiled at her. 'What would you consider to be your strengths?'

'Oh, gosh… Well, not job interviews, that's for sure!'

She laughed, self-deprecatingly, thinking they'd join in—only they didn't. They looked at her with amusement, but didn't laugh.

This is not going well.

'I'm a good nurse practitioner. I am. It may not seem like it. I don't think I'm giving you the best impression. But that's my weakness, you see? I babble when I'm nervous, or I go silent completely—which, looking at you now, I'm guessing you wish was the case today. But... I make a mean cup of tea and I'm kind and considerate. I *love* talking to my patients and building a trusting relationship with them and...'

Suddenly her brain went astoundingly blank and her mouth gaped open as she fought desperately for something positive to say that would make them change their minds.

'I'm...er...'

She closed her mouth, looking down. She saw the hole in her trousers and thought about how badly this was going. Felt herself deflate. Felt all the fight go out of her.

'I'm a good person...' It was all she could manage.

The rest of the interview didn't go any better.

With her fight gone, and her sense of optimism about getting this job disappearing faster than a bullet from a gun, Hannah felt she waffled her way through all their questions. Never saying anything persuasive and certainly not saying anything that would make these two think they ought to employ her.

'Do you have any questions you'd like to ask us?' said Lucy at the end.

And even though she'd practised many of them in the car, such as, *Would I get the opportunity to run training courses regularly to maintain* she figured she'd failed at this interview anyway, so what did it matter?

'When do I start?' she said, and laughed, joking.

Her smile died on her face when she saw the two of them look at each other once again, before looking back at her quizzically.

'Look, I would like to thank you for seeing me. I appreciate your time. But I could have done much better.'

She stood and shook their hands. Then she took one last final look at Dr Zachary Fletcher, just so she could imprint his face on her memory and go home and tell her best friend Melody all about him. Not that she'd be likely to forget his face…it was just so attractive. But it would have been nice to think she could look at it for as long as she wanted if she got this post.

'You're welcome. We'll be in touch,' he said, and that Scottish burr soothed her jangling nerves.

She headed back out into Reception, thanked the reception staff, and then put her bag on a waiting room chair so she could search for her car keys. Once she'd found them she headed outside, and walked straight into the young mother she'd seen earlier, colliding with her.

'My baby! She's choking!'

What?

Hannah dropped her bag and rushed over to the mother's car—and, yes, the young mum was right. Her baby was strapped into her car seat and appeared to be choking on something.

She turned and said urgently, 'Go into the surgery—get more help!'

She wrestled with the safety lock, unfastening it and pulling the baby free. The obstruction couldn't be seen, and she didn't dare risk putting her finger in to hook the obstruction in case she forced it down further. She supported the infant on the length of her arm, face down, and began to deliver some blows to her back, between the baby's shoulder blades.

The baby still coughed and spluttered, and just when Hannah thought the child was in danger of passing out, the obstruction flew out of the baby's mouth and landed on the car park concrete. Half a grape.

The young mum came running out of the surgery, followed by Dr Fletcher and Lucy and another male—a doctor, by the looks of it, armed with a go bag. Their faces relaxed when they heard the baby burst into tears after such a shocking and scary experience.

'She's okay now. She's okay,' Hannah said, handing the upset baby back to her mum. 'But maybe you ought to get one of the doctors to give her the once-over, just to be sure.'

The young mum nodded and walked over to the other medic, another handsome young man, with a fashionable short trimmed beard.

They headed back into the surgery and Dr Fletcher watched them go, then turned back to appraise her and smiled. 'Well done. You just saved that baby's life.'

'Oh, anyone would have done the same.'

'A lot of people would have panicked, seeing a baby choking like that. You showed some skills, and best of all you remained calm and did what needed to be done.' He seemed to think about something, then grinned. 'How quickly can you give notice?'

'I'm sorry?' She stared at him, not sure she was understanding. He had to be joking, right?

'Would you like the job?'

When he smiled, his whole face lit up…eyes sparkling.

'This one? Here?' She pointed at the surgery, trying to make sure she understood correctly.

'That would be the one I am referring to, yes.'

'You're sure?'

'One hundred percent.'

She laughed. This was crazy! *Really?* Was he just offering her the job out of sympathy?

'But I did awfully in the interview!'

'You were nervous.' He shrugged.

'I was terrible!'

'No.' He shook his head, and as he turned to go he laughed and said, 'You were *tip-top*.'

CHAPTER TWO

Present day

ZACH HAD WORKED extremely hard to build this team, this family feel at the Greenbeck surgery. He'd not wanted to start a practice where a bunch of people just came into work each day, did their hours and then clocked off. He'd wanted to create a place of work where people looked forward to coming in every day. Where the people he employed were more than team players. Where they were like family—only without all the arguments or secrets or jealousies.

Hannah had been a strange, energetic, babbling, nervous bundle of energy at her interview, but she had made him smile in a way he hadn't smiled for a while. He'd known she was perfectly qualified and had the experience he was looking for just from seeing her application form. What he'd wanted to judge was her character, and whether she would fit into Greenbeck with them all.

Her job interview had been...well, a *disaster*. He'd seen in her eyes the moment she'd thought she'd lost them, and even though he'd kept asking her questions to show her that he was still interested, that she still had time to pull things back, he'd realised her confidence had taken one hell of a knock. Something had knocked the stuffing out of this beautiful young woman, and he'd found himself wanting to help her.

But the interview had ended so badly he'd begun to think that maybe he was wrong. Maybe she'd be perfect in a year or two, when she had built up more confidence in herself? And then she'd astounded him when she'd saved that baby's life in the car park on her way out. It had been in that moment, when Hannah had passed the baby back to the mother, that he'd seen in her eyes the confidence she had in her skills and her ability to know what the right thing to do was.

She'd known how to handle the panicking mother, she'd managed to send for help, and afterwards she hadn't seemed to want any accolades for what she had done. She had been humble. As if it was an everyday occurrence. And he'd known there and then that she was the nurse he'd been looking for.

Now he was waiting for her and the new doctor, Dr Stacey Emery, to arrive for their first day. They both had appointments today, but their time allotment for each patient had been doubled from ten minutes to twenty, to give them time to get used to being somewhere new. If there was anything they weren't sure of, it would give them extra time—to find necessary items or go and ask for advice—without the appointments falling behind and creating long waits for the patients who were still in the waiting room.

For some reason he felt nervous, but he told himself it was because he wanted today to go well. And that worked until he saw new advanced nurse practitioner Hannah Gladstone walk into the main reception area, holding a plastic tub filled with what looked like cookies, and smile at everyone. Just watching her introduce herself to everyone made his mouth go dry and his heart pound hard in his chest as she came closer and closer to him.

Just excited to actually see her here. That's all. Building the work family. Glad my instincts were right.

He noticed an almost imperceptible limp. Her left leg. From

the accident she'd mentioned? She seemed to be in a little discomfort but hid it well.

'Good morning, Dr Fletcher.' She stood before him, her eyes twinkling with excitement and nerves. 'Cookie?'

He held up his hand to refuse. He was trying to watch what he ate, and it was too early for him to have sugar. 'Zach, please. All moved in okay?'

'Yes! Thank you. It's a little weird, waking up to birdsong and cows mooing outside my window, rather than car alarms blaring or sirens, but I'm sure I'll get used to it.'

'Mrs Micklethwaite will take good care of you.'

'Well, I was just lucky she had a room that I can lodge in. Trying to find a place in Greenbeck is extremely difficult.'

He nodded, agreeing. Their other new member of staff, Dr Emery, was going to lodge in Dr Daniel Prior's annexe as there weren't very many places to rent that weren't holiday lets at exorbitant prices. Greenbeck had been named as one of England's top ten most beautiful villages, and since then prices had soared and empty properties were impossible to find.

Zach tried not to notice the shine of her thick, dark brown hair, nor the intriguing fact that she had a central heterochromia that he hadn't noticed before. Her eyes were greyish blue on the outside, but dark hazel in the centre. They were so different and strange, and it made him want to stare at them more and more to note their subtle colour changes.

What on earth am I doing? Concentrate, man! She doesn't need me staring into her eyes like some wee lovesick pup!

Zach began introducing her to the admin team and Hannah gushed at them all. Smiling, shaking their hands. Laughing with them. Joking. Offering cookies. Apologising for being nervous. He noted the limp again. She favoured her right leg. He wished he'd asked her further questions during the interview, but at the time it hadn't seemed right. Maybe he'd find out more soon?

'Would you like tea or coffee, Hannah?'

'Oh, let me! Does anyone else need one?'

She bustled through to the small kitchenette and began getting out mugs and filling the kettle with water. He noticed her wince once, hiding it with a smile, and laughing at not knowing where the spoons were.

He thought he heard footsteps coming down the corridor and stepped out into the hall, spotting the new doctor. 'Dr Emery! Pleased to meet you in person at last! Let me introduce you to everyone.' He led her back into the small staffroom. 'Daniel you already know. Our HCA is Rachel, our resident vampire is Shelby, and this...' he turned to face Hannah once again '...is our new advanced nurse practitioner Hannah. It's her first day, too.'

He stepped back to let everyone say hello to one another, and then he showed Dr Emery to her room and left her to it, going back to grab the coffee that Hannah had very kindly made for him.

'Shall I show you your room?' he asked.

'Yes, please!'

Zach led the way to the end of the corridor. Hannah's room was situated between his room and the fire exit out into the car park where the staff parked. It was bright and airy—in fact, it was a little larger than the other consulting rooms. On one side it had a desk, with computer and printer, and on the other side all the medical equipment she'd need and an examination bed, so that the two zones, administrative and medical, were separate.

'This is where the magic happens,' she said, draping her handbag over the back of the chair and trailing her finger across the desk, before opening the cupboards and seeing what was inside.

Equipment for taking blood samples, swabs, bandaging supplies for wounds. Oxygen masks and a multitude of other medical equipment that she would no doubt use on a daily basis.

'I'll just be next door, if you need to ask any questions. Or if I'm not available Daniel is a couple of doors away. But ask anyone. You never know who might know the answer.'

'I'll do that. Thank you.'

'I guess I'd better leave you to settle in, then.'

But he found himself lingering and he wasn't sure why.

'Are you…um…in any pain?' he asked.

Her cheeks flushed red. 'Pain?' she said, as if she didn't understand.

'You seem to be in some discomfort. With your leg.'

'Oh! That's nothing. I'm used to it. Don't worry. It won't affect my work.'

'No, of course not. But if there was something I could help you with you'd come to me, yes?'

She nodded. 'Of course.'

And still he lingered.

What am I doing?

'Right, then. I'd better—'

'Can I just…?' Hannah bit her lip and stepped towards him. 'Can I just thank you, Zach, for offering me this job? I never got to say it before, and I just want you to know that you have no idea how grateful I am that you've given me this chance. I promise I won't let you down.'

And she looked into his eyes so deeply, and so earnestly, that he found himself lost for a moment. Lost in looking into those blue-hazel depths, pulled in until he suddenly realised that maybe he ought not to be.

'I know you won't. That's why I hired you.' He was lost

for words, wondering why his brain seemed to have stopped
working. 'Have a good morning, Hannah.'

'You too.'

He nodded and closed the door behind him, stopping briefly
in the corridor to try and work out just what he was feeling
and why he was feeling so out of sorts.

Her smile?

Her eyes?

Don't be a great eejit.

When the door closed behind Zach, Hannah let out a huge
breath and tried to slow the rush of her runaway heart.

For three months she'd been telling herself that Dr Zachary Fletcher could not, and would not, be the handsome devil
she remembered from the interview. Because her mind had
been all of a fluster back then, what with her nerves from the
interview, and she hadn't been thinking straight. So she'd told
herself that she'd simply imagined how gorgeous and handsome he was—because no man could actually look that perfect
and not be some sort of celebrity living in Hollywood, right?

Only she'd been mistaken. Zach was *exactly* how she remembered! She hadn't made him up, or imagined him, or exaggerated his looks or his accent. He was… He was…

'Exquisite. A feast for the eyes,' she murmured, squeezing
her eyes tight shut and trying to tell herself that it would all
be just fine…

Dr Zachary Fletcher was obviously married, and no doubt
a fabulous loyal husband and father to a perfect family. And
they'd have a cat and a dog, and maybe chickens or ducks in
the back garden. His children would be angelic and admired
by all, and he'd be the envy of all the other parents at the local
school, and no doubt make everyone's mouth water when he
competed in the parents' races on sports day, or helped out at

the cake sale and made all the local ladies salivate when looking at him, rather than at the delectable edibles he'd have on the table before him, and they'd all be jealous of his beautiful, model-like wife...

Sinking into the chair behind her desk, she shook her head, trying to clear it, knowing she had to get into work mode, see who was on her list for the day...what she'd be tackling.

Thinking about Zach... Well, that would have to wait. Even though she knew that, realistically, she wouldn't be able to ignore him for long.

Could a man like him be ignored?

Probably not.

And he'd noticed her limp. Already. So much for her trying to hide it. His medic's antennae must have been going crazy, and she was a fool to have thought she could hide her injury from everyone here. Clean slate? Hah!

She had eight people on her list this morning. The first one due in fifteen minutes. So she took off her cardigan, hung it on the back of the door, and began to set up the clinical side of her room the way she liked it to be before calling in her first patient of the day.

Miss Petra Kovalenko came in and Hannah could immediately see what the issue was. But she didn't want to just presume.

'Good morning. I'm Hannah. How can I help you today?'

'It's my eyes. They've been really sore and itchy since Friday evening, and this morning when I woke up I couldn't open them without soaking them first in warm water.'

'I can see they look inflamed. They're very red. Are you normally fit and well?' she asked.

Petra nodded.

'Have you been around any children with eye infections?'

She laughed grimly. 'I teach in the infants' school.'

'Ah. That'll do it! I can see there's a lot of green discharge stuck in your eyelashes, which would suggest that this is bacterial conjunctivitis. Have you had a cold recently? Earache?'

'A bit of earache…but I put that down to the sound levels at work. Children can squeal really loudly.'

Hannah smiled. 'I'm just going to check your ears and throat—is that okay?' She looked into Petra's ears using the otoscope and saw a mild redness in her right eardrum, but her throat looked clear and her tonsils were fine—as were her temperature and blood pressure.

'Okay. I'm going to prescribe you some topical antibiotics. Are you allergic to any medications?'

'No.'

'You're going to need to make sure you wash your hands regularly, as this is contagious.'

'I can still work, though?'

'Yes, you can. Just be careful with hand hygiene, and don't share towels or pillowcases at home—that kind of thing. If you start sneezing or coughing, cover your mouth with a tissue and make sure it goes in the bin.'

'I will. Thanks. When should it start to clear?'

'Antibiotics should work within a few days. If you're still getting gunky eyes after four or five days then get back in touch. But this definitely seems bacterial, so these antibiotics should knock it right out.' She handed Petra the prescription.

'Thanks. I appreciate it.'

'No problem. You take care.'

'You too.'

When Petra was gone, Hannah let out a big sigh of relief. First patient done! And it had been wholly satisfactory. This was what she enjoyed about her job. Yes, she dealt with many acute conditions that people might consider boring, like coughs and colds or sore throats, but she felt as if she could do something about them, even if it was just to reassure a patient.

She worked steadily through her list, treating a urine infection, a migraine, a case of athlete's foot and a painful verruca before she was able to take her morning break. She headed to the small staffroom and filled the kettle with water to make some tea. As she waited for the kettle to boil she began to shift her stance, to take the weight off her left leg, just as Zach came in.

'Hey, how's it going? Everything okay?'

There was something about his smile… It was so broad, so genuine. And his eyes were so bright… And just seeing him made her have a funny feeling in her tummy.

It's just nerves. I just want to be liked. It's the people-pleaser in me.

'Yes! All good, thanks.'

'I'm glad to hear it. Just thought I'd grab a quick cuppa, and you've already got the kettle on, so…' He sank down into a chair.

Hannah smiled at him, not sure what to say. 'Do I…um… detect an accent there?'

He nodded. 'You do! I was raised in Bathgate. West Lothian.'

'Oh, really? How long were you there for?'

Zach shrugged. 'For most of my childhood. I went to Edinburgh to study medicine, and then came to England.'

'Quite a big change.'

'I guess… What about you?'

'Oh! Nothing as interesting, I'm afraid. Born in Surrey. Raised in Surrey. Worked in Surrey.' She rolled her eyes at how boring her life sounded. 'It was time for a change,' she added, hoping he wouldn't dig any more than that.

It hadn't just been time for a change. She'd needed to get

away. From everyone who knew her. The humiliation had been too much to bear. She'd thought the time right after her non-wedding had been the worst, but honestly it hadn't. It had come much later, after the gossip had spread, when weeks and months had passed by and people kept looking at her with pity, as if she were the eternal underdog or something…

Her parents and her best friend Melody had all told her just to power through, but it had become impossible. She'd felt as if everyone was looking at her. Judging her from afar. Knowing every intimate detail of her life. She'd been laid bare before them all and she'd needed some privacy back. Some dignity. The fresh start that this opportunity at Greenbeck had afforded had been worth the upheaval of moving and leaving her old life behind.

Her mum had begged her not to go. Told her it didn't matter and that she should hold her head high as she'd done nothing wrong. But that was easy for Mum to say. She wasn't the one who had to face everyone and see that look in their eyes. See all the questions they had and were dying to ask. It was the worst feeling in the world.

'A change is as good as a rest, huh?' said Zach. 'Isn't that what they say?'

'Yes…' She rubbed at her left leg, trying to be casual about it, hoping he wouldn't notice.

'Everything okay?' He looked down at her leg, clearly concerned.

'I'm fine. Think I overdid it jogging at the weekend.'

Jogging? Hah! I don't jog! Why did I say jogging?

'Well, I mean… I *say* jogging… It was probably more of a fast walk. And when I say fast walk…what I actually mean is…'

She bit her lip. Her nerves were making her babble, searching for the right word, the right explanation to put him off the scent, determined not to let him find out.

She stopped talking. Chuckled. 'My leg just aches sometimes.'

'The accident?'

He'd remembered. From the interview. She was impressed. And also concerned.

'Yeah…'

'What happened? If you don't mind me asking?'

What happened ruined my life, that's what.

And she did mind. Big-time.

'I had an accident at a theme park.'

His face clouded. 'Nothing serious, I hope?'

The urge to tell him was tremendous. To just get it out into the open…not to have to hide. She was so sick of hiding. But this was her fresh start! Did she really want him knowing all about it on her first day?

She wrinkled her nose and shook her head. 'No. Just a small prang.'

Behind them, the kettle had finished boiling.

'Were you after tea or coffee?' Hannah offered brightly.

'Coffee would be great, thanks.'

'Milk? Sugar?'

'Just milk, thanks.'

'Sweet enough?' She turned as she joked, not realising that he'd got up and was standing close by.

His blue eyes were so intense! Sparkling like tanzanite. Thick, dark eyelashes emphasised their brightness. And he was such a perfect specimen of a man. Tall. Broad. Fit. His fitted blue shirt emphasised his musculature. He was…*solid.* That was a good way to describe him.

Solid, not perfect.

Exercise-conscious, not fit.

Easy on the eye, not delectable or delicious or stunningly edible!

Feeling a little unsettled by her reaction to him, she turned away, let out a slow, silent breath, and concentrated hard on making the drinks, hoping her hands wouldn't begin to tremble. She could not afford to be attracted to this guy! He was her boss, for goodness' sake! And, more than that, she'd come here to get away from men and romance and all the complications that came with them.

'I don't know about that,' he said, coming alongside her.

She made his coffee. Stirred it and passed it to him. Trying not to brush his fingers with hers and hoping that he couldn't tell that her respiration rate had increased or that her face was flushed.

'Thank you.' He took a sip. 'Perfect. Right… Back to work we go. Remember, any problems you can just come and knock on my door.'

'Yes.'

No.

She watched him go, her breath exiting her body in a loud huff once she felt he was out of earshot.

Zach took his coffee back to his consulting room, closed the door behind him and sank into his chair, rubbing his hands over his face and through his hair.

Hannah was perfectly qualified, yes, and he felt she'd fit into the small Greenbeck family as he'd expected her to, but…

What was it about her that made him long to just sit and look at her and listen to her speak for hours? She was funny. Nervous, clearly. But he was sure that was only because it was her first day.

When she got nervous she spoke quickly, and a lot, and somehow he got dragged into her orbit. He found it hard to tear himself away when she got lost like that. Wanted to see where she would take him with her stories. But…

He wasn't ready to be attracted to someone else. Not after the catastrophic failure of the relationship he'd had with Milly, the local veterinarian. He'd only just begun to hold his head high again.

Now when he saw Milly in the village, smiling and laughing, holding Hugh's hand, he was able to just drive by and not grimace too hard and wonder why he'd not been enough. And people had moved on and stopped asking him about her. Patients had stopped checking that he was okay. Life had begun to return to normal for him and he *liked* to be that way. Unnoticed. Alone. Living a simple life.

But Hannah…

Was she going to endanger the normality that he'd craved for so long? Was she going to be a wrecking ball in his life? A grenade?

Should he have hired one of the other applicants? That ANP only five years away from retirement age? Or the guy with excellent references but a terrible dandruff problem? Would that have been easier?

But, no. Hannah had made a huge impression on him. Both in her interview and in saving that baby's life. Her babbling and her smile and her sparkling personality and her wonderfully exotic eyes had dug into his psyche and refused to budge, saying, *Pick me! Pick me! Pick me!*

And so he had.

'You are in trouble,' he said to himself, clicking on the name of his next patient so that the screen in the waiting room would tell him that he could make his way to Zach's room.

As he sat waiting for Mr Mackenzie Parsons and his dodgy knee to arrive he became acutely aware of Hannah's laughter in the next room. He had to fight the urge to go and see what she was laughing at. He wanted to be a part of it, wanted to see her face light up for himself, but he knew he wouldn't. Couldn't. For self-preservation he needed to stay exactly where he was.

As if on cue, the door opened and there was Mr Parsons. Hobbling in, using his walking stick. 'Morning, Doc!'

'Mr Parsons! How are you today? Take a seat, young man.'

'Not so young these days,' his patient complained, groaning as he sank into a chair.

'How can I help you today?'

'I need you to take a look at this. I don't think it's right.' Mr Parsons leant forward, grabbed his trouser leg, and pulled it up over the most swollen, red and inflamed knee Zach had seen for a long time.

His eyebrows rose. 'Okay... How long has it been like this?' he asked. He wheeled his chair forward to examine the knee, gently palpating the joint, exploring it, trying to feel for the underlying structures beneath the swelling and the infection that had clearly set in.

'Started Saturday night.'

'As bad as this?'

'No, no. Just an ache then. But Sunday morning... Ooh, it really began to hurt, and I've been popping paracetamol since. My daughter wanted to take me to A&E—but I didn't want to bother them with this.'

'I don't think they'd have thought you were bothering them, Mack. Did you bang your knee in any way?'

'I did some gardening Saturday morning. Pruning back some climbing roses that had got out of hand. My Matilda had let them run wild and free in her garden for years. They were a mess and she finally let me at them.'

'Did you catch yourself on any thorns?'

'Maybe a little. Just there—look.' He pointed at a small puncture hole to the right of the kneecap that looked dark and purple.

'I see it.'

Mr Parsons' knee was hot to the touch. Most definitely an

acute infection had got in. Maybe complicated by some cellulitis, too.

'We need to get you on some antibiotics. Do you still have a full range of motion in the leg?'

'Oh, yes. It feels a bit stiff, like, but I can move it.'

'Let's take your temperature… Any chills? Sweats?'

'Now you mention it, yes…'

'Nausea?' Zach reached for his digital thermometer and placed a new disposable cover on the tip before placing it in Mack's ear.

'No.'

It beeped. His temperature was raised, and Zach didn't like it. He feared that this might be a case of septic arthritis and knew that Mr Parsons needed to be put on an antibiotic drip.

'This isn't good, Mack. Especially with your artificial knee joint. I'm sorry to say I think you need to receive those antibiotics in hospital. Is there anyone who can take you to A&E? Your daughter Matilda?'

'She's had to go to Southampton today.'

'Right. Then I'm going to ask Reception to call an ambulance for you. I want you to go straight there. It probably means a bit of a stay, I'm afraid.'

Mr Parsons nodded his head. 'I thought it might be the case. Well, you know best, Doc. As long as I can go home first to lock up?'

'I'll just go and have a chat with Reception. Get them to ask the ambulance to pick you up from home within the next two hours?'

Mack nodded.

'You stay here a moment.'

'Will do.'

He went to ask one of the ladies on Reception to order an ambulance for pick-up from Mack's house in two hours, and gave her Mr Parsons' medical details so she could provide them to the ambulance service. Then he returned to his consulting room.

'All done. When you get home, I want you to keep that leg raised up on a chair—understand?'

'Yes, Doc. I do. And thank you for taking the time to see me. I appreciate it.'

'No problem. And next time go straight to A&E with something like this. Please don't wait.'

Mr Parsons nodded.

'When did you last take painkillers?'

'About three hours ago.'

'Right…'

He ended the consult and began to write up Mack's notes. He feared that Mack might need surgery to replace the artificial joint, depending on how bad the infection actually was, but no one could know at this stage. He hated it that Mr Parsons might now have a long road in front of him just because he'd decided to tackle some overgrown roses.

But that was how life was. Sudden, unexpected events could overtake you at a moment's notice. Even if you'd been in a relationship for over a year with someone and felt secure at last, life had a way of spoiling everything…

When the notes were written, Zach called for his next patient, hoping that the rest of the day would be uneventful, but no sooner had he sat down and begun to make a start on his admin tasks did an alert pop up on his screen. Dr Emery, their new GP, had an emergency on her hands.

He dropped everything and went rushing to her room, to discover that her patient, Sarah Glazer, was about to give birth unexpectedly.

'What can I do?' he asked Stacey. He didn't want to step on her toes. This was her patient. But he also understood that this was her first day here, and she might be overwhelmed, so he would help in any way she needed.

'Call an ambulance.'

'I'm on it.' he disappeared back to Reception. 'Charlotte? I'm going to need you to call another ambulance.'

'Two in one morning? Are we going for a record?'

'Maybe! It's for Sarah Glazer—she's on Dr Emery's list. Tell them she's about to deliver a baby and we'd appreciate an emergency ambulance as quick as they can.'

He went back to Stacey's room and saw that now Daniel was there with her, helping her, and knew he'd only be in the way.

'Daniel? I'll take your last patient so we can clear the surgery.'

He went to Daniel's room and explained to Mrs Robotham why he was stepping in. She didn't seem to mind, so he went through the rest of the almost completed COPD review that Daniel had been doing and then sent her on her merry way, with the promise to see her again in a year's time.

'We'll call you—don't worry.'

'Thank you, Dr Fletcher.'

As he headed back into the corridor he met Hannah, who was watching as Sarah Glazer was wheeled on a stretcher from Dr Emery's room.

'It's all go here, isn't it? So much for a quiet little village surgery.' She smiled.

'Absolutely. We may be small, but we are mighty!'

Her smile lit up her eyes, and briefly he found himself staring again. Deliberately he followed the paramedics outside, just to give himself some space from the gorgeous new advanced nurse practitioner.

He checked to make sure that Dr Emery was okay, and asked if she needed to chat, but she said she was fine, that it was all in a day's work, and he was reassured that he'd made the right choice in choosing her.

When he got back inside the surgery Hannah was making everyone a hot drink. 'I think we all deserve it,' she said, as all the staff filed into the small staffroom for lunch now the front doors had been locked.

He went to help her. Show her where the trays were. But when he bent down to get them out of the cupboards so did she, and somehow they banged their heads together.

'Ow! Are you okay?' he asked.

She was rubbing at her head. 'I think… Yes. I'm okay.'

'Let me check.'

He reached for her head, let his fingers slide into her soft hair as he checked to make sure there were no breaks in the skin, or any bumps, but she seemed fine.

She looked up at him, her eyes meeting his, and he let go, stepped back, feeling his cheeks colour. 'You're all right.'

Him, on the other hand… Not so great.

He pointed at the low cupboard. 'Trays are in there…on the side.'

'Thanks.'

'I'll leave you to it…unless you need a hand?' She looked a little pale.

'I'm fine. You go and sit down. It sounds like you doctors have had a busy morning.'

He smiled at her, and then sat down so that he had his back to her. This confusion he was feeling over Hannah…it needed to stop. He didn't want it. Or need it. It was a distraction when he needed to be clear-headed, to help his two new staff members settle into their jobs on their first days.

Both he and Stacey had needed to order an ambulance. It happened… There'd been a day last July when the surgery had ordered three ambulances in the course of a few hours! A suspected heart attack, a severe asthma attack and a woman he'd suspected of having suffered a stroke. They probably wouldn't need an ambulance now for days...weeks... Or maybe they'd need another tomorrow? Who knew?

Being on the frontline of primary healthcare, you never knew who might walk through your door. A patient might think that they were just having a bad headache—they wouldn't know that perhaps they were having a transient ischaemic attack, or TIA, which was a mini stroke. They might come in complaining about a pain in their leg and discover that they had a deep vein thrombosis. A clot which might prove dangerous. Some patients played down their ailments. Others exaggerated them. It was what they faced day to day.

Hannah came past him and stooped to lay the tray of tea-and-coffee-filled mugs onto the table. Her cookies were nearly all gone. Just one or two left on the plate. Did he want to try one and be blown away by her baking skills, too?

He noticed her wince and rub at her left leg again, but chose not to mention it. She'd say if there was a problem.

She sat in a chair opposite and picked up one of the mugs, sighing with satisfaction after taking her first sip. 'That's lovely.'

'How's your first day going, Hannah?' asked Charlotte from Reception.

'Good, thank you. How is it on Reception?'

'Busy. But we're lucky we can offer more appointments now that you and Dr Emery are here. We've had to turn people away or make them wait, and not everybody understood that we simply couldn't fit them in.'

'I hope people weren't too mean to you?'

'There'll always be one or two bad apples who try to make life difficult, but thankfully the people of Greenbeck are understanding. And everybody knows everybody, so they really can't get away with being rude or horrible.'

Hannah smiled and nodded, sipping from her mug.

Zach had his lunchbox in the fridge, and now that Hannah was nowhere near the vicinity of it he went to fetch it. Then, with his mug of coffee in hand, he went back to his consulting room to eat in private.

He couldn't sit in that room with her. If he did, he'd want to look at her. Ask her loads of questions. And the poor woman was trying to have lunch. It was her first day, and she'd be trying to make a good impression on everyone. She didn't need him prying too.

No, it was best if he ate alone. It wouldn't be seen as strange. He often ate in his room. He'd done it a lot after his relationship with Milly had broken down. So many people had wanted to ask him questions and he'd just not wanted to deal with it. Not right away. Not when it was all so raw.

Sighing, he put down his sandwich and picked up the phone, dialling a number he knew off by heart.

'Hello?'

'Evelyn? It's me.'

Evelyn McDonald wasn't his real mum. But she was the woman he'd given that honorary name to. Evelyn was one of the many foster parents he'd lived with growing up in Bathgate, and the only one with whom he'd stayed in touch. She was kind and gentle, and she'd taken him in when he was fifteen and got him through his school exams before he'd been moved on elsewhere.

'Zachary! It's been so long. How are you?'

'Not bad. Thought I'd check in.'

'Okay. Normally when you call me to just check in, there's something going on. Do you need to talk about it?'

'No. Aye. Maybe…' He leaned back in his chair, running his hand through his hair. 'It's just one of those days, you know?'

'Is it Milly?' she asked quietly.

Evelyn had never been keen on Milly. It was as if his foster mum had had a sixth sense about her not being right for him from the beginning.

'No. It's not her.'

'There's someone else?' she asked, surprised.

'No.' He shook his head, thinking of Hannah.

'Oh. I thought there might be.'

'No. I've had two new members of staff start today and it's been a complicated morning, that's all. There's a lot of expectation on a first day.'

'Are they nice?'

'The new staff? Aye. They're bonny. A new GP who's come down from Scotland, actually, and a nurse from Surrey.'

'Mm-hmm. Single, are they?'

He laughed. 'Yes, but it's not like that. One's a single mum and the other…' He couldn't think of how to describe 'the other' without giving anything away.

'I understand. Look, Zach, you've been on your own for some time now. No one would blame you if you started noticing someone else.'

'I'm not noticing someone else!' he protested.

'Okay, I believe you. Maybe.' He heard her chuckle. 'But if you like this nurse, then…why not?'

'Who said it was the nurse?'

'You did…when you paused.'

'Evelyn, You see and hear too much that isn't there.'

'Och, it's there, laddie, you just can't admit it yet.'

He shook his head in exasperation. 'How are things there?' He paused. 'Were Lachie's bloods good?'

There was a sigh. 'Not bad. They're letting him start chemo again, so that's bonny.'

Lachie, Zach's foster father had recently been diagnosed with brain cancer. They'd discovered a large tumour after he'd begun complaining of excruciating headaches and dizziness, but his chemo had been stopped for a while after he'd developed an infection and been admitted to hospital. Fate had not been willing to give the man an easy time of it, and had allowed him to contract C Diff whilst he was in there. Clostridium Difficile was a bowel condition that caused pain and extreme bouts of diarrhoea.

'Good. And you're both okay?'

'Apart from that, aye. I saw Mrs Fincham the other day and she sends her best wishes to you.'

Mrs Fincham had been his science teacher at secondary school. 'She was a good teacher,' he said.

'She was.'

'Well, I'd better get on. Lunch breaks only last for so long.'

'Okay. Well, you take care. And remember—you can call me just to check in and say hi. You don't have to wait for a reason.'

'All right.'

'And, Zach? Be kind to yourself. You're worth it.'

He smiled. Evelyn knew him well. He was his own worst critic.

Wishing her goodbye, he got off the phone and finished his lunch. His drink had gone tepid and he needed another one before afternoon clinic started, so he headed back to the staffroom, expecting it to be empty as everyone prepped for the afternoon shift.

And it was—except for Hannah, who clearly thought she was alone as she sat with her head bowed, as if in pain, and rubbed at her left leg.

'Hannah?'

Her head shot up and her cheeks flushed bright red. She tried to hide the movement of rubbing her leg, pretending to straighten out her trouser leg. 'Oh! You surprised me.'

'You're in pain.'

She screwed up her face and wrinkled her nose, as if what he'd just said was Grade A ridiculousness. 'What? No!'

She moved to stand, but as she put weight on her left leg she winced and sucked in a breath.

He was at her side in a heartbeat. 'What is it?'

'It's nothing!'

'You're wrong. It's clearly something. Now, you're either going to have to tell me or I'm going to insist on having you examined.'

Hannah bit her lip. 'By you?' Her voice quavered.

'I could. But if you'd prefer a female doctor to check you over, I'm sure I could get Dr Emery to take a look.'

Hannah sighed, closing her eyes before looking up again. 'No. It's bad enough that you'll have to know. I don't need everyone knowing about it. This is so embarrassing… And on my first day as well.'

'Pain isn't embarrassing. Let me know how I can help you.'

She nodded. 'Okay, but I don't want anyone else to know. And it's probably best if I show you…' She looked away, seeming almost embarrassed.

'Only if you're sure.'

'I am. But…not here. Could we go to your room?'

Intrigued, he nodded.

Even though he offered his arm, she told him she wanted to walk unaided to his room. She was clearly limping, and when they got to his room she grimaced and went to the examination bed, pulling the curtain across for some privacy.

'You remember I mentioned an accident?' her disembodied voice called from behind the blue curtain.

He did remember. 'You said you had a prang at a theme park.' He began to wash his hands, just as something to do.

'Yes. That's right. Well, it was more than a prang.'

'I kind of guessed.'

He was pacing slowly, back and forth...back and forth, his mind racing. Had she had leg surgery? Maybe her bones had been pinned? Comminuted fractures could be terrible injuries to recover from. Perhaps she was missing some muscle? Or had had skin grafts?

He heard her get onto the examination bed. 'You can come in now.'

He stared at the curtain, suddenly incredibly anxious. 'Okay...' He stepped forward, pulling open the corner of the curtain and trying not to show on his face any reaction to what he'd *not* expected.

Hannah had a mid-thigh prosthetic.

She was an amputee.

CHAPTER THREE

'I WAS ON a roller-coaster. It was a new thrill ride. It had only been open a few months and I was keen to try it. But the braking system failed and we ploughed into a stationary car ahead of us. I got my legs trapped.'

More than anything, she'd not wanted to reveal this. Some people changed once she'd told them she was an amputee. They looked at her differently. Or even, as in one particular case, dropped you like a hot potato because you didn't fit the image of the hot fiancée he'd prided himself on having any more.

Zach, to his credit, didn't let any shock cross his face. He simply nodded. 'Are you having phantom pains?'

She shook her head. 'No, it just feels really sore around the socket.' She pulled it free of her leg and noticed that the liner she wore inside had folded over. That was what had begun to cause an irritation. 'Damn it!'

'Here…let me.' Zach gave her room by placing the prosthetic on the floor and then examined the skin around her upper thigh.

She tried not to flush at the fact that he was touching her upper leg with his bare fingertips. Or the fact that he was being so gentle and nice. Or that, this close, he smelled like a summer breeze.

Zach probed the reddened skin. 'There's no sore, but the skin is irritated. I'll put a dressing on it to help protect it.'

'I can do that,' she said, feeling that she'd revealed more about herself than she'd ever wanted to on her first day, and not wanting him viewing her as helpless.

But he stopped her. 'Stay where you are. Sit back. I can do this. I don't very often get to play around with bandages. Why should you nurses have all the fun?'

He winked at her before bending to pull out drawers and look in cabinets, but came up empty-handed.

'Bandages are in *my* room,' she told him. 'Cupboard under the sink.'

'Hmm… You're right. Stay there. Don't move.'

He glanced at the clock to check the time and so did she.

They had about five minutes before afternoon clinic started. If she gave him two minutes to find the right bandage, another minute to put it on and the last two minutes to get her prosthetic back on, then she might be able to start her afternoon clinic on time. She didn't like to run late.

As she waited, she gazed around his room, but saw nothing that gave any clues about his personal life. No photographs of family. No model wife. No cherubic children. Not even a picture of a beloved pet. There was no relaxing art on the walls—just good health posters and information about flu, shingles and Covid jabs.

Zach Fletcher was a mystery man. Or just a private one.

Doesn't make any difference. He's just a colleague.

The door to his consulting room opened and he came back in, smiling broadly, his arms full of supplies. 'I wasn't sure which would be best…'

'That one.' She pointed at a packet to the left, keen to get this over and done with. It was exposing, her sitting there. What if someone walked in?

'Ah. Thanks.'

After opening the packet, he began to apply the dressing to her leg, relieving the pressure on her irritated skin. 'How's that?'

'Not bad. We'll make a nurse of you yet.'

He picked up her prosthetic, checked the lining wasn't folded this time, and helped her place it back on.

'I'll let you get dressed,' he said.

He left the bed area, pulling the curtain over for her privacy again, even though he'd just seen her without her trousers on and might even have noticed her knickers. Black. Sensible. Comfortable. She'd stopped wearing sexy knickers after the accident, having not felt sexy since.

Flushing, she adjusted her clothing and shifted off the bed and back onto both feet, testing the leg to see how it felt.

It did feel better.

Pulling the curtain open, she saw him at his desk, his back to her.

'Thank you, Dr Fletcher.'

'It's Zach. And the pleasure is all mine.'

No. She couldn't call him Zach right now. Not after he'd seen her exposed like that. Limbless. In sensible knickers that her mother might wear. He had to stay as Dr Fletcher.

'Well, I appreciate it. I'd better get off and start my afternoon clinic.'

'Okay.'

'And you promise not to tell the others?' she asked.

He made a zipping motion across his mouth. 'Patient confidentiality.'

But she wasn't his patient. Not really. He'd helped out a colleague.

She left him to his clinic.

It was a strange afternoon. Zach got through it, like he did any other day, but he couldn't help thinking about Hannah and what she had gone through.

She'd been through a terrible trauma. Life-changing. And yet she remained optimistic and bright and funny.

And beautiful.

He'd be lying if he told himself he hadn't noticed that. He'd noticed it on day one, but it had not factored in his decision to offer her the job. She'd simply seemed a good fit for Greenbeck. But by obtaining this good fit for the surgery, had he made his own life incredibly complicated?

Already he was questioning himself. Worrying about her. Why had she not told him about the accident properly before? Probably because she didn't know him well enough to share something so personal. But had she felt she might be discriminated against if she had? He hoped not. He wasn't that type of guy. Wasn't that type of employer. Or was it more to do with the fact that people often hid facts from him? Patients lied every day. Milly had lied to him...

She had told him once that she loved him, but that had been untrue because she'd been sleeping with someone else. Hugh. Someone he'd considered a friend. He'd found them together and even then, in that moment, with the evidence right before his eyes, she'd tried to lie. Hugh had tried to lie. Said it meant nothing. Told him it wasn't what it looked like. Had they thought him stupid?

He'd never discovered the truth about his own parents, either. Evelyn had said his mum hadn't been able to cope with him and had placed him into care when he was two years old. He had no memories of his biological mother. And apparently his father had never stuck around and there'd been no other family.

He'd been cast adrift in the world as a child *and* as an adult. Alone. Unloved. Abandoned. So it had remained easier to stay on his own. To be the best doctor he could be and care about people in a professional way. Without risking his heart.

Evelyn had told him he shouldn't have to live that way. That he deserved love and that one day he'd find happiness with someone. But he wasn't sure he could trust anyone enough for that any more. He could live without love. Hannah could live without a leg. People went without all the time and it was fine.

There was some leftover chilli in his fridge at home, from the day before, so he began to bake a large potato in the microwave to go with it, and stood there, staring at it, watching it go round and round, his mind wandering through an imaginary theme park.

Picturing a crashed ride and a crushed leg.

And the hot salty tears that must have run down her face because, being a nurse, she would have known what her injury must mean.

'*Start!* Start, you stupid thing!'

Hannah had been at Greenbeck for two weeks and had really begun to feel like part of the family already. Everyone was so lovely. So kind. Welcoming and warm. And apart from the blip with her prosthetic on that first day with Zach, no one else knew and everything had gone perfectly.

Until now, when her car wouldn't start to take her back home for the evening.

The engine sounded dry and croaky every time she tried to turn it on. It made vague attempts to sound as if it was desperately trying to start. A couple of times she even thought that luck might be on her side as it nearly caught, but then it just died on her, and when she turned the key an array of lights lit up on her dashboard.

She had no idea what they might mean. She could diagnose a urinary tract infection, prescribe medication and bandage the worst of diabetic leg ulcers and help them heal—but diagnose what had gone wrong under the car bonnet? Understand what all those orange and red lights meant?

No chance.

She smacked the steering wheel in frustration, then jumped when someone rapped their knuckles on the passenger window and bent down to look into the car.

Zach.

Her heart was thumping fast, because he'd scared her, and his warm smile merely accelerated it further.

She got out. 'I think it's died on me. Do you know car CPR?'

'I've not taken that particular training course. You're going to have to call the breakdown people. Unless you want me to take a look at it?'

She raised an eyebrow. 'You know how to fix cars?'

He bobbed his head left, then right. 'No, but I could pretend, if it would make you feel better.'

She laughed, and bent down to find the lever that popped the bonnet. She had no idea what she was looking for either. Walking to the front of the car, she watched him lift the bonnet up, set the catch to hold it in place and then have a good look. Touching different bits. Checking the oil. Making a lot of humming noises as he thought.

'Any clue?'

He turned to look at her. 'Not at all.'

She laughed with him. 'I guessed as much.'

'I strongly suspect that cars might be more complicated than people. Especially since they all run via computer chips these days.'

She nodded. 'I'll call the breakdown service.'

'Want me to wait with you?'

'Oh, no, you don't have to do that. You must have plenty of things to do.'

'It's no problem. It wouldn't seem right, just leaving you here on your own. Listen—why don't we go over to The Buttered Bun? They're open till late today. We can grab a cup of coffee and you'll be able to see the breakdown guys arrive if we sit by the window.'

Sitting with Zach? In a café? Away from work? Like... friends?

She could think of a million reasons why not, but just one look at his twinkling eyes and his cute yet oh-so-friendly smile and she just couldn't say no.

'Sure. Why not?'

She locked up her car and they made the short walk across the green to the café. A sign on the door stated that tonight was the Knit and Natter group, and anyone was welcome. When they went in, they waved and said hello to a group of smiling middle-aged and elderly ladies and one gent, who were all working their magic with pointy needles and a variety of wool, before grabbing a window seat.

'Just coffee?' Zach asked.

'I'm a bit peckish. I'd love a sandwich if they have any left?'

'I'll check.'

She watched Zach go to the counter and talk to the young lady behind it, who had the same stunning red hair that their new GP Dr Emery had. It was almost as if they could be sisters.

'No sandwiches left, but Jade says she can do you a toasted currant bun?'

'Perfect. Thanks. You must let me pay.' She stood up to get some money out of her purse, but Zach held up his hands.

'No, no. My treat.'

Hannah settled back down into her seat. He was being very kind—which wasn't helping with her attraction to him. If he was prepared to sit and wait with her, did it mean that there was no one at home waiting for him? She'd overheard a couple of the receptionists mentioning the name 'Milly' alongside Zach's the other day, but she hadn't caught the whole thing. Nor did she want to get embroiled in workplace gossip. But she kind of wanted to know if he had someone. Because she didn't want this to look like something it shouldn't.

Right now she had no certainties, and it left her feeling on edge around him. Nervous. Because she liked him. A lot. Something she'd not taken into consideration when she'd applied for a new job.

Zach brought over the tray. A mug of coffee for her, a small teapot for him, and two hot toasted currant buns for them to share.

'Looks great.'

The wonderful aroma of the sweet toasted bun alongside that of melted butter made her mouth water.

'Tuck in.'

She took a bite and made a pleased sound of satisfaction, then dabbed at her mouth with a napkin. 'So, do you need to call anyone?' she asked. 'Tell them you'll be late home?'

'No.'

'Oh.'

Shoot.

'You?' he asked.

'No.' She took a sip of her coffee. It was hot and strong and almost burned her tongue.

He raised an eyebrow. 'How are you enjoying being at Greenbeck?'

'Oh, I love it! It's just what I needed.'

'Are all your family back in Surrey? Do you miss them?'

'They're not far... Only an hour or so away.'

But she didn't want to talk about herself. He already knew far too much.

'What about you?' she asked. 'So far away from home in Scotland.'

'Ah, well...' He smiled, clearly considering how much to tell her. 'I don't actually have any real family. There are some foster parents I still speak to when I can. I ought to arrange some time to go back and see them, but you know how it is. You get busy...'

'You do. So...you were in care?'

He nodded.

'What was that like?'

'Not the greatest barrel of laughs, but it taught me a lot about life. About what's important.'

'Life lessons are important. I know *I've* undergone a few.'

'Your leg? That must have been quite an adjustment?'

She nodded. 'Something like that. I felt lonely a lot. Like no one else could understand what I was going through. At least until I joined a support group. That's why I'm always keen to establish them at my place of work. Having a chronic illness or injury can be isolating.'

'You're right. I felt a similar thing when I was at school. Everyone else seemed to have parents and families and places to go at the weekends. Birthday parties and huge family Christmases and Hogmanay celebrations. Me...? I went back to the children's home. And even though there were always other kids there, it was one of the loneliest experiences of my life.'

'Well, aren't we a couple of Cheery Charlies?' she said, and smiled.

He laughed.

She took a sip of her drink.

'I've learned from it, though,' she went on. 'I've learned that I used to waste so much time, waiting for the *right* time, but there's no such thing. Whilst you're waiting—whilst you're being afraid—time is slipping through your fingers. You need to take action. Go after what you want and stop waiting for everything to be perfect.'

'What were you waiting for?'

She looked away from him. Where were the breakdown

people? Why weren't they here yet? Did she really want to tell him this?

'I was waiting for myself to be whole.'

Zach frowned. 'How do you mean?'

She sighed. The fight to hold back was so easily lost when she was with him. It was dangerous.

'I was engaged when I had my accident. The wedding was only a month or so away, so we pushed it back. Initially the doctors thought they could save my leg, and I had three surgeries whilst they tried. Then infection set in and they needed to amputate. I told Edward to push the wedding back further, which he gladly did. In fact he seemed relieved by my decision, which should have been a red flag, but I was too busy focussing on my recovery. I thought we would get married when I had learned to walk unaided with my prosthetic. I visualised his reaction to seeing me walk down the aisle all by myself. I romanticised it. I thought he'd be proud of me. Realise just how much he loved me. But it turned out that Edward was happy to push the wedding back because he wasn't sure he could be married to an amputee. He said he loved me, but wasn't *in* love with me, and that physically he didn't fancy me any more. He sent a text on the morning of our wedding, to say it was over.'

Zach had exactly the right reaction. He frowned, looking angry on her behalf, and also incredulous that anyone could react in such a way. 'What an idiot,' he said. 'Sounds like you had a lucky escape.'

She smiled sadly. 'I didn't think so at the time.'

'I know that feeling. If it makes you feel any better, you don't hold any exclusivity on terrible past relationships.'

'I'm glad. What happened with you?'

Zach took in a big breath and sighed. 'Her name was Milly. *Is* Milly. She's the local vet—no doubt you'll run into her at some point. We were together for a year…got engaged. Everything seemed perfect.'

'What happened?'

'We were so busy planning our wedding we forgot to talk about what we wanted from our marriage, and when I did ask Milly informed me that she didn't want children. *Ever.*'

'And you do?'

He nodded. 'I've never had a family. Not a blood family. When I was young I always held on to the fact that when I became an adult I could start one. It's hugely important to me. And Milly had seemed perfect for me until that little bombshell. I tried to work it out with her. Asked her if there was any chance she'd change her mind in the future…'

'And there wasn't?'

'No. There didn't seem to be any wiggle room at all. I tried. I hung in there. Seriously considered not having children myself and thought Milly would be enough for me. I told myself she would be. But things had changed between us. There was tension. An atmosphere. She told me that she would always feel guilty for not giving me what I wanted—and then I found her in bed with one of my friends, so that was the end of that. And it didn't take long for the news to get around in such a small place as Greenbeck.'

'I'm sorry.'

'Don't be. Like you, I had a lucky escape. I didn't think so at the time, but I do now.'

It was astonishing to Hannah that someone would have cheated on him. And even more amazing to learn that he was single. So…both of them single people. Both looking for love.

She shivered at the thought. It was actually a little terrifying. Upsetting too. Like Zach, she'd dreamed of settling down one day and having a family of her own. But who would she find to love her without seeing the great empty space where her leg ought to be? And what about the fact that her prosthetic represented the emotional baggage that she carried with her everywhere?

But Zach would have the chance to find someone else, right? He had been nothing but kind and welcoming. He was warm and friendly. He took time for people and was clearly a dedicated doctor who wanted the best for his patients. And he'd helped her with her prosthetic. Done everything humanly possible to make her feel comfortable about him seeing it. He'd come to her aid when her car wouldn't start, and now he was sitting with her, keeping her company until the breakdown service arrived.

He was a gentleman, and as far as she was concerned this Milly had made a terrible mistake in letting this man slip through her fingers.

Zach's attention was suddenly snagged by something out of the window. 'Oh. They're here.' He pointed over to her car. The breakdown service had arrived.

'Oh, right. Well, thank you for keeping me company. And for the hot buns.' She smiled, realised what she'd said, then blushed madly. 'I mean—'

He laughed. 'I know what you mean.'

When he smiled the way he was doing now—truly smiled, broadly, widely, his eyes crinkling at the corners, shining bright—he was the most handsome man she had ever seen. She could have stared at him all day.

'Why do I keep saying silly things in front of you?' she asked. 'It's like my brain stops working.'

And then she blushed some more, because she wasn't sure if she'd just admitted something to him that she shouldn't have.

But if he thought so, he didn't let on. He let her off the hook, standing up and waiting for her to follow. 'It's fine. But I'm not going to leave you yet. What if they can't fix it? You'll have no way to get home.'

Now she was scrabbling. He made her nervous. He made her say stupid things. She would much prefer it if he went away.

'You've done more than enough already. I can't ask you to waste more time waiting around for me.'

'It's not wasted time. Making sure you're all right is important.'

She thanked him as they made their way out of The Buttered Bun and walked over to the staff car park next to the surgery.

She explained the situation and the breakdown woman popped the bonnet and started running some diagnostic tests.

Hannah leaned back against the low stone wall next to Zach and gave him a friendly nudge with her elbow. It was the safest way she could think of to touch him.

'You're a good man, Zachary Fletcher. I hope you don't let this Milly take up too much room in your head.'

'I don't. Like I said, I've learned from it. There'll be someone out there who's perfect for me—who wants the whole she-bang. Marriage, kids…grandkids one day. When I'm ready to trust again. And no doubt there'll be someone out there who is perfect for you, too. We've just got to be open to it when they show up.'

'Absolutely.'

'Mind you, with my track record I'm not sure I'll be all that great at trusting anyone. And if the trust isn't there…' He shrugged, indicating that such a relationship would be likely to fail.

'I know what you mean,' she said. 'It's a huge risk, isn't it? Putting yourself out there… Making yourself vulnerable…' Her voice cracked on that last word and she swallowed down tears. She'd not thought she'd be so emotional, but Zach had opened up her emotions like no one had in a long time. It was weird and strange and terrifying.

'Then perhaps we should make a pact?' he suggested.

She wiped away a stray tear. 'A pact?'

'Yes—an agreement.'

'About what, exactly?' she asked, amused by the turn of their conversation.

'Earlier, you said everyone needs to stop waiting for the perfect time and the perfect person. But we both know we're going to hold off until we feel…ready. The dating world is full of imperfect people and perhaps it will never be the right time for us both to get back out there. Perhaps we need to somehow practise in a safe way? To grow our confidence? Make sure that neither of us dates the wrong person or ignores any red flags? Maybe we can teach each other how to find love and happiness with someone who truly adores us without question and wants exactly the same things as us.'

'Oh? As simple as that, huh? Okay. How do we do that?'

'We date each other.'

'I'm sorry—what?' She almost choked.

Zach laughed at her reaction. 'Hold your horses! I'm not saying we actually *date* each other. I meant we practise being *on* dates. Together. That way, if one of us does something wrong, or ignores what could potentially be a red flag, the other one can point it out with no recriminations and no hurting the other person.'

'Oh…' Well, that didn't sound too bad. 'Like an experiment?'

'We'll test hypotheses. See what works. What doesn't. Then, when someone perfect for us comes along, we'll be so well prepared we won't lose them, and they'll think we're amazing because we will have trained ourselves to be.' He smiled. 'What do you think?'

It was a crazy idea! Ridiculous! But it was tempting, too… because what if he was right? What if he could help her feel like more than she was?

'I think you might be on to something.'

'Great. We're both adults, so we know what we're doing, but we've also both experienced abandonment, which can really screw a person over. So we promise to make sure that the other person gives love a chance when it arrives. You can be my guinea pig and I'll be yours.'

She nodded. That sounded just fine. Being each other's test subject meant that she wouldn't actually ever go out with him, right? It would just be practice. To see how they came across on dates. And it didn't sound as if he was interested in *her*.

'Cool. You've got yourself a deal.' She held out her hand and he shook it, smiling.

But this was too close to him…with those smiling eyes and that gorgeous grin. And touching him…

She broke the contact and stared at the mechanic as she analysed Hannah's car. Eventually she signalled them to come over.

'I'm afraid it's your alternator. It's completely dead and isn't sending out any electrical signals, so your battery is dead, too. I can replace the battery, but not the other. I'll call out a tow lorry and have your car taken to the local garage.'

'Barney's?' asked Zach.

The woman nodded.

Zach gave Hannah a lift back to Mrs Micklethwaite's. When he'd parked up, he looked at her awkwardly. 'So…when should we start our experiment?'

She shrugged. 'Maybe we should start as we mean to go on? No messing about. No waiting for the perfect time to start before we get cold feet. This weekend?'

He nodded.

Much later, she slumped onto the bed in her room, telling herself she'd done the right thing, agreeing to a fake date. They were going to meet at the pub. They'd agreed it was a perfect first date location. Public. They would eat. Drink. Talk. Play darts or pool. Maybe go for a walk later...

They both deserved to find love.

To find the one.

What was the worst that could happen?

CHAPTER FOUR

MR JERRY FISHER sat down opposite Hannah and reached into his pocket, pulling out a piece of paper.

Oh, no, he's got a list.

'I'm experiencing some dizziness. Room-spinning stuff.' His thumb moved down the paper. 'And I get tingling, and this foggy feeling, and sometimes it takes me a long time to find my words.'

She glanced at his medical file. Jerry was eighty-two years of age and was always at the doctor's with a string of mild complaints. He'd been in yesterday to see the HCA to have his earwax removed. A couple of days before that he'd been in complaining about ringing noises in his ears.

'Okay… I can see you have a list there,' she said, 'and we only have a short time together, so why don't you pick the two most important things that are bothering you and we'll go from there.'

'They're all bothering me, though.'

'I know…' She reached forward and held out her hand for the list.

He passed it to her.

'There are *twelve* items on this list, Mr Fisher, and I have only ten minutes with you. It's just not possible for me to provide you with the most effective care if I try to cover them all at once.'

'But what if they're all connected?'

She glanced at the list. 'With the greatest of respect, I don't think a blackened toenail and a suspicious mole are connected. You do seem to be having a lot of trouble with your ears, though. Let me look at those.'

Hannah glanced at his ears, using the otoscope, but could see absolutely nothing wrong. The eardrum was as it should be after treatment from the HCA. No extraneous wax. When she checked his temperature it was perfect, and so was his blood pressure.

'Is there a chance, Mr Fisher, that…well…that you may be a little lonely?'

Jerry looked down at the ground and she knew she'd hit the nail on the head.

'Things just haven't been the same since Beryl died.'

'That's your wife?'

He nodded. 'I just wanted to speak to someone. I'm sorry, Nurse, for wasting your time.'

He got up to go.

'Mr Fisher—wait.' She laid her hand on his arm. 'Loneliness can be a serious issue, and if you're creating medical complaints just to have someone to talk to here, I'm assuming that you're doing this elsewhere?'

He looked at her, shamefaced. 'I go to the library and ask them to order me books I don't want. I go to the local shop just so I can talk to the girl on the checkout. She's nice. And often I'll sit in The Buttered Bun and nurse a coffee all day, just to be around people.'

'Don't you have friends? Family?'

'They're all gone. I was the youngest of my family and I've had to bury them all. Beryl's family, too. The friends I used to have are either dead as well or in care homes.'

Hannah felt terrible for this old man. But she had a solution.

'I just may have the answer to your problem, Mr Fisher. I've recently started a support group here at the surgery for people like yourself, who are looking for companionship and friendship. And the best bit is that I've teamed up with a local dog rescue centre, who are prepared to bring over some of their long-term residents so that you can sit and play with the dogs, or maybe take them for a walk through the woods up to the castle.'

'Really? I used to have a dog... I've felt too old to take on another one.'

'Then this is ideal. Shall I put your name down? They meet once a week, on Saturdays, just after lunch.'

'Yes, please do.'

She smiled. Jerry Fisher looked brighter already. Just the thought of having some companionship was enough to put a sparkle back in his eyes.

'If you do have any serious health niggles, though, Mr Fisher, you'll need one ten-minute slot per issue, okay? I'd be happy to see you again.'

'You've been very kind. And understanding.'

'It's my pleasure. I know what it's like to feel alone.'

'A young thing like you?'

'You'd better believe it.'

'Will you be at this friendship group?'

'Yes, I'm going to come. As the organiser, I want to make sure it's working.'

'Then I'll look forward to seeing you, Nurse. Thank you.'

'Take care, Mr Fisher.'

With her patient gone her clinic was done for the morning, so she performed a few stretches to get the kinks out of her back and for just a moment sat in her chair, in her room, enjoying the peace and quiet.

She closed her eyes, hoping to meditate for a moment or

two. But all she could think of was her upcoming practice date with Zach.

They'd not really established any rules. Did they have to treat it like a proper date and get dressed up? Or could they just be relaxed and test each other with questions over a pint of beer and a packet of crisps?

She was going to be at the new support group first, with the patients she had identified as lonely. She could hardly turn up to that in a little black dress…

On Saturday morning she was nervous. She'd arranged to meet the dog rescue people and the companionship group outside the surgery, as they couldn't have animals inside the practice, and as lunchtime passed she saw a group of about eight people begin to gather, amongst them Jerry Fisher.

At that moment a van pulled into the car park, emblazoned with the logo of the local dog rescue centre, and two women got out. They were both young and blonde, one with her hair up in a high ponytail, the other with hers down.

'I'm Dee—this is Elle,' said the one with the ponytail.

'Hannah. Great to put a face to the name,' Hannah replied.

'We've brought a variety of dogs. Smaller and older ones, mainly. Not likely to pull.'

There were spaniels and cockapoos, a Yorkshire Terrier and a West Highland White, and soon everyone was part-nered up with a dog.

Hannah was walking a King Charles Spaniel named Fudge, and she led the group towards the public footpath that would wind its way up through the woods towards the castle. She knew they probably wouldn't actually make it that far. It was quite a steep climb, by all accounts. But she'd been told by Shelby, the phlebotomist at the surgery, that there was a path that led off the main one and remained level, leading in a large circular route, taking in a small lake.

She noted that Jerry had the Yorkie, and a big smile on his face as he chatted with an older lady by the name of Pearl.

'This is lovely,' said Dee. 'I've not been out this way before.'

'Where do you live?' Hannah asked Dee.

'Near Beaulieu.'

'Oh. Isn't that where the motor museum is?'

'That's it.'

'Are you into cars?'

Dee laughed. 'No. Not my thing. I much prefer dogs.'

Hannah nodded. 'It must be lovely in your job…when you get to see a dog connect with a family and find a new for ever home?'

Dee smiled. 'It is. It makes me want to wave a magic wand over them all, so they'll all get a new family and a loving home, but the world doesn't work that way, does it?'

'No. And if we had something like that, I think we humans would use it on ourselves first.'

'Ain't that the truth? Imagine finding another human who would totally adore you and be loyal to you for the rest of your life. Think it can be done?' Dee laughed.

'Probably not.'

And that was why she had to do this practice dating with Zach—because if she thought it truly was impossible to find someone who could love her and be loyal to her, then perhaps *she* was the one who needed training and re-educating?

She refused to acknowledge the strange feeling that came over her when she considered her date with Zach. The discomfort… The desire to call him and cancel… Because it didn't matter what she felt. Hannah was not going to get involved with anyone again.

She wasn't whole. She wasn't complete. Who would find her

attractive now, with an entire leg missing and a thigh stump that had healed oddly so there was a weird dimpled scar on the end of it? Even she could barely look at it sometimes. Why would any man? Edward certainly hadn't wanted to know, and he had loved her, so…

Zach had seen it, of course. She tried to forget that. The way he'd put his carefully composed doctor face on when he'd seen she was an amputee. She recognised that look. All medical professionals had it. It was a carefully curated look. One you used at work to show that nothing a patient showed you could shock or appal or make the patient feel embarrassed in any way.

He'd worn that look.

What must he have really felt?

Thought?

It doesn't matter. We're just practising. It doesn't mean anything. I'm just his test run for when the real thing comes along. And I'll be happy for him.

CHAPTER FIVE

ZACH HAD OFFERED to walk his neighbour Marvin's German Shepherd dog, Rebel, whilst Marvin was in hospital. Marvin had called him to ask if he could let Rebel out into the back garden to do his business, and feed him morning and night, but Zach loved dogs and so had offered to take Rebel for a proper walk, if Marvin was okay with that?

'Sure thing—if you don't mind? They're saying I can come home tomorrow.'

'No, it'll be good for me. Don't you worry about Rebel. I'll keep him with me until you're home. I'm not on call this weekend, so it's easy for me to keep him with me, fed and watered.'

'You're a good man, Zach.'

'So are you, Marvin.'

He'd decided to take Rebel up to the castle and back. He knew that Hannah was taking her social group there, with the rescue dogs, and they were supposed to be meeting later for their first practice date. He figured she'd feel more comfortable if he was dressed in casual dog-walking clothes, too.

He wasn't sure why he'd suggested this fake dating thing. Maybe it was because he'd not liked the way Hannah had kept her injury from him. That had niggled slightly. Clearly she had some issues in her past, as everyone did, but he didn't like secrets and he'd always thought he was the type of person others could be honest with. And if he wanted a perfect working team at the surgery, then he needed to be honest with her. So he'd opened up about his own pain with Milly.

When he'd heard about Edward, Hannah's ex, and how he'd treated her a rage had built inside him and he'd wanted, desperately to show Hannah that she was worth someone's time and effort. She was important. Not worthless. Which was how this Edward had obviously made her feel. It would be his duty, hopefully as her friend, to help her heal. So he'd offered to help her find love again. He wasn't doing it for himself. He wasn't ready to find love at all. But he'd play along until she found someone.

It was a decent distance to the castle and would be a great cardio workout—going up that hill and back again. He usually jogged up to the castle, so it was nice that today he'd taken his time to get up to the castle, to calm his nerves and go exploring down paths he didn't normally take. There was a pretty bridle path that took him past the edge of a sheep farm, and a field with a mix of donkeys and horses that he hadn't even known was there. Rebel seemed interested in them all, and wagged his tail excitedly every time he saw a horse up close.

Zach checked his watch when he began to feel hungry, and realised he ought to head back down to Greenbeck so he could meet Hannah later, go to the pub and get something to eat.

As he and the dog strolled down the hill he enjoyed the relaxation of just being present in nature. A dappled light glinted through the verdant foliage, and the earthen floor was scattered with small sticks and old pine cones that Rebel occasionally picked up and carried in his mouth, before dropping to go and sniff at something more interesting.

It felt good. He'd always wanted a dog, but had never got one as he didn't think it fair to leave it cooped up all day whilst he was at work. Maybe one day, when he found the right woman to settle down with and they began their family, getting a dog was something they could discuss?

It was easy to hypothesise when it wasn't actually happening. When he really tried to imagine it—finding someone, trusting someone—he got a little nervous.

As they got to the bottom of the path he became aware of voices and saw a group of people walking dogs. He heard laughter and conversation and knew he'd come across the social group.

Hannah's group.

He felt his heart begin to race and a smile crept across his face almost without him realising. He raised his hand in a wave, saw Hannah smile and wave back, and could not explain the feeling he experienced at that.

The others began to wave too.

'Dr Fletcher!'

'Hey, Doc!'

Rebel happily greeted all the other dogs, and there ensued a lot of wagging tails and sniffing of butts.

'Hey, how's it going?' he asked Hannah.

'Great. I didn't know you had a dog,' she said in surprise.

He laughed. 'Oh, I don't. This is Rebel—he belongs to my neighbour. I'd love a dog, but with the hours we work...' He smiled at her, loving how relaxed and happy she looked. He wasn't used to seeing her in normal clothes. She normally wore her uniform. But today she looked amazing. A sleeveless white blouse, fitted blue jeans, boat shoes... And her dark brown hair was loose and flowing.

'Zach? This is Dee. Dee—Zach. Dee has helped me set up this group for some of our patients.'

He shook Dee's hand. 'Pleased to meet you.'

Dee was pretty, and the way she was looking at him, eyeing

him up and down, gave him the feeling that she liked him. It made him feel a little nervous.

'Pleased to meet *you*, Zach.'

He nodded, and then extracted himself from the conversation by putting Rebel back on his lead, clipping him on securely.

They began walking again—out of the woods, into the lane that led to the surgery car park.

Dee and Elle got water bowls out for all the dogs to take a drink before they loaded them back into the vans. Hannah was giving everyone hugs and thanking them for coming and telling them she hoped they'd show up again next week.

Dee and Elle said their goodbyes and promised to see Hannah next week, and then they were gone, too.

'Just us, then. And Rebel,' she said, scooting low to give the dog a head-rub.

'Are you hungry yet?' he asked.

She looked at him. 'Actually, I am.'

'Still up for the pub? You could back out, of course, but I would point out that it's not good behaviour to back out when you've made a date with someone.' He grinned.

'Okay. And you should know that women often have second thoughts about going on a date, but often push through just to give the guy a chance.' She smiled sweetly. 'Let's go to the pub now. Sit in the beer garden. There'll be shade and water for Rebel.'

'Sounds good to me.'

The Beck Canal ran along the bottom of the garden at the Acorn and Oak pub. There were ducks, geese and swans meandering about on the grass, or gliding smoothly across the water's surface, whilst people sat chatting on wooden benches and occasionally threw crisps onto the ground for the birds to eat.

'How's your car?' asked Zach.

'Back up and running again, thank you. For a while there I contemplated buying a pushbike to get around, but Barney managed to fix it.'

'A bike's a good idea. I've got one. There are some good trails around the village and this area. I could show you.'

'Oh. Actually, that sounds interesting. I ought to do more exercise, and it does seem silly to drive to work each day when I could bike it in probably the same amount of time.'

'What sort of bike would you be thinking of? Racing? Mountain?'

'I haven't thought about it. Though I guess one suited for roads as well as off-roading on trails?'

'A mountain bike, then.'

'Perhaps.'

'I could come with you. Help you pick a good one. If you want.' He shrugged and took a sip of his beer.

Hannah appreciated that he was trying to help. But spending more time with him looking at bikes... Going out on rides together... Would that be too much? Probably not. He was just doing it as a friend—he wasn't interested in her in any other way.

'Thank you...that'd be very kind.'

'Don't mention it.'

Wow. He had such a wide, generous smile. It truly lit up his eyes and made them sparkle, and in turn made happy feelings twirl in her gut. He was just so...

What was the word?

Gorgeous. There. She'd admitted it. Zach Fletcher was gorgeous. The most attractive man she'd ever met. The kind she could fall hopelessly for. The kind she could just sit and stare at for hours with a dreamy expression on her face and...

Dear God, am I doing it now?

'This bike shopping thing,' she said. 'And going on rides together. That would be as friends? Or as part of our practice dating?'

'Friends, for sure. I don't think taking a girl bike-shopping would be her idea of a good date.'

'Gold star, Dr Fletcher.' She smiled.

Thankfully, the server arrived at that moment, bringing them the cod, chips and mushy peas they'd both ordered from the menu. It looked perfect. Thick-cut, twice-cooked chips, beer-battered cod and a small pot of mushy peas topped with mint sauce.

'Thanks.' Hannah picked up her knife and fork. 'This looks good.'

'It does.'

For a brief moment they ate in silence, tucking into their food.

'You must have been very happy with the way your group went?' Zach said eventually. 'Lots of people showed up.'

'I am. I'm hoping that once word spreads it will get bigger, and people who wouldn't normally talk to one another will.'

'Those dogs were great.'

'They were good as gold. Like Rebel, here.' She smiled at the German Shepherd, who sat by their table, hungrily watching each mouthful they devoured.

A couple walked past them and sat down at a far table. Hannah noticed Zach's face change. It had lost some of its sparkle.

'Everything okay?' she asked, glancing at the couple.

'Milly and her new beau.'

'Milly? As in…? Do you want to go inside?'

'No. Of course not. It's fine. It's just…'

'A little in your face?'

He nodded and took a sip of his drink. 'It just niggles because she wasn't honest with me. I thought we had a truthful relationship and we didn't. So… End of, really. Sorry—I shouldn't be talking about an ex on a first date.'

She leaned in. 'Are you kidding? Bashing exes is the fun part! You get to explain to your date all the ridiculous stuff that they did, and then you bond and laugh together and promise not to be like that.'

'Are you sure?'

He was looking at her so intently that it began to make her second-guess herself.

'Well, I'm not sure now… Perhaps that's where I've been going wrong? Okay. No talk about exes. Especially not on a first date. We save the horror stories for when we know a person better. How does that sound?'

'Better.' He took another sip of his cold beer. 'This finding happiness lark is complicated, isn't it? Full of potential minefields.'

'You're telling me… I once went on a date with this guy and he…' She trailed off, blushing. 'On second thoughts… that's a horror story, too.'

Zach laughed. 'See?'

'Absolutely!'

She ate a chip, looking at Zach, her mood thoughtful. Did a first date really want to hear about her horrible history with men? She'd thought they did, but maybe they were being polite? She didn't want Zach to relive his upset with Milly. The betrayal. The lying. The deceit. Nor did she want to imagine him with her.

Looking at Milly, at first glance Hannah thought she was beautiful, and could understand why Zach might have fallen for this long-legged blonde sylph. But when she stopped to look properly Hannah could sense a meanness to her features. Her eyes were too sharp. Small. Dark. Her lips were too thin.

There were too many angles to her face, and she pouted a lot as she listened to her companion.

Milly glanced over now. Saw her sitting with Zach. Curiosity crossed her features and then she turned back to her companion and laughed.

Hannah wanted to see Zach happy more than anything. Not reliving his past. If she saw him happy, it would give her hope that maybe one day she could have happiness, too.

So, who would be her ideal man?

Someone tall and dark-haired, like Zach? With that tousled look. Blue eyes. They always looked nice with dark hair. And a broad, genuine smile that made his eyes sparkle and twinkle. Someone kind and considerate. Clever. Someone who made her laugh. Someone she could talk to and just be herself. Someone who shared the same values as her. Someone who loved animals and wanted pets. Someone who didn't care that she was incomplete. That she was an amputee. A man who saw her for who she was, and not just a woman missing a leg. A man she could just sit and shoot the breeze with in a pub. A man who made her feel warm and fuzzy inside. Who could make her heart race. A man who made her think she could do anything.

Like Zach…

Zach. I've just described Zach.

She put down her knife and fork and dabbed at her mouth with a napkin. 'Could you excuse me for a moment?'

'Of course.' He stood when she did. 'Gentlemen do stand when women get up to leave?'

She nodded. 'I just need the loo.'

He nodded and she hurried away to the ladies' room, face flaming with the sudden reality of the fact that Zach exactly fitted her description of the perfect guy.

Physically, maybe. In character, perhaps. But what was he

like in a relationship? He was still showing her his good side. Maybe there was another?

He was her boss. Her colleague. And she wasn't ready to fall for anyone else. She'd agreed to this fake dating thing knowing that, and was only doing it because she wanted to help Zach find someone and be happy. She wasn't ready to do that *herself*. Couldn't bear the idea of experiencing all those emotions again...developing feelings for someone only to have him cast her aside, like Edward had.

I have a lot to offer someone—I know I do. But what if I'm found wanting?

She would not allow herself to fall for Zach. Because, if she was being honest with herself, it would be easy to do so. Zach was extremely easy on the eye, he was incredibly warm and friendly, and he was funny and clever and handsome and...

Oh, dear Lord, he's all the things!

She felt cowardly. But she was protecting herself. She'd given her whole heart to Edward and she'd thought he'd be there for her after the accident. She'd wanted to show him how grateful she was for all his support. She'd wanted to learn to walk up the aisle unaided as a surprise on her wedding day. She'd been so excited about it! All those hours of practice... imagining his face when he turned to see her...the way his face would light up. Perhaps he'd cry?

But no. Instead she'd received that text from him on the morning of their wedding, telling her that he didn't want to get married, that he wasn't in love with her. That he just couldn't get past her amputation.

'I'm sorry. I can't do this. It's over.'

He'd given her no chance to ask questions. He'd simply turned his phone off.

She'd thought that maybe they could just postpone the wedding if he wasn't ready...get married later, perhaps. But no, again. Edward had moved on quickly. And now he had a girl-friend who was tall and leggy and fun. Someone who didn't need to remove her leg and prop it up against a wall at night before bed.

The devastation he'd left in his wake…the loneliness he'd left her with…the feelings of inadequacy…

No. She couldn't go through all that again. Couldn't risk putting her whole heart on the line again. Because she wasn't sure she had a whole heart any more, and any man—most especially Zach—deserved a whole heart being given to them.

That was why she was doing this. For him. Because he'd been so kind.

Hannah splashed water on her face, dried it with a paper towel, then headed back outside, feeling apprehensive. As she neared the table, she saw that Zach was on his phone.

'Aye, that would be great…okay. See you then. Bye.' He clicked off the phone and smiled at her as she returned. 'Tell me—is it good etiquette to take phone calls from the person you call your mother during a date?'

She laughed. 'Hmm… I don't know. Maybe. It depends on the reason for the call. If it's an emergency, then obviously that's okay. If she's ringing to tell you some good news, then that's also okay. But if she's ringing to tell you that you mustn't be home late and she's already laid your clothes out for you to-morrow morning… Probably don't mention that to your date.'

He grinned. 'Then I'm okay. She was ringing with good news.'

'That's great.'

'Am I allowed to share it with you? What's the protocol on that?'

'You can tell me if you want to. I guess it depends on how you think the date is going and whether or not you like the person.'

'Hmm… Well, let me see… I do want to. I think the date is going well and right now I do like the person,' he said, with a grin.

Were his cheeks reddening? she thought. He was trying to hide it by taking a long drink of his beer. Dutch courage?

She blushed herself. 'Then please share. I'm all ears.'

'My foster father got through his chemo this week without any adverse side effects and he's going to ring me tomorrow.'

'Chemo? What type of cancer is he fighting?'

'Brain.'

'I'm so sorry. What stage is it?'

'Three.'

She nodded. 'Do you want to talk about it?'

He shook his head. 'Maybe later. I'm mindful that I don't want to drag down the date by bumming everyone out talking about illness and death.'

She nodded. 'Good call. For a practice date, of course. But as a friend I'm here any time you want to talk about it.'

Her own grandfather had died from cancer. For him it had been lung cancer that had metastasised. She barely remembered him—only snippets—but she did remember the toll it had taken on her mother. Cancer was difficult for all the family.

They suddenly became aware of panicked voices behind them and both turned. An elderly couple near the canal were staggering to their feet. The old man was struggling to breathe, his hands blindly shooting out and knocking over his drink. The glass smashed as it rolled off the table and hit the paving slabs beneath it.

Ducks scattered wildly and his partner, the older woman, shouted. 'He can't breathe! Someone help!'

Hannah and Zach leapt to their feet and raced over.

The man was having some sort of asthma attack. A serious one. He was already on the ground, weak from not being able to get enough oxygen.

As Zach attended to him Hannah called for an ambulance. When the paramedics arrived they checked the man out, placing a nebuliser and mask over the man's face. The man—Donald—began to breathe a little easier.

After the excitement had died down, and the man was on his way to hospital, the landlord of the pub gave Hannah and Zach a free slice of cheesecake each. It was banoffee cheesecake. Rich and decadent.

'Never a dull moment when you're a medic,' Hannah said.

'No, there isn't.'

'And, you know, saving someone's life when you're on a date kind of makes them think that you're an amazing hero.'

'Not sure what the ethics would be in always having someone on hand to get into a medical crisis for you to solve… Probably dubious and best to avoid.'

Hannah laughed. 'Agreed! Unless it happens naturally.'

'Good point. Now, should I offer to walk you home?'

She nodded. 'That would be gentlemanly and nice—thanks.'

He smiled. 'I'm trying my best.'

CHAPTER SIX

IT WAS WEIRD, walking side by side with Zach and the dog. They walked slowly, taking in people's gardens, admiring flowers, waiting for Rebel to sniff various posts and garden gates, and it felt as if she was walking with a boyfriend.

Only normally if she walked with a boyfriend she'd hold his hand, or have her arm around him, but she couldn't do any of that with Zach. Technically, this was only a first date. And a practice date. Not even the real thing. So she stuck her hands in her pockets as it felt the most comfortable thing to do with them.

Up ahead she spotted Dr Emery, with her son Jack, coming towards them.

'Hey...' Hannah greeted them.

'Hi! What a gorgeous day, huh?' said Stacey. 'We're off to feed the ducks.'

'Sounds good,' said Zach.

Hannah crouched down to make eye contact with Jack. 'You must be Jack?' she said. 'I've heard so many amazing things about you from your mum.'

She'd also heard some horrible things. Stacey had told her that they'd come here after some bullying that Jack had experienced at his previous school, due to the large birthmark he had on his stomach.

Jack looked intrigued.

'She said to me that you're the best reader and the bravest boy she knows,' Hannah went on.

'I do like to read.'

'Me too! Perhaps you could recommend some books to me one day.'

Jack nodded shyly.

She stood and smiled at Stacey. 'How's he settling in?'

'He's doing all right. I'm trying to think of ways to help him feel he fits in more. Daniel suggested scouts, but I'm not sure…'

'That would be *great* for him. He'd enjoy that.'

She looked down at the little boy. He was cute. Freckled, with the same red hair as his mum. She hated to think that he felt isolated and different. She knew how that felt.

Her sympathy for what he was going through suddenly made her brave. She addressed the little boy again. 'Hey, Jack, want to see something cool?'

Jack nodded.

'I've got a super-secret that makes me special and unique. Want to see it?'

'Sure.'

She raised her trouser leg to reveal the prosthetic, glancing at Stacey with a smile.

'Whoa…' Jack was fascinated.

'I lost my leg a short while ago. It changed my life. Made me think that everyone was staring at me. But you know what? They're not. People are so worried about themselves, they're not thinking about you or me. Once, I hated what had happened to me. I was very sad. But now… It's a part of me. It's what makes me special and different and I'm *better* for it. It showed me who my true friends were. So, if you ever want to talk I'm here for you, okay?'

Jack nodded.

Hannah looked at Stacey, who mouthed *Thank you*.

'Shall we go and find those ducks, then?' she asked her son.

'See you Monday,' said Zach.

Stacey and Jack said goodbye, and then they were alone again. Zach kept looking at Hannah, smiling broadly.

'What?' she asked.

'That was a good thing you just did for that little boy.'

'Well, I know how it feels to be different. To feel that you're not as good as everyone else.'

'You know you are, though? Miles better.'

She blushed at his compliment. 'Thanks.'

'I mean it.'

'Well, you're very kind. And I mean that.'

They walked a little further. Getting closer and closer to Mrs Micklethwaite's.

'I guess I should ask…is getting my prosthetic out on a first date the right thing to do?'

'Why not? But you don't have to show them. You could tell them about it, and if they have a problem with it then it's best to know sooner rather than later, right?'

She nodded, reaching down to scratch behind Rebel's ear. 'That's for sure. But what if it freaks them out?'

She remembered coming round from her amputation surgery. Slowly opening her eyes to see her family gathered around her bed, all of them happy, smiling. Except Edward, who'd looked as if he was really struggling with what had happened.

'Then you'll know they're not for you. Honesty is the best policy—isn't that right?'

'Yes. You're right. Okay… Rule number one for me, then, is to be upfront. Tell them about my leg.'

'It doesn't need to be the first thing you speak about.'

She laughed. 'Maybe not. *Hi. I'm Hannah. I'm an ampu-*

tee. Want to look? Yeah, I agree…it doesn't come across as romantic, huh?'

He shook his head with a smile, and then they were back at Hannah's place. They stopped at the garden gate.

'Well, this is me. Thanks for the meal.'

'You're welcome. I enjoyed it.'

'You're probably sick of the sight of me. You see me all week, and now we've met at the weekend…'

'Are you sick of the sight of *me*?'

She looked at him. 'No. I'm not.'

'Then ditto.'

Hannah laughed. 'What's the protocol for ending a first date?' she asked nervously. 'Shake hands? Peck on the cheek?'

She had to force herself to stop giggling nervously. Because even the idea of kissing him on the cheek was…

Oh, my God. I can't even describe what that would feel like!

'I guess…if it's gone well and you like them and you feel comfortable…a peck on the cheek is reasonable.'

'And if you like them a lot?' she asked.

Were her cheeks red? They felt red. Hot. Flaming. Was there a colour hotter than red?

'Then a short kiss on the lips would be acceptable,' he replied, his face flaming also as his eyes met hers.

Then he gave an embarrassed laugh that was oh-so-endearing, and she looked away because she couldn't meet his eyes.

'Okay. Should we do the kiss on the cheek thing, then? We're just practising, and I think it would be…' she swallowed hard '…*awkward* if we did anything else.'

He nodded thoughtfully. 'You're right.'

Smiling, he leaned in and she proffered her cheek.

Or that was what she meant to do. But something right at the last moment changed her mind, and she turned instead and their lips met.

His lips were soft. He smelt good.

Heart pounding madly, she couldn't believe what she was doing! Kissing Zach on the lips?

She opened her eyes as he pulled away in surprise, and laughed and shrugged. 'It was a good date. And I like you,' she tried to explain, cheeks still blazing with heat.

He stepped back, a little uncertain. 'I guess those were the rules...'

Now it seemed awkward.

She chuckled nervously. 'I'd better get in. Lots to do,' she said, stepping away regretfully, but trying not to show it by grinning madly.

'Yeah, I'd better get back,' he said, indicating the path behind him and beginning to walk away.

Why did this feel like the end of a real date? *Why?* She found her gaze dropping to his mouth, eyeing his lips, and found herself laughing nervously again.

'Enjoy the rest of your weekend, Zach.'

'Yes. You too. But you're going to have to go inside. I'm not leaving until you are. That's what a gentleman would do. So you should watch for that. When you're dating for real.'

'Yes! When it's for real. Right. That's good. That's good advice.'

She gave him a small wave, lifted the latch on the gate and headed for the front door. She rummaged in her bag for her key and unlocked the door, then stepped inside, turning at the last moment to smile and wave one more time before closing it.

When the door had closed, she felt a long, low breath escape her and she fell against the door, face pressed hard against the wood. It was cool and smooth and she wanted to stay there and never move—yet she also had to fight the urge to unlock the door, fling it open and rush back outside.

Instead, she lifted her head and peeked through the small

glass window in the door shaped like a diamond. She saw that Rebel was looking up at Zach, head tilted to one side, as if to say, *What are you doing? You missed a trick there.*

'What would you know?' she heard him say, glancing at the house one last time and then walking away.

Hannah's next patient was a seven-month-old baby brought in by her dad, who'd noticed some lumps and bumps. She smiled in delight as Mr Asher walked in with his daughter, who was in her pushchair, kicking her legs and holding on to a cuddly plush horse.

'So this is Amy?'

The dad sat down. 'Yes.'

'And how can I help you today?'

'She's been a little off for a few days, and then this morning, when I was changing her, I noticed these little raised lumps. They look like blisters.'

'Okay. And is she normally fit and well?'

'Yes.'

'I can see from her record that she's had all her vaccinations. Is she eating and drinking?'

'Drinking fine, but she's a little off her food.'

'Okay… And is she urinating as usual. Filling her nappy?'

'Yes, that all seems the same.'

'All right, I'll just check her temperature.'

Hannah slotted the thermometer into the baby's ear and pressed the button. It beeped back a reading that informed her that Amy did have a slightly raised temperature.

'Let's take her over to the bed and you can show me these bumps.'

She let the dad undress his daughter whilst she washed her hands at the sink. Then she donned gloves and went over to the examination bed to coo at the baby and gain her trust before she did her examination.

She didn't like to traumatise babies if she could help it. If she could establish a good rapport with her younger patients they would sense that she wasn't someone to be feared. And even though Amy was only seven months old, and would not remember this visit at all, she still wanted to make this experience comfortable for Amy.

'Hello, there! Oh, look at you! *Look* at you! Aren't you adorable?'

She could see the lesions on the baby's skin, clustered mainly around her mid-section, her armpits, her nappy area and legs. Hannah tickled her slightly to make Amy laugh and then shone a light into her mouth.

'You're such a good girl! Oh, yes, you are.'

She straightened and placed her stethoscope in her ears and listened to Amy's chest whilst smiling at her and wiggling Amy's arm, as if she was playing.

'Thanks. You can get her dressed now.'

Hannah removed her gloves, washed her hands again and settled down in her seat.

'Amy has chicken pox.'

'Oh, the poor thing.'

'Yes. She's going to feel a little uncomfortable for a while, and she'll be infectious until these blisters began to scab over. It's probably best to keep her away from people—especially vulnerable people—and don't go near any pregnant mothers.'

'I wonder where she's caught it from?'

'You don't know anyone with the virus? She's not at nursery, or a childminder's? Anyone in the family?'

'No. Yesterday we took her to a baby massage group, because we thought with her being grizzly it might help. Could she have got it there?'

'It sounds like she already had it, if she'd been a little off. If you have the number of her baby massage group you ought to give them a call and inform them, so that the other mums and dads can be alert for an outbreak.'

He nodded. 'I will. Sounds like I've got my own little Typhoid Mary.'

Hannah smiled. 'She has a few spots in her mouth. That's probably going to put her off her food, if her mouth's sore. Just give her plenty of fluids, infant paracetamol if you think she needs it, and you might want to make sure you keep her fingernails trimmed so that she doesn't scratch. You can use mittens or socks on her hands at night.'

'Okay.'

'You can use calamine lotion to help with the itching. Or there are other soothing creams you can get from the pharmacist. If you speak to them, they can advise you on what the best topical application is to use.'

'Thank you.'

'When you bath her just use cool water, not too hot, and when you dry her don't rub her with a towel, just pat her dry. That'll help. And use a moisturiser or lotion afterwards.'

'Got it.'

'And if you have any concerns or worries, or you think she's getting worse, then give us a call and we'll see her for another check-up, okay?'

'Perfect. How long do you think she'll be like this?'

'Maybe five days or so?'

He sighed. 'Long time for a little one.'

Hannah nodded. 'She'll probably cope with it a lot better than you will. Parents naturally worry, but it's good for her to get it now. Saves her from having a bad case as an adult.'

'True. Okay, thanks, Hannah.'

'You're very welcome.'

She smiled as they exited her room and began to type her notes into the system.

Little baby Amy had been an absolute delight. Hannah loved babies, and hoped one day to have her own. But she couldn't see that happening for a while. For that to happen she'd have to be serious with someone, and she couldn't imagine that happening yet either. She'd have to find someone she could open up to. Someone she could be vulnerable with. Someone who didn't care about her missing leg. Someone who wanted the same things out of life as her. Someone who could make her smile and laugh…who gave her warm feelings.

Zach's smiling face came to her mind and she pushed it away.

Again.

He'd been in the forefront of her thoughts a lot just lately and that couldn't be good. Since that date at the weekend she'd felt that…well, that he was amazing! But she couldn't fall for him, right? He was her boss. Her colleague. She'd just started here. Getting into another relationship doomed to failure was not the way to go.

They were practising for *his* benefit, not hers, that was all, and she had to keep telling herself that time spent with Zach was only borrowed. One day he would feel comfortable enough to ask a woman out, and it wouldn't be her… So be it. Maybe she should try to quicken the process and get it over with? Or, maybe, considering how he'd made her feel since that day, she should avoid having another date with him for a little while?

No. A long while.

'Do you have any balloons?'

Zach's ears pricked up. He'd recognise Hannah's voice anywhere.

He was in the Greenbeck village store. A place that had been run by the Riley family ever since he'd been there. George and Lucinda Riley had been stocking it with the same stuff for years. Bread, milk, fruit and veg, tinned goods—that kind of thing. But recently he'd noticed a few different things creeping into their stock. Things that he strongly suspected were down to the current member of staff behind the counter— Stephen, their youngest son.

There were postcards now. Calendars featuring Greenbeck. Touristy bits and pieces. Keychains. Sunglasses. SIM cards! He'd been talking about trying to bring his parents into the twenty-first century and it looked as if the tide was beginning to turn. And Stephen had grown fond of telling every customer, 'If it's not on the shelf, I can order it in.'

Zach had popped into the store to pick up some dog food for Rebel, whom he was still looking after. He'd used up what Marvin had had left in his cupboards, and he'd also needed something for his own meal that evening. Stephen might not have persuaded his parents that Greenbeck was ready for fresh pasta in the shop yet, but he'd found some dried farfalle, some fresh chicken, bacon, cream and a single lemon.

Now Hannah's voice drew him out from the shadows at the back of the store like a moth to a flame. 'Hello again.' He placed his wire basket of goodies on the counter next to hers.

Her smile of greeting was genuine. 'Hello! What are you doing here?'

'Same as you, I imagine. Shopping.' He looked at the contents of her basket. Cheese. Sausage rolls. Crisps. 'Having a party?'

'No, but Shelby will be. It's her birthday bash this week, remember?'

'Oh, that's right!' Shelby was their phlebotomist. 'You must have drawn bringing the snacks?'

She nodded. 'And the decorations. Because Anna on reception is poorly, so I said I'd pick them up for her. What did you draw?'

'Non-alcoholic fizz.' He pointed at a couple of bottles behind the counter. 'Three of those please, Stephen.'

'Can do.' Stephen filled his basket.

'So…balloons? Streamers? Anything like that?' Hannah asked Stephen.

'I can get you some.'

'When?'

'Tomorrow. Come by after work.'

'Perfect. Just those, then, please.' She indicated the snacks, and the sad-looking pre-made sandwich, the single packet of crisps and the bottle of water.

'I hope that's not your dinner?' Zach asked.

'This?' She laughed and blushed. Paused. Nodded. 'Actually, it is. Mrs Micklethwaite is having a family dinner and won't have time to cook for me, so…'

'Why not come to mine? I've got more than enough for two. Chicken farfalle. What do you say?'

She smiled at first. Seemed to think for a while. For a very brief moment he feared she would say no. Part of him *wanted* her to say no. It would let him off the hook. He'd not been able to stop thinking about her lips since the weekend and it was extremely distracting. And their practice date had been terrifying. But one look at her sad little meal and the invitation had just rolled right out, before he could stop to analyse what his mouth was saying.

'Just dinner. And maybe you can help me walk the dog afterwards.'

'You've still got Rebel?'

'Marvin's developed some complications. They're keeping him in.'

'Oh. Poor Marvin. Nothing serious, I hope?'

'He spiked a fever, so they're just taking precautions.'

'Right. Well, that's sensible.' She glanced at her sandwich. The lettuce looked a little droopy. The cheese a little plastic. The tomato a little mushy. 'Fine. Okay. Dinner… What time?'

He swallowed. 'Oh. Um…about six?'

'Sounds great.'

Stephen had finished ringing up her purchases. She paid him, said goodbye to the two men, and left.

Zach watched her go, before turning back to a grinning Stephen.

'Just dinner?' he asked, with a raised eyebrow.

'Och, get away with you. She's a colleague, and anyone would have done the same thing.'

Stephen nodded. 'Sure! Absolutely.'

Zach shook his head as Stephen chuckled. Once his items were in the bag Zach had brought from home, he hefted them from the counter.

'Just don't forget to order her stuff,' he said.

Stephen saluted. 'Yes, sir.'

What had she agreed to? She'd not thought about running into him at the village store! She'd thought Zach would shop away from the village, at a large superstore, or something. Not there. Anywhere but there.

And now she had agreed to go to his place for dinner.

Was this part of their practice dating thing? She wasn't sure. But he hadn't said anything about it being a date so she decided she would make it absolutely clear that it wasn't by dressing really casually, not bothering with make-up, and generally being…what? Friendly? Casual? Colleaguey? Was colleaguey a word? Probably not, but that was what she would be.

She glanced at the clock. Five-fifteen. Forty-five minutes before she had to be at his house. She stood in front of her wardrobe and began pulling out clothes. Dress? No. She didn't often wear dresses anyway—what the hell were these doing in her wardrobe still? Tossing them to one side, she began looking at her blouses. The blue one was nice. It had that frill. But that was too feminine, and she didn't want him looking at her and being reminded that she was a woman. T-shirt? Hmm...

She pulled out a claret T-shirt. It was plain. Not too tight. And—oh, yes!—khaki linen dungarees. They were casual. Covered her figure. And they were comfortable. There was even a small bleach stain on the leg that said, *You're not important enough to make me want to dress nicely for you.*

Good. That would do. Trainers as well.

Dressed, she sat in front of the small mirror that she'd perched on top of the small bedroom table. Hair up? Or down?

Down is probably best.

She grabbed her cleansing wipes and began to remove her make-up, eliminating every last trace. Her earrings were removed too. She automatically reached for her perfume, then stopped. No, this was an anti-date.

Hannah stood in front of the mirror, turning this way. That. She looked as if she was about to start painting and decorating a room. Which was perfect.

'Good. Nothing about me screams, *Be attracted to me!*'

She was about to leave the room when she suddenly thought she ought to take a gift to Zach's. If you turned up for dinner, wasn't it polite to take something? A bottle of wine?

I'll have to buy one on the way.

Hannah set off at a casual pace to Zach's. Walking seemed best. She didn't want to get there too early, and she could waste some time perusing the wine.

When she got to the village store Stephen was still behind the counter. 'Hi,' she said.

'Hello,' he replied. 'Twice in one day! I must be popular. What can I get for you?'

'I need wine.'

He grinned. 'Don't we all? Is this for dinner with the doc?'

She felt her face flush. 'It's just a meal. I don't want to arrive empty-handed.'

'Well, I happen to know that Dr Fletcher likes this one.' He swept a bottle from behind the counter, presenting it to her almost as if he were a sommelier. 'It's his favourite and would go well with the chicken.'

He took a step in front of her, smiling. She perused the bottle, considering. If she turned up with his favourite wine, what would that say? She decided not to take any chances, shook her head, and said, 'How about that one?' She pointed at another behind the counter.

Stephen shrugged, picked up the other bottle. 'Sauvignon Blanc. Good choice.'

'Thanks. How much?'

She paid him and walked out of the shop, happily feeling that she'd dodged yet another bullet. It was a decent bottle, but it wasn't his favourite, so he wouldn't think that she'd been asking about him at the shop. He'd view it as a casual choice. Nothing important. It was vital to Hannah that he did not think she was interested in him.

'Because I'm not. I'm not. *I'm not,*' she muttered to herself as she lifted the latch on his gate and sucked in a strengthening, empowering breath before knocking on his door.

Inside, Rebel barked, and she smiled. The dog would be a good buffer. Because right now she felt like a small fly, about to set foot on a giant spider's web. This was Zach's home. His territory. Hardly neutral ground. He'd be feeling comfortable here. She…? She would be less so.

His outline appeared, coming down the hall, and when he opened the door Rebel rushed out to greet her.

'Hello, boy,' she said, ruffling his fur and making a big fuss of him before she looked up at Zach.

Wow. He looks amazing.

Dressed casually in blue jeans and a white fitted tee, he looked as if he'd stepped out of a jeans commercial or something. He was barefoot. *Barefoot!* And his clothes moulded his body with absolutely no thought or concern for how it might affect her.

She managed a weak smile as her heart rate accelerated, and with no other working thought inside her head she thrust the bottle towards him. 'To go with the chicken.'

He examined the bottle and smiled. 'Ah, my favourite! How did you know?'

His what?

Her mouth gaped open slightly as she recalled Stephen's slight smirk, and how he'd positioned himself behind the counter so that the only remaining bottle of white was the one that she'd picked out.

Zach's favourite.

'Erm… Stephen helped.'

He nodded. 'I bet he did. Come on in!'

Zach stepped back, allowing her passage, and her embarrassment lessened as curiosity to see what kind of place he lived in took over.

CHAPTER SEVEN

HANNAH LOOKED…AMAZING. There was no other word for it, really. She was wearing cute khaki dungarees and her hair was loose. At work, she usually wore a little bit of make-up. Eyeliner. Mascara. Stud earrings. But without make-up she looked even more beautiful. Fresh and appealing. *Au naturel*. It did something to him. Stirred his blood even more.

Once he'd closed the door behind her, he wasn't sure what to do. Take the wine into the kitchen? Make her a drink? But the words that came out were, 'Want a tour?'

She turned and swept her hair over her shoulder in a wave. 'Sure.'

So, his heart hammering in his chest so much he feared an arrhythmia, he led her into the lounge, glad he'd done a tidy-up before she got here. He wasn't an untidy person, but he'd wanted to make a good impression. He'd cut some flowers from the garden and they sat in a vase on the mantelpiece, and he'd switched on the corner lamps rather than the main light, for a little ambience.

He wondered what she'd make of his choice of art. A fondness for Art Deco posters was something he'd always had.

But did she notice any of those?

No.

'What is that?'

She'd gone over to his corner unit and lifted off the cuddly toy that sat on top.

He laughed. 'That's meant to be a baby haggis.'

She smiled. 'It's cute.'

Then she headed over to his bookshelf, and he watched her as she perused the titles. He had a mix of most things, but a particular fondness for historical fiction that had some sort of crime or mystery at its heart.

'You've read all of these?' she asked.

'Most of them.'

He showed her the kitchen, and then led her into the garden. He'd never been one to have green fingers. He could keep people alive, but plants had always been a problem. But then he'd got this garden, and his neighbours and the local garden centre had been so helpful that he'd finally been able to grow things successfully. He was pretty pleased with it.

'It's lovely, Zach. What are those?' She pointed at a small pot of flowers in various shades of pink, purple, yellow and white. They looked like large daisies.

'Mesembryanthemums,' he told her. 'They've started to close up for the night, but in the daytime they're at their best.'

She smiled and raised an eyebrow at his knowing their name. 'They're very pretty.'

Like you.

But he managed to refrain from letting that slip out.

His cottage wasn't very large. Only two bedrooms, though both of those were a decent size, and he'd maximised the space by having fitted wardrobes made to fit around the chimney breast. He showed her the guest room first, before his own room, and tried his hardest not to imagine what it might be like to lay her down upon the soft cover of his bed and see her hair splayed out over his pillows.

'I'd...er...better go and check on the pasta.'

She gave a nod, looking just as relieved as he to leave the bedroom space.

Downstairs, as he approached the kitchen, he turned to her. 'Can I get you a drink? Tea? Coffee? Something stronger?' He wiggled the wine bottle she'd brought.

'Wine would be great.'

'Perfect.' He grabbed two wine glasses and checked they were perfectly clean before undoing the screw cap and pouring them both a glass. He passed her one over.

'Thank you. So what are we having? Chicken…?'

'Chicken farfalle. My recipe calls for pancetta, but there wasn't any of that at the village shop, so we've got bacon that I've cut into small strips. And Dr Emery's grandfather gave me a whole bunch of asparagus the other week, so I'm adding some of that, too.'

'Sounds lovely. Can I help with anything?'

'Nope. Take a seat—it's nearly done.'

He busied himself for a while and that helped to calm his nerves. He so wanted this meal to be perfect. He didn't want the chicken to overcook and go dry, or for the pasta to be too soft, and he got so into what he was doing he almost forgot that she was behind him.

Almost.

But she was there. In his periphery. And he knew that she was watching him. He didn't normally get nervous like this and knew he had to calm down. This wasn't a date. This was just one colleague inviting another to dinner. That was all.

'How are things at Mrs Micklethwaite's?' he asked.

'Oh, you know… It's a bit like living at home with your parents. There's a curfew. I can't have the television on in my room after ten o clock at night and she doesn't like me to have visitors. No smoking. No drinking. And no longer than thirty minutes in the bathroom.'

He turned. 'You're kidding?'

'I wish I was.'

Zach laughed. 'Sounds like the care home I lived in on and off. The rules there were on laminated sheets stuck on the walls in every room. No chewing gum. No ball games after eight o clock. Breakfast between six a.m. and eight a.m.'

'Wow. You must have been so happy when you got to leave and stay at a foster place?'

He shrugged. 'Sometimes. It depended if the foster parents were nice. Not all of them were. You could tell which ones were doing it for the money.'

'Did you speak to your foster father? The one going through chemo?'

She'd remembered. 'Yes. He was doing all right. A bit tired, but that's to be expected.'

Hannah nodded. 'When did you last see him?'

'I went up in February. Stayed for a weekend. I try and go a couple of times a year. How about you? When are you going to visit your family next?'

'Oh, you know… When I can get some time off from work. My boss can be a real bear.'

He turned and smiled. 'I hope you're talking about Lucy and not me.'

She laughed. 'Of course!'

He turned back to the stove, put butter and cream into a pan and let it bubble until it thickened. Then he tipped in the cooked chicken and asparagus. Then he drained the pasta and added it to the creamy chicken mix, stirring well. It was looking good. He was pleased with it. He ground some black pepper on it, sprinkled a little nutmeg and some parmesan he'd grated earlier.

'Here we go. Done.'

Zach filled two bowls. Topped each dish with a little of

the crispy bacon and a few more shavings of parmesan and it was done.

'*Voila. Bon appetit!*'

'This looks amazing, Zach! You can cook!'

'Well, you don't know for sure yet. It might taste awful.'

'Let's find out.' She speared a piece of chicken and swirled some creamy pasta onto her fork, then tasted it.

He watched her face intently. He wanted her to love it. It was one of his favourite dishes to cook. It would mean something to him if she liked it.

Her eyes widened and she made an appreciative sound. 'Oh, my goodness, that's amazing!'

Zach beamed with delight and took a forkful himself. 'Thank you. I do my best. Much better than that sandwich you had planned.'

'You're telling me… Listen, if ever the doctor thing doesn't work out for you, you can fall back on being a chef.'

He laughed. 'I'll bear it in mind.'

She took a sip of her wine and looked at him consideringly. Curiously. 'What made you become a doctor? Did you always want to be one?'

'No. I dreamed of being an astronaut. I liked that idea of escaping earth for a while and floating around in space without a care in the world. And then I got to school and learned science, and realised that if you were in space you'd have plenty of things to worry about! But science—chemistry and biology—was a subject I really enjoyed at school. When I was fostered at Evelyn's I began to get interested in medicine, and it just kind of grew from there. What about you? What made you become a nurse?'

'Oh, gosh, I always wanted to be one—ever since I was a little girl. I can't tell you where it came from, but I do remember playing with my dolls, and instead of having tea parties with them I got them to attend clinics and hospital appointments instead. I was always bandaging them. I even had this one doll with soft arms, and I would get a sewing needle and thread and give her stitches!' She smiled at the memory.

He could imagine that. Her as a little girl, playing with her dolls like that. It was cute.

'I remember thinking that the human body was such an amazing thing. It could do so much, but it could break so easily. I really liked the idea of helping people. Does that sound clichéd?'

He shook his head. 'No. Not at all.'

'I did think about being a doctor. Once, anyway.'

'You did?'

She nodded. 'But it seemed like so many years of training and I was impatient. I wanted to get started. I wanted to be hands-on, and I felt that being a nurse would allow me to do that.'

'You could still be a doctor if you wanted to.'

'Oh, no, thanks! I love what I do. I can't imagine changing that.'

'Well, we're very lucky to have you.'

'Thanks.'

They both ate quietly for a minute or two.

'So...um...when do you think we ought to do our second practice date?' he asked, knowing he needed to break the silence, and also knowing that it would probably make her smile. He liked doing that. He liked seeing her smile.

'Gosh, I don't know. Um...when's good for you?'

'I don't know either. What's the etiquette for asking for a second date? How long do you wait? Where do you go?'

She blushed. 'I've been out of the dating world for so long I'm not sure my answers are applicable.'

'Well, we had a sort of late lunch last time. We're having dinner now—though this is just as friends and not as a date.'

She pointed her fork at him. 'Exactly.'

'So…something else, then? A film? Bowling? Ice skating?'

'Have you seen me try to skate?' she asked, going red in the face and laughing.

'No. But now you're making me think I want to.'

'Can *you* skate?'

'Never tried it, but it could be fun. Shall we?'

She shook her head. 'I'm not sure that's the best activity for me.' She looked down pointedly at her leg.

'You can do anything you want,' he said softly. 'Don't let it hold you back. The world is your oyster—prosthetic or not.'

She sipped her wine, considering his words. Maybe he was right? 'Sure! Why not?'

'Okay. Next weekend? Saturday? Say three o'clock? After your social group's walk? We can drive over to the nearest town. There's an ice rink there.'

'Zachary Fletcher… You do know we're both liable to come back with loads of bruises from falling over all the time?'

'But we'll have had fun—and isn't having fun together the point?'

She nodded. 'I guess it is.'

'Then it's a date.'

Zach and Rebel walked her home. It was such a lovely evening it seemed a shame to take the car.

'And, look…it's only nine forty-five, so you'll get back before your curfew,' he joked.

She smiled, wishing he wouldn't joke. Because he was just so cute, and just so perfect all the damned time! He was a doctor. He could cook. He loved animals. He cared for people. He smelt good. Looked good.

Did he taste as good?

I bet he does.

But she didn't want to think about that.

Zach deserved someone who could give him the whole of her heart. The whole of her being. And she simply didn't feel good enough for him. Besides, he was her work colleague and her boss, and that just had red flags all over it, didn't it?

She'd not been enough for Edward. Maybe she wasn't enough for anyone?

She'd begun to suspect lately that maybe her relationship problems with Edward had been there *before* the amputation, but she'd blamed everything on losing her leg. There'd certainly been a few arguments before that day at the theme park. He'd complained about the hours she spent at work. About how her patients seemed to come before him. Said that she always chose work over him.

'Do you think that we, as medics, always put work first?' she asked now, and looked at Zach, a slight frown between her brows.

'I don't know. Some of us, for sure. Being a medic can be a vocation. A calling. It's got to be. We certainly don't do it for the money or the long hours.' He smiled. 'Why do you ask?'

'It's something someone once said to me.'

'Your ex-fiancé?'

She nodded. 'Edward. We used to argue about it all the time.'

'What made you think about that?'

'What we're doing... The fake dating.'

'How so?'

'Well, we're trying to help each other out, right? Make sure we say the right things on dates. Do the right things. And it just got me thinking... Edward always used to argue that I kept a piece of myself held back. Like he never got all of me.'

Self-preservation, she'd called it, but where had it come from? It wasn't as if her parents had a bad marriage. She'd grown up in a wonderful home and had very happy memories of her childhood.

But as she began to think about it a bit more, she remembered her mum's story. How she'd once been an incredible young woman. Intelligent. Worthy of going to university. She'd wanted to study astronomy. Had spent years staring at the stars through her father's telescope. But then she'd met and fallen in love with the man who had become her father, and her dreams, and the woman she was, had disappeared as soon as the ring had been slipped onto her finger. She'd become a housewife and a mother. And there was nothing wrong with either of those things, but she knew her mum had lost who she was. Had lost her passions and her dreams as she'd raised her children.

'Do you think that was true?' Zach sounded curious.

'I don't know. Maybe. But what if it was? What if all my relationships are doomed to failure because I hold a piece of myself back? What if we do all this fake dating and it doesn't make a blind bit of difference to me? What if I'm just faulty and can't be fixed?'

He turned to look at her. She could see him thinking and wondered what was running through his brain. Was he glad that he wasn't really dating her? If he'd wanted to date her then he would, but no, he was using her as practice for when the real love of his life came along.

'Have you considered the idea that you might have held a piece of yourself back from him because you knew deep down, subconsciously, that he wasn't the right man for you?'

Hannah stopped walking and turned to stare at him. No. She hadn't considered that. She'd been so focused on what might be wrong with *her* that she'd never considered there might be something wrong with Edward.

'Huh…'

'What?'

'I hadn't considered that.'

'So, let's think about it. Was there ever anything about this Edward that made you hesitate?'

'I don't like talking badly of people.'

'We're not. We're analysing. It's to help you. Consider it a fake date bonus.'

She nodded. 'Okay… Well, maybe he could be a little self-absorbed sometimes.'

'Okay. Good start. What else?'

'Selfish on occasion. Inconsiderate. A little rude to waiters.'

Zach smiled as he listened.

Her list began to grow, the more she thought about it. 'He wasn't keen on animals, and he told me that when we got married he'd never want a pet. Said they were too much work. Took up too much time. Made a mess. That kind of thing…'

'Deal-breaker right there, if you ask me.'

She laughed, but now she was on a roll. 'He'd eye up women when we passed them—even with me right there, holding his hand. He spent more time in front of the mirror than me, and before we'd leave the house he'd always ask me if his collar was straight. If his nostrils were clear. If his ears were clean. Honestly, he'd stand in front of me and expect me to check them! What was I? His mother? Why couldn't he look for himself, in that mirror he loved so much?'

Zach laughed along with her. 'There you go!'

'He wanted me to give up work when we had a child. I'd forgotten that. All those little things that he did that drove me up the wall. I was so focused on my recovery. On this image I had of myself getting to the church and getting out of my wheelchair and walking up the aisle. I was hoping to see an amazing smile light up his face. For him to cry with happiness… Oh, my God, Zach! I was in love with a fairy tale! Not the real-life version of us.'

She stopped walking as realisation hit. She couldn't believe it. Why hadn't she seen it before? Zach had helped her see with just a couple of simple questions and his support, telling her that it was okay to talk about it. That she wasn't doing anything wrong in bashing the 'brave fiancé' who had stood by her through her surgeries and amputation.

Because *he hadn't*. Not at all.

She looked at him in all seriousness. 'You're going to be an amazing guy for the right lady. When you find her. You do know that, don't you?' she said, wanting him to know it.

He looked at her strangely. 'And you'll be an amazing woman. When the right man comes along.'

At her lodgings, she decided not to drag out the whole goodbye thing. The last time had been awkward. The more she had stood there, the more she had wanted to do something. Give him a peck on the cheek, just as friends. But, terrified he might think it meant something more, she'd stopped herself—and then had lain awake for hours, reliving that moment and cringing.

So tonight she simply smiled, thanked him for walking her home, placed her hand on his arm as a grateful gesture, then gave a brief wave and hurried inside.

Was that better than before?

Easier?

The answer was a resounding *no*.

CHAPTER EIGHT

PETER LAYMAN WAS an eighty-year-old gentleman who had come in for one of his monthly chats with Zach. He never came to talk about himself. Peter, despite his age, was still sturdy and strong, and the most that had ever been wrong with him was his Type Two diabetes, and he even seemed to have that nicely in control. No. He came to talk about something else.

Someone else.

'Hello, Peter!' Zach shook the man's hand as he came into his consulting room and bade him sit. 'How are you today?'

'Not bad, Zach. Not bad at all…'

He always said that. Zach sometimes thought the man's legs could be on fire and he'd still say, *Not bad. Not bad at all*.

'And how's Ellen?'

'Oh, you know how it is… The same, mostly.'

Ellen was Peter's wife of sixty years. At the age of seventy-six she'd been diagnosed with Alzheimer's. They'd dealt with it alone for the first couple of years, but then Peter had begun to struggle with the behaviour and the moods, and after Ellen had nearly burnt the house down after leaving a chip pan un-attended he had finally made the difficult decision to put his wife into a specialist care home.

It was a decision that Peter had struggled with immensely. He loved his wife, and felt it was his responsibility to look after her and do the best by her, and even though Zach had tried to present the idea of her going into a home as being best for her, as well as Peter, his guilt had weighed him down terribly.

'I went to see her yesterday,' he told Zach.

'How did that go?'

Peter shrugged. 'She didn't recognise me at first. That's always a blow. Sixty years with that woman at my side, and when I went into her room she just looked at me blankly and asked, *"Who are you?"* It's a hard thing, Zach. A very hard thing. She just doesn't see me.'

Zach nodded. He couldn't imagine loving someone for that long and then having that person not know who he was.

'Did she remember eventually? Did you tell her who you were?'

'Oh, yes. I got the photo album out. It took ten minutes, but then she said my name and everything was fine again. She even slipped her arm into mine and laid her head on my shoulder.' Peter smiled. 'That was nice.'

'Good. I'm pleased. How are her legs doing?' asked Zach. 'She had cellulitis, didn't she?'

'The doctors over there have been very good. Had her on antibiotics and it seems to be clearing up. Her skin's very dry, though, and the district nurse comes and has given the staff some cream to apply.'

'Good. It all sounds very positive. And how are *you* doing at home? Everything all right there? Any problems?'

'No. You know me… I can look after myself.'

'I know, but I have to ask. Are you lonely?'

'Sometimes. When you live with someone for that long you're used to just turning to them and making a comment about something, or asking a question. But when I turn around, even now, after all this time, I'm still surprised there's no one there.'

'Well, if you're interested, our nurse Hannah is running a group each Saturday for people on their own who want a little companionship. They meet here, and the local dog rescue centre brings over some of their dogs, and everyone walks together. It's very good and everyone has a wonderful time.'

'Ellen and I used to have a dog. Little white toy poodle. Suzy, she was called. Nice little thing… What time does this group meet?'

'After lunch.' He reached for one of the flyers from his desk drawer and passed it over. 'All the details are there. Take a look. I think you might enjoy it.'

Peter nodded. 'I might give it a go. I got out of the habit of being with friends after Ellen got sick. And a few have since died, which you expect at our age. But this sounds interesting. I'll certainly give it a go. Thanks, Zach.'

'No problem. And if you ever need to talk—about anything—just call Reception and we'll fit you in, okay?'

Peter nodded and got to his feet. 'Same time next month?'

Zach smiled. 'Same time next month. Or any time.'

Peter shook his hand again and Zach walked him to the door, giving him a wave as he disappeared down the corridor.

He tried to imagine what it might be like to have been married for sixty years. What that would feel like. What a deep love it would have to be, to last that long… To build such a relationship, over time, only for it to slowly be eaten away by a disease that took that other person from you a little at a time, day by day.

Was that harder than losing them in an instant?

He didn't know.

On an impulse, he knocked on Hannah's door.

'Come in!'

He opened it and smiled to see that she didn't have a patient with her. 'Morning. How are you doing?'

'I'm good! How are you?'

'Great. I think I've got another person interested in your dog walking social group.'

'Oh?'

'Gentleman who's had to put his wife in a care home. Alzheimer's,' he explained.

'Oh, bless him. How is he?'

'He's managing. Just lonely, I think. He took a flyer—said he'd try it out. His name's Peter Layman. Just thought I'd better let you know that you might have one more this weekend.'

'Okay. I'll notify the dog rescue centre.'

'You still up for our ice skating?'

'I think so. You?'

'Yes. I did think about backing out for a brief moment. Because that's probably what I'd do if it was a real date.'

'You'd get cold feet about ice skating?' she said, and laughed nervously.

He nodded, smiling at her laughter.

He'd been an idiot to suggest ice-skating and force her into it. But he'd meant what he'd said. She could do anything. He wanted to make her feel that she could.

'Well, if you put it like that... But I realise this is all about helping you find *The One*, so I'm going to be there.'

'It's meant to be helping you, too! Hey, I'm off to the bike shop tonight, to look for a decent mountain bike.'

'Want me to come along?' he asked. 'I said I would.'

'Oh! Well, that's very kind of you—if you're sure? I'd hate to keep taking up your time.'

'I don't mind. A promise is a promise.'

'Okay. I'm heading there straight after work in my car. It should only take half an hour or so.'

'Sounds perfect. I'll meet you after we've both seen our last patient.'

He left Hannah's room and then went out to deal with his little secret.

* * *

It felt strange to see Zach get into her car and smile at her before putting on his seatbelt. She appreciated him offering to come along and share his expertise on bikes, but she hadn't really expected him to do so. It was something he'd mentioned only casually—*'Oh, I'll help you, if you like.'* She'd never thought he actually would.

Edward had used to do that.

'I'll help you clear out that room. Don't want you throwing something important away.' Or, *'I can go shopping with you if you like.'*

But when the time came he'd always be too busy, or he would have made other plans, or he'd say he was too tired and he just wanted to relax and could they do it later?

'Which shop are we going to?' asked Zach.

'I thought the one in Cherringham.'

'Chrissie's Bike Shop?'

'That's the one.'

'I know it well. I got mine from there.'

She began to drive through Greenbeck, past the village green, over the Wishing Bridge, and then up the hill that would take them past the castle. Cherringham wasn't far. About a fifteen-minute drive. And Chrissie's Bike Shop sat in the centre of the small town, open that night until eight o'clock.

'Any news on Marvin?' she asked.

'Yeah, looks like he's developed quite an infection. They've put him on intravenous antibiotics to help get rid of it.'

'Poor guy. And your foster father? How's he doing since his chemo?'

'Yeah, good… He's had a couple of difficult days, but Evelyn said he was doing much better today.'

'That's good news. What are you doing with Rebel whilst you're at work?'

He laughed. 'Can you keep a secret?'

'Of course!'

'I brought him to work today. Settled him down in the old bike shelter behind the surgery, with a blanket, some toys and a bowl of water, and popped out in between patients to give him a quick cuddle and a toilet break.'

She laughed. '*That's* why I saw you out the back! For a minute there I thought I was going mad. But that *was* you in the woods?'

Zach grinned. 'Yes. Don't tell Lucy. You'll get me in trouble.'

'Hardly. You're the senior partner.'

'But Lucy's the practice manager and she used to be a nurse—you never mess with a nurse.'

'You'd better believe it!' She laughed with him, enjoying the fact that she was sharing his secret. 'Was Rebel all right?'

'He was fine! He was in the shade all day, and I took him food and snacks and toys…we had a walk. I think he enjoyed himself.'

'You love having a dog, don't you?' she asked softly.

He nodded. 'I do. I want Marvin to be better, but I'm really not looking forward to handing that dog back when he is.'

'I get that…'

They drove on in companionable silence for a little while as the traffic got busier heading into Cherringham. They got stuck behind a learner driver for a while, who stalled the vehicle at traffic lights, but they were in no rush so neither of them was bothered.

After finding a parking space in the town centre, they began their short walk to the bike shop.

'So, you say you're looking for a mountain bike?' said Zach.

'Yes. But I don't need anything with loads of gears and features. It's just to get me to work and back, and the occasional trail ride.'

'Have you got a helmet?'

'No.'

'Then you'll definitely need one of those. Safety first.'

'Good thinking.'

She pushed open the glass door to Chrissie's and they headed inside. Instantly they were surrounded by the smell of brand-new rubber and shiny, colourful bikes in all shapes and sizes. The young woman behind the counter looked up at them and asked if they needed any help.

'Not yet,' said Hannah. 'We're just browsing, thanks.'

'Well, I'm here if you need me.'

She beamed a smile, and Hannah couldn't help but notice how the young woman kept sneaking looks at Zach. Did he notice things like that? He had to, right?

She noticed when guys looked at her. The appreciative smile. The second glance. The way their eyes would run up and down her body, as if she were some sort of commodity and they were trying to work out if she were worth pursuing.

She suspected that most would go running in the opposite direction after one look at her stump. Prosthetic legs were interesting, sure. And people admired you for having one in some ways. But not everyone found a missing leg to be physically attractive. She got that. So it was going to take a special kind of man who wouldn't be bothered by it. A man who would see beyond her physical disability. Beyond her missing limb. A man who found the woman behind it worth loving and much more important than anything physical that was missing.

Because she still felt whole. Wanted to believe that she *was* whole. It had taken her some time to feel that way and head out into the world like a brand-new person, but technically she was, and it had taken her time to get to know the new her.

'This one looks good.'

Zach was directing her attention to a silver-framed mountain bike. Looking it over, she kind of liked it. The style... The look...

He hefted it easily. 'It's lightweight. Want to try it?'

She grabbed hold of the handlebars and tried to swing her left leg over the crossbar. But her prosthetic foot didn't lift high enough and she stumbled, off-balance, and suddenly found herself caught in Zach's arms as he pulled her back to safety.

'Are you okay?' he whispered, his mouth by her ear.

Her heart thudded painfully in her chest, and even though her mouth was dry, and her body was going crazy at being in Zach's arms, she somehow managed a nod, her cheeks flaming red.

He seemed to be looking intensely into her eyes, and the feelings it created were crazy! His lips parted.

To kiss her?

'You need a lower crossbar,' he said, his voice strangely low.

He let go of her now that her balance was back. Of course. He was probably worried about her reaction to him holding her. He wasn't attracted to her in the least! They were here about bikes!

He walked over to another bike. Red, with a silver and black streak of colour across the frame. It looked a lot easier to get on, and the seat didn't look as if it would slice her in two, either.

'Great.'

'Give it a try.'

Zach held the bike steady whilst she tried to get her leg over the frame and she did so easily. A label was hanging from the handlebars.

'"*Ten gears, lightweight aluminium frame, broad, deep-tread tyres, front suspension, disc braking system...*"' he read aloud. 'Sounds good to me.'

'What's the price?' she asked, still feeling slightly unsteady after what had just happened.

He turned the tag to show her.

'Not bad.'

'How does it feel?'

'Comfy. Surprisingly.'

'It's one of our most popular brands,' said the sale's assistant, who'd now come over, sensing a sale.

The name tag over her left breast said her name was Tayla, and she smiled at Zach once again.

'Could I test it out?' asked Hannah.

'Sure. We've got an area out at the back. Follow me.'

Tayla took hold of the bike, removed it from its rack and began to wheel it towards the rear of the store. They passed through a door marked 'Staff Only', walked down a long corridor and then out through a fire exit, to where there was a large car park and, beside it, a small bike trail that went in a rough loop and included some small hillocks. No doubt for those who liked to perform jumps.

'Here you go.' Tayla removed the sales information from the handlebars and passed the bike to Hannah. 'Take it for a spin.'

A broad smile crept across Zach's face as Hannah set off down the track, wobbling slightly to begin with as she adjusted her balance and found the right place to situate her prosthetic foot on the pedal. Her hair streamed out behind her and he could hear her laughing as she went up and down the small humps on the track.

'You're doing great!' he called out, when she risked a quick glance at him and gave him a wave.

'It suits her,' said Tayla, glancing at him.

He had to agree. She looked amazing. But then again, she always did.

'Is she your girlfriend?'

The question pulled him out of his thoughts and he turned to look at the salesgirl. 'Er…no. She's a work colleague.'

'She's wearing a nurse's uniform. Are you a nurse, too?'

'I'm a doctor.'

'Oh? In a hospital?'

'No. A GP surgery.'

He whooped and clapped his hands in support as Hannah passed them once again.

'I wanted to be a nurse once.'

'Oh?' He gave the girl a quick smile, then turned back to watch Hannah.

'Didn't get the grades I needed for university.'

'That's a shame. You could always retake them, if that's what you really want to be.'

'Yeah, but it costs so much now, and I'm not sure I want that student debt hanging over my head.'

'It can be a worry.'

He didn't get to say any more. Hannah came to a stop in front of him, cheeks flushed red and an intense gleam of happiness in her smile.

'I love it! I'll take it!' she said, dismounting.

He couldn't help himself. He stepped forward and held his hands out, as if waiting for her to fall again, but Hannah frowned at him and, taking it as an admonishment, he stepped back.

'Oh, that's great!' said Tayla.

'Do you sell helmets?' she asked.

'We do.'

'I'll need one of those.'

They followed Tayla back into the shop and were shown to the helmet selection on the back wall.

'Wow, there's so many to choose from,' said Hannah.

'Which one do you fancy?' he asked.

'I don't mind, as long as it doesn't make me look silly.'

He wanted to say that it wasn't possible for her to look silly, but he held back, picking up a neon yellow and white one and placing it on her head, laughing as it pressed some of her hair down over her face.

Hannah laughed in response and adjusted the curtain of hair that had covered her face. 'What do you think?' She turned this way. Then that. Almost as if she was trying on a hat for a wedding. Then she looked in the small mirror at herself. 'Hmm… Not sure about the colour.'

Zach took the helmet off her and passed her a black and silver one, pressing it down onto her head and comically rapping on the top of it with his knuckles. 'How does that feel?'

'Actually, it feels all right.' Hannah adjusted the buckle under her chin and checked the fit and the look in the mirror. 'What do you think? I like it.'

She turned to him for his opinion. He knew he was smiling. Broadly. Did he ever stop smiling when he was with her?

'Looks good.'

'Doesn't wash me out?'

'No.'

'I don't look awful?'

'No.' He wanted to tell her she looked beautiful, but didn't dare. He didn't want to come across as if he was interested in her.

'Wow… Save that charm for the practice dates.' She undid the clip and looked back in the mirror, so she didn't see the look that crossed his face.

She was more than beautiful. And she was one of the most

courageous people he knew. Sure, he hadn't known her long, but even after all she'd been through she still had a wonderful outlook on life. After her accident she could have become bitter, or depressed, even angry. No one would have blamed her for that. But no. She'd fought hard to get back to a normal life. She still took care of others. She remained positive. And she was still looking for her happy ending.

She was beautiful inside and out. Losing a leg hadn't changed her. Being abandoned on the day of her wedding had been the thing to damage her, cause her to be afraid of being abandoned by anyone she had feelings for.

Something he understood all too well.

There'd been a long time as a boy when he'd not felt wanted. He'd never been adopted, though other children in the care home had been, and it had left him wondering what it was about him that made him unlovable? Was it because he was bigger than the other boys? More rough-and-tumble? Was it because he'd sometimes got into trouble at school? Or because he had dyslexia?

When he was fifteen, his first ever girlfriend had cheated on him. And during the upset Evelyn and her husband had fostered him. Maybe she'd taken pity on the young boy sitting in the corner with the sad eyes? She'd given him hope for a while, that maybe there wasn't anything wrong with him except for the fact that he wanted to belong. Because he'd always felt on the outside of everything.

Then his second girlfriend had also cheated on him. She'd said he came on too strong. Was too fast and too quick in telling her that he loved her and wanted to make all these plans. And maybe he had been. But he'd just been searching for a person to settle down with.

To make a family with.

To belong to.

So that finally he'd feel that he had a family of his own.

He'd gone to university determined to stay single. To hold himself back...to remain separate. He'd learned that people he got close to only hurt him in the long run. He'd come top of his class, year after year, and although there'd been the odd date with other medical students during placements at the hospital there'd never been anything serious. He'd deliberately kept things casual. Fun. One night only. Until he came to Greenbeck.

In Greenbeck he'd worked hard to establish himself—and then he'd met Milly. Fun, energetic Milly, who understood what it was like to have patients and to put your work first, and he'd begun to believe that they shared a bond no one else could understand. He'd fallen for her hard. And he'd begun to believe that maybe he'd found the one.

Only to be wrong again.

'I'm going to take this one!' Hannah called out to Tayla.

'Great! I'll get everything rung up for you.'

Whilst they waited Hannah turned to him and smiled. 'Thanks for coming with me.'

'No problem.'

'We should meet up and go on a bike ride together sometime.'

He nodded. 'Sure! I'll look forward to it.'

Instantly his mind began to think of all the great places he could take her. Planning beautiful routes they could share. Maybe they could take a picnic and enjoy a day out? But he had to tell himself not to keep rushing ahead. He did this all the time—and she was not the right woman to rush ahead with. She was just his friend, nothing more. If she'd wanted to be with him she'd have shown him a sign, but she hadn't. They were each other's test subjects. Each other's guinea pigs. She did not want to go out with him!

So hold your horses. She's never going to be yours.

CHAPTER NINE

MRS JANET HANCOCK hoisted herself up onto the examination bed and Hannah adjusted the back for her, so she was sitting up comfortably with a pillow supporting her lumbar region.

'I think it might be better... It feels better, anyway,' she said, as Hannah began to unwind the bandage that had been wrapped around her right foot by another member of the surgery team the last time she'd come in to have her diabetic ulcer checked.

'No pain at all?'

'No, nothing.'

People with diabetes could develop peripheral neuropathy, which meant that they lost sensation in their feet. No pain wasn't always good. Humans felt pain for a reason. It was a good thing. It told you to keep away from fire. It told you if you'd stepped on something prickly. Some diabetics caused damage to their feet because they couldn't feel that there was anything wrong, and the damage increased until it was too late to do anything about it.

After removing the bandage, Hannah carefully removed the gauze pad that had been used to cushion the underside of the heel bone, where there was normally a layer of fat. The pad was discoloured, and the wound had clearly oozed quite a bit. She tried not to show anything on her face when she saw the extent of the damage the ulcer had caused.

'This doesn't look good to me, I'm afraid, Mrs Hancock.'

'No? Oh, dear… How bad is it?'

Hannah could see bone—that was how bad it was. And the bone itself didn't look good either. If this infection had gone all the way into the bone and she'd got osteomyelitis…

'I think I'll need to get your GP to take a look at this as I'm not happy with it. Who's your doctor?'

'Dr Fletcher.'

'Okay. I'm just going to see if he's free. You stay there and don't move, all right?'

'All right…'

Hannah gave her a smile and then headed to Zach's room, knocking gently on the door.

'Come in!'

She opened the door and saw that he was alone.

'Just emailing a patient,' he told her. 'What's up?'

'Janet Hancock.'

'Yes?'

'Her ulcer's bad. I need you to take a look, but I'm pretty sure she needs to go to hospital.'

He sighed. 'Right. Okay… Two minutes and I'll be in.'

'Thanks, Zach.'

She headed back into her own room and began to wash out the wound, trying to get a clearer picture of what they were dealing with. The ulcer was sizable. At least two centimetres square at the staged edges. And Mrs Hancock's notes stated that she'd missed her last wound-check over two weeks ago.

Could they have done something more if she'd come in and not missed her appointment? Hannah had seen this kind of thing before. The patient couldn't feel anything wrong, so they ignored appointments and check-ups, but it was vital that they attended every one. Mrs Hancock had put her foot at risk. If the infection in the bone had gone too far, she could lose the foot—and Hannah knew how it felt to be told that sort of news. Knew how it felt to wake up from surgery and discover that there was a part of her missing for evermore. An empty space. The knowledge that you would never be the same again.

A knock on the door announced Zach's arrival and he came in. He said hello to Mrs Hancock and then had a good look at her foot. 'I think this needs to be looked at by a consultant, Janet,' he told her.

'You think so?'

'Yes.'

'You can't just give me some antibiotics and send me on my way?'

'No. Once the infection gets into the bone, it gets a lot more serious than a GP can deal with. And we want to be able to do everything we can to save your foot.'

'Save it? You think I might lose it?' Her voice filled with horror.

'Let's not go there just yet. Let's see what the consultant says. I'm going to give the hospital a call and then I'll contact you at home, to let you know what's happening. In the meantime, Hannah here will bandage you up and get you comfy again.'

'Right... Okay...'

'Try not to worry. I'll call you as soon as I've spoken to the hospital.'

'Thank you, Doctor.'

Zach gave her a nod and left the room, and Hannah began to rewrap Mrs Hancock's foot.

'That's scary...what he said. Do you really think I could lose my foot?' asked her patient.

'I don't know, Mrs Hancock. Let's hope not.'

'Don't know what I'd do! Woman of my age going through something like that.'

It was no fun for anyone of any age.

'Let's be positive. We have no idea if that's even going to happen. But from now on I want you to make me a firm promise.'

'What's that?'

'That you'll attend every single appointment given to you. Even if you feel okay. Even if everything feels fine. Can you do that for me?'

Mrs Hancock nodded. 'I can.'

'Good.'

'I'll be quick. Just a few words.'

Zach had called the staff to attention. They'd all been milling about in the main reception area, where Shelby's birthday lunch was being held. The reception desk itself was covered in various trays of food and drink, and helium balloons had been hung behind it.

All the staff, who'd spent ten minutes loading up their paper plates and mingling, settled down somewhat and waited for Zach to speak.

'First off, I just want to say how proud I am of all of you. We work hard here as a team, looking after the people of Greenbeck, so when we get the opportunity I like us to celebrate each other. Celebrate the time, the care, the effort you put in to take care of our patients. Sometimes it can be difficult, when a person is alone, or in pain, or frightened, but I know that you guys can handle all of that. You reassure. You help. You care. And I couldn't ask for a better team. Shelby? It's your birthday! And even though you're at work…' he smiled '…I hope you have a fabulous day and that we see you bright and early tomorrow morning without a hangover.'

Everyone laughed good-naturedly.

'I'll try, but I can't promise,' Shelby said, raising her glass of non-alcoholic fizz.

He covered a few surgery updates. Read out a couple of feedback forms they'd had, praising members of staff. Then said, 'Okay, let's eat!'

Zach settled down in a seat next to Hannah. 'I've had an update on Mrs Hancock's foot,' he told her.

'You have?'

'It's definitely osteomyelitis. They're treating it with antibiotics at the hospital and she's going to have surgery for debridement and to remove an abscess. They're hoping that will be enough.'

'Fingers crossed, then.'

'Yes. She's upbeat, they say. I thought I might pop in and see her after her surgery.'

'Could I come along?'

He nodded. 'Sure. I think she'd like that.'

'I know how scary it can be. You know that the doctors are doing what they can to save your limb, but if an infection gets hold it can be touch and go.'

'I can only imagine…'

They watched as Shelby oohed and aahed over the cake that had been brought out.

'Who made that? Was it you, Gayle?' she asked, addressing one of the receptionists who often brought cakes in on a Monday for everyone.

'No, not me.'

'Then who?'

Daniel raised his hand. 'I made it. With help from Stacey.'

Shelby looked surprised. 'Who knew you had this in you?'

Zach noticed Daniel glance over at Stacey and wink at her. It was a friendly, conspiratorial wink. Then he caught Zach's eye.

He raised an eyebrow at Daniel as a rousing chorus of

'Happy Birthday' was sung. Afterwards, when Shelby cut into the cake and discovered that it was a rainbow cake, she made a strange squeak.

'A rainbow cake! Oh, wow, this is awesome!' And Shelby threw her arms around Daniel, surprising him, hugging him, before she turned and did the same to Stacey. 'You two are awesome!'

It made Zach happy to see his crew getting along so well. This was what it was all about. Family didn't always have to mean blood. And after his list of dating disasters he'd come to Greenbeck to find that he belonged somewhere. He belonged here.

'Daniel seems happy,' Hannah said.

'Yeah...' Zach smiled. 'I think Stacey and her young son Jack are giving him something to be happy about.'

'Really? Daniel and Stacey? I think that's great! They suit one another.'

'Well, I don't think it's official yet, and they think no one else has noticed, so let them keep that notion until it's announced for sure.'

Hannah nodded, and mimed a zipping motion across her lips.

'Are we still okay for ice skating?' he asked.

Hannah laughed. 'I guess so. I can't actually believe you've talked me into going.'

'It's important to not let anything hold you back—or so I've been led to believe.'

'You're right. I've heard that, too.'

Zach's plate was nearly empty. 'I'm going to load up on some more sausages and things. Sneak them out for Rebel. Cover for me?'

'Sure!'

He smiled a thank-you and got up to refill his plate with

meaty treats. Then he successfully mimed getting a call on his mobile and headed off down the corridor, where the noise lessened. Soon he was at the fire exit and heading outside.

Rebel had been sleeping, but he woke at the sound of Zach's footsteps and got to his feet with a waggy tail and a wobbly butt.

'Hey, boy...'

He made a big fuss of the dog and lowered the plate for him to eat. He sat beside Rebel on the low wall, waiting for him to finish, and then they played for a short while. Rebel rolled onto his back for a belly-rub, which Zach happily gave him. They had another twenty minutes before afternoon surgery, so Zach decided to take him for a short walk.

He clipped on Rebel's lead, and when he stood noticed that there was someone at the window, watching.

It was Hannah, and she gave him a wave.

He waved back and headed off on his walk, his steps light and carefree, a broad smile upon his face.

Ice skating.

Hannah had her doubts about the whole enterprise.

She hadn't been ice skating since she was a little girl and she'd not been good then, with two legs. How on earth was she going to manage with a prosthetic? Would she even be able to get the prosthetic into a skate? The whole date could be a disaster before they'd even started!

But a practice date was a practice date, so she had to make the effort and not back out, because they'd promised one another and Zach was counting on her.

She was hoping not to develop any further feelings for him. Because Zach was great and she... Well, she was playing a dangerous game in continuing on with this charade.

The more time she spent with him, the more she found herself imagining what it might actually be like to be going out with Zachary Fletcher for real. How could she not? He was a great guy. But he didn't see her that way. Not in the way she would want him to. And even if he did, would she be brave enough to take that step? To put herself out there on the line? Knowing he could break her heart in two?

Because if it did all go wrong, then where would she be? Stuck in the surgery, working with him day by day, and everyone knowing they were exes. It would be as awkward as hell.

She'd spoken to Stacey and heard all about her last relationship with a fellow colleague which had gone wrong. The way Stacey had felt ousted from the practice because people took sides. That sounded horrific, and she couldn't imagine how Stacey must have felt.

If that were to happen to her, she had no doubt that people would take Zach's side, no matter how much they liked her. Zach was their boss. He was the senior partner and everybody loved him. He was kind and considerate and a great employer, and he really looked after his staff. They wouldn't risk losing any of that just to side with her. Would they? And then where would she be? Alone again. Rejected again. And she loved it here.

No. She had to tread carefully. To remember exactly why she was here with him at all. She was his practice buddy. His dry run. His guinea pig. She was the person he wanted to discover all his mistakes with, so that when his real true love came along he'd be perfect, and confident, and know that he could be the person she would need him to be without panicking about losing her. Without worrying that he'd say or do something stupid that would ruin it all.

He deserved that chance. He'd experienced heartache, just like her. And Hannah was his marker. She was his dummy run. She was there for him to get things wrong with, so that she could point out what he needed to do to be right. She was the one who would bear the scars and the oopsie-daisies and the awkward moments, so that he could shine like the star he was when the right woman came along.

And when that happened she'd be left behind.

To watch him fly.

With someone else.

She was his teacher, his instructor—nothing more. And she should teach herself distance. She would be good at that. It would make it easier when he sailed off into the sunset with another woman.

But what to wear today? She'd received a text from Zach two days ago saying that it was Disco Hour at the ice rink. Would everyone make an effort to dress up? She didn't want to stand out. It was going to be bad enough as it was, with her slipping and sliding everywhere and holding on to the barrier for dear life.

Throwing open her wardrobe, she looked at the possibilities. She did have an old pair of bright purple shorts that she'd owned since she was a teenager and never thrown away, but she didn't want her prosthetic leg on display so she dismissed those. Skirts and dresses were out of the question, too. She owned a rainbow-striped top. Would that do? Paired with some jeans?

If she remembered correctly, she had a pair that… She rummaged in the back of her wardrobe. Ah! Yes! There they were. Jeans with silver sequins along the leg seams. She'd bought them ages ago, thinking they were fun, but had hardly ever worn them after the accident. They were wide-legged, so should fit over her prosthetic easily.

Dressed, she looked in the mirror and smiled, turning this way, then that. She put her hair up into a high ponytail, put on some sparkly eye make-up and some large, dangly yin and yang earrings, and felt her look was complete—clashing and loud and out there.

It would have to do. Zach would no doubt laugh, but hadn't he said that dates were meant to be fun? If she was going to spend her time practising with him, then why shouldn't she have fun whilst she was doing it?

Downstairs, the doorbell went, and she heard the heavy footsteps of Mrs Micklethwaite as she went to answer the door.

'Er... Miss Gladstone? Dr Fletcher is here!'

Hannah's heart pounded, her stomach rolling in fear and excitement. If she went downstairs dressed like this and he was just standing there in jeans and a tee, she'd feel terribly embarrassed.

'I'll be down in one minute!'

Hannah sprayed a small mist of perfume onto her neck and fastened the high-top trainers she'd put on.

'What am I doing? What am I *doing*?' she muttered to herself as she gave her reflection one last look.

It wasn't too late to back out, was it? She could quickly change and go downstairs, tell him she'd changed her mind. That she didn't feel well, or something. Ice skating was going to be a risk. What if she made an absolute fool of herself? It would be hugely embarrassing!

But she wanted to spend more time with him.

She *wanted* to.

And that urge overrode her fear completely.

Hannah headed downstairs, her nerves getting worse with every step, until she reached the bottom and saw him, still at the front door. Dr Zachary Fletcher. Dressed in a perfectly white suit with a black shirt underneath with wide lapels that almost reached the width of his shoulders. As soon as he saw her, he grinned and struck a pose. One hand on his hip, the other hand pointing up into the air.

Hannah instantly laughed. 'Oh, my goodness! That's perfect!'

'Think I'll be the only one there dressed like this?'

'Maybe!'

He smiled and looked her up and down. 'You look great.'

'Thanks.'

Zach gave her a small peck on the cheek, and then bent down to pick something up from the porch. It was a small bouquet.

'Tradition states a guy brings flowers.'

'They're beautiful. Let me put them in the kitchen. Do you want a tea or anything first?' she asked hopefully, wanting to put off arriving at the rink for as long as possible, so that Zach didn't get to experience her shame for a while.

'I'm good. Unless you want something?'

'No, I'm good too.' She smiled back at him, not sure what to say next.

Mrs Micklethwaite stood looking at both of them as if they were crazy. 'Maybe you ought to get going? I don't want the neighbours thinking I'm running some sort of retro lodging house.'

Hannah rolled her eyes good-naturedly. 'Okay. Thanks, Mrs Micklethwaite. See you later.'

'No later than ten,' she said, closing the door behind them with a solid finality.

'Your carriage awaits.' Zach indicated his car, parked at the end of the path.

On the back seat, she could see Rebel sticking his head out of the window. 'Rebel's coming, too?'

'Kind of. Next to the rink is a shopping centre with doggy daycare. I've booked him in there for a couple of hours. Didn't want to leave him home alone.'

'You're spoiling him!'

'Absolutely, I am. He loves being with other dogs, so I thought he'd enjoy it.'

Zach walked her to the car and opened up the passenger door for her. 'My lady.'

'Thank you, kind sir.'

He grinned, and once he'd made sure she was in safely closed the door and hurried round to the driver's seat.

'So, where did you find the outfit?' she asked. 'Or has it been lurking at the back of your wardrobe for years?'

Zach laughed. 'I hired it.'

'Really?'

'Of course! You think I had *this* lurking at the back of my wardrobe?'

'I had these,' she replied. 'Back home, we used to do a lot of dressing up. Halloween parties, Seventies dinner parties. Pirate and princess days. There was even a fairy hen party once.'

'Really?'

'Yep. In Amsterdam. I had to stand in Heathrow Airport dressed as a wood nymph for a whole hour before anyone else turned up.'

'Did you think they'd abandoned you?'

'I thought they were winding me up and they'd turn up in normal clothes and just the pink sash we were all supposed to be wearing.'

'But everyone turned up as fairies?'

'Yep.'

'I would have liked to see that.'

'I think I have a picture on my phone. Hold on…' She rummaged through the photo files on her mobile until she found the day in question. It held fond memories.

As he looked at the pictures she found herself looking at him. Studying him. He was just so…so…*perfect*.

'This was before your accident?'

'Yes.'

Of course, yes. Her fairy outfit had been short. He had to be looking at her legs, she thought. Wishing she were still the same now.

'You look amazing!'

She took the phone back and nodded. Of course he'd think that. She'd been whole then. Normal. Her life hadn't been destroyed by Edward, or a faulty roller coaster, or a stupid little bacterial microbe that had refused to submit to antibiotics. Clearly Zach thought she'd looked amazing then. She'd thought so too, and confidence had oozed out of her every pore. Back then she'd been young, pretty and carefree. With her whole life ahead of her. Possibilities galore. And the correct amount of limbs.

She wasn't like that now.

She was crippled. Not just by her body, but also by her emotions.

'Are you okay?' he asked.

Hannah forced a smile. 'Yes. I am. Come on! We don't want to be late for Disco Hour.'

Rebel put his head forward between the two seats and licked the side of Hannah's face. She turned and gave him a quick cuddle. Dogs always seemed to know when you needed cheering up. Perhaps she could do with an emotional support dog?

'Lie down, Rebel,' said Zach.

The dog lay down, and Zach started the engine and began the drive over to Cherringham.

'Let's hope we don't get stopped by a police officer. I'd hate to have to explain these clothes.'

Hannah smiled. 'That would be interesting! We could say we were time travellers from the past.'

'Yeah? And what have we come forward in time for?'

'To see what it's like? See if we're happy?'

'What if it was the other way round? What would you be doing if we travelled into the past? Would you do anything different?'

'Personally?'

He nodded.

'Hmm… I don't think I'd have got on that roller coaster.'

'Then you'd be married. To Edward.'

Hannah frowned. He was right. She would be. How would that be? Knowing now that she'd always had doubts about him, she wondered if she would have gone through with it.

She'd kept on planning the wedding after the accident because it had been a positive goal, to keep her optimistic and her mind off her injury. Planning the wedding had kept her sane! But marriage to Edward? Would it have been rocky? Would it have failed before it had even begun?

'What would you change if you went back into the past?' she asked Zach.

He shrugged. 'I'm not sure. I guess I'd have liked to know my real mother. And who my father was. If she'd have kept me, my life might have been different.'

'Perhaps she couldn't. Perhaps she gave you up because she knew she wasn't in a good situation to look after you and she wanted you to have a chance in life.'

'True…'

'You might never have become a doctor, either. Might never have arrived in Greenbeck.'

'It's strange, isn't it? The *What would you go back and change?* question. It's tempting to think you would change your life for the better, but when you really examine it you discover just how much you'd lose from your present if you did.'

'Exactly. So, what are you grateful for right now? What's wonderful in the world of Dr Zachary Fletcher?'

He smiled. 'My foster parents. Greenbeck. Rebel. My work. You.'

She blushed. 'At least I'm in there somewhere! Although if this were a real date and she asked you that question I hope that you'd put her higher up the list.'

'Ah—noted! Anyway, I wasn't listing them in order of importance. I was doing it alphabetically.'

'Were you?' She thought for a minute, running his answers through her mind. 'Oh, yeah! Clever sod.'

'What about you, Hannah? What are *you* grateful for right now?'

'Hmm, let me see… *You!*' She laughed. 'Greenbeck. My family. My job. The freedom to just be me.'

'Disco Hour at the Cherringham Skating Rink?'

'Of course! It's given me the opportunity to see you dressed up like that.' She indicated his white flare-legged suit and wide seventies lapels. 'They're going to think we're weird when we take Rebel to the doggy day care first.'

Zach laughed. 'Maybe.'

They'd entered the outskirts of Cherringham. The skating rink was located in a large retail park that also contained a cinema and a bowling alley. Zach managed to find them a decent parking space, not too far away, and she became aware of the sideways looks they got as they walked Rebel to the Waggin' Wheels Doggy Daycare Centre.

'Disco Hour?' asked the young girl on Reception, smiling at their clothes.

'How did you know?' asked Zach.

'They have it every first Saturday of the month. You should see what some people wear! You two… You're not too crazy.'

'Glad to hear it. We'll collect him in an hour or two.'

'See you then.'

They walked out of the doggy day care centre and towards the skating rink.

'See? That wasn't too bad,' he said.

'No. I guess not. Oh, my gosh, look at that!' Hannah pointed at a young man wearing a psychedelic jumpsuit heading into the skating rink. 'I guess we're not going to be the odd ones out, after all.'

He laughed and held the door open for her.

'Thank you.'

She smiled and they headed inside to buy tickets.

Her nerves were beginning to build. Getting dressed in weird clothes was one thing. Going skating was another. Would she be able to get the skate on over her prosthetic? she wondered again. If she couldn't this whole date would be ruined. If she knew anything about dating it was that ruining a date did not go down well, and they were trying to teach each other how to date well.

So she pasted on a smile and stood in the line with Zach as they waited to get their skates. Once acquired, they went over to the wooden benches to put them on.

Hannah spent ages loosening the laces, so Zach had his skates on well before her. She'd only got the right skate on, and was thinking about how best to tackle the left.

'Want some help?'

She looked at him, grateful that he understood. 'Please.'

And Zach got down on his knees, held the skate in one hand and her prosthetic foot gently in the other, and slowly began to guide it in.

Was this what Cinderella had felt like? In that moment with Prince Charming was at her feet, sliding her dainty toes into the glass slipper? At least Cinderella had known her foot would fit!

'If it doesn't fit we can do something else,' she said, trying to sound reasonable and *Hey, I don't mind.*

He looked up at her, smiled. 'It'll fit. Trust me.'

His blue eyes sparkled and held such warmth. She wished she could feel his hands on her foot, her ankle, her lower leg. Feel the pressure of his fingertips against her skin. But all he was touching was plastic. Yet despite that she could still feel a rush. Could imagine what it would feel like. And when he slid her foot into the skate she felt a surge of happiness.

'You did it!'

'Of course!' He began to lace up the skate for her.

Hannah resisted the urge to reach out and run her fingers through his hair. To stroke the side of his face and say thank you. She wanted to—so much! Instead, she just beamed a smile at him when he was done, and he got to his feet and held his hands out to help her up.

She stood, expecting him to let go of her immediately, but he didn't.

'How does that feel?'

She knew he meant how did it feel to wear the skate on her prosthetic when she was only used to wearing a shoe? But her brain was registering what it felt like to be standing there holding on to his hands.

'It feels great.'

'Need me to hold your hand whilst we walk to the rink?'

'Er…yes, please,' she answered—simply because she wasn't ready to let go of his hand just yet.

And actually, as they began walking, she was glad she hadn't let go, because walking in ice skates was completely different from normal walking when you had a prosthetic.

She wobbled a little. Felt unsteady. Her hand clutched his arm tightly. She felt muscle. She felt solidity and strength and felt protected and safe.

'Okay?' He looked at her intensely. Caring etched deeply across his features.

'I'm good.'

They neared the entrance to the rink and Hannah looked out at the icy expanse, seeing all the other people dressed in disco outfits, whizzing here, there and everywhere. Everyone looked so capable—and she was not. Seventies music was playing, blaring out from the speakers, and there was a disco ball above the rink, splintering light in all directions.

Zach stepped out onto the ice first, getting the feel of it and holding on to the side with one hand as he helped her out on to the slippery surface.

She bit her bottom lip, expecting to fall on her bottom almost immediately, but Zach held her steady.

'I've got you. Don't be afraid.'

She nodded.

Zach didn't let go once. He held her left hand, whilst she held onto the barrier with her right, and slowly they began to skate forward.

It was halting, at first. She stumbled once, almost fell, but Zach steadied her, laughing, and she rebalanced herself and carried on. Soon she began to get swept up in the atmosphere as her confidence grew. The clothes, the music, the ice. But most of all in just being with Zach and holding his hand. It meant the world to her that he didn't let go, and she could tell, seeing how much easier he found it, that he could have easily skated on ahead.

Only he didn't.

He stayed by her side, making sure she was safe, and they were smiling and laughing and enjoying each other's company.

'Want to let go of the side?' he asked.

'I don't know…'

'Come on. Give it a go! I believe in you! I promise I won't let go.'

She nodded, and tentatively let go of the side, shrieking and wobbling and laughing so hard that she clutched at his arm and overbalanced. Her skates went out from under her and she grabbed onto him so hard she pulled them both down onto the ice.

Zach took the brunt, landing on his back, and she fell onto him.

They were both still laughing, but then she saw a look in his eyes that stopped her, and she stared into those blue depths and wondered, ever so briefly, ever so daringly...

'You know...if this were a real date, it would be the perfect moment to kiss.'

He gazed back at her. 'I think so too. Or else we'd awkwardly try and get back to our feet and pretend the moment had never happened.'

He was telling her what they should do, and he was right. Because it suddenly felt as if the moment had passed, and she became aware of people whizzing by them. She remembered that they were in a public rink, and probably causing an obstacle to other skaters, and reluctantly she got to her knees, grabbed the side barrier and hauled herself to her feet.

She held out a hand to help Zach up, and watched as he brushed ice crystals from his clothes.

'You okay?' he asked.

'Yeah.'

She smiled, feeling awkward, wishing she'd been brave enough to kiss him. Only she hadn't. Because this wasn't a real date. So she'd hesitated, frightened. What if she *had* kissed him? He'd clearly not wanted that, and then the whole day would have been awkward. Work would have been awkward!

No. I did the right thing. I think...

'You want to go it alone, or…?'

He proffered his hand again, but he couldn't meet her eyes, and she just knew, right there and then, that she had made him feel awkward with the way she must have looked at him. Suddenly she felt appalled and embarrassed. He'd obviously known that she'd thought of kissing him!

Shame flaming her cheeks, she held on to the barrier grimly and said, 'I think I'll try it on my own. You go on ahead. It's okay.'

He nodded. 'You're sure?'

'Yes. I just need to get my balance a bit better—you go and have fun.'

'Okay…'

She could tell he still had some reluctance at leaving her, but leave her he did.

Hannah gulped back tears as she watched him skate away. It was faltering, and he was clearly still trying to keep his balance, but he was doing it.

A thought entered her mind. She could take this moment of blessed relief, turn around and go home. It would be fine. She could get a bus, or a taxi. By the time he discovered she was gone it would be too late.

I'd never get this damned skate off!

And also she'd only be postponing the inevitable. There'd still be awkwardness at work. Trying to avoid each other. No, she had to stay. Had to hope that letting him move away and skate on his own would mean that by the time he caught up with her again the moment would have passed and they could pretend that it had never happened.

Besides, avoiding running away was the whole point of this practice dating endeavour!

Using the barrier, she pulled herself along, adjusting her balance, occasionally feeling steady enough to let go and test herself. It was exhausting, the amount of mental energy she was putting into her balance, concentrating on not falling. She barely noticed the music, or the other people. Didn't even have time to enjoy everyone else's costumes.

She stopped to rest and turned to see where Zach was. She saw him instantly. On the far side of the rink, helping a young woman dressed in a silver sequinned dress get back to her feet. He was a gentleman like that. Good. Kind. Always trying to help.

The young woman had taken his hand, and even at this distance, Hannah could see her broad smile, the way she was laughing, the way she flicked her hair and kept laying her hand on Zach's arm as they laughed and joked about something. Hannah could see it was an obvious flirtation. This woman liked what she saw in him, that was for sure.

A surge of jealousy swept over her and, determined to ignore it—and what it meant—she continued to pull herself along the side of the rink. It was nothing to do with her. Zach could flirt with whomever he liked. It was quite clear that he didn't want to flirt with *her*.

She was so busy concentrating on what she was doing and making her first lap that she jumped when she felt a hand touch her arm.

Zach.

'Just me. How are you getting on? Any better?'

'A little. You were doing quite well.'

'Do you think so? I felt like a baby deer on ice.'

'No, you were doing brilliantly. I saw you helping that woman. Was she okay?'

'Och, she was fine.'

'She liked you. You should ask her out.'

There. She'd said it.

Because if she pushed him away and made him ask someone else out, then these ridiculous practice dates could stop and she could get some distance from him and stop all these ridiculous thoughts she kept having about him. Plus, hopefully, it would make him see that she hadn't meant it about kissing him when they'd fallen over. She'd just been speaking hypothetically—that was all.

Zach smiled and shook his head. 'I don't think so. Besides, I'm here with you, and I'm sure it's bad form to ask another woman out on a date when you're on one with someone else.'

'But you're not. Not really. This is a practice date. Why not see if you're ready for the real thing? Go and ask that woman out. I'm sure she'd say yes if you asked.'

He shook his head. 'No. I'm with you and… I'm not ready.'

'Well, at least go and get her number for when you are.'

'She's not my type,' he said firmly.

He sounded sure of himself. Certain. Determined. And his tone implied that he wanted her to end this conversation. She felt a little taken aback by it.

'Okay. Just thought I'd mention it. Fancy a break? Shall we get a drink?'

Suddenly Hannah wanted to get off the ice for a bit.

'Sure. I need a break.'

CHAPTER TEN

ZACH STOOD IN the café queue, waiting to buy a couple of hot chocolates, and saw Hannah had grabbed them a table. The ice rink's café sat alongside the rink itself, so the customers could still see everyone on the ice and watch people skating whilst they had a break themselves.

He'd needed to get off the ice. For a change of scene. A break. So many thoughts…so many feelings…had reared up in his mind over the last hour or so and he was feeling confused and worried.

It had begun way before the fall, to be honest. But with Hannah losing her balance, and him somehow catching her, overbalancing himself and pulling her down with him onto the ice… She'd knocked the wind out of him in more ways than one.

Something had happened in that brief moment when she'd lain half on top of him, staring into his eyes, and he'd looked into hers. There'd been an awareness. A wanting. If his life had been a romcom, that would have been the perfect moment to kiss her and change the course of the entire movie, and maybe his desire had been all too clear, because she'd said, *'You know…if this were a real date…it would be the perfect moment to kiss.'*

He'd even agreed! Out loud! Which had ruined everything. Because he'd seen the alarm in her beautiful eyes, the way they'd widened in surprise, and he'd realised all too quickly what a mistake he'd made. So he'd suggested an alternative idea instead.

'Or else we'd awkwardly try and get back on our feet and pretend the moment had never happened.'

And that was the face-saving option they'd gone with. Much to Hannah's relief, no doubt.

When she'd suggested he skate on his own, he'd agreed. Happily. Needing some space to get away and think. To calm down. To decide what to do.

Had he come up with any answers? No.

And then she'd said he ought to ask that woman out! The one he'd helped to her feet. Well! That was a clear indication from Hannah that she didn't want him to get any ideas about kissing her in the future! She was trying to get him to ask out another woman! Clearly she was embarrassed by him, and the sooner they stopped having these practice dates the better.

'Two hot chocolates, please,' he said.

'Marshmallows and whipped cream?'

He nodded and looked back. He could see that Hannah was looking away from him, towards the ice and the other skaters. See? She couldn't even look at him now. He'd been such a fool!

He'd been an idiot to think that maybe…just maybe…there could be something more with Hannah. He'd wanted to kiss her so much! But fear—his damned fear—had got in the way! He'd hesitated. And he couldn't help but think where they'd be right now if he'd just acted on impulse and done what he'd wanted to do.

I know where we'd be. Avoiding each other. After I'd apologised. She clearly doesn't want me.

She'd told him straight. *'This is a practice date… Go and ask that woman out…'*

She wouldn't have said that if she'd wanted to be with him,

would she? She was clearly trying to politely steer him away from her. She was the only one of them thinking clearly. Thank goodness for her.

Zach paid for the two drinks and carried them over to the table on a tray. 'Here you go. Two hot chocolates with all the trimmings.'

'Oh, wow! These look great.' She smiled at him, eyes sparkling, and then looked back at the rink again, watching the skaters. The ones who could twirl and pirouette and spin.

He took the opportunity to look at her and realised that no matter how much he wanted her he would never be able to have her. Hannah was simply doing him a favour. She was his practice date and nothing more. As he was for her. That was all. It was simple.

He needed to stop letting his thoughts and feelings run away with him, as they so often did in his secret yearning to find the one perfect woman he could create a family with. He often saw things that weren't there. It was a flaw. He needed to face it. Confront it. And wasn't that the whole point of these practice dates? Perhaps if he showed her that he was learning from them, and changing, they could end these things and he wouldn't have to torture himself by spending time with her?

'So, what did you think to your first skating experience?' he asked, trying to get her to engage with him at the table.

She turned to him. 'It was…interesting. Harder than it looks on TV.'

'Definitely. It seems to hurt more when you fall as an adult.'

Hannah nodded, taking a small sip of her hot chocolate. It left a little line of cream along her top lip, and he didn't know whether to reach out and wipe it away with his thumb, or just mention it.

'You have a…erm…'

He pointed at his own mouth and she quickly grabbed a napkin and dabbed at her face.

'Thanks.' She blushed.

'I'm sorry if I pulled you down with me,' he said. 'I was trying to stop you from falling, but I overbalanced. I just wanted to say sorry for that.'

'It's fine.'

'No, it wasn't. It led to...' He swallowed hard as he saw fear and uncertainty wash over her features. 'To you falling on me. And there was a moment there that... Well, I guess we both know it was awkward, right?'

Hannah looked down at the floor, cheeks flushing with a heat that he knew was nothing to do with the temperature of her drink.

'You thought I wanted to kiss you,' he said. 'I know you did. You said so yourself that that would have been the perfect moment. I'll admit the thought did cross my mind, but... it would have been the wrong thing to do—obviously. I don't know why I even thought it.' He smiled ruefully. 'So, I'm sorry. It was a learning experience, though! Honestly. And I want to thank you for that.'

'Oh! Well... I'm glad I'm helping, then.' She gave him a brief smile that left her face as quickly as it came. 'You've helped me and I've helped you—and that's what this is all about, huh?'

'Absolutely.'

'Maybe we're cured?'

He managed a small laugh. 'Maybe.'

'Perhaps we should try dating other people properly now? Now that we've had our eyes opened by each other?'

Zach nodded slowly, not liking the idea one bit. But maybe she was right? Maybe they had become too close through this process?

'I guess we should…'

They both sipped their drinks quietly.

Hannah picked up her teaspoon and began to take small mouthfuls of cream and marshmallow. Eventually she said, 'You know… I'm kind of tired. Would you mind if we went home soon?'

'Not at all. Shall we finish these, then go?'

'That'd be great. Thanks.'

She'd not been able to wait to get home. After leaving the rink they'd collected Rebel, who'd been overjoyed to see them, licking them both profusely before he could be calmed down enough to get his lead clipped back onto his collar, and then they'd got back in the car for the drive back to Greenbeck.

Thank heavens for the radio, playing softly in the background, otherwise the journey might have been made in utter silence.

Now, as Zach pulled up outside Mrs Mickelthwaite's, she pasted on a huge smile and gushed about what a wonderful time she'd had, thanking him.

She was about to get out of the car when Zach had said, 'Hannah, please wait.'

She frowned, looking at him, wondering what he was going to say. Hopefully something that would clear up this mess that had come since their fall at the rink. Would he say something about the near-kiss? Something that would make seeing each other at work easy.

But he looked tongue-tied. Was frowning slightly as if he was searching for the right words. And then he looked at her, sighed, and reached for her and pulled her lips to his in a sudden kiss.

She almost gasped, she was so taken by surprise. But her

shock soon gave way to enjoyment as she sank into everything he was making her feel.

He was a fine kisser. A very good kisser. His bristles tickling her face, his hand in her hair at the nape of her neck…

She needed to breathe. Didn't want to breathe. Didn't want to stop this. Who needed air? Not her.

And as the kiss deepened she felt her body come alive. Every nerve-ending was firing into life, her body demanding to be touched, or caressed or teased.

His kiss was everything she'd imagined it could be and more. Gentle. Passionate. Expert. Delightful. Arousing.

Goodness me, this man is a gift!

And then he broke away. Met her gaze. Looked at her uncertainly, not sure of her response. He let go of her, sat back in his seat.

She stared at him, her mouth still open, still breathless. She wasn't sure what she was supposed to do now. Or say!

'If that had been a real date, then that's how it should have ended. Just so you know,' he said.

She nodded and got out of the car.

Hannah got to work early on Monday, locked up her new bike in the bike shed, and was very much relieved to see that Zach's car wasn't there yet. In her room, she hung up her jacket and bag on the back of the door and began to prep for the day.

Her first patient was a stitch removal. She didn't normally deal with that—usually the HCA took care of it—but there was a note on the system to say that everyone else was fully booked and they'd needed to place this patient with Hannah. Lucy, the practice manager, had approved it, and Hannah was glad to do it and have something practical to focus on first thing.

Normally when she arrived for her working day she would spend some time in the staffroom. Get the kettle boiled, make everyone drinks and socialise for a bit. But not today. Any time she spent with Zach was going to be awkward, and she didn't want other people to notice it and start commenting about it. Or even gossiping. Not that she thought that anyone would do so maliciously, but it happened even in the nicest of places.

She wanted to forget their last practice date, but she couldn't get the image of his face out of her mind. She'd practically been lying on top of him. Their faces inches away from each other. There'd been an awareness in each other's eyes. That look of uncertainty. *Temptation.* That had been the most difficult thing. Had he seen the temptation within her?

And then that kiss in the car. That had been…out of this world! But it hadn't been real. He'd said, *'If this was a real date, then that's how it should have ended...'* And he was right. They hadn't been on a real date. But a man who could kiss like that…

Her computer beeped to let her know that her first patient had arrived so she called them in.

Mr Souness ambled into the room and gave her a smile. 'Morning, Nurse.'

'Good morning, Mr Souness! How are you today?'

'Not bad…not bad. Carrying on, as you do.'

She smiled. 'And how's the leg been?'

'Fine! Nothing to report—and I hope you don't tell me anything otherwise once you've seen it.'

'Shall we get you on the bed?'

He nodded and clambered up, and she helped him lift his legs. The injury was on his lower leg, and it stated on the system that the wound was near the ankle, so she didn't need him to remove his trousers.

'Let's take a look, then. Remind me how you did this?' she asked, as she began to unwind the bandage.

'Chasing after a young woman,' he said, and chuckled.

'Really?'

'Well, kind of.' He blushed. 'I met someone. Someone I hadn't seen for over fifty years. But she was my first love— and you never forget your first, do you?'

'That's what they say,' she said, knowing that she'd never forget Edward, but maybe for entirely different reasons than him being her first true relationship. His abandoning her at the altar would be the primary reason.

'I was on a cruise to the Norwegian fjords. One of those singles cruises. I wasn't looking for love, just friendship. Companionship, you know?'

She nodded as she removed the last of the bandaging and began to take off the gauze pad to expose the seven stitches that lay in a line just above his ankle.

'And there was Stella. We knew each other at school when we first went out, and I'd never forgotten her. But life got in the way, and we both got married to other people, and then we both lost our spouses and ended up on the same cruise. Oh, it was so good to reconnect! To speak to someone who I felt really got me, you know?'

Hannah examined the wound and found it to be perfectly healed. No sign of redness or weeping or infection. The stitches were good to come out.

'We had nine wonderful days together, and then, when we docked in Southampton, I was trying to catch up with her as we headed back onto dry land. I tripped and fell and caught my leg on another person's luggage.'

'Causing this wound?'

He nodded. 'Apparently I've got friable skin—whatever that means.'

She smiled. 'It means your skin easily tears or breaks down. Or it can bleed if gently manipulated.'

'Oh. Well, that sounds about right. Poor Stella felt so guilty for rushing ahead, but she was so keen to see her grandchildren, who were waiting to pick her up from the ship, she couldn't help but go faster than me.'

'Well, it all looks fine to me, Mr Souness. I can take these stitches out, if you're happy for me to go ahead? It shouldn't hurt.'

'Please do.'

She grabbed the knot of the first stitch with her tweezers and used the stitch cutter to cut it and pull it free. 'So, it's been about twelve days since your accident. How are you and Stella now?'

'We're okay... I think. You'd think it'd be straightforward at our age. That we'd both know what we want. And we do. But trying to combine our lives when we've both got so much baggage between us is proving a little tricky, if I'm honest.'

'That's understandable.'

'And it's real now. On the boat, it was a different world. Like reality had been suspended. We could pretend we were fine and ignore all the little niggles.'

'I can understand that.'

It was similar to her pretending to date Zach. Reality, who they really were, didn't count. They could both be someone else before reality came back to bite them both on the butt.

'I do love Stella, and perhaps I always have, but I'm different now. I've been through things. Losing my wife was one of the most horrific life events I've ever had to get through. On the boat, it was fun. It was casual. It was good to get to know her again. But if we carry on seeing each other...' His voice trailed off.

'You don't want to get close in case you lose her, too?'

He nodded. 'Yeah... We're not young whippersnappers, either of us. And she's had cancer once. Breast cancer, she said. It's terrifying, to be honest. And look at me. I've already got my first wound.' He pointed at his leg and chuckled to lighten the moment.

Hannah wasn't sure what to say to him. Was she even qualified to advise about love? Was anyone?

'I guess you've got to take it day by day,' she told him. 'Don't rush into anything until you're absolutely sure. I'm sure she feels the same way, too, and has the same hesitations.'

'Happen you may be right.'

She removed the last stitch, very happy with the procedure. 'There you go. All seven stitches. You should be fine going about your daily routine, but be careful and don't knock this ankle, okay? You don't want to open it up again.'

Mr Souness smiled and nodded. 'Thank you, Nurse. And thank you for listening.'

'My pleasure. And I hope that you and Stella get to find the happiness you both deserve.'

'Thanks, love. You take care.'

'I will.'

She helped him off the couch and he ambled back out of the room. She quickly cleaned the bed and her instrument trolley, wiping everything down, and then sat at her computer, inputting notes into the patient's record. She liked Mr Souness. He seemed a nice chap. And it was obvious from him that, no matter your age, relationships weren't easy.

You'd hope that by the time you reached your sixties or your seventies you'd have everything worked out, but maybe love was never meant to be simple? Maybe something worth having had to be fought for? Had to be difficult? Otherwise you wouldn't cherish it as much? If love was easily attainable, maybe it would hold less value?

Her next patient had a urinary infection, for which she prescribed some nitrofurantoin. And after that she saw a child with bronchitis. Then came a woman with tonsillitis and tonsil stones.

Hannah had quite a productive morning, whizzing through her appointments steadily, until she reached eleven-fifteen, her morning break time, and she realised that she was terribly thirsty. She'd had nothing to drink since seven that morning, and she'd been working hard and talking a lot.

It was essential to chat to her patients in order to make them feel at ease, but she also wanted to get to know them better. They were hopefully going to be her patients for a long time, and she wanted a good relationship with them all.

She had no water in her bag, and she knew she'd have to get herself something from the staffroom. But all the clinical staff at Greenbeck had their morning break at eleven-fifteen, and she was worried that Zach would be in there. Pulling up the patient lists, she saw that Zach hadn't yet ticked off his last patient, so hopefully he was still in his room treating him. Doctors often ran late, as some patient consultations took longer than the allocated ten minutes.

So she got up and headed to the staffroom, walking quickly to the small kitchenette and grabbing herself a glass so she could get some water. Ideally she wanted tea, but that would mean waiting for the kettle to boil and Zach could come in at any time.

Hannah filled her glass and smiled at Daniel as he came into the staffroom, saying good morning, and then headed back to her room. Just as she was passing Zach's door it opened. A patient came out, gave her a smile, and then there he was, looking at her, a hesitant smile on his face.

'Good morning.'

'Morning.'

Would it be rude to go straight to her room? She managed a quick smile and held up her drink, as if to say, *Must get on.*

Busy. Sorry... And then she headed to her room, closing the door behind her with relief.

She'd just sat at her desk with a heavy sigh when there was a knock at her door.

Her heart jumped in her chest. 'Yes?'

'Can I come in?'

Zach.

If she said yes, they'd be alone in the room—and goodness only knew what he wanted to say! But if she said no...she'd feel awful. And she'd be making everything worse! Better to face it and get it over and done with.

'Sure—come on in.'

He opened the door, looking stunning, as always, in dark trousers and a pale blue shirt that had a faint white check patterning. It brought out the blue of his startlingly gorgeous eyes. His thick dark hair looked slightly mussed, as if he'd been running his fingers through it recently, and she couldn't help but think what it would be like to run her own fingers through it...

'What can I do for you?' she asked.

'I need us to be as we were before.'

Heart. Pounding. Maddeningly.

'I'm sorry?' she said, as if she didn't quite understand him.

'Things are different...since the ice rink incident. And the car. I'm sorry. I should never have...' His voice trailed off and he swallowed hard. 'What happened in the car...we were still pretending, right? And you're my friend, and I don't want to feel like we need to avoid each other. Not here. I won't allow it. This should be our safe space. Our *comfortable* space. And I want back the bubbly, happy Hannah that I first met. Tiptop Hannah.'

He smiled.

She smiled, too. Remembering that first day. That first embarrassing day when she'd thought all was lost, when actually it hadn't been. He was right. They shouldn't have to avoid each other. Not here or anywhere. They were grown-ups, for crying out loud. No one had died. Nothing terrible had happened. They'd just kissed. And, even though that kiss had been the most spectacular thing she had ever experienced, it had been just pretend.

Hannah nodded. 'You're right.'

'We're good?'

'We're good.' She smiled at him, and he sank into a chair opposite her.

'Great. I'm glad to hear it. I missed being able to talk to you this morning.'

'I missed that, too. And my morning cup of tea!' She jiggled her almost empty glass of water in front of him.

He laughed. 'Well, we can't have that. Want me to go and make you one?'

He was so kind.

'I'll come with you.'

And they headed back to the staffroom together.

Zach was thrilled that they were on talking terms again. It wasn't exactly as it had been before, but it was close to it. And he knew that with a little more time it would return to normality. They just had to wait for the awkwardness to get out of the way first.

To accelerate that process, he'd asked Hannah if she wanted to join him on a trail ride, using her new bike. She'd agreed, after a brief hesitation, and he was now waiting for her to arrive.

He'd initially wanted to meet her at her house and cycle from there, but he'd held back from suggesting that, not wanting it to seem like a date. This was just two friends...meeting up to enjoy a little bit of exercise and then going their separate ways.

So he'd suggested they meet at the village green. By the bench next to the duck pond. It seemed a nice, neutral spot, and now he'd arrived he could see that the team responsible for organising the village fete had begun their decorating. He could see lines of bunting going up, and from where he stood he could also see Walter and Pauline, the two stalwarts of any village organisational team, standing at the bottom of a ladder, issuing suggestions to a young man at the top of it, who was trying to attach a banner that went over the main road into and out of Greenbeck.

Pauline held a clipboard, whilst Walter was giving instructions. 'Higher. Lower. To the left. No. Not that left. My left.'

He smiled, and then his gaze was caught on a movement to his right and he saw Hannah pedalling towards him, a big smile on her face as she gave him a little wave.

Zach waved back and waited for her to come to a halt in front of him. It was a Thursday evening and thankfully they still had plenty of daylight hours left.

'Hey. Looking good! How are you enjoying it?' he asked, indicating the bike.

'Great! I've had to adjust the seat position, but it feels much better now.'

'Aye, you'll have to tweak a lot of things at first, until you get used to it. What sort of ride do you fancy? A road ride? Or a trail? There's a good one through the woods that's not too much uphill.'

He couldn't help but notice how great she looked. Normally he was used to seeing her in her nurse's uniform, but now she wore a tight cycling top and long sports leggings that covered her prosthetic down to her mid-calf. He tried not to stare. The clothing accentuated her curves, which he knew he was already drawn to. The figure-hugging sportswear was doing him no favours.

'Trail sounds good. Why don't you lead and I'll follow?'

'Okay.'

He pulled on his helmet, fastening it beneath his chin, and mounted his bike. It would be better for him to lead. Then he wouldn't have to worry about how distracted he'd get if he had to follow behind her.

Setting off, he glanced behind him to make sure she was matching his speed, and then steered them towards the woods behind the surgery.

At this time of day the heat had begun to wane, but sunlight still glinted through the gaps in the canopy above. It was perfect. His nose filled with the aroma of earth and leaves and pine cones.

The beginning of the trail was slightly uphill, and he could feel his heart pumping hard to get up the slight incline before they took the path that would level out and lead them along the valley in which Greenbeck nestled.

'You okay?' he called.

'I'm doing great!' she called back, and he grinned, steering off to the left slightly as the trail widened, so Hannah could catch up and ride alongside him.

He gave her a smile, and she smiled back, and in that moment he thought she looked beautiful. Her brown curls were escaping from beneath her helmet. She looked happy. Sunlight shining down on her face. Sparkling eyes. A truly gorgeous and wonderful woman. He felt lucky to be with her. To have her by his side. He hoped it could be like this always.

Tearing his eyes away, he glanced forward, avoiding a tree root that was quite prominent, steering around it and then continuing on.

'Isn't this great?' she asked.

'It is. There's nothing like it.'

'Where does this trail take us?'

'It takes us parallel to Greenbeck and then further out into the valley…past a few farms. We can do a giant loop—it's about fifteen kilometres in total. Is that okay?'

'As long as we can stop somewhere to rest!'

He nodded. 'There's a pub around the halfway mark. The White Rabbit.'

'Sounds perfect.'

They continued their ride together. Talking. Laughing. Just enjoying being in each other's company.

After about three kilometres the woods opened up into a green valley and fields, and before they knew it they'd come across a farm filled with alpacas. Hannah asked if they could stop to take a look.

They pulled to a halt and parked their bikes against a fence, and Zach watched as Hannah held out her hand to a white alpaca that was standing by the field's edge, curious about its new visitors.

'Oh, my gosh, aren't they cute?'

He laughed. 'They are.'

He pulled at some long grass growing on their side of the fence, passed some to Hannah, and she fed the alpacas, chuckling at the way they chewed, how their ears flicked back and forth, and how they kept a curious eye on both of them.

'I think I read somewhere that alpacas can be used to protect other farm animals. They keep foxes away from chickens and ducks—that kind of thing.'

'Really? That's cool.'

She reached out to stroke a chocolate-brown one that had joined them at the fencing. He saw it was missing a leg.

'Oh, Zach…look!' She pointed.

But the alpaca was doing just fine. In fact, it was bigger

than the others, and ambled about the field without any difficulties. He watched Hannah as she gazed at it, marvelling, and then she let out a huge smile.

'It doesn't matter to the alpaca, does it?'

'No.'

'It just carries on. Doesn't let it hold it back. In fact, it looks like it's the one in charge!'

She was right. The bigger alpaca seemed to be herding the others away from the fence, as if it were telling the smaller ones to be careful.

'It's what you do with them that counts...' she mumbled.

'Sorry?'

She looked at him. 'My dad. After my accident, he told me there's a saying. *It's not the cards you're dealt that matter—it's what you do with them that counts.*'

Zach nodded. 'Sounds like a wise man.'

'He is.' She paused. 'Zach, have I been letting this hold me back?' She knocked on her left thigh with her knuckles.

'No. I don't think so.'

'But I have, though! I might not show it, but I'm worrying about my leg all the time! I know a part of me is missing and I let it affect me. This alpaca doesn't! Those hundreds of cute videos you see of three-legged dogs and cats don't either! They're still full of joy...they still live their lives to the fullest...and yet I've allowed this thing that happened to me to mark me out in some way, as if I'm different. I'm not. I'm differently abled, and that's all. But I've allowed it to cripple me emotionally! I've held back from things because I'm scared all the time!'

'Hey...' He touched her arm, then let go. 'You're not scared. You're the bravest person I know.'

'You're just saying that because you have to. Because you're my friend and you like me.'

'No, I'm saying it because it's true. Because I mean it. Do you know how many people would still be suffering from depression because of an accident like yours? How many who'd be bitter? Or angry? And yet you're always smiling. Always determined to find the silver lining in everything. And you help other people feel brave. Look at how you spoke to Jack, Stacey's son. Look at how you create support groups for people and take an interest in their lives and try to make them better. Look at how you've tried to help *me*! You're a gift to this world, Hannah, and don't you forget it!'

He'd not meant to get angry, or passionate, but he couldn't bear to see her second-guess herself like this. To see herself as weak. Because she wasn't. She never could be. She'd been through so much, and if this was how she'd come out the other side then he could only hope he'd have been half as brave as her.

She stared at him. Shocked. He saw her gaze drop to his mouth and then she turned away, looking back at the now retreating alpacas.

'Thank you.'

He let out a breath. 'You're welcome.'

He wasn't sure where they went from here. Why was he always ricocheting about in his emotions when he was with her? Moments of calm. Moments of happiness. Then moments of terror and surprise and desperate frantic panicking and then relief again. Calm again. Certainty. Happiness.

He realised he couldn't bear to see her question herself. Couldn't bear to see her sad. Or regretful. She was beautiful. Inside and out. Her heart was kind and thoughtful and generous. She made him smile all the time. Made him laugh. Made him feel content. When he was with her, he felt…complete.

His heart pounded at the realisation.

'We should make a move,' he said quickly.

She nodded and they got back on their bikes and continued to cycle down the trail.

He led the way once again. But instead of being able to enjoy the countryside, the green fields, the tidy little farmhouses tucked away into the hills, the flowers and the occasional rabbit they saw dart across their trail, his mind was focused on Hannah and what she meant to him.

She meant a very great deal, and he knew he would do whatever was in his power to make sure she was happy. Even if it was at great cost to himself.

The rest of the week had been uneventful. Hannah felt that she and Zach were returning to normal, which was great, because she knew that things had got awkward between them after the ice skating and that kiss. The bike ride had helped—spending time together with no expectations other than cycling and enjoying being out and about in the evening air.

And then there'd been her small revelation when she'd seen that three-legged alpaca. It had given her a new outlook. A change of perspective. And she'd decided, there and then, that she was not going to let her lost leg hold her back. If she wanted something, then she'd go for it. If she met someone she liked, she'd ask him out. And if *he* had a problem with her leg, then that was going to be *his* problem. Not hers.

It had lifted a weight from her shoulders. Put a spring in her step. Something she felt had been missing for some time.

'I just wanted to say how much I've been enjoying this group, Hannah,' said Peter, the patient that Zach had introduced to her dog-walking group, whose wife was in a care home facility with Alzheimer's.

'Oh, I'm glad,' she replied.

'I got to chatting with Alma and Geoff the other week, and

it was so nice to have a proper conversation again. It's funny how you miss simple things like that when you're alone.'

She nodded.

'Geoff told me about how he goes fishing on a Sunday, over at Cherringham Lake. And, by golly, I hadn't been fishing since I was a boy. So he's offered to take me and we're going to make it a regular thing.'

'That's fantastic! I'm so pleased! I hoped this group would help people make new friends and connections.'

'And what about yourself?' asked Peter.

Hannah frowned, amused. 'What do you mean?'

'Well, surely you don't want to hang around with us old people each weekend!' He smiled. 'You must have friends, or someone special to share your time with?'

'I'm more than happy to spend time with you, Peter. Age doesn't come into it if you're with people you like.'

He smiled back at her. 'Ooh, here we go—the boss is coming. Look lively!'

She looked up and saw Zach approaching with Rebel. The sun was behind him and he looked gorgeous in blue jeans and a white shirt, his sun-tanned skin revealing dark chest hair at his throat.

'Zach! I wasn't expecting to see you today.'

'Well, Rebel seemed restless, and it looks like Marvin will be out of hospital tomorrow, so I thought I'd bring him out for one last big walk. I'm going to miss him.'

Hannah noticed that Peter had hung back to walk with the rest of the group, perhaps so that she and Zach could talk together in private. 'You'll still get to see him,' she said. 'He'll be right next door.'

'I know, but when you've developed a bond it's not the same thing, is it?'

'I guess not...'

She understood. She'd got used to seeing Zach with Rebel, too, and couldn't imagine seeing him without him. Or saying goodbye to the dog.

'You might have to get your own dog.'

'Maybe… One day, anyway.'

'Don't put it off. If you want something, go for it,' she said, thinking of her own new resolve.

Why shouldn't Zach have a dog? Yes, he worked long hours each day, but he could get a dog-sitter. Or put it into doggy daycare. Or bring it to work with him and train it to sleep in a corner whilst he saw patients? Well, maybe not the last thing. But he could find a way if he really wanted a dog of his own.

Lives were short. Time was short. You never knew when your life could change in an instant. You could get hit by a bus. Or have a roller coaster accident. And then you'd wish you'd taken the chance when you had it. Life was too short for regrets.

At the end of the walk she said goodbye to everyone and helped Elle and Dee load the borrowed dogs back into the van, until finally she was alone with Zach and Rebel.

'Want to join us for a last walk together?'

He had such a charming smile. Such a way with him that she couldn't resist. And honestly, she thought, why shouldn't she? She liked spending time with Zach, and Rebel was a lovely dog, and it was a beautiful day, and she didn't want to go back to Mrs Micklethwaite's yet. Her landlady was having her hall redecorated, and the workmen there had had their radios on and had been singing quite loudly when she'd left. She wasn't ready to go back to that noise.

'Why not?'

The village green was looking lovely. All the bunting was up now, and hanging baskets and lights had been strung up around lampposts and telegraph poles as the village prepared for the fete.

Zach let Rebel off the lead as they headed onto the green, and Hannah could see that in the duck pond today the small water fountain was working, sending up a spray of water in the centre. It was all very pretty.

Rebel went over to sniff at another dog—a small cockapoo that one of the locals was walking.

'The house is going to seem weirdly empty when he's gone,' said Zach.

'I bet.'

'I guess you never know what you've got until it's not there any more.'

Hannah nodded. She felt she knew that life lesson more than anyone.

'I've been thinking... About our practice dating.'

'Oh?' She turned to look at him briefly. Warily.

'I think we should stop,' he said.

'Oh. Okay...' It should be a relief. Why wasn't it a relief? Why was it disappointing?

He nodded. 'I think we both need to take the plunge. Stop practising and get real.'

She stared at him. What did he mean? With other people, surely? He didn't mean get real with each other? As in *each other*?

'Um...' She struggled to think of what to say. Not sure what she should say.

But Zach's gaze was pulled from her as the sound of splashing and barking came, and they both turned to see Rebel bounding through the water of the duck pond, sending ducks quacking and flapping in all directions, as he headed for the centre of the pond and the fountain!

'Oh, damn...' Zach ran over to the edge of the duckpond. 'Rebel! Rebel, come on, boy!'

Hannah smiled at first, then laughed as Rebel continued to utterly ignore everything Zach was saying. He was having tremendous fun, leaping about in the water, trying to catch the water droplets that shot from the fountain. The dog was having the time of his life.

'I think you might have to go in and get him.'

Zach turned to her, laughing. 'I'm not going in there.'

'It's just water.'

'Then you go in.'

'It's not my dog.' She smiled.

Zach grimaced and nodded. 'Rebel? Come on, boy! Biscuit! Look what I've got!'

He pretended to draw a biscuit from his pocket, but both he and Rebel knew that he was lying.

Rebel continued to leap about and play in the water. Zach sighed. 'Fine. Watch my shoes?'

Hannah laughed and nodded as Zach sat down to pull off his shoes, then his socks, and rolled up his jeans to his knees. He had nice legs...

He stood and let out a big sigh, staring at the playing dog for a moment, before he placed a foot in the water. 'Ooh, it's cold!' He pulled his foot out and turned to her, laughing.

Hannah smiled. 'Go on. Go and get him.'

'This isn't going to end well. I can feel it...' Zach took a tentative step into the cold pond water, grimacing as his toes touched the bottom. 'I don't know what's on the bottom of this pond, but I'm guessing it's not nice.'

She laughed. This was hilarious! His face was a picture, and her stomach hurt from laughing so much as he waded across the duck pond.

Other people stopped and stared, smiling and pointing, getting the attention of the people they were with and telling them to look at Zach as he waded through the water to an oblivious Rebel, who was still dancing and prancing and barking. Some people got out their phones. Began recording.

Zach wobbled, almost losing his balance. 'It's slippery!'

'You'll be fine!' she called, watching his progress as he got closer and closer to the happy, bouncing German Shepherd. Whatever happened, this dog was going to be exhausted after this walk!

Zach was getting close. He stopped. Obviously thinking about how to approach the dog. He unhooked the dog's lead from around his waist, where he'd clipped it to a belt loop, and took an unsteady step forward through the water.

But Rebel continued to bounce and splash and jump about, and when Zach stretched out to try and grab Rebel's collar the dog veered away, pulling at Zach, who was refusing to let go. Suddenly there was a yelp. A splash. A huge wave of water as Zach lost his footing and disappeared into the green murk.

Hannah burst into fresh laughter, bending double, as Zach burst to the surface, soaking wet and covered in algae and weeds and a brown silty substance that she didn't want to guess at.

He sat there in the middle of the duck pond and wiped his face free of water. And then he turned around and grabbed Rebel more securely this time and hooked on his lead.

Around the pond, everybody cheered—including Hannah— as a soaked Zach stood and took a bow and began to wade back through the water towards her. She had tears of laughter streaming down her face, and she'd also pulled her phone from her pocket and taken a picture of Zach emerging from the pond with Rebel like a rather more domestic-looking Poseidon.

'Are you okay?' she asked, still laughing, wiping away her happy tears with her sleeve.

'Bonny! Can't you tell?'

'You look like a swamp monster.'

He looked down at himself and laughed. 'Aye. I do a bit.'

'Let's get you back to your place. I'll get the dog cleaned up whilst you take a shower.'

Zach laughed and nodded.

CHAPTER ELEVEN

AS SOON AS he got through the door of his house Zach began to strip off his clothes, pulling his shirt over the top of his head.

'What are you doing?' asked Hannah, looking slightly alarmed.

Oh. He'd been so desperate to get out of the damp, wet and dirty clothes, he'd not thought twice the second his front door had closed behind him.

But Hannah was trying not to look, and her cheeks were bright red, and he realised he must look a sight.

'Sorry. I'll take these off upstairs and grab a shower. If I leave them outside my bedroom door, would you be able to stick them in the machine for me?'

She nodded. 'And I'll put Rebel in the garden.'

'There's a hose out there. Could you wash him down?'

'Sure thing.'

She grabbed Rebel's lead and led him through the kitchen to the French doors, unlocked them and headed out.

Zach let out a breath and trotted upstairs, undoing his trouser button and zip as he went and stripping down to nothing once he got into the bathroom. He dropped the dirty clothes on to the landing area, and then turned on the shower and stepped under the lovely fresh and clean hot water spray.

It was a boon to his body, which had grown sticky and uncomfortable on the walk back from the duck pond. He had no doubt he was the talk of Greenbeck by now, and by Monday everyone would be talking about it at work.

Well, he could deal with that. He'd been the centre of gossip before. It passed. One day you were the hot topic…the next the village had moved on to bigger and better things. At least this time it was something funny.

The shower was making him feel much better, and he used plenty of shower gel to get rid of the 'Eau de Pond' smell he'd brought home with him. Shampoo. Conditioner. Body-wash. Within a few minutes, he felt clean, and he stepped out and wrapped a towel around his waist, ran his fingers through his hair.

He was just about to go to his room to pick out some clean clothes, when he heard a shriek downstairs.

'Hannah? You okay?'

He heard a groan and, fearing she'd hurt herself, ran as fast as he could downstairs. He found her sitting on the kitchen floor.

He rushed to her side. 'What happened?'

She didn't answer. Not to begin with. She was staring at him, slightly open-mouthed. 'Erm…the floor was wet. I… um…slipped.'

Was she hurt?

She looked him up and down, seeming rather perturbed. 'You're wearing a towel,' she said.

He nodded. 'Aye.'

She swallowed hard and flushed. 'It's not much.'

'No, it's not.' He stared back at her, suddenly realising… Was she…*attracted* to him?

Hannah licked her lips and tore her gaze away, looking everywhere but at him. 'I should…um…go. Leave you to it. To get dressed. To…um…'

She glanced at him one last time and his gaze locked with hers.

'Hannah…?'

'Yes?' She was looking up at his face, her eyes wide and dark, her breathing rapid.

He felt the stirring of desire and knew that she was feeling the same. Had he been wrong about her feelings after all this time? He'd fought his for so long. His feelings for her. And now she was here. And he wasn't sure he could deny himself again.

'Please stay.'

She nodded.

And stepped forward into his arms.

When Zach had gone upstairs to get showered and changed Hannah had stood outside, hosing down the dog which had kept on trying to catch the water stream with his mouth. She had tried not to think of a naked Zach. She'd thought she'd been quite successful, too.

When the dog had been clean, and had shaken himself multiple times to shed the excess water trapped in his fur, she'd headed inside to the kitchen to find a towel to dry him with. Only instead, she'd slipped on the floor. Gone head over heels and landed on her bottom with a thump.

Pain had shot up her coccyx, so she'd not really heard Zach calling her name. And then suddenly he was there, running into the kitchen half-naked, clad only in the towel around his waist.

It had been quite a moment.

The pain in her coccyx had been forgotten.

The beauty of the man standing before her, pebbled with water droplets all over his wonderful muscles and dampening and darkening his chest hair, had been as if she was held in a mesmerising tractor beam, unable to tear her gaze away.

He'd held out his hand and pulled her to her feet, and that was when the delicious aromas had hit her nose. Whatever he'd showered with smelt divine. Sandalwood? Cedar with a hint of spice? Whatever it was, it was intoxicating!

He'd asked her a question, and she thought she'd answered, but she wasn't sure. She might even have said something obvious, about him only wearing a towel, and then her fight or flight instinct had kicked in and she'd known she ought to leave before she did something incredibly stupid. But then he'd asked her to stay, and there had been something in his eyes that melted her heart...

Now their fingers entwined as she stepped towards him. Hesitant. Uncertain. Doubtful. Because she could be misreading his attentions. Surely he couldn't want her? Could he?

But then he slipped a hand to the nape of her neck and pulled her close.

She closed her eyes and felt the soft warmth of his lips against hers. And her body woke up from the hibernation it had been in for far too long. A surge of electricity ignited all her nerve-endings and they waited, expectant, for his caress. No mere fireworks here—instead Hannah felt as if she was the birth of a new star. A supernova. She was blinded, stunned, shocked by how he made her feel, and all logical thought went out of the window as he pressed her back against the kitchen cabinets and ran his lips down the length of her throat.

She felt his hardness against her. She was lost. Overwhelmed. She'd fought this for so long, not believing for one minute that he had any interest in her, and now this... She couldn't fight it. Nor did she want to. Because she wanted him. Desperately!

She had tried to persuade herself that it could never happen, but now it was, and she really didn't want it to stop because it felt so unbelievably good. *He* felt good. Strong. Solid. She ran her hands down his back, came to the towel and pulled it open, dropping it to the floor and taking him in her hand.

She heard him draw in a shuddering breath. It was powerful. *She* had done this to him. *Her. Hannah.* She had turned him into this passionate, desirous man. He wanted her and she wanted him and nothing could stop them now. Reality? No. Sensibility? What was that?

She began to stroke him, and the growl in his throat was enough to send her over the edge. It felt as if she'd been waiting for this man for so long. Had been kept from him for far too long. And yet at the same time she had been tempted and teased by him during those ridiculous fake dates they'd been having. So near and yet so far. He'd been a delicious temptation and now he was a delight she could savour—because all the pretence was gone now.

All the practice that they'd been hiding behind was out of the window. This was real. Very real. And she was going to savour every moment. Every kiss. Every touch. Every breath. Each moment was to be enjoyed to the full.,

His hands pulled her free of her top, his fingertips leaving a delicious trail over her skin, her shoulders, her back as he released her bra, gently and delicately removing the lace. And then her breast was in his mouth, and she realised she wanted his mouth elsewhere, too…

Could he read her mind? Because suddenly he got to his knees, kissing and licking a trail down over her stomach as he began to undo her trousers.

She felt an edge of panic, remembering her leg. Her prosthetic. But he'd seen it already—it wasn't as if it was a surprise. It wasn't going to put him off, was it?

Still she felt fear. Apprehension. Was it enough to make her call a stop to this?

No.

She wanted him. Far too much.

And when his lips pressed to her sex through the thin slip of her silken underwear her doubts fled. Disappearing like smoke. And then she was standing there, in his kitchen, in just her underwear, and he was kissing her *there*. With feather-light touches. Dampening the fabric with his hot mouth. Or maybe it was her own heat?

And then his fingers grasped the edge of the silk and slowly rolled it down, exposing her slowly. Kissing her. Licking her. Finding that sensitive spot and making her gasp out loud and clutch his hair...

She felt a vague awareness that they were in his kitchen, during daylight hours, with no curtains closed, but she couldn't remember if any houses overlooked Zach's back garden or not. She didn't think so. She thought they were safe. And one quick glimpse told her that the only being looking in on them was Rebel, who lay by the back door, panting from his exertions in the pond and looking at them quizzically.

A smile touched her lips as her head went back, and she breathed Zach's name as he pulled her trousers free from her legs. This was it. The moment in which he saw her leg not through being a doctor and her being his patient, but as a sexual partner. As someone he desired. Would it dull his response?

Clearly the answer was no, as he stood and brought his mouth back to hers, hungry for her, hitching her up onto the kitchen counter, parting her legs and moving between them.

'Wait...we need a condom...' she said breathlessly, one hand on his chest.

'I don't think I have... Wait... There might be one upstairs. Hold on.'

And he scooped her up, held her around his waist and began to carry her up the stairs.

Hannah began to laugh. 'Seriously?'

'You bet,' he said, and he carried her as if she weighed no more than a feather up the stairs, across the landing and to his bedroom, where he gently lowered her onto his bed and reached across her to yank open the drawer of his bedside cabinet.

He rifled through books, papers, pens. Pulled out a few charging cables, tossing them to the floor, and then made a satisfied noise as his hand reached for a square packet that had been lurking right at the bottom.

'Aha!' He peered at it, turning it this way and that. 'Do these things have expiry dates?'

'Probably.'

'It's old.'

'How old?'

He grinned at her. 'Not so old. It's in date. Just!'

He showed her the expiry date. It expired in one more month. Which made it okay. And then he used his teeth to tear the packet open and pull out the condom and she helped him put it on.

'Now, where were we? Oh, yes. I remember...' He grinned and kissed her again.

The bed was better than the kitchen counter. And when he finally entered her she clutched him to her and thought she would never let go.

To finally have Zach in her arms, wanting her, desiring her, was more than she could ever have hoped for.

Hannah woke much later, when the room was dark and quiet. Next to her, Zach was fast asleep, one arm flung over the top of his head, and for a brief moment she just watched him breathe.

He was a beautiful man, and what they'd shared had been beautiful. Truly. But now that her brain was no longer clouded by the joyous fog of oxytocin and endorphins, the reality of their situation began to encroach.

They had breached the barriers of friendship, work colleagues, boss and employee, and taken things to another level. They'd had sex. Seen each other. Tasted each other. Had laid each other bare, exposed themselves, and added a new, complicated dimension to their relationship.

They would have to face each other at work. Pretend nothing had happened. Hide it from everyone else. Because she didn't want people knowing about this! It would be different if they were in a romantic relationship, but neither of them had set forth any demands of what they wanted from this.

What if it had just been lust?

What if he woke up and regretted it? Panicked? Had second thoughts like she was doing now?

The sex had been wonderful—of course it had. But it had placed them in jeopardy. If they both wanted more, then great. Maybe… But what would that mean? And when one of them wanted it to stop how awkward would that be?

They worked together! Would Hannah end up in the same situation as Stacey had once faced? Feeling ousted from a surgery she loved because people took sides? And although she thought she was liked, the village would take Zach's side, and living here in Greenbeck would become a miserable affair if the villagers took against her.

It all felt so uncertain, and yet her feelings for Zach ran so deep. The idea of losing him…

But she didn't want to outstay her welcome. Didn't want to…

Oh, my God, did we leave Rebel outside?

Hannah crept out of bed and grabbed a robe off the back of his bedroom door and slipped into it. She carefully opened the door—and almost fell as she tripped over a furry hazard.

Rebel got to his feet and looked at her curiously.

Zach must have woken up and let him in before going back to bed.

Crouching, she ruffled the dog's head. 'Hey, boy.' she whispered. 'Sorry about leaving you outside earlier.' She smiled. 'We were busy, huh?'

Rebel licked her cheek in response.

She smiled, then stood up. Her leg ached. She didn't usually sleep with her prosthetic on, but she must have drifted off after the sex. Lying in Zach's arms, she'd not wanted to leave them. They'd felt like the most perfect place to be.

So what to do now? Go back to his bed? Get a drink? She did feel thirsty...

Hannah tiptoed downstairs and found her clothes neatly folded on the back of a kitchen chair. Zach must have picked them up when he came down to see to the dog.

He was a good man. Maybe the best man.

And that scared the hell out of her.

If she went back up, what would that mean? She'd be signalling that she was happy. Content. Wanted more.

And she did want that.

But...

What if he didn't? What if last night had just been a fun interlude for Zach?

He didn't seem the type of guy who would be like that. He seemed genuine. But then she'd thought the same of Edward and she'd got that terribly wrong.

Could she trust her instincts this time?

As she dithered she heard noises upstairs. Unfamiliar creaks. Too late she realised that Zach was coming downstairs.

'Hannah?'

His voice came from the hall and she stood there, caught in the kitchen, holding her clothes to her chest.

He appeared in the doorway. Saw her holding her things. 'Are you *leaving*?'

'Um… I thought maybe I ought to. Before it gets light. I don't want people gossiping.'

'I don't care what other people say. Do you?'

'Yes. I know I shouldn't, but I do. Look, yesterday was great, but…'

He looked down at the floor, then up again. 'But?'

'I don't know if we made a mistake. Maybe we shouldn't have done what we did. Taken our relationship beyond being friends. We were just meant to be practising! Maybe we got caught up in the moment, like when we were skating, and maybe the feelings…none of them are real, and…'

Her voice trailed off as she saw the pain in his eyes, and briefly she wondered if *she'd* made a mistake. Had it been real for Zach? Did he want them to be together?

But then he ruined that illusion. 'Maybe you're right. If I've made you feel uncomfortable, I'm sorry. Perhaps we need some space from one another? We can do that—though I'd like to think we can be professional at work?'

His face was like stone. Blunt. Hard. Emotionless.

It broke her heart to know that she'd been right. It *had* been a mistake, and now everything was ruined and she had to get out of there!

'Of course. I need to get dressed…'

She pushed past him and headed into his living area and closed the door. She threw her clothes onto the couch and stripped off his robe as quickly as she could. The sooner she got out of here the better!

Tears pricked her eyes at the knowledge that she'd got it so horribly wrong with him, and that he had done a reverse turn just as quickly as she had. Now everything would be different, and by giving in to their desires and not thinking straight they had potentially ruined it all.

She sucked in a breath, wiped her eyes, picked up his robe, folded it and placed it on the couch. Then she relaxed her shoulders and opened the door.

Zach was in the kitchen making coffee, as if nothing had happened, and it hurt that he could be so casual about this. So unaffected. It almost made her angry, and she wanted to beat her hands against his chest.

'I've left your robe on the couch,' she said.

'Uh-huh.' He sipped from his mug without looking at her.

'Give my best wishes to Marvin.'

He said nothing.

'I'll see you on Monday.'

And, with her heart breaking into millions of tiny pieces, she turned away from him, opened his front door and left.

When the front door had closed, Zach put his coffee mug down and propped himself against the counter, letting out a huge breath.

She'd said last night had been a mistake.

A mistake!

The fact that she thought the most beautiful thing he'd ever experienced in his entire life was a mistake astounded him! Shocked him to his core. How could she view what they'd done as something to regret and walk away from him when he had absolutely fallen hook, line and sinker for the woman? Had he been wrong? Again?

I thought I was right about her, but I was wrong. I'm so stupid!

Perhaps human beings were doomed to keep repeating the same mistakes they always made? Because it was hard-wired into their systems to learn from falling? They couldn't move forward without the scars to prove it.

But when do we have enough scars?

He'd thought she felt the same as him. That somewhere along the line their practice dating as friends had brought them closer and closer together. But yet again he'd been rejected. She knew he had a fear of rejection and yet she'd done this to him! It was cruel. It was…

He sighed and banged a fist down on the counter, making Rebel flinch.

'Sorry, boy.' He crouched down and Rebel came to him. Sat beside him and licked his leg. 'I've got to say goodbye to you today, too, haven't I?'

When Marvin came home he'd lose Rebel, too. No Hannah. No Rebel. No close friend. And awkwardness at work, no doubt.

He leaned back against the kitchen cabinets and watched the clock until it was time to fetch Marvin from the hospital.

CHAPTER TWELVE

HANNAH ALMOST CALLED in sick on Monday morning. But she knew she couldn't let down all those people who were booked in for appointments and so she went in early. Head down. Staying in her room. Taking in enough food and drinks so that she didn't have to venture into the staffroom with everyone else.

With Zach.

A knock at her door on at lunchtime scared her to death. What if it was Zach? But it wasn't. It was Stacey—Dr Emery.

'Just checking to see if you're okay? I haven't seen you all morning.'

'I'm fine!' she said brightly, relieved that it was her and not a tall, brooding, rejected Dr Zachary Fletcher.

'You sure?'

'Absolutely! Just catching up on some admin and a few referrals from last week.'

'Okay. Well, if you need anything…'

'Thanks.'

She let out a huge sigh when Stacey left.

As the days passed, she kept hearing Zach's deep voice through the walls, from his consulting room next to hers. Occasionally she heard him laugh out loud, and realised that he was absolutely fine with what had happened! She almost wanted to storm next door and rant and rave at him, ask him why he was so unaffected. Wasn't he supposed to be afraid of being rejected? Like her?

It was eating her alive!

She wasn't sleeping. Wasn't eating.

But worst of all she missed him so much!

Zach had become her everything. Not just a great boss and colleague, but an amazing friend and someone she enjoyed spending time with.

One morning, when it had become very hot in her room, she stepped outside for some fresh air, standing where Zach had used to keep Rebel. Seeing the empty space where the dog had been almost broke her heart. Her bottom lip began to tremble and quiver, and it took a huge amount of energy to force the tears away.

Everything had changed, and people were starting to ask questions. They'd noticed a difference in her. They were being respectful and keeping their distance, not being too pushy, but she could see that people cared. Which was nice. Although the one person she wanted to talk to the most, she couldn't.

There'd been an awkward moment that morning, when one of Zach's patients had come to see her about some headaches she'd been having. When Hannah had performed a blood pressure check, she had discovered her BP was through the roof. Dangerous levels. She'd had to knock on his door and ask him what he wanted her to do. Usually with a high blood pressure they'd send a patient home with a monitor to check their BP twice a day, every day for a week, but this patient's readings were so high Hannah had been worried about the stroke risk.

And Zach's face on seeing her appear in his room... He'd looked shocked, then uncomfortable, and then he'd been businesslike. Abrupt.

It had hurt.

She couldn't be like this with him. She wanted them to go

back to the way they'd been before. Carefree. Happy. Joyful. Spending time together. Seeing him smile and knowing that she'd caused it. Going for a walk and hearing him laugh at some silly thing. Holding his hand. Being in his arms again…

I love him.

The realisation was startling. But she'd known the truth of it, deep down, for some time. She'd just been ignoring it. Pretending it wasn't really happening. Because if it was, then it was putting her heart in jeopardy. It was a hopeless love. A fatal love. It couldn't live. He didn't want her. Not the way she wanted to be wanted. Fearlessly. Hopelessly. Eternally. Unconditionally.

And if I love him, and can't have him, how do I get through my days?

It was the morning of the village fete. The sun was shining, the sky was blue, birds were singing and the bunting was dancing in the breeze. Children were smiling…families looked happy. He should be feeling joyful, but Zach was feeling anything but.

He felt lost. Unmoored. Alone. He was surrounded by friends and people who liked him, but it didn't seem to matter a jot without Hannah being there.

How had it all gone so wrong? He'd thought, when they'd finally given in to their desires and slept with one another, that their path would be smooth. There would be no hiding any more, they'd each shown that they wanted the other, so surely it ought to be plain sailing from there?

But no. He'd caught her trying to creep out of his house. Without a goodbye. And she'd looked regretful. Said that they'd made a mistake. He'd realised suddenly, startlingly, that he was being left behind again. Not good enough.

It had hurt so much, like being stabbed in the heart, that he'd immediately gone on the defensive. His walls had gone up, he'd gone quiet, as he always did, and then later, he'd collected Marvin from hospital.

Even Marvin had asked him if everything was all right. Said that he seemed different. And then he'd had to say goodbye to the dog.

He was only next door. Zach could hear him in Marvin's garden. But he missed him. Rebel had been his companion as his relationship with Hannah had developed. Or he thought it had developed...

Wasn't he supposed to have learned from his past? Wasn't he supposed to have learned from his mistakes in trusting that a woman he desired felt the same way as him?

He'd been so sure she felt the same way that night! Being with her physically, he'd felt they were equals, that they were both there because it was what they wanted. So much!

This past week had been a torment. She'd been avoiding him. People at work had noticed she was staying in her room and asked him if he knew what was going on, if anything? He'd had to shrug. To pretend he didn't know. He'd told them to give her time, that maybe she just needed some space. When all he'd really wanted to do was go to her, wrap his arms around her, and whisper into her hair that everything was going to be all right.

Only he couldn't, and that was tearing him in two.

And now he had to judge a babies' fancy dress competition. With Stacey and Daniel. He had to go to the fete and paste on a smile and pretend that everything was hunky-dory in his life. When it wasn't. When what he wanted was to find Hannah. Tell her that... Tell her...

Tell her I love her? And make her run away some more?

She'd probably leave the surgery. Leave Greenbeck. And that was the last thing he wanted to happen. He needed her in his life, and if it was to just be his friend, then that would have to do. Even if it meant seeing her with someone else.

No, that's not true. I don't think I could bear that. So, should I tell her?

Although saying *I love you* to Hannah seemed fatalistic to him, she thought they'd made a mistake. Telling her would just make her think that he couldn't let go and refused to be abandoned again. Wouldn't it?

But what if she was just as afraid as him? He knew she could be, because she'd been abandoned, too. Maybe her re-action that morning was because reality had set in and she hadn't seen a way forward? What if she needed *him* to declare how serious he was about *her*? She'd been humiliated in love before. Had thought her ex was putting just as much as she was into the relationship. And she'd been wrong. What if she was just scared?

She'd stood in front of a mirror wearing a wedding dress, getting ready to show the world that she wanted to marry her man, and he had made a fool of her. Jilted her on their wed-ding day via a cowardly text message. *A text message!*

Maybe she would be afraid of what she felt for him until she knew for sure what he felt for her was just as strong?

His mind began to race. Going backwards and forwards on *what ifs* and *maybes*.

If he could somehow show her what she meant to him. Tell her. Let the whole world know that he loved her and that he would put himself out there for her, no matter the risk to him…

Would that be enough?

Would that win him the girl?

His love?

Because if she loved him, too—and he hoped that she did—then she would make him the happiest man on the planet.

The question was…was he brave enough to risk it?

CHAPTER THIRTEEN

HER INSTINCT HAD been not to go to the Greenbeck village fete.
Zach would be there. He'd been asked to judge a babies' fancy
dress competition, so he would definitely be there. And she
missed seeing him. Missed just being near him. And because
there would be plenty of crowds she thought she'd be able to
lose herself in them and he wouldn't notice her watching him.

I just want to make sure he's okay.

He probably was.

People seemed to have no problem in walking away from
her.

But her heart ached for him so she decided to go. It would
be better than staying in the house. Mrs Micklethwaite was
out for the day, and she didn't want to sit at home alone. Was
it better to be lonely surrounded by other people? Probably.

She cycled there, propping up her bike by a lamppost and
locking it, knowing it would still be there on her return. She
didn't plan on staying long. Just long enough to reassure herself that he was okay.

The fete seemed to be in full swing when she got there. Full
of marquees, and people milling around, the air filled with the
scent of candy floss and burgers and coffee.

As she passed the refreshments tent she felt a hand upon
her arm.

'Nurse?'

'Mr Fisher! Hello, how are you?' Jerry Fisher was the gentleman who had joined her dog-walking group after coming to see her with imagined ailments because he'd been so lonely. He was standing next to another gentleman, who was holding on to the lead of a dog she recognised.

'Rebel?'

'This is Marvin. He's just come out of hospital,' said Jerry, introducing them.

Zach's neighbour. 'Of course. How are you, Marvin?'

'Much better now I'm out of that place. All you doctors and nurses do a wonderful job, but there's nothing quite like being at home, is there?' He smiled, patting the dog's head. 'You know Rebel?'

'I got to know him when Dr Fletcher was minding him for you. They came on our group's walks once or twice.'

Marvin nodded and smiled. 'Oh, there he is! Dr Fletcher!'

Hannah froze, her heart thudding in her chest.

'Oh, I don't think he heard me,' said Marvin, shrugging. 'I'll get a hold of him later, no doubt.'

Hannah let out a tense breath. 'I must be off. Nice seeing you both.'

She smiled and slipped away from the tent, glancing in both directions to see which way Zach had gone. It was hard to see, because there were so many people, but she thought she could see him up ahead. He was quite tall, compared to most people. Logic told her to walk in the other direction, but her heart propelled her after him. She tried to tell herself that she would keep her distance. But the need to be near him was overpowering.

A group of people emerged from the beer tent and she lost sight of him. She struggled to make her way through the crowd, to keep track of him, but he was lost.

As the crowd thinned out, Hannah let out a short, frustrated breath.

'Hannah?'

She turned. 'Zach...'

He was there. Right there. Standing before her, looking as handsome as ever, and she knew in that moment that her heart was hopelessly lost to him and always would be.

'I thought it was you,' he said. 'How are you?'

She swallowed. How to answer? Lie and tell him she was fine? Or tell him the truth? Tell him that she *had* made a mistake. A mistake in thinking that the right thing to do was walk away from him because she was afraid.

'I've been... I don't know how I've been. Confused, mainly.'

He nodded.

Behind them one of the organisers, Walter, was up on a dais with his megaphone, asking all competitors for the babies' fancy dress competition to make sure they were at the main tent for one o clock.

Zach stared at her. It was too loud for him to speak. Then, when the noise lessened, he said, 'I've missed you.'

Her heart skipped a beat. 'Me too.'

He looked at her then. And his eyes were filled with hope.

'What happened between us was not a mistake, Hannah. Nothing that amazing could be a mistake. What we did afterwards? Absolutely—for sure. But *before*? Being with you... getting to know you...enjoying spending time with you... All of that was perfect. All of that was *meant to be.*'

Her heart filled with joy at his words.

Zach stepped closer to her. One step. Two. And then he reached for her hands, entwining his fingers around hers.

'I'm sorry if I ever made you feel like you weren't enough. I never meant to. Because you *are* enough. You are more than that. *Enough* doesn't sound like a big enough word for what you mean to me, so I want to show you. I want to prove to the world what you mean to me—what you will always mean to me.'

Hannah was beaming, happy tears in her eyes, and she nodded, speechless.

Zach smiled, and turned to take hold of Walter's megaphone as he stepped down from his dais. 'Can I just borrow this for a moment, please, Walter?'

He stepped on to the dais.

What was he going to do?

Hannah squeezed his hand and stood beside him on the platform, suddenly nervous.

'Can I have everyone's attention, please?' said Zach.

She almost froze as everyone turned to listen to him. All eyes were on them.

Zach was smiling. He had the look of a man who was determined to do something, no matter what, and knew that the adrenaline of the moment would carry him through.

'My name is Dr Zachary Fletcher. Most of you know me. I work at the Greenbeck village surgery and this lovely woman to my left...' he turned to smile and wink at Hannah '...is our advanced nurse practitioner, Hannah Gladstone. She is not only a stunning nurse but a wonderful human being, and I want you all to know...' He paused, turned to her. Looked her directly in the eyes. 'That I love her with all my heart.'

She stared at him. The villagers forgotten. The fete forgotten. All she saw was him. All she heard...all she felt...were his words and their meaning.

He loved her.

He loved her!

'I love you, too,' she said, and everyone around them began to clap.

She took a step towards him, threw her arms around his neck and kissed him—right there and then on the stage.

His arms went around her, his eyes sparkled with happiness and delight, and she kissed him again and again.

'I knew I was right about you,' he said.

She smiled. 'How do you mean?'

'From that very first day we met. You told me you were absolutely tip-top.'

And Hannah smiled and laughed and kissed him again.

EPILOGUE

HANNAH STOOD IN her wedding dress in front of the mirror, smiling at her phone and the latest text from Zach.

I love you. I can't wait to marry you. See you at the end of the aisle!

He'd sent so many texts. There'd even been a video message from him. A compilation of shots of him getting dressed for their wedding. His clothes laid out on the bed. The pink rose for his buttonhole. Zach wearing just a white shirt, boxer shorts and dark socks, with Daniel helping him do his tie. The next was him buttoning his trousers. Shrugging on his jacket. Fastening the cufflinks. Checking he had her wedding ring with a big smile on his face. All set to music she loved.

She had no fear today.

This wedding day was the one she'd been practising for. Her real wedding day. The one she'd been meant to have.

But Zach knew how scary this day would be for her. How she might have flashbacks to the last time she'd stood in a wedding gown. And he was doing everything in his power to make her know that he would be there at the end of the aisle.

She did not doubt him.

She had no second thoughts.

No cold feet.

Because her love for him was absolute and it knew no bounds. Everyone said they were perfect together and she knew they were right.

Stacey, her maid of honour, was dressed in a soft pink gown and came up to her to fiddle with her veil. 'Are you ready?' she asked.

Hannah nodded. 'I am.'

Another text beeped into her phone.

Don't be too late. I've already waited far too long in my life to find you. I love you.

Smiling, she typed her reply, and once she'd pressed 'send', Stacey took her phone from her.

'That's enough. You're going to see him in a few minutes and then you can spend the rest of your lives showing each other how much you love each other.'

'I can't believe I'm about to marry him.'

'No? I don't see why. We could all tell it was going to happen.'

'Really?'

Stacey nodded. 'Now, come on. I need this ceremony to be on time. Baby Esme will need a feed in exactly sixty minutes.'

Esme was the beautiful baby girl that Stacey and Daniel had had together. Another workplace romance… The people in the village had begun calling the surgery Cupid's Bow, which made them smile.

They'd all come to Greenbeck to find something. They hadn't known what it was, but here they had found their true love. Their happiness. One another.

The sleek grey car didn't have far to go to take Hannah

and her father to the church. She knew half the village was going to be there, and could feel butterflies dancing in her stomach.

Alighting from the car, she posed for the photographer a few times, then Stacey handed over her bouquet of pink roses and she began to walk up the small curving path towards her destiny.

Inside, the organ began to play 'The Wedding March' and she heard the scuffle of many people getting to their feet. She looked at her father.

'Okay?' he asked.

'I'm more than okay.'

They stepped forward into the church and all eyes turned to her.

Hannah blushed at the attention, but then she set her eyes on Zach at the end of the aisle and he turned to see her, his face breaking out into the broadest smile she had ever seen, and that was all she needed to see. All she was aware of after that.

Her husband-to-be.

Dr Zachary Fletcher.

And at his feet their adopted dog, Bonnie. A black Labrador who had stolen their hearts from the moment they'd first seen her at the shelter. She had a pink bow tied around her neck to match the buttonholes.

Zach looked so handsome, and she saw him wipe away a tear of happiness as she walked towards him.

When she got level with him, he leaned in. 'You look beautiful. I'm so lucky.'

She beamed. 'So am I. The luckiest girl in the world.'

She wanted to lean in and kiss him. Kiss him now. But there would be a time and a place for that in this ceremony.

Her next kiss with Zach would be as his proud, happy, and eternally in love *wife*.

They turned to face the vicar, hand in hand. Dog at their feet. Tail wagging. And they began to say their vows.

* * * * *

COMING SOON!

We really hope you enjoyed reading this book. If you're looking for more romance be sure to head to the shops when new books are available on

Thursday 8th June

To see which titles are coming soon, please visit

millsandboon.co.uk/nextmonth

MILLS & BOON®

Coming next month

TWIN BABIES TO REUNITE THEM
Ann McIntosh

A tidal wave of arousal crashed over Saana as her gaze dropped to that full, wide mouth—unsmiling now, but no less sinfully sexy for that fact.

Against her will, her head suddenly filled with scenes, scents, sensations of being held in Kenzie's arms. There, her every sensual need had been met, ecstasy lifting her higher and higher, until it became irresistible and she was flung into the stratosphere.

Taken to the stars.

Suddenly weak-kneed once more, Saana knew it was time to bring this surreal encounter to an end. The sustaining anger had waned, leaving her floundering and sad.

But she wouldn't allow that to show.

The one person she'd ever completely trusted had betrayed her and deserved nothing but cool dismissal.

Getting a grip on both her emotions and her traitorous body, and although her legs still felt weak, she walked around the car to the semicircular staircase leading to her front door.

"Well," she said, aware of Kenzie's gaze following her

and refusing to meet it again. "This has been delightful, but I'm afraid it's time for you to leave."

She was two steps up when Kenzie replied.

"Saana, I need your help."

Pausing, Saana felt the words echo, shockingly, between them. In fact, it was almost impossible to believe she'd heard them correctly.

Unable to resist, she looked over her shoulder, saying "As surprising as it is to hear you, Miss Independence, say that, I'm sorry. I'm not interested in offering assistance."

Then, as she turned to climb to the next step—wanting to hurry now, to get away—she heard Kenzie say, "I'm pregnant with twins. And I really need your help."

She froze where she stood, trying to process the words, her first impulse to spin around and look at Kenzie to judge whether she was telling the truth or not. To let loose all the questions firing around her brain.

Pregnant? By whom? Had she started a new relationship without telling Saana? Decided she wanted a family with someone other than the wife she'd promised to love and cherish always but had then left behind?

Continue reading
TWIN BABIES TO REUNITE THEM
Ann McIntosh

Available next month
www.millsandboon.co.uk

LET'S TALK

Romance

For exclusive extracts, competitions
and special offers, find us online:

f MillsandBoon

𝕏 @MillsandBoon

◎ @MillsandBoonUK

♪ @MillsandBoonUK

Get in touch on 01413 063 232

MILLS & BOON

THE HEART OF ROMANCE

A ROMANCE FOR EVERY READER

MODERN

Prepare to be swept off your feet by sophisticated, sexy and seductive heroes, in some of the world's most glamourous and romantic locations, where power and passion collide.

HISTORICAL

Escape with historical heroes from time gone by. Whether your passion is for wicked Regency Rakes, muscled Vikings or rugged Highlanders, awaken the romance of the past.

MEDICAL

Set your pulse racing with dedicated, delectable doctors in the high-pressure world of medicine, where emotions run high and passion, comfort and love are the best medicine.

True Love

Celebrate true love with tender stories of heartfelt romance, from the rush of falling in love to the joy a new baby can bring, and a focus on the emotional heart of a relationship.

Desire

Indulge in secrets and scandal, intense drama and sizzling hot action with heroes who have it all: wealth, status, good looks…everything but the right woman.

HEROES

The excitement of a gripping thriller, with intense romance at its heart. Resourceful, true-to-life women and strong, fearless men face danger and desire - a killer combination!

JOIN US ON SOCIAL MEDIA!

Stay up to date with our latest releases, author news and gossip, special offers and discounts, and all the behind-the-scenes action from Mills & Boon...

 @millsandboon

 @millsandboonuk

 facebook.com/millsandboon

 @millsandboonuk

It might just be true love...

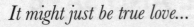

MILLS & BOON

MODERN

Power and Passion

Prepare to be swept off your feet by sophisticated, sexy and seductive heroes, in some of the world's most glamourous and romantic locations, where power and passion collide.